NIGHT'S BLACK AGENTS

SOLO OPS

BY GARETH RYDER-HANRAHAN

CREDITS

Publishers: Simon Rogers and Cathriona Tobin

Author: Gareth Ryder-Hanrahan

GUMSHOE One-2-One system designed by Robin D. Laws

Night's Black Agents designed by Kenneth Hite

Editing: Colleen Riley, Cathriona Tobin

Art Direction: Gareth Ryder-Hanrahan, Cathriona Tobin

Cover Artist: Jérôme Huguenin

Interior Artists: Gislaine Avila, Lauren Covarrubias, Leanna Crossan, Evanleigh Davis, Marisa Erven, Jen McCleary, Georgia Roan, Runa I. Rosenberger, Jorge Fernández Sanz, Ernanda Souza, and Quico Vicens-Picatto

Layout: Jen McCleary

Playtesters: Stacey Abbott, Nathaniel Bennett, Peyton Bradley-Ryder, Jym Brier, John Buckley, Susan Carlson, Dave Choat, Natalie Daumen, Michael Daumen, Diane Donaldson, Bryant Durrell, Michael Duxbury, Sandra Ellison, Eric Ferner, Mike Fraser, WOoDY GamesMaster, Adam Gauntlett, Fritz Jahnke, Kelly Monroe Johnston, Jon Lane, Jeanna Lundgren, Robert Lundgren, Johan Lundström, Chris Miles, Laura Moussa, Karim Muammar, Lisa Nunheim, Erik Otterberg, Lisa Padol, Kelly Pawlik, Ken Pawlik, Catherine Ramen, Christopher Rinderspacher, Scot Ryder, Emily Savidge, Liam Scanlon, Emily Springer, David Springer, Fiona Tatchell, Sarah Wood.

Pelgrane Press is co-owned by Simon Rogers and Cathriona Tobin.

CONTENTS

4

AGENTS

Do not look back; you are never completely alone.
— The Moscow Rules: Rule 4

In ***Night's Black Agents: Solo Ops,*** a lone spy uncovers and thwarts the sinister schemes of a world-spanning conspiracy, and hunts its vampiric masters. It adapts the ***Night's Black Agents*** roleplaying game and combines it with the GUMSHOE One-2-One rules to produce a game experience where a single badass spy — the player — faces off against the forces of darkness, as orchestrated and choreographed by a Director. The Director portrays all of the people, places, and perils encountered by the Agent. The Director holds all the secrets — he knows what's really going on. It's up to the player to muster the courage and the cunning needed to beat the vampires on their native soil.

The default protagonist for ***Solo Ops*** is **Leyla Khan**, an ex-spy who fell under the supernatural influence of a vampire and was brainwashed into working for the conspiracy. Now, she's broken free and is trying to stay ahead of her former masters while assembling the information and allies she'll need to bring them down. In the course of this desperate struggle, she must:

- Uncover the extent of the vampire conspiracy, mapping its branches and personnel
- Survive attacks by the vampires and their minions and pawns
- Recover her fragmented memories
- Ensure she doesn't fall back under the sway of the vampires by securing methods to defend herself against their psychic commands.
- Discover the nature and weaknesses of the vampires
- Detect and prevent ongoing or ad hoc vampire or conspiratorial operations
- Weaken the vampire conspiracy by striking at its main branches or key personnel
- Finally, destroy the vampires at the heart of the conspiracy

Any of these goals can provide the seed for an operation, one chapter in Khan's story. Sometimes, her operations will be active ones, where she's moving forward against the vampires by investigating their operations, thwarting their goals, and attacking their conspiracy. Other operations will be reactive, where the vampires are the ones moving forward — attacking some other group, infiltrating some new city, or striking directly at Khan.

However, the player may prefer to create her own vampire hunter. As the sample ***Solo Ops*** scenarios in this book are tailored for Khan, the Director will need to create new operations for this original character (or adapt ideas from Khan's stories).

GETTING STARTED

This book assumes that the Director is experienced in basic roleplaying concepts, ideally having run at least one multiplayer game. GUMSHOE One-2-One makes an ideal introduction to roleplaying for a player entirely new to the form. The best way to show your player what roleplaying means is to run her through a scenario. This shows, rather than tells, what it's all about. Espionage thrillers — and vampire fiction, for that matter — are full of formulaic elements like car chases, shootouts, tailing suspects, sneaking around airports, and staking undead horrors, giving the player a familiar set of reference points to help navigate the story.

MEET LEYLA KHAN

The easiest way to get started is to play our pregenerated protagonist, Leyla Khan: her character card is on p. 269, and her background handout is on p. 268.

The three sample operations in this book star Khan as the vampire hunter.

YOUR OWN AGENT

Alternatively, the player may prefer to create her own fictional avatar. In that case, guide the player through the character creation rules starting on p. 8, and then either create your own stories based on that player, or adapt our prewritten adventures to your player's chosen backstory.

A NOTE ON PRONOUNS

In the text to follow "you" sometimes means you, the player or Director, and sometimes "you," the character you're playing. From context, you'll see which is which. Normally, game books skirt this dilemma by using the plural for players, but in GUMSHOE One- 2-One there is only one.

Every now and again, clarity requires us to pick genders for the player and Director. In these passages we call the player "she" and the Director "he," though of course anybody can take on either of these roles. Please bear with us, mentally editing the text to reflect your pronouns of choice.

SETTING UP

The GUMSHOE One-2-One system uses cards to track injuries, assets, and other special conditions. Before starting play, you need to print out and cut up the generic cards on p. 258 as well as any cards associated with the operation you're running.

The player needs either Leyla's character sheet on p. 269, or a copy of the blank character sheet on p. 267, the rules summary sheet on p. 271, and at least two six-sided dice. Add beverages, snacks, notepaper, soundtracks, and other accoutrements as desired. As **Solo Ops** takes place in a cinematic, monster-haunted approximation of the modern world, some Directors like to have a tablet or laptop to hand to call up street plans and images. Others prefer to enjoy the increasingly exotic experience of going a few hours without checking Twitter.

QUICK RULES REFERENCE

This summary quickly presents the game's essential rules concepts, which we'll go on to explain in greater depth.

Are you an experienced GUMSHOE GM who'd like to start by seeing how One-2-One differs from its predecessor? Flip to p. 270 in the Appendix.

Your character attempts actions in the storyline by using abilities. Abilities come in two types: Investigative and General.

Investigative abilities (p. 11) allow you to gather information. The animating principle behind GUMSHOE states that *failing to get key information is never interesting.* If you have the right ability and you look in the right place for clues you need to solve the mystery, you will always find the information you seek. If you lack the relevant ability, your character can talk to a Contact (p. 45), who might also provide guidance and assurance as needed. Some Contacts are trustworthy and reliable; others carry an element of risk.

A piece of information need not be critical to the case for you to gain it without chance of failure and at no cost. Much of mystery-solving lies in sorting the important from the tangential. If only the crucial clues came for free, it would give the game away.

In some situations, you can spend a resource called a Push (p. 13) to gain an additional benefit that clears the character's path through the story, such as favors from witnesses, knowledge that keeps the character safe, prior relationships to central figures, lucky breaks, or clever stratagems that an experienced spy can exploit to tip the odds in her favor.

You start the game with **3 Pushes**, and can gain others during play.

General abilities (p. 25) determine whether you succeed or fail when trying to take actions other than gathering information, usually in an event called a test. The most important kind of test is the Challenge (p. 34.)

Whenever it might be as interesting for you to fail as it would be to succeed — say, fighting an assassin, running away from the militia, or trying to sneak into a vampire's castle undetected — you roll dice.

The game uses standard six-sided dice, which roleplayers sometimes refer to as d6s.

You've got two dice in all General abilities. You can earn more dice by taking on Extra Problems or tapping your other abilities to perform dramatic Stunts.

When rolling multiple dice, roll one at a time: you may succeed without having to roll all of them.

At the end of the Challenge, your die roll total may match or exceed that of an Advance (the best result) or a Hold (an okay or middling result). If not, your Outcome is a Setback, which means that something bad happens.

On an Advance you will probably gain an Edge (p. 38): an advantage you can use later in the scenario. As a reminder, you gain an Edge card. The card's text will tell you how it works. Often, you must discard the card to gain the advantage.

If you reached the Advance threshold without rolling all of the dice you were entitled to, you also gain a Push.

On a Setback, you often gain a Problem (p. 38), representing a dilemma that might cause trouble for you later. Again, you receive a card to remember it by — a Problem card. Certain cards might lead to a terrible end for your Agent should you fail to get rid of, or Counter, them (p. 39) before the scenario concludes.

Every so often you'll make a simple roll, called a Quick Test (p. 40), to see if you succeed or fail, without the possibility of Advances, Edges, Setbacks, or Problems.

In addition, you start with **three Mastery Edges**, special Edges representing your Agent's extensive training and expertise. Each Mastery Edge describes what it does on the card.

The rest is detail. You don't have to learn any special rules for combat or mental distress, as you would in standard GUMSHOE and most other roleplaying games. The Challenge system, with its descriptions of Outcomes and its resulting Edges and Problems, handles it all.

CREATING YOUR CHARACTER

Build your character by picking abilities from a list, and bring it to life by adding specific details like your spy's name, exceptional talents, and personality quirks.

You start with the following Investigative abilities: **Bullshit Detector, Charm, Intimidation, Notice, Reassurance, Research, Streetwise, Urban Survival**, and **Tradecraft**, and two dice in each General ability.

You may then pick another six Investigative abilities, for a total of 15.

STARTING MASTERIES

You begin play with 3 Mastery Edges (sometimes just called Masteries). As an elite spy, you've mastered your skills to an extraordinary degree and that opens up options and techniques beyond the reach of most people.

You can change your choices of Mastery Edges during play if you wish – see p. 25 for more on Edges of all kinds, including Masteries.

If you're not sure which Masteries to take when starting out, we recommend the following for Khan: Unshakeable (Cool), Painkillers and Vodka (Medic), and Trained Reflexes (Athletics).

LEYLA KHAN

INVESTIGATIVE ABILITIES

Bullshit Detector, Charm, Criminology, Electronic Surveillance, High Society, Human Terrain, Intimidation, Notice, Outdoor Survival, Reassurance, Research, Streetwise, Tradecraft, Traffic Analysis, Urban Survival

GENERAL ABILITIES

Athletics 2, Conceal 2, Cool 2, Cover 2, Driving 2, Evasion 2, Fighting 2, Filch 2, Infiltration 2, Mechanics 2, Medic 2, Network 2, Preparedness 2, Sense Trouble 2, Shooting 2, Surveillance 2

CORE ABILITIES

The particular mix of Investigative abilities possessed by a *Solo Ops* player character varies. Contacts cover any Investigative abilities that the player doesn't hold directly. So, one spy might be an expert in **Electronic Surveillance**, but relies on her contact in the Ministry to handle **Bureaucracy**-related clues. Another spy might know all about how to pull strings and get things done with **Bureaucracy**, but has to call on her technogeek sidekick to plant bugs and gather information with **Electronic Surveillance**.

However, there are a few core Investigative abilities that are common to all player characters in **Solo Ops.** These are:

Bullshit Detector, Charm, Intimidation, Notice, Reassurance, Research, Streetwise, Urban Survival, and **Tradecraft.**

Why these abilities? They're all either informal, universal ways of manipulating people (**Charm, Intimidation, Reassurance**), information-gathering abilities that are best used in the moment (**Bullshit Detector, Notice**), absolutely integral to the espionage genre (**Streetwise, Tradecraft, Urban Survival**), or a catch-all failsafe investigative skill (**Research**).

USING INVESTIGATIVE ABILITIES

Investigative abilities give you information. They're how you interrogate the world around you. Think of them as questions you can ask the Director. Investigative abilities always work – you never need to roll to spot a clue. The challenge in *Solo Ops* is assembling the facts you uncover into a coherent understanding of what's going on and choosing how to act on that information.

You've got a number of Investigative abilities in different fields, reflecting your particular talents as a spy. Descriptions of what your Investigative abilities do come later in this section.

When a scene starts, your Director will describe what you can tell about it right off – what you see and hear, what you recognize, what inferences you can reasonably draw from obvious clues.

> *Director: Okay, you walk into the nightclub. Electronic dance music assails your ears, and it's alternately dark and blinding as strobe lights flash. The dance floor's packed – a mix of partying tourists and a few locals, mostly women – but there's a higher tier of tables over there that's nearly empty apart from a few older men in suits, and it's clear that's where the real business of the club happens. There's a big guy – shaved head, leather jacket – lounging at the bottom of the stairs up to that higher tier, and you can guess he's a bodyguard or bouncer.*

You can then explore the scene further by asking questions. Sometimes, you'll be able to pick up more information by examining a facet of the scene more closely. The Director might volunteer this extra information, or you could ask

if a particular Investigative ability tells you anything more. For example, the Director might say:

> *Director: With your* **Streetwise**, *you recognize a few of the gangsters on the upper tables. Mostly Mafioso-types operating out of Varna.*

Or you might ask:

> *Player: Can I tell anything about these guys with* **Streetwise***? Or* **Criminology***? Do I spot any faces from an Interpol Most Wanted list, maybe?*

Sometimes, you'll need to describe how you're using an Investigative ability. You never just read the names of your abilities off your character card and wait for more description.

> *Player: Okay, I'm going to* **Intimidate** *the bouncer. I want to see who's in charge, so I'm just going to walk up towards him, projecting menace. Really draw attention to myself, just be as scary and tough as possible. I'm not trying to threaten him; I'm guessing that he'll look towards his boss for a cue on how to respond, and then I'll know who's running the show.*

Sometimes, the Director may ask you to elaborate on how you know a particular piece of intel. In that case, you're free to extemporize on what aspects of your character's experiences or background gives insight into the current situation. Treat these as opportunities to flash back to significant or illuminating moments in your character's murky past (and possibly set up future Contacts).

> *Director: With your* **Military Science***, you recognize these guys as Czech special forces. Is that just from reading briefing documents, or have you had personal experience with them?*
>
> *Player: So, I was part of a counter-terror investigation, and we'd traced a terrorist bomb-making operation to a farmhouse outside, er, let me Google, Vitkovice... I worked with a Czech spec-ops team to storm the farmhouse.*
>
> *Director: Sure. Okay, your liaison with that team was a guy named Karl Virek, and you spot him with the other soldiers in the bar...*

Sometimes, you discover clues just by describing your character completing simple tasks. This happens when no special training or method is required.

> *For example, if there are financial documents taped to the bottom of a desk, and you say, "I look under the desk," the Director replies, "You find an envelope taped to the underside of the desk top."*

For certain clues, ones that an expert character with specialized training would not miss, or ones that are indispensable to the mystery, the Director gives you time to ask. Before the scene ends, the Director describes you noticing whatever the clue happens to be, even if you didn't specifically ask. That gives you the opportunity to have the fun of discovering the clue, without painting your spy as incompetent or unaware.

Clues that you *must* find to progress through the operation are called **core clues**.

ON CLUES

The GUMSHOE engine, which powers the *Night's Black Agents* rules, separates the business of discovering information from the business of confronting (or escaping) the opposition. In espionage novels and films, the emphasis isn't on finding the information in the first place. Usually, the heroes are awash in facts and intel, trying to piece them together to deduce the opposition's plans, or to plan a counterstrike.

When you do see information withheld from characters, it's seldom portrayed as a failure on the part of the competent, fact-gathering hero. Instead the writers show an external force preventing the hero from applying their abilities. In a spy thriller, you might get stonewalled by your enigmatic boss, or find a witness dead when you return to question them. Information is only withheld when it makes the story more interesting — usually by placing the hero at a handicap while they move forward in the storyline. In GUMSHOE terms, they're not trying to get an available clue and failing; they're either using an ability for which no clue is available, or the failure itself is the clue: the boss' stonewall is a **Bureaucracy** clue that your own agency is involved, the dead witness provides information on their killers' methods via **Forensic Pathology**.

Of course part of the fun is saying things like "Keyhole satellite imagery shows a heavy Revolutionary Guard presence at the black site" or "Chatter indicates an upswing in Al-Qaeda activity in Romania" or "I sweated the meeting place out of their bagman." You can still say, and do, all of those things in **Solo Ops**. It's just that GUMSHOE doesn't make you roll to succeed in doing them: those are automatic successes with (in the above examples) **Data Recovery**, **Traffic Analysis**, and **Interrogation**. But what do you do with that intel? What plan do you foil? What strike do you launch? The action really starts after you gather the clues.

Intelligence operations are not about finding clues. They are about interpreting the clues you do find.

Figuring out the conspiracy, or planning an operation, is hard enough for a group of analysts, without someone withholding half the pieces from them. GUMSHOE, therefore, makes the finding of clues all but automatic, as long as you get to the right place in the story and have the right ability. That's when the fun part begins, when the players try to put the components of the puzzle together.

Investigative games often bog down into speculative debate between players about what **could be** happening. Many things **can** be happening, but only one thing **is**. If more than one possible explanation ties together the clues you have so far, you need more clues.

Solo Ops operations are designed so that there's **always** a path to the final confrontation. There'll **always** be at least one open line of investigation telling you where to go next. Often, this will point you into danger, but that's the rhythm of the thriller. Information leads to danger, and if you survive that danger, you obtain more information.

Whenever you get stuck, **get out and gather more intel, even if that means taking risks.**

PUSHES

The character starts each scenario with three Pushes. In certain situations, the player may spend a Push to use an Investigative ability to gain something above and beyond basic information.

For example, you might:

◆ spend a Push on **Bullshit Detector** to guess the motivation behind a character's deception

◆ spend a Push on **Architecture** to discover the ideal place to set up a sniper's nest

◆ spend a Push on **Bureaucracy** to convince the clerk not to tell anyone you were ever there

◆ spend a Push on **History** to declare that you happen to know a lecturer at the local university who's an expert in the obscure cult you're investigating

Often, Challenges give a list of abilities that can be Pushed to gain a bonus to the roll.

The Director may tell the player that she could use a Push now (*"Do you want to Push your Bullshit Detector?"*), or the player might ask if Pushing would be viable in the current situation (*"Can I Push my Occult Studies to, uh, know the proper way to lay a ghost to rest?"*). If a Push won't help, the Director tells the player that – you can't "waste" a Push by using it if a benefit isn't available.

Sometimes, a scenario might suggest appropriate Pushes or categories of Pushes. For example, if a scenario says that the player can get past a guard with an **Interpersonal** Push, then that's shorthand for "any plausible **Interpersonal** ability will do – you could **Intimidate** the guard, or **Charm** him, or bribe him with **Negotiation**, or bluff past with **Cop Talk**, or..."

INVESTIGATIVE EDGES

Some Edge cards let you mimic an Investigative ability that you don't normally possess. For example, locating a copy of an Interpol report might let you find a clue as if you had **Criminology**, or a weird prophetic dream might grant you a one-shot use of **Vampirology**. Finding Edges like these enables you to rely less on Contacts.

CONTACTS

When a scenario calls for an Investigative ability that you don't have, it's time to turn to your Contacts – experts and allies with the specialized skills you need. Contacts exist to convey information to you, so your character does not seem ridiculously well-informed in every field of knowledge. They also give you and your Director a chance to play out relaxed, lower-key scenes featuring supporting characters who aren't trying to kill your Agent. These supply the camaraderie that springs up between player characters in group games.

To find a Contact, you usually use the Network ability (p. 30). You may also run into Contacts in the course of an operation – for example, if you rescue a journalist from the conspiracy, you might ask the Director if she can count as a free Contact.

Each Contact is represented by a Contact card that lists that Contact's main Investigative abilities. Contacts may also have a few General abilities, but the primary use of a Contact is to provide you with information and assistance, not to get into peril on your behalf. (For that, you need to spend Pushes for favors – see p. 14).

Contacts are ephemeral – they're people you know from your former life or people who move in the same clandestine circles that you do, people with information or talents you need. If you follow a clue to Baghdad and you want a local expert to tell you about the criminal underworld in Iraq, then you'd need to seek out a Contact to provide that information. Contacts usually don't last longer than one story – either you vanish from of their lives as suddenly as you appeared, or they get killed.

If a Contact survives, and the character was sufficiently interesting and memorable to warrant a return appearance, the Director may bring that Contact back in future adventures, or you might choose to call upon an old Contact when a situation warrants.

CONTACTS AND CLUES

If a clue can only be obtained using an ability possessed by a Contact, the Director will tell you that you need to get the information to the Contact so they can find the clue. The challenge here is grabbing and extracting the raw intel. For example:

> Director: *You break into the building. It's some sort of pharmaceutical lab. Chemical experiments, glassware full of bubbling liquids, computers doing some sort of modelling of molecular interactions, thick binders full of printouts and case notes. The place has been abandoned in a hurry.*

Player: Can I tell anything about what they're working on?

Director: As far as you can tell, it's something to do with hemoglobin bonding, but you'd need **Pharmacy** *and* **Diagnosis** *to make sense of it.*

Player: Okay. This is a case for my contact, Dr. Hoske. I'm going to grab some samples and take photos on my phone.

Later...

Director: Dr. Hoske recognizes the work – it's based on research by a Professor Lemuel, who was working on synthetic blood. He's in Berlin – looks like he's the person to talk to next...

Sometimes, you'll be able to tap your Contact's knowledge directly, over the phone or through some other remote communication.

Player: All right, I'm going to climb down into the catacombs under the haunted castle. I'm going to use **Preparedness** *to have brought along a wireless body camera and a radio, so my archaeologist buddy can track my progress.*

Director: Climbing through the dark tunnels, you come across a tomb. There's a smooth stone on top of it, and it looks like there are teeth marks on it. (As the archaeologist contact) Wait, go back. Shine a light there... that stone. There's a folk practice of burying suspected vampires with a stone jammed in the corpse's mouth, to stop it rising again. That stone might be one of those.

Player: So who took it out?

Other abilities may require that you get your Contact into position to use their skills on your behalf.

Director: You need **Cop Talk** *to get the files from the morgue.*

Player: I'll call my Contact Detective Grey and have him get them for me.

Director: Over the phone, Grey sounds hesitant, and says that there's a lot of scrutiny of the case right now. He's worried about internal affairs taking an interest in him.

Player: I'll spend a Push to reassure him – I tell him that he'll get the credit for catching the "serial killer" once we take down the vampire.

FAVORS AND ASSISTANCE

By spending Pushes, you can obtain favors and other help from a Contact. The Contact might provide you with weapons or equipment, or get you into a secure location, or pull strings within whatever groups they're associated with, or help out with some other part of your mission. Such favors are always limited in scope and duration – you can't bring a buddy along with you for a whole mission, or get a friend to solve the whole mystery for you. (And your Director should definitely avoid the horrible situation where a Contact has to have a conversation with another character, as nothing's worse than a scene where the Director has to talk to himself.)

Possible favors include:

♦ the loan of specialized equipment, including weapons
♦ breaking the law or bending the rules
♦ providing shelter and support

♦ helping out on a challenge
♦ providing a distraction
♦ gathering information off-screen

Sometimes, your Contacts will help you out in Challenges by contributing their General ability dice to yours. For example:

Player: Okay, I need to break into that office. Can I find a place nearby where I can stash my getaway car that won't be found by security?

Director: Maaaaybe. You've already seen they've got heavy security – and you haven't countered that "High Alert" Problem you picked up earlier. If you leave a car nearby, there's a good chance it'll be found.

Player: Change of plan, then. I'll get Detective Grey to drive by and pick me up – I'll arrange a rendezvous time.

Director: You'll have to spend another Push to get Grey to play along.

Later, Khan finds herself running from pursuers. As she runs (an **Evasion** *challenge), the player suggests that she be allowed make a* **Driving** *stunt using Grey's dice – she describes how his police car pulls up alongside her, and she dives in through the open window while he drives off at speed.*

CONTACTS AND CHALLENGES

Some Contacts have the right General abilities to help out with Challenges – see p. 45 for these rules.

INVESTIGATIVE ABILITY DEFINITIONS

The definitions in this section describe the kinds of clues you can gather with each ability, and how you might go about doing that. Each ability name appears next to two icons. The first tells you which category the ability falls into: Academic **A**, Interpersonal **I**, and Technical **T**.

"You" in these descriptions always refers to the character.

Ability descriptions consist of a brief general description, followed by examples of their use in an operation. Creative players can propose additional uses for their abilities as unexpected situations confront their characters.

Certain specific actions may overlap between several abilities, ideally providing many possible ways forward in the scenario. For example:

♦ you can enhance image resolution with **Data Recovery**, **Electronic Surveillance**, or **Photography**

♦ you can analyze (or synthesize) a designer drug with either **Chemistry** or **Pharmacy**

♦ you can identify a smuggled artifact with **Archaeology**, **Art History**, or possibly **Occult Studies**

♦ you can tell what gun made that exit wound with **Criminology**, **Forensic Pathology**, or **Military Science** — or with an Investigative use of **Shooting**

♦ you can pick out the real leader of a Chechen gang with **Human Terrain** or **Streetwise**

♦ you can bluff your way into a hospital with **Bureaucracy**, **Diagnosis**, an Investigative use of **Cover**, or using **Forgery** to create a false ID card

Some abilities, like **Notice** and **Research**, are broadly useful, and will crop up constantly. Others may be called for many times in the course of

INVESTIGATIVE ABILITIES

ABILITY	TYPE	ICONS
Accounting	Academic	A C
Archaeology	Academic	A C
Architecture	Academic	A C
Art History	Academic	A C
Astronomy	Technical	T C
Bullshit Detector	Interpersonal	I
Bureaucracy	Interpersonal	I C
Charm	Interpersonal	I
Chemistry	Technical	T C
Cop Talk	Interpersonal	I C
Criminology	Academic	A
Cryptography	Technical	T C
Data Recovery	Technical	T C
Diagnosis	Academic	A C
Electronic Surveillance	Technical	T
Forensic Pathology	Technical	T C
Forgery	Technical	T C
High Society	Interpersonal	I C
History	Academic	A C
Human Terrain	Academic	A
Interrogation	Interpersonal	I C
Intimidation	Interpersonal	I
Languages	Academic	A C
Law	Academic	A C
Military Science	Academic	A
Negotiation	Interpersonal	I
Notice	Technical	T
Occult Studies	Academic	A C
Outdoor Survival	Technical	T C
Pharmacy	Technical	T C
Photography	Technical	T C
Reassurance	Interpersonal	I
Research	Academic	A
Streetwise	Interpersonal	I
Tradecraft	Interpersonal	I
Traffic Analysis	Technical	T C
Urban Survival	Technical	T
Vampirology	Academic	A C

one scenario, and not at all in others. Abilities that are especially suited for Contacts are called out with a Contact icon **C**, but this is a suggestion, not a hard-and-fast rule; if you want a spy who's an expert codebreaker or art historian, go for it.

ACCOUNTING (ACADEMIC)

You understand bookkeeping and accountancy procedures; you can read and keep financial records. You can:

◆ tell legitimate businesses from criminal enterprises

◆ reconstruct financial histories from old records (uncovering, say, slave-trading or smuggling)

◆ spot the telltale signs of embezzlement, bribes, blackmail, or shell companies

◆ track payments to their source

◆ launder funds and set up numbered accounts

◆ interact with bankers and money launderers as a professional equal

ARCHAEOLOGY (ACADEMIC)

You excavate and study the structures and artifacts of historical cultures and civilizations. You can:

◆ tell how long something has been buried and date its construction

◆ identify artifacts by culture and usage

◆ distinguish real artifacts from fakes

◆ navigate inside ruins and catacombs, including finding secret doors and hidden construction

◆ describe the customs of ancient or historical cultures

◆ spot well-disguised graves and underground hiding places

◆ interpret site maps and archaeological dig records

◆ estimate the market value of, and likely customers for, a smuggled artifact

◆ interact with archaeologists and museum curators as a professional equal

ARCHITECTURE (ACADEMIC)

You know how buildings (and infrastructure generally) are designed and constructed. You can:

◆ guess what lies around the corner while exploring an unknown structure or sewer system

◆ deduce or discover where sewer, power, phone, cable, and gas lines enter or pass beneath a structure, and trace them within it

◆ rough out a floor plan and interpret blueprints

◆ judge the relative strength of building materials

◆ identify a building's age, architectural style, original use, and history of modifications

◆ deduce the existence of hidden rooms, bricked-over sewers, or secret crypts

◆ construct stable makeshift structures

◆ identify elements vital to the structural integrity of buildings, sewers, dams, or bridges

◆ interact with architects and civil engineers as a professional equal

ART HISTORY (ACADEMIC)

You're an expert on works of art (including the practical arts such as furniture and pottery) from an aesthetic and technical point of view. You can:

◆ distinguish real works from fakes

◆ tell when something has been retouched or altered

◆ identify the age of an object by style and materials

◆ accurately estimate the price of, and likely customers for, an *objet d'art*

◆ call to mind historical details on artists and those around them

◆ call to mind details of stolen or missing artworks

◆ interact with art collectors and museum curators as a professional equal

ASTRONOMY (ACADEMIC)

You study celestial objects, including the stars and planets. You can:

◆ decipher astrological texts

◆ recall the phase of the moon and time of sunset and sunrise without looking it up

◆ use a telescope, including large reflectors

◆ plot the movement of stars and planets, including which ones are overhead at any given time

◆ predict eclipses, comets, meteor showers, and other regular astronomical phenomena

◆ calculate flight paths for ballistic missiles or rockets

BULLSHIT DETECTOR (INTERPERSONAL)

Not all lies are verbal. You can tell when a person is attempting to project a false impression through body language, using the human capacity to judge and sense motives and character. Basically, this ability allows you to tell if someone is lying to you, and (with a spend) make a decent guess about their motives. This doesn't tell you what they're lying about specifically, or let you see through their lies to the truth.

This ability works best on nervous, guilty, or unpracticed liars, especially civilians or petty criminals.

Certain individuals — con men, actors, expert deep-cover agents, professional gamblers, and similar — may be so adept at lying that they never set off your built-in lie detector, or

WHY NO LYING ABILITY?

Unlike many other RPG rules sets, GUMSHOE does not treat lying as an ability unto itself. Instead characters employ it as a tactic while using any of the various Interpersonal abilities. With **Bureaucracy**, you tell functionaries what they want to hear. A little **Flirting** persuades the attractive stranger you admire her politics. Using **Interrogation**, you convince suspects that you're really just trying to help them out, and so on. There's a little bit of deception in nearly every successful Interpersonal interaction — at least that's how it works for covert operatives.

overload it by being "always on." Some people believe their own falsehoods. Psychopathic and sociopathic personality types and brainwashed vampire cultists lie reflexively and without shame, depriving you of the telltale tics and gestures you use to sense when a person is deceiving you. Many of the undead, or those who have tasted their blood and been changed, will occasionally "read wrong," but will similarly fail to send any useful signals to a human watcher.

You can also use this ability to cold-read a mark for fortune-telling scams, phony séances or mentalist acts, and the like.

BUREAUCRACY (INTERPERSONAL)

You know how to navigate a bureaucratic organization, whether it's a government office or a large corporation. You know how to get what you want from it in an expeditious manner, and with a minimum of ruffled feathers. You can:

♦ convince officials to provide sensitive or inconvenient information
♦ gain credentials on false pretenses
♦ find the person who really knows what's going on

♦ develop and maintain contacts within a bureaucracy with which you have regular dealings
♦ locate offices and files
♦ borrow equipment or supplies
♦ convince third parties subject to a bureaucracy that you have a legitimate work order or request

Bureaucracy is not a catch-all information gathering ability. Bureaucrats wish to convey the impression that they are busy and harried, whether or not they actually are. Most take a profound, secret joy in directing inquiries elsewhere. When characters attempt to use **Bureaucracy** to gain information more easily accessible via other abilities (such as **Research**), their contacts simply lose the request and go to lunch early.

For a Contact who will really stick their neck out (so to speak), use the **Network** ability (see p. 30).

CHARM (INTERPERSONAL)

You're good at getting people to help you by complimenting them, as subtly or blatantly as they prefer. You can quickly size up someone in conversation and discern areas of pride or of hidden shame (both susceptible to your approach). You can get them to:

♦ reveal information
♦ perform minor favors
♦ regard you as trustworthy

If the target of your **Charm** finds you sexually attractive (and this ability covers social awareness and lets you pick up on subtle signals and unconscious tells), you can use this ability to play on that attraction.

CHEMISTRY (TECHNICAL)

You're trained in the analysis and manipulation of chemical substances, and have a working knowledge of such related sciences as biochemistry, genetics, geology, and metallurgy. Given suitable lab facilities, you can:

♦ among a wide variety of other materials, identify drugs, pharmaceuticals, toxins, and viruses
♦ create simple explosives, incendiaries, poisons, gases, and acids
♦ analyze unknown substances, soil samples, minerals, alloys, compounds, gene sequences, etc.
♦ match samples of dirt or vegetation from a piece of evidence to a scene
♦ perform chemical document analysis on ink or paper
♦ safely handle (or knowledgably advise against handling at all) hazardous materials
♦ interact with physical scientists and lab techs as a professional equal

COP TALK (INTERPERSONAL)

You know how to speak the lingo of the police, and to make them feel confident and relaxed in your presence. You may be a current or former cop (or national police agent), or simply pose as the kind of person they immediately identify as a solid, trustworthy citizen. You can:

- coolly ply cops for confidential information
- get excused for minor infractions
- imply that you are a colleague, authorized to participate in their cases
- tell when a cop is lying to you or holding something back
- pose convincingly as a cop when dealing with a civilian

CRIMINOLOGY (ACADEMIC)

You study crimes, and the methods for solving crimes, from laboratory techniques to psychological profiling. You can:

- recall details of past art thefts, bank robberies, serial murders, and everything in between
- plan a criminal enterprise successfully
- make accurate guesses as to the upbringing and pathology of criminals or killers based on their known modus operandi
- predict criminals' future actions based on their past behavior, researched or observed

- detail or predict the organizational structure, leadership, and activities of known organized crime rings
- note relationships between objects at a crime scene, reconstructing sequences of events
- transfer, take, and match fingerprints using the naked eye or software; you are familiar with all major fingerprint databases
- match typewritten materials to a given machine, handwriting to a known sample, tire tracks to specific models or vehicles, etc.
- bag and tag objects for forensic analysis without contaminating your samples
- perform ballistics and gunpowder analysis of bullets or other residue
- perform blood and fiber tests on crime scene evidence

CRYPTOGRAPHY (TECHNICAL)

You're an expert in the making and breaking of codes in any language you can read, from the simple ciphers of old-school espionage to the supercomputer algorithms of the present day. Shown a code, you can guess who might be using it. Given some time and a dictionary, you may be able to puzzle out foreign alphabets, translating languages by brute force. You can:

♦ break most ciphers, given time
♦ recognize encryption systems and know which agencies and groups commonly use them
♦ solve complex puzzles and problems with practiced ease
♦ spot patterns and shapes in apparently random data, and tell encrypted text from random noise

DATA RECOVERY (TECHNICAL)

You use computer and electronic technology to retrieve and enhance seemingly inaccessible information or imagery on hard drives and other media. You can:

♦ recover hidden, erased, or corrupted computer files
♦ increase the clarity of audio recordings, zeroing in on desired elements
♦ miraculously find detailed, high-resolution images within a blurry video image or pixilated JPEG
♦ interpret and enhance spy plane and satellite imagery, or even provide a real-time feed from a series of satellite downlinks

Actually *tasking* a spy plane or satellite involves getting a hacker to break into the system.

Simply discovering information (including commercial satellite imagery) in a computer or electronic database is **Research**.

DIAGNOSIS (ACADEMIC)

You diagnose human disease, injuries, poisonings, and physical frailties, and may be broadly acquainted with veterinary medicine as well. You may have a medical license. You can:

♦ diagnose diseases, poisonings, and other ailments
♦ prescribe treatment for a treatable condition
♦ deliver a baby
♦ identify the extent and cause of an unconscious person's trauma
♦ detect when a person is suffering from a physically debilitating condition such as drug addiction, pregnancy, or malnutrition
♦ establish a person's general level of health
♦ identify medical abnormalities
♦ understand medical jargon
♦ interact with medical professionals as a peer

At the GM's discretion, you may be trained in a more complex specialty, as well as the sort of general practice indicated here. The GM may or may not allow very elementary **Forensic Pathology** ("the killer used a blunt instrument; death was instantaneous") with this ability.

ELECTRONIC SURVEILLANCE (TECHNICAL)

You're adept at the use of sound and video recording equipment to gather intelligence. Given proper gear, you can:

♦ trace phone calls and GPS signals
♦ plant secret listening devices or hidden cameras
♦ create ad hoc listening devices using cell phones or other street technology

♦ locate secret listening devices, sensors, or cameras planted by others
♦ make high-quality audio and video recordings
♦ enhance the quality of audio and video recordings, isolating chosen sounds or images

Actually tapping a phone line or fiber optic cable may require a **Mechanics** test. Evading electronic surveillance systems is almost always an **Evasion** or **Infiltration** test.

FORENSIC PATHOLOGY (TECHNICAL)

You study crime scenes and perform autopsies on deceased subjects to determine their cause and circumstances of death. You can use skeletal evidence to reconstruct the physical details (age, sex, medical condition, sometimes occupation) of the deceased.

Among other things, your examination can identify:

♦ the nature of the weapon or weapons used on the victim, if any
♦ the approximate time of death
♦ the presence of intoxicants or other foreign substances in the bloodstream or on the skin
♦ the contents of the victim's last meal

In many cases, you can:

♦ reconstruct the sequence of events leading to the victim's death from the arrangement of wounds on the body
♦ determine time (and sometimes place) of death by studying the insects at the scene (or the eggs and larvae in the body)
♦ perform DNA analysis on samples found at crime scenes, matching them to samples taken from targets

FORGERY
(TECHNICAL)

You fake things. Given time, originals (or good images), suitable materials, and work space, you can:

◆ create a false passport, driving license, visa, or other government credential

◆ forge handwriting with a sample to work from

◆ fake a book, pamphlet, newspaper, or other published work

◆ forge a painting, sculpture, or other *objet d'art*

◆ artificially age paper and ink

◆ undetectably open and re-seal a sealed envelope, document pouch, or other "soft" container

◆ create an attractive, if uninspired, work of art on a subject of your choosing

It takes less time and effort to create a fake credential that will never be checked: an employee ID badge for an office building, a fake police shield to get past a doorman, etc.

HIGH SOCIETY
(INTERPERSONAL)

You know how to hang with the rich and famous, and how to chat them up without getting security called. You are comfortable with "old money" aristocracy, with the Davos elite, with the televised chattering classes, and with the crassest of nouveau riche vulgarians and celebutantes. Yachts, Gulfstreams, and four-star restaurants are your seeming natural habitat. You can:

◆ dress fashionably for any occasion

◆ get past the velvet rope at exclusive clubs and parties, or past the concierge at a four-star hotel

◆ drop brand names, allude to current trends, and generally blend in culturally with rich scenesters of all types

◆ identify the best wine, liquor, food, jewelry, and other luxury goods

◆ successfully schmooze for an introduction to a celebrity, elected official, or financier

◆ recall specific or relevant gossip or news about the tastes, lifestyles, or sordid behavior of a rich or famous person

◆ know where and when the best parties, most culturally important openings, or other gala events in any city are due to happen

◆ score drugs or otherwise find the seamy side (if any) of high-society functions, happening nightclubs, etc.

◆ interact with the rich and famous as an accepted equal

Note that this ability does *not* necessarily convey any actual wealth or fame. The GM can, if he wishes, allow an Agent to use family connections or a liberated company slush fund to explain it.

HISTORY
(ACADEMIC)

You're an expert in recorded human history, with an emphasis on its political, military, economic, and technological developments. You are also an expert in the tools historians use: documents and books. You can:

◆ recognize obscure historical allusions

◆ recall important or relevant events in a given country, city, or region

◆ identify ancient languages and scripts

◆ perform textual analysis on a manuscript or book to date it or identify the author

◆ determine the age of a document

◆ tell where and when an object made during historical times was fashioned

◆ identify the period of an article of dress or costume

◆ interact with historians and similar academics as a peer

HUMAN TERRAIN
(ACADEMIC)

The U.S. military's counter-insurgency strategy called for "human terrain mapping," along with the more conventional physical terrain mapping involved in combat operations. The "human terrain" includes the "areas, structures, organizations, cultures, people, and events" of a region: mapping and exploiting that terrain comprises disciplines like anthropology, sociology, theology, social psychology, political science, and propaganda.

As a trained and knowledgeable mapper of human terrain, you can:

◆ identify artifacts and rituals of living cultures

◆ describe and predict the customs of a foreign group or local subculture

◆ predict the behavior of a given crowd, mob, or militant faction

◆ supply information about religious practices and beliefs

◆ quote relevant tags from the major scriptures

◆ recognize the names and attributes of various saints, gods, and other figures of religious worship and veneration

◆ identify whether a given religious practice or ritual is orthodox or heretical

◆ identify temples, meeting places, or other locally important structures

◆ analyze political and social structures — including identifying key figures, rivalries, and weak points — in a given group or society: e.g., a warlord's militia, an academic conference, a labor union, or a majority-Muslim *banlieue* in Paris

◆ develop a strongly appealing political or religious message for a given subculture or society

◆ detect, or conspire at, election rigging

INTERROGATION (INTERPERSONAL)

You extract information from subjects fearful of your authority, cruelty, or power. To use this ability, you must place the target in custody, or in a situation evocative of constraint and punishment. You might borrow an interrogation room from local cops, or construct a makeshift one in an abandoned shipping container or a disused Balkan cement factory. Through threats, persistence, and the occasional deception, you gradually establish a bond with your targets, convincing them to identify with you psychologically, and that giving up the information you seek — even if it's a confession — is their only remaining option.

INTIMIDATION (INTERPERSONAL)

You elicit cooperation from targets by seeming physically imposing, invading their personal space, and adopting a psychologically commanding manner. Intimidation may involve implied or direct threats of physical violence, but is just as often an act of mental dominance such as a stare down or a well-directed taunt. You can:

♦ gain information
♦ inspire the target to leave the area
♦ anger the target into involuntarily revealing information
♦ quell a target's desire to attempt violence against you or others

LANGUAGES (ACADEMIC)

You're fluent in a number of obscure or difficult languages or dialects. These might be living languages from distant parts of the globe or dead languages like Sumerian. You can read and translate texts from these languages, and pick up on subtle linguistics or cultural ambiguities.

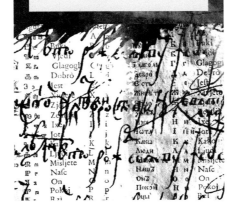

OF COURSE I SPEAK RUSSIAN

As a former international spy, you're assumed to speak a number of common languages so fluently you could pass for a native speaker, and be able to get by in conversation in a few more. Save the **Languages** ability for obscure or extinct languages – for cases where your need for a translator is an element of the plot. Alternatively, take **Languages** as one of your own Investigative abilities if your conception of your character has them as a brilliant multi-linguist.

LAW (ACADEMIC)

You know the criminal and civil laws of your home jurisdiction well, and are broadly acquainted with foreign legal systems. You may be (or impersonate) a bar-certified attorney. You can:

♦ assess the legal risks attendant on any course of action
♦ understand lawyerly jargon
♦ argue with police and prosecutors
♦ interact with lawyers, magistrates, and court officers as a professional equal

MILITARY SCIENCE (ACADEMIC)

You are a student of warfare, probably trained as such in a military academy. This expertise includes a knowledge of military history, strategy, and tactics, and the weapons, technologies, and engineering techniques of the battlefield. You can:

♦ identify uniforms and insignia
♦ identify an unknown military or paramilitary force by examining the weapons they use
♦ deduce a soldier's training and assignment history from his demeanor and use of slang and jargon
♦ spot weaknesses in an enemy's fortifications or tactics
♦ note relationships between objects and damage at the scene of a firefight or battle, reconstructing sequences of events
♦ use **Military Science** as an Interpersonal ability to interact with military and paramilitary personnel

NEGOTIATION (INTERPERSONAL)

You are an expert in making deals with others, convincing them that the best arrangement for you is also the best for them. You can:

♦ haggle for goods and services
♦ gauge likely prices of items, including what someone else will pay for them
♦ successfully and politely bribe a corrupt official or policeman
♦ mediate hostage situations or diplomatic crises
♦ sell something to a potential buyer
♦ swap favors or information with others

NOTICE (TECHNICAL)

You're adept at casing a scene and at finding important clues. This is the generic ability for spotting a hidden clue, general situational awareness, or noticing a non-threatening visual anomaly. You can:

♦ spot hidden objects or objects of interest (including bullet casings under a car or drops of blood behind the desk) at a crime scene or other investigation site
♦ case a location to spot guards, cameras, rear entrances, security procedures, potential police response, weapon mounts, etc.
♦ note entrances and exits from rooms you're in, and who's near them
♦ notice signs of a previous search of the location
♦ find and transfer fingerprints, fiber evidence, or other physical clues in a scene

Spotting enemy surveillance or monitoring a location is **Surveillance**; sensing a sniper lurking in the shadows is **Sense Trouble**. Searching for a deliberately hidden object that is *not* a core clue is **Conceal**.

OCCULT STUDIES (ACADEMIC)

You're an expert in the historical study of magic, superstition, and sorcery from the Stone Age to the present. From the Templars to numerology to the Golden Dawn, you know the dates, the places, the controversies, and the legends. You can:

♦ identify the cultural traditions informing a ritual by examining its physical aftermath
♦ guess the intended effect of a ritual from its physical aftermath
♦ fake a fortune-telling session, séance, or other occult activity
♦ read and cast a horoscope
♦ supply historical facts and anecdotes concerning various occult traditions, cult groups, demons, and legends
♦ identify occult paraphernalia, grimoires, symbols, and codes
♦ identify occult activities as the work of informed practitioners, teenage posers, or *bona fide* vampires

This ability does not cover vampire lore per se, which is handled by **Vampirology**.

This ability does not allow you to work magic or summon supernatural entities, even if the campaign admits the existence of magic. You may believe in the occult or not; the skill functions just as well in either case.

At the GM's discretion, this ability also covers UFO lore, cryptozoology, conspiracy theory, zero-point physics, and other fringe sciences. In a campaign heavily involving such matters, the GM may instead add a **Fringe Science** ability paralleling **Occult Studies**.

OUTDOOR SURVIVAL (TECHNICAL)

You have worked and lived outdoors and in the wild, possibly during a rural upbringing or extensive military service "in country." You can:

♦ tell when an animal is behaving strangely
♦ tell whether an animal or plant is native to a given area
♦ find edible plants, hunt, and fish
♦ ride a horse
♦ make fire and survive outdoors at night or in bad weather
♦ navigate overland, albeit more easily with a compass and a map
♦ track people, animals, or vehicles across grass or through forests
♦ hunt with dogs, including tracking with bloodhounds, assuming you have friendly dogs available

PHARMACY (TECHNICAL)

You are able to identify and compound drugs and medicines. You can:

♦ identify drugs and potions, and recognize their side effects and contraindications
♦ identify a drug addict after a brief interaction
♦ identify poisons and determine antidotes
♦ given the raw materials, manufacture morphine, heroin, cocaine, ecstasy, methamphetamine, and other controlled substances

PHOTOGRAPHY (TECHNICAL)

You're proficient in the use of cameras, including still, motion-picture, digital, and video photography. You can:

- take useful visual records of sites of interest or surveillance targets
- spot manual retouching or digital manipulation in a photographic or video image
- realistically retouch and manipulate images
- use filters and lights to capture images only visible in infrared or ultraviolet
- develop film if you're, like, stuck in 1967 or something

Interpreting satellite or aerial photo imagery uses **Data Recovery** or the ability connected to the imagery's subject: e.g., **Archaeology** for a dig site, **Architecture** for a terrorist compound, **Military Science** for a missile silo.

You don't need **Photography** to just snap a few quick shots through a telephoto lens, but if you require specialist techniques or full coverage, you need this ability.

REASSURANCE (INTERPERSONAL)

You get people to do what you want by putting them at ease. This may involve fast talk, genuine sympathy, or just a calming presence. You can:

- elicit information and minor favors
- allay fear or panic in others
- convince frightened or worried witnesses that they saw nothing unusual
- instill a sense of calm during a crisis

RESEARCH (ACADEMIC)

You know how to find factual information from books, records, official sources, and the Internet. You can ferret out information from collections of books, records, files, archives, newspaper morgues, or big piles of unsorted papers. If the information lies within, and you have access to the collection, you can find it. You're as comfortable with a card catalogue and microfiche reader as with a search engine. Your smart phone address book brims with exotic and informative contacts.

This skill covers any open source intelligence (OSINT); if the information is protected, you likely need **Data Recovery**, **Infiltration**, or an asset in place to get at it.

Research often involves Taking Time (p. 39). In effect, you can substitute **Research** for other academic abilities like **History**, **Law**, **Chemistry**, **Astronomy** and the like, but the trade-off is that it takes a lot longer to track down the clues you need.

STREETWISE (INTERPERSONAL)

You know how to behave among crooks, gangsters, druggies, hookers, grifters, and other habitués of the criminal underworld. You can:

- deploy criminal etiquette to avoid fights and conflicts
- identify unsafe locations and dangerous people
- recall which gang or mafia claims a given area as turf
- deal with fences, black marketeers, drug dealers, arms runners, and so forth
- successfully price illegal goods such as drugs, stolen items, or weapons
- get hired for a criminal operation
- tell when practiced criminals and con men are lying, as with **Bullshit Detector**
- gather underworld rumors

TRADECRAFT (INTERPERSONAL)

You know how to utilize the techniques of conventional espionage agents, and how to talk to them if you must hold a meet. You can:

- set up and check a dead drop
- spot or conduct a brush pass or car toss
- determine which agency trained a covert operative by examining their tradecraft, surveillance methods, etc.
- identify good places for recognition signs, cleaning passes, etc.
- recall notorious or relevant episodes of spying, covert ops, etc.
- gather rumors in the covert ops world
- make contact with operatives without scaring them off
- convey information or threats elliptically without tipping off eavesdroppers

TRAFFIC ANALYSIS (TECHNICAL)

You know how to boil down a mass of data — probably raw signals intel, a tranche of phone records, or possibly a whole lot of surveillance tapes — and extract its meaning and patterns. Given the data, you can:

- determine which numbers in a set of phone records are calling who, when, about what
- determine which cars in a city's traffic pattern are driving where, when, and how long they're staying there
- find patterns in the data flow, e.g., more murders in August, or the same museum guard on duty during all the incidents
- work out the daily (and weekly, monthly, etc.) routine of an office, military base, museum, etc. and answer questions like: When is payroll made? Who takes delivery of parcels? When does the cleaning staff arrive?
- find anomalies in the data flow, e.g., missing records or "dogs that didn't bark"
- find weak spots in security that follow regular patterns
- identify the source of information (or disinformation) by tracking its route through the system
- assemble a communications or organizational picture of a social network such as a criminal conspiracy, academic email list, or division of border guards

URBAN SURVIVAL (TECHNICAL)

You are familiar with working and living in cities, especially their seamier underbelly, possibly as the result of an urban upbringing or extensive police service walking a beat. You can:

- tell when crowds or passers-by are behaving strangely
- tell whether a passer-by or bystander is native to a given neighborhood
- cadge spare change, Dumpster dive, and otherwise survive on the streets if need be
- navigate an unfamiliar urban street layout and locate buildings without looking like a tourist
- find open manholes, dangling fire escapes, and conveniently unlocked doors
- interact on friendly terms with the local homeless or vagrant community
- find (or avoid) a neighborhood where you can use **Streetwise** to good effect

In addition, you can recall specifics (streets, restaurants, shortcuts, etc.) of any city you've ever spent more than a few days in, and are familiar with its layout, police patrol patterns, etc.

VAMPIROLOGY (ACADEMIC)

The subset of occultism dealing directly with vampires. You know the traditional lore from Hercegovina to Hammer Films, the great names, and the legendary spoor of the undead. You can tell actual vampire attacks from those of mere serial killers or the affectations of goth wannabes.

Your popular knowledge may or may not initially apply to actual vampires, although as the campaign goes on, your **Vampirology** ability will apply to your monstrous foes.

In some games, the GM may not allow this ability at character creation, either to maintain initial suspense or because very few spies know much about vampires. In such campaigns, you may buy **Vampirology** with experience after encountering vampires.

USING GENERAL ABILITIES

When attempting actions that don't directly gather information, and which can lead to engaging story possibilities whether you succeed or fail, use your General abilities.

General abilities fall into four categories:

- ◆ ■ **Manual**, drawing on a combination of skill training and fine motor skills
- ◆ ★ **Mental**, drawing on mostly on intellectual study, perception, thought, and/or memory
- ◆ ▲ **Physical**, using your gross motor skills
- ◆ ● **Social**, relying on appearance, social awareness, and ability to blend in

General abilities are measured by the number of ability dice you possess in that ability (0, 1 or 2). You roll these dice, one by one, attempting to avoid a bad result (a Setback), hoping to improve your position (an Advance), but sometimes settling for a middle-ground result (a Hold). Tests are explained on p. 34

The benefits of Edges and penalties imposed by Problems often specify that they apply to a particular one of these three categories.

To see if you succeed with the use of a General ability — and, if so, how well — you'll engage in a Challenge, which we'll explain shortly. That will make more sense if we first show you what each ability does.

MASTERY EDGES

You have access to special techniques and training called Mastery Edges. These Mastery Edges reflect your intensive training and cinematic badass nature as an elite spy. You start each game with three Mastery Edges; you can pick any Edges you wish from the list on p. 273.

Each General ability has two or three Mastery Edges associated with it. You can take multiple Mastery Edges from a single ability if you wish.

CHANGING MASTERY EDGES

You can swap one Mastery Edge for another in the middle of an operation when you move from one city to another, or when you take a period of downtime to prepare for an impending confrontation (this counts as Taking Time; see "Taking Time" on page 39). If you've discarded a Mastery Edge in the course of play, you don't get a replacement card and have to make do with your reduced hand size until the end of the operation.

For example, you might start a game in London with three Masteries. You spend two of your Masteries, then fly to Rome. While traveling, you swap out one of your unused Masteries for one you expect will be more useful when hunting vampires in the catacombs...

GENERAL ABILITIES

ABILITY	CATEGORY	ICON
Athletics	Physical	▲
Conceal	Manual	■
Cool	Mental	★
Cover	Social	●
Driving	Manual	■
Evasion	Physical	▲
Fighting	Physical	▲
Filch	Manual	■
Infiltration	Physical	▲
Mechanics	Manual	■
Medic	Manual	■
Network	Social	●
Preparedness	Mental	★
Sense Trouble	Mental	★
Shooting	Physical	▲
Surveillance	Social	●

GENERAL ABILITY DEFINITIONS

ATHLETICS

Athletics allows you to perform general acts of physical derring-do, from running to jumping to throwing grenades to rappelling down the side of a building to dodging falling or oncoming objects. Any physical action not covered by another ability probably falls under the rubric of **Athletics**.

EDGE

Trained Reflexes

ATHLETICS MASTERY

You've got astounding reflexes, and can dodge or minimize the effects of almost any blow. Discard to gain +1 Athletics die for one Challenge.

EDGE

Unstoppable

ATHLETICS MASTERY

Discard to immediately exchange 1 or 2 Injuries for a Hurt Problem.

CONCEAL

You can hide things from view and conceal them from search. Your methods might include camouflage, hiding items on your person, snaking things into drawers unobserved, building secret compartments into cars or briefcases, or even altering a thing's visual signature with paint or plaster.

Among other things, you can also:

- discover things intentionally concealed, including bugs, cameras, or bombs
- mask an infrared or scent signature, given suitable equipment such as insulated cloth or coffee grounds

- efficiently pat down a target or, given time, conduct a thorough strip search
- "clean" a crime scene or safe house of evidence indicating your presence there
- detect signs of a previous careful, professional search
- plant a listening device, hidden camera, or bomb

Wiring or building a bug or hidden camera uses **Electronic Surveillance** or **Mechanics**. Setting a bomb uses **Mechanics**. Discovering a camouflaged object in a reconnaissance photo is **Data Recovery**. Tapping a phone or fiber optic line is **Mechanics**.

You can also use **Electronic Surveillance** to detect bugs and cameras, especially those aimed at other targets.

EDGE

Perfect Conceal

CONCEAL MASTERY

You've always got something up your sleeve. Discard to produce any one small item (a lockpick, a knife, a cigarette lighter, a cell phone), even if you've been thoroughly searched or passed through a security scanner.

EDGE

Cache

CONCEAL MASTERY

Discard to have already stowed a cache of equipment where you can now retrieve it. This cache may contain weapons, passports, money, vehicles, medical supplies, or obscure equipment.

COOL

You're able to remain calm, detached, and focused even when under stress. Use **Cool** to:

- stick to your cover when questioned or interrogated
- avoid temptations and resist emotional appeals
- stay on target during a crisis
- keep calm in a firefight
- avoid giving yourself away under pressure
- resist supernatural forces attempting to influence your behavior

---
EDGE

Unshakable

Nothing touches you.
Nothing leaves a mark.

COOL MASTERY

If you still hold this card at the end of the operation, discard it to Counter any Problem.

EDGE

Ice Cold

You stay calm under pressure and don't let anything slip.

COOL MASTERY

Discard to ignore all penalties to a test.

COVER

This ability represents your ability to disguise yourself by taking on the identity of another person. You've got an established stash of cover identities, including the associated documents. At any time, you may reveal or remember the existence of a cover identity that you established previously: perhaps during your old life, or while freelancing since, or even earlier during the campaign.

Provide the Director with as many details as he needs to work it into the campaign.

If you want your cover to have an especially useful position or background ("Oh, the ambassador knows me as his old drinking buddy"), then the Director may either ask you to Push the appropriate Investigative ability, or else take a Problem to compensate for this advantage. ("The ambassador knows you as his old drinking buddy... who had an affair with his wife.")

You can also use this ability to disguise yourself by changing your clothing, mannerisms, and so forth. A quick disguise doesn't have the depth or documentation of an established cover identity, but can help you avoid detection or Heat in certain circumstances.

EDGE

Connected Cover
COVER MASTERY

You've got several well-established alternate identities. Discard when undercover to have a GMC recognize you as your alternate identities. The GMC vouches for you ("I know this guy – he's a gambler, not a spy").

EDGE

Quick Disguise
COVER MASTERY

Discard to automatically find the elements of a basic disguise in a scene; you'll always be able to find a lab coat in a hospital, an army uniform in a military base, a battered leather jacket near a biker gang. You automatically Hold on one Cover test.

DRIVING

You're a skilled defensive driver, capable of wringing high performance from even the most recalcitrant automobile, pickup truck, or van. You can:

- evade or conduct pursuit
- avoid collisions or minimize damage from collisions
- successfully drive off-road without bogging down or wrecking, assuming even minimally hospitable terrain
- maintain high speed under unfavorable weather conditions
- perform jumps, drifts, reverses, and other driving stunts
- spot tampering with a vehicle
- conduct emergency repairs

Driving doubles as an Investigative ability when used to:

- evaluate or estimate the performance or condition of a motor vehicle
- predict, evaluate, or plan highway or Autobahn routes between cities
- determine the street value, visibility, or availability of a stolen vehicle
- interact with drivers and similar gearheads as a professional equal

You can also pilot a small plane, helicopter, motorboat, or other vehicle.

EDGE

Grand Theft Auto
DRIVING MASTERY

Discard to automatically and instantly steal a car. There's no test and no delay – it's as easy as pulling open the door and sliding in behind the wheel. There'll always be a vehicle to hand when you use this card.

EDGE

Wheel Artist
DRIVING MASTERY

Discard to gain +1 **Driving** dice in a Challenge.

EVASION

You're good at escaping pursuers and avoiding detection, either by losing yourself in a crowd, hiding in the shadows, or running like hell. **Evasion** can incorporate stealth, but it also covers getting the hell out by jumping through windows and charging through packed streets. You can:

- escape when being chased by bad guys
- vanish when someone turns their back
- avoid arrest when chased by police
- outrun a pursuing monster
- evade detection when people are looking for you
- lose a tail when you spot someone shadowing you

For car chases, use **Driving**.

EDGE

Vanish

EVASION MASTERY

If you're out of sight of your enemies, you can escape from a scene. You can't bring anything or anyone with you — this is the dramatic equivalent of an ejector seat.

EDGE

Dodge This

EVASION MASTERY

Discard to gain +1 **Evasion** dice in a Challenge.

FIGHTING

You can hold your own in a hand-to-hand fight, whether you wish to kill, knock out, restrain, or evade your opponent. For this purpose, **Fighting** covers all sorts of unarmed combat, from aikido matches to bar brawls to Muay Thai kickboxing bouts, as well as the use of melee weapons like knives, clubs, swords, police batons, fighting sticks, or stakes.

For firearms, use Shooting.

EDGE

Martial Arts Expert

FIGHTING MASTERY

Discard to gain +2 **Fighting** dice in a Challenge when fighting bare-handed.

EDGE

Weapons Expert

FIGHTING MASTERY

Discard to gain +2 **Fighting** dice in a Challenge when fighting with a weapon.

EDGE

Grit

FIGHTING MASTERY

Discard this card to ignore the penalties from any Injury or Hurt cards for the rest of this scene.

FILCH

Your nimble fingers allow you to unobtrusively manipulate small objects. You can:

- pilfer small items from desks, counters, crime scenes, or museum displays, even under the supposedly watchful eyes of a guard or police officer
- walk out openly with a briefly unguarded bulky and low-value item as if you were entitled to it, e.g., steal a security guard uniform from the locker room
- given a diversion, lift almost anything you can carry under your clothing, e.g., cut a painting out of its frame and stuff it under your jacket
- pick pockets
- slip cell keys from guards' belts, lift ID badges from lapels, etc.
- surreptitiously relieve opponents of their weaponry
- plant objects on unsuspecting targets
- switch two similar objects (like two briefcases) without being noticed

---
EDGE

Sleight of Hand

FILCH MASTERY

Discard to declare retroactively that you palmed some small object — a key, a memory stick, a credit card, a poker chip — that was mentioned in an earlier scene.

EDGE

No Slip-Ups

FILCH MASTERY

Discard to automatically Hold in a **Filch** Challenge.

INFILTRATION

You're good at placing yourself inside places you have no right to be. You can:

- pick locks (including handcuff locks)
- deactivate or evade security systems
- enter and hotwire a locked car
- move silently
- hide in shadows or cover
- avoid visual security, whether guards or cameras
- find suitable places for forced entry, and use them

Despite its name, **Infiltration** is as useful for getting out of places undetected as it is for getting into them. If you're spotted, though, **Infiltration** is of no use.

Use **Infiltration** to hide in cover or to creep around unnoticed. To hide in a crowd or to stealthily follow a target, use **Surveillance**. To shake or outrun a pursuer through speed, not stealth, use **Evasion**. To rappel onto a roof, or climb a fence, use **Athletics**.

EDGE

Open Sesame

INFILTRATION MASTERY

Discard to automatically Hold in an **Infiltration** test involving a door, lock, or similar obstacle.

EDGE

Stealth Operator

INFILTRATION MASTERY

Discard to automatically Hold in a **Fighting** challenge when ambushing from hiding.

MECHANICS

You're good at building, repairing, operating, and disabling mechanical, electrical, or electronic devices, from catapults to DVD players to key parts of a city's power grid. Given the right components, you can create jury-rigged devices, booby traps, or weapons from odd bits of scrap. This ability also covers using heavy machinery and equipment such as cranes or artillery.

This ability includes explosives, so you can:

- defuse bombs and traps
- handle nitroglycerin or other dangerously unstable materials with relative safety
- given time, blow open safes or vaults without damaging the contents
- mix explosive compounds from common chemicals
- safely construct and detonate explosive devices or booby traps of your own
- implode, or selectively destroy one part of, a structure with explosives
- set a reliably hot and destructive fire

Effectively, any time you reach for the duct tape, you're probably about to use this ability.

EDGE

Boom

MECHANICS MASTERY

Discard this card at any point after you planted a bomb. The bomb goes off, and you get to describe the explosion – and pick who takes the brunt of the blast. If it's part of a test, you automatically Advance.

EDGE

Duct Tape Ninja

MECHANICS MASTERY

Discard to assemble a solution out of objects at hand. As long as you can justify it, you Hold in any **Manual** or **Physical** contest.

MEDIC

You can perform first aid on sick or injured individuals. You can also use this ability on yourself, although your options there are more limited.

See p. 49 for how to use **Medic** to treat Injuries.

EDGE

Painkillers and Vodka

MEDIC MASTERY

Discard to make a **Medical Attention** (p. 49) test without having to Take Time.

EDGE

Battlefield Medic

MEDIC MASTERY

Discard to Push **Diagnosis**, **Forensic Pathology**, or **Pharmacy**, or to gain a bonus **Medic** die.

NETWORK

This ability represents your network of professional contacts. You've got friends and former assets all over the world, and you can draw on them for assistance as Contacts. The better your roll, the more reliable a Contact you produce. See *Network Tests*, p. 45.

EDGE

What Are You Doing Here?

NETWORK MASTERY

Discard to make a **Network** test to create a Contact when you wouldn't normally be able to make such a test. For example, if you're imprisoned in a vampire's dungeon, you could whistle up a helpful Contact — a fellow prisoner, a turncoat jailer, a thief robbing the place — by playing this card. Your **Network** test is at a -4 penalty.

EDGE

You Never Knew Me

NETWORK MASTERY

Discard when a Contact betrays you to reveal that you'd planned for this eventuality. Either describe how you avoid the effects of the betrayal, or gain 4 dice that can be applied to any Challenges arising from the betrayal.

PREPAREDNESS

You expertly anticipate the needs of any operation by packing a kit efficiently arranged with necessary gear. Assuming you have immediate access to your kit, you can produce whatever object you need to overcome an obstacle. You make a simple test (p. 40): if you succeed, you have the item you want. You needn't do this in advance of the adventure, but can dig into your kit bag (provided you're able to get to it) as the need arises.

Items of obvious utility to a covert operation or anti-undead hit job do not require a test. These include but are not limited to: smart phones, weapons, detonators, flashlights, binoculars, batteries, gloves, zip cuffs, duct tape, rations, cigarettes and lighters, multi-tools, magnifying glasses, pocket mirrors, garlic, stakes, and crucifixes.

Other abilities imply the possession of basic gear suitable to their core tasks. Characters with **Diagnosis** have their own first aid kits or medical bags; **Photography** comes with a camera. If you have **Shooting**, you have a gun; **Data Recovery**, you have a laptop, and so on. Preparedness does not intrude into their territory. It covers general-purpose investigative equipment, plus oddball items — a Ouija board, a baseball, a tube of super glue, a gas mask — that suddenly come in handy in the course of the story. The traditional "rappelling line just long enough to get me down off this building" is a classic **Preparedness** feat of the spy thriller genre.

The sorts of items you can produce at a moment's notice depend not on your rating or pool, but on narrative credibility. If the Director determines that your possession of an item would seem ludicrous, anachronistic, or out of genre, you don't get to roll for it. You simply don't have it. Any item which elicits a laugh from the group when suggested is probably out of bounds.

Inappropriate use of the **Preparedness** ability is like pornography. Your Director will know it when he sees it.

EDGE

The Nick of Time
PREPAREDNESS MASTERY

Discard this card to reveal you took some action in advance — you planted a bomb, you bribed a cop, you researched the route of a parade that you now use to cover your escape.

EDGE

The Reptile Fund
PREPAREDNESS MASTERY

Discard to have access to money. This can be a duffle bag stuffed with non-sequential bills, the fruits of credit card fraud, or a box of ancient gold coins looted from some Transylvanian tomb. It's enough for one sizeable purchase or bribe.

SENSE TROUBLE

This ability allows you to perceive (either with sight or other senses) potential hazards to yourself or others. For example, you can:

♦ hear the click of a safety being taken off
♦ see a flittering shape cross the moon
♦ smell the charnel reek of a ghoul's breath in the windowless warehouse
♦ notice the tiny marks on the inspector's wrist
♦ have a bad feeling about that glassy-eyed border guard at the seemingly deserted checkpoint

The Director should never require the use of this General ability to find clues to the problem at hand. Instead, use Investigative abilities, defaulting to **Notice** when no ability seems more appropriate. **Sense Trouble** is for a scenario's action-oriented sequences. In short, if not seeing something will get you attacked, it's **Sense Trouble**.

Sense Trouble can also be used to specifically locate the source of an already-discovered problem: the ticking bomb, the concealed sniper, the soul-drinking rune.

EDGE

Intuition
SENSE TROUBLE MASTERY

Discard to gain +1 **Sense Trouble** dice in a Challenge.

EDGE

En Garde
SENSE TROUBLE MASTERY

You've got an uncanny knack for sensing the presence of the supernatural. Discard when you gain a Shadow Problem to refresh all your dice pools.

SHOOTING

You are adept with personal firearms, including field stripping, repair, and identification. This skill also, for game-mechanical simplicity, covers crossbows and similar trigger-operated missile weapons, as well as RPGs, squad weapons (mortars and machine guns), shoulder-fired missiles, and the like.

EDGE
Sniper
SHOOTING MASTERY

If you have a chance to prepare and aim, discard to gain +2 dice in a **Shooting** Challenge.

EDGE
Two Guns Blazing
SHOOTING MASTERY

Discard for +1 **Shooting** dice.

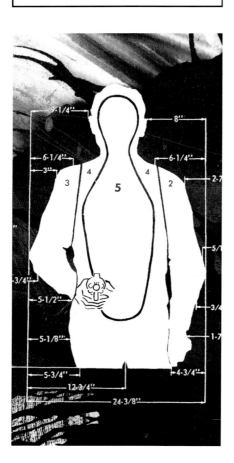

SURVEILLANCE

You're good at watching and following targets without revealing your presence. You can:

◆ guide a team to follow a target for short periods, handing off to the next in sequence, so the target doesn't realize he's being trailed

◆ use telescopic viewing equipment to keep watch on a target from a distance

◆ find undetectable vantage points for single-point coverage by eyeball or video

◆ maintain a stakeout without rousing your target's suspicion

◆ anticipate blind spots in your coverage and plan for them, or use them to "dry clean" your own shadowers

◆ determine a target's regular pattern, including any chokepoints suitable for ambush or snatch jobs

◆ hide in plain sight or blend into a crowd

◆ listen at doors or windows without being overheard yourself

◆ spot a tail, stakeout, or other non-electronic surveillance of another person

Spotting a tail or other non-electronic surveillance of yourself might be **Surveillance** (if spotting the tail probably won't lead to combat) or **Sense Trouble** (if it will lead to combat); the Director should use his best judgment.

Use **Infiltration** to creep around unnoticed and to hide in cover. To hide in a crowd or blend into the background, to sneakily or cleverly shake a pursuer, or to stealthily follow a target, use **Surveillance**. To outrun a pursuer, use **Evasion**.

EDGE
Pavement Artist
SURVEILLANCE MASTERY

Discard to retroactively declare that some seemingly innocent person in the scene is actually working with you and is also spying on your target. Make a **Network** test afterward to determine how reliable this contact is.

EDGE
Total Situational Awareness
SURVEILLANCE MASTERY

Discard to gain +1 **Surveillance** dice in a Challenge.

WHEN GENERAL ABILITIES GO INVESTIGATIVE

Every so often a General ability becomes a more likely avenue for information-gathering than any of the Investigative abilities. Like a straight-up Investigative ability, the player gets the information by looking in the right place for it. No Challenge or roll occurs.

When this happens in a published scenario, we boldface the name of the ability and note that it's being used as such.

"**Driving** (*as an Investigative ability*) *reveals that no ordinary tool cut the brake line.*"

DIGITAL INTRUSION

Hacking, as an Investigative ability, is available only through Contacts. While intercepting messages and breaking into systems is obviously a key aspect of modern-day espionage, too much reliance on it makes for a dull game. It's an action thriller – you're supposed to be double-tapping with a pistol, not double-clicking with a mouse. If you need to break into a computer network, then you either go to a suitable source, or obtain the requisite passwords through guile or intimidation.

A talented hacker can enter secure networks without formal access, and read, download, alter, or delete data and records therein. A hacker can:

♦ obtain files and databases
♦ intercept message traffic, download message archives, and filter through them for useful intel
♦ track the movement of network-connected devices
♦ tap into security cameras

With a Push, the hacker can:

♦ monitor or even take control of electronic and computerized networks and systems, such as traffic signals, a building's security system, or the RFID readers in a subway
♦ hack digital locks, assuming you can find access to them
♦ clone a cell phone's SIM card
♦ write viruses, worms, or other hostile code to disable a computer system
♦ identify security flaws in a computer system
♦ piggyback on existing wireless or computer networks
♦ transfer electronic funds, book "free" plane tickets and hotel reservations, commit credit card fraud, and the like
♦ provide a digital "paper trail" for a forged identity
♦ engage in **funkspiel**: impersonate another user's electronic "fist," sending pattern, or digital behavior
♦ blend in socially on hacker bulletin boards and at "black hat conferences

A digital intrusion attempt can attract Heat if it makes waves, steals valuable data (or cash), or otherwise has notable effects on the system or the outside world, or if it's detected by the target network's security systems.

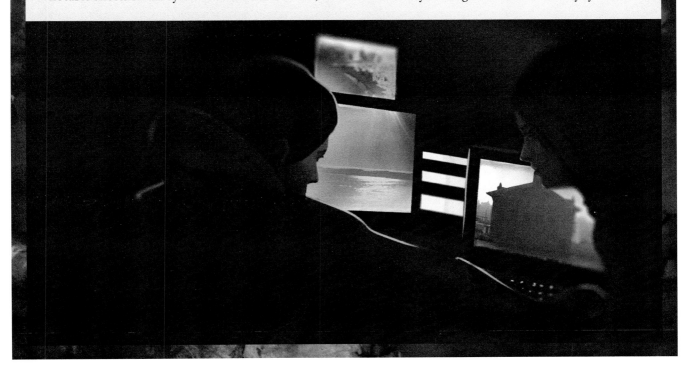

RULES

TESTS

A **test** determines what happens when you try to do something that might not work. Your Director decides whether your proposed action requires a test. If it doesn't matter to the outcome of the investigation, or if your failure to perform the action offers no interesting story choices, you succeed, no test required.

Two types of tests appear in the game: Quick Tests and Challenges. Challenges are more interesting and require a little more explanation, so we'll start there.

CHALLENGES

Challenges occur in situations where degrees of success or failure can send the story into different possible branches, each of them interesting in its own way. Examples include:

- trying to sneak into a vampire's crypt without waking it up
- tailing the German spy back to her safehouse
- disarming the bomb before it blows up the ferry

Sometimes you know that you'll get what you want, but you are only determining the costs of success (if any).

When you make a test, you describe what your Agent is trying to do. You might directly suggest the General ability you're using, or your Director may infer it from context.

DIE ROLLS

Make a test by rolling a die. (GUMSHOE always uses an ordinary 6-sided die). Each General ability has a number associated with it — for starting characters, always 2. This number indicates how many times you may roll the die when testing that ability. Roll dice one at a time, adding to your total as you go.

Depending on the situation, it may be rewarding to describe each individual die roll as a part of an ongoing action scene. Roll a 6 on the first die in a **Fighting** Challenge, and describe how you throw the bad guy across the room,

then vault over the table to kick him in the face. Roll a 1, and maybe you throw him across the room, but he flings the steel refrigerator door open to block your follow-up attack and you smash head-first into it, stunning yourself.

In other situations, describing each die roll may be redundant ("*I bandage myself with* **Medic**. *And then I bandage myself more, because the first bit of bandaging was only a die roll of 2.*")

OUTCOMES

Your final total determines the **Outcome** of your action. You either:

- **Advance**, succeeding especially well. This might grant you an Edge card, or allow you extra leverage in the situation at hand.
- **Hold**, which generally leaves you no worse off than you were before, or allows you to move forward, though without additional benefit. (The occasional especially daunting Challenge may present a Hold that puts you in a tough spot, but which is not nearly as bad as the Setback.)

♦ endure a **Setback**, worsening your situation. It may saddle you with a Problem card. Or it might simply make your immediate dilemma worse in some way.

Your Director tells you the number you need to meet or beat to score an Advance.

EARNING ADDITIONAL ROLLS

After rolling any die, you may gain additional dice by

♦ taking on an Extra Problem

or

♦ executing a Stunt

The Challenge will describe if an Extra Problem or Stunt (see below) is available.

You can also get extra dice if you've got an appropriate Edge to spend, or if you've got a Contact that'll help out.

You can't get more than three bonus dice in a Challenge (one from an Extra Problem, one from a Stunt, and one from an Edge or Contact).

Some highly constrained or specialized Challenges won't have any Extra Problems, Stunts or suitable Edges available. In such situations, when you can't earn bonus dice, you've nothing to rely on except your own General abilities.

DEPLETING ABILITIES

Once you've used an ability, it's at a -1 die penalty in future challenges until you next Take Time (p. 39). So, if you undertake a **Shooting** challenge, then you've only got one **Shooting** die for the rest of the scene. The ability is referred to as Depleted.

EXTRA PROBLEMS

When you take on an Extra Problem, you commit more to the task, but at a price. Think of it as going into debt,

incurring future trouble to overcome your current obstacle. If you Advance or Hold, you leave the situation with only that Problem hanging over your head. If you suffer a Setback, you could wind up with two new Problems: the one listed in the Setback description, and the one you voluntarily took on. You can incur only one Extra Problem per test. Most represent minor setbacks, but a few turn out to be truly nasty. The Director does not reveal the nature of the Extra Problem until the end of the test, making the choice fraught and uncertain.

STUNTS

A Stunt allows you to use a different General ability than the one called for in the Challenge. You justify your use of an unexpected ability by couching it in terms of a cinematic action move or clever reversal. For example, when making a Driving Challenge to catch a fleeing villain, you could use your **Mechanics** ability to get another **Driving** die by describing how you expertly push the engine to its limits, or you could use your **Surveillance** ability to spot a shortcut down an alleyway only millimeters wider than your vehicle.

A Stunt costs two dice of a General ability to get one die of the relevant ability (two **Mechanics** to get one **Driving** die). Using an ability to pull off a stunt Depletes it, leaving you with only one die in that ability until you Take Time. That means, generally, that you can only Stunt with each ability once per scene.

(You can spend Edges to get bonus dice in one ability, and then translate those into a bonus die in another ability by Stunting. Similarly, if a card lets you reroll dice of a particular ability, you can use that card to reroll a converted die. So, if you're using two **Athletics** dice to get a die of **Fighting**, you could use an Edge like an Athletics Mastery (p. 26) to reroll that converted die.)

BONUSES AND PENALTIES FROM EDGES AND PROBLEMS

Some Edges add a bonus to your Outcome for as long as they remain in your hand. Add this bonus to the first roll.

Others grant a bonus if you choose to discard the card. You can decide to do this at any time.

Problem cards in hand may impose penalties to the Outcome. Factor these in after the first roll. In some cases, a card's text applies only to your next test of an ability, and the card may then be discarded. Other, less obliging Problems hang around until you Counter them in some other way.

BONUSES AND PENALTIES FROM CONTACTS

Some Contacts have General abilities listed on their Contact cards: you can use these Contacts like Edges to get their dice as bonus dice. You don't need to discard the Contact, but you usually have to spend a Push.

*For example, your Contact Alain the jewel thief has **Infiltration** 2 and **Filch** 2, in addition to the Investigative abilities of **Art History** and **Streetwise**. You spend a Push to convince Alain to help you break into a gallery. His assistance gives you +2 Infiltration dice.*

GAINING PUSHES

When you reach an Advance with dice from the active ability still unrolled, you gain a Push (p. 13). This might well mean that you got both an Edge and a Push.

If you have an Edge card that allows you to roll an extra die on a test, or gain bonus dice from an Extra Problem or Stunt, you can spend these dice before rolling any of your ability dice, or wait until you've rolled them all. The first option increases your chances of earning a Push. The second lets you wait and see if you really need to spend that resource on this Challenge, giving you the option of holding onto it for later.

BACK TO THE STORY

After you have either:

♦ equaled or surpassed the number needed for an Advance, or

♦ rolled the die as many times as you are allowed and not scored an Advance

...the Director describes the story result of the Outcome, paraphrasing from the narrative text provided in the Challenge (or, if improvising Challenges on the fly, the Director describes the Outcome extemporaneously).

CHALLENGE QUICK REFERENCE

On an Advance:

♦ You always get a special benefit, usually including an Edge.

♦ If you still have unrolled dice, you **also** get a Push.

On a Hold:

♦ You end up neither worse nor better off, taking neither penalties nor benefits.

On a Setback:

♦ Something bad happens to you in the story, often represented by a Problem.

To increase the chance of gaining an Advance,

♦ You may take on an Extra Problem, allowing you to roll an additional die.

♦ You may attempt a Stunt, spending two dice from another ability to roll an additional die.

If you use an ability, it's Depleted (-1 die) until you Take Time.

CHALLENGE FORMAT

Published investigations present Challenges in the following format:

NAME OF CHALLENGE
NAME OF ACTIVE ABILITY

Bonus: If applicable, lists a bonus applied to your first die roll under certain circumstances. Often, applies when you've got a particular Edge, or gives the opportunity to Push a relevant Investigative ability.

Penalty: If applicable, lists a penalty applied to your first die roll under certain circumstances. Most often applies when you have a particular Problem card.

Advance #+: Quick description of what happens in the story when you advance. A published scenario, like the one in this book, may refer you to the main text for more detail. The number is the test's target to Advance. Any result equal to or higher than that lets you Advance. Often you earn an Edge; if so, it is named here.

Hold #-#: Description of what happens when the Outcome is a Hold. The numbers show the range in which a Hold occurs. The second number is always 1 less than the target to Advance.

Setback # or less: Description of what happens in the story when the Outcome is a Setback. Numbers show the range in which a Setback occurs. Names the Problem you incur, if any.

Extra Problem: Describes the most obvious Extra Problem the Agent can take on to gain an additional die against this Challenge.

Stunt: If the player's allowed to use dice from another General ability, then the answer here is "Yes." We may even suggest a few likely abilities that fit here. If a Stunt isn't appropriate (either because it's hard to think of a cinematic way to resolve the challenge, or because the Director wants to put the player in a bind), then the answer here is "No."

Write Challenges in the second person, as if addressed to the character. Here's an example:

SPOTTING THE SNIPER
SENSE TROUBLE

Bonus: +2 if you Push Architecture

Penalty: -2 if you've got the Problem "Face Full of Tear Gas."

Advance 8+: You spot the sniper on the roof of a nearby apartment block. You race up the stairs and burst out onto the roof before he gets a chance to fire. He drops his gun and flees across the rooftops. Gain Edge 3, "Sniper Rifle."

Hold 4-7: You spot the sniper on the roof but he hears you coming. By the time you reach the roof, he's already stowed his weapon and fled across the rooftops. You can chase him, but he's got a lead.

Setback 3 or less: The sniper spots you first and takes a shot at you. Gain Problem 5, "Grazed."

Extra Problem: Problem 6, "Prime Suspect."

Stunt: No.

EDGE

Sniper Rifle

You've got the sniper's weapon — the weapon used to murder the ambassador. You might be able to find useful intel through a forensic examination of the rifle, but if you're caught holding it, you'll be a suspect in the investigation. Discard for a bonus die in any **Shooting** challenge at extended range.

PROBLEM

Grazed
INJURY

You've been shot in the side. It could have been a lot worse.

PROBLEM

Prime Suspect
HEAT

You were seen near both shootings; the police want to question you about the ambassador's death.

IMMEDIATE CONSEQUENCES

Some Advances confer a bonus or extra die on another test that will happen right away. Some Setbacks impose a penalty. Since they are resolved right away and don't need to be tracked from one scene to the next, they don't require the use of Edge or Problem cards.

VOLUNTARY LOSSES

The player can always decide not to engage in a test, but instead to accept the consequences of a Setback result. This might happen when the player decides that failure introduces an interesting or challenging story possibility. Cool tests are the most likely to inspire a player to take a voluntary loss.

READING RESULTS TEXT

Snippets of text portray the Advance, Hold, and Setback results as second-person narration, directed at the Agent. In some cases, usually in **Cool** tests, they may even suggest the character's perceptions, emotional responses, or thoughts. Although the Director can always read them out verbatim, usually the player will find it more natural to hear them paraphrased into a less polished, but more spontaneous, narration. Where possible, the Director should break this text into small chunks, inviting the player to participate in a back-and-forth dialogue. See the example below.

CHALLENGE EXAMPLE

You undertake the Challenge "Spotting the Sniper," above. You have two ability dice in **Surveillance**. *The Director tells you that you need an 8 to Advance, and that there's both a bonus (from spending a Push) and an Extra Problem available. You roll the first of your dice and get a 5. That isn't enough, so you roll again and get a 2, for a total of 7 — still short of your target. You can either accept a Hold result, or take on an Extra Problem in order to get the third die roll that will assure an Advance, or Push* **Architecture**. *You decide to spend the Push – guessing that any Problem involving a guy pointing a sniper rifle in your direction is going to be bad, and gain the Advance (and its "Sniper Rifle" Edge).*

The Director paraphrases the Advance text, leaving you spaces to contribute additional narrative detail. "You scan the skyline, looking for the places a sniper might hide out. There's one apartment block up there that offers a good field of fire. How are you getting up there?"

"I run into the alleyway and parkour off a wall so I can grab onto the edge of the fire escape. I

haul myself onto the fire escape and then race up the stairs."

"He hears you coming – you see him drop his sniper rifle, turn, and run. He jumps over the alleyway, scrambling up the sloped green roof of the adjoining building. You're nearly at the top of the fire escape – do you chase him across the rooftops immediately, or do you want to grab the rifle he dropped first before someone else finds it?"

"Can I do both? Grab the rifle, and take a snap shot that brings him down without killing him?"

"Er. Sure." (The Director hastily converts his planned "Chase the Sniper" **Athletics** *Challenge into one based on* **Shooting**.)

HANDLING PROBLEMS AND EDGES

These notes guide you in using Edges and Problems during play.

FORMATTING

The cards in this game use the following format:

Story material comes first; this is italicized under the heading, and provides a description of what prompts the card. Next comes rules material, in regular style; this includes the ability the card relates to, and then the Outcome of an Advance, Hold, and Setback result. Any Extra Problems which can be taken are listed at the bottom of the card.

Some cards might not have both — cards omit the story material when their title says everything there is to say: "Stabbed" or "Vampire Bite" require no further elaboration. Other cards present only story material, leaving the player and Director to weave them into the narrative in the course of play.

WHAT "NEXT TEST" MEANS

Some Problems apply a penalty to the character's next test, or next test of a particular type. As a player, you can't burn off the penalty by using it on a pointless test with no meaningful bearing on the storyline. Only tests called for by the Director or the scenario, or which make narrative sense and threaten to put you in a worse position on a Setback, count as "next tests" for this purpose.

WHEN INSTRUCTIONS DIFFER

When the text of an Edge or Problem card contradicts that of a Challenge, treat the card as an exception that takes precedence.

> *For example, the text of a Challenge may specify that Edges applying to tests of General/Physical abilities, or* **Evasion** *in particular, can be applied to the present test, in which the spy and an innocent bystander are running away from ghouls. If, however, the player has an Edge called Ghoul Lore, which can be applied to any test where ghouls are present, the card wins out, ignoring the apparently more restrictive Challenge text.*

Where the text of a Problem and an Edge conflict, the Edge takes precedence.

DUPLICATES

Except where indicated, if you get an Edge or Problem you already have, it is duplicated, adding an additional copy to your stack. In the case of an Edge, this represents a benefit you can use more than once, and/or one that conveys an additional benefit. For a Problem, it means your dilemma has doubled in intensity. You must Counter each card separately, reflecting a dilemma that has just become twice as bad as it was.

Bonuses and penalties "stack," to use gaming parlance. Add together all *active* penalties and bonuses when applying them to a Challenge. (Most Injuries, though, only apply in the scene you acquired them in.)

CONTINUITY

Some cards have the Continuity keyword. These cards are part of your character's ongoing story, and aren't discarded at the end of the mission. Keep these cards until expressly allowed to discard them.

CLUES

Some cards have the Clue keyword. These cards are important to the current operation: you can't discard these cards until the clue's purpose in the operation has been completed, or at the end of the operation if you choose a different path through the adventure.

HEAT, SHADOW, INJURY, AND HURT

Some cards – all Cumulative Problems – have one of these keywords. These are Problems that build up over time, reflecting some ongoing peril. The more Heat Problems you have, the more trouble you're in with the police and other authorities. The more Shadow you accrue, the more exposed you are to supernatural danger. See p. 46 for more on these special problems.

COUNTERING PROBLEMS

Problems may reduce your range of options in the story at hand. For example, "Prime Suspect" makes approaching the police much more risky – you can't find the real killer if you're stuck in a police interview room.

Problems left unaddressed at the end of the story can lead to a downbeat ending. To prevent your adventure from ending in remorse, dissipation, bruises, or macabre demise, do your best to Counter your Problems before the mystery resolves.

To Counter a Problem, you must do something that would credibly get it out of your way. This may require a successful test or the expenditure of a Push or Edge.

> You can't give the police the real killer – he crumbled to dust in the sunlight – but you need to get rid of this cloud of suspicion. You arrange for one of your Contacts to provide you with a solid alibi. He agrees, but at the cost of a Push.

TAKING TIME

The most common way to Counter a Problem is to Take Time. When Taking Time, the Agent momentarily puts the investigation aside to deal with the issue raised by the Problem.

> You've escaped from the vampire's castle by climbing down the sheer cliff, but you had to leave all your equipment behind.

PROBLEM

Empty-Handed

You escaped the castle with nothing but your nightclothes. You need to acquire some supplies — and a wardrobe.

You can't Push Interpersonal abilities, and automatically fail **Preparedness** tests. Counter by Taking Time to gather gear.

How exactly you overcome this problem is up to you. You might call on a contact who'll help you out. Maybe you declare that you've got a safe deposit box with a cache of supplies in town. Perhaps you stole a few ancient, dusty gold coins from the castle, or maybe you just scavenge clothing from a laundromat and shoplift up some gear from an army surplus store. How you get back in the game is up to you, your General abilities, and your conception of the character. You discard the card.

In a few cases, Taking Time may require a Quick Test or Challenge. More often the player simply describes a brief interlude scene. The text of certain Problem cards explicitly indicates what this scene might look like. The GM may decide that your alternate solution works better than the suggested one. Players can also suggest ways to Take Time to get rid of Problems whose text doesn't describe a Counter at all.

Refreshing Abilities: When you Take Time (for any purpose), any Depleted abilities refresh to full. So, if you've used your **Cool, Shooting**, and **Athletics** abilities (reducing them by one die each), they pop back to full when you Take Time.

Healing: When you Take Time, you can exchange Injury cards for Hurt Problems (p. 48).

Laying Low: If you stay hidden and off the streets when taking Time, you can discard one Heat Problem.

Travel: You can also Take Time to travel from one city to another, or to wait for sundown or sunup. In a game

of spies and vampires, having the cover of darkness or the reassuring safety of sunlight may be worth risking Blowback.

BLOWBACK

Taking Time is not without cost. Some scenarios may find your character working against the clock to accomplish a particular end: getting the formula before the conspiracy releases the toxin into the water supply, finding the blackmail material before the bank has to pay the ransom, or rescuing the kidnap victim before the vampires devour them.

Without a deadline, Taking Time typically gives enemies, rivals, and nuisances time to make moves against you they otherwise couldn't. These incidents, called Blowback, are described for Directors on p. 86. Every time you Take Time, there's a chance that the bad guys strike back, or do something that will make your task even harder. You've got to balance the advantages of Taking Time to get rid of annoying Problems against the danger of damaging Blowback.

A high Heat or Shadow Score (see p. 46) on your part unlocks nastier Blowback for the Director to use against you. Be careful of Taking Time if either your Heat or Shadow Score is 3 or higher.

QUICK TESTS

On occasion, you may face a very straightforward obstacle where you can only succeed or fail, with no particular ongoing advantages or disadvantages arising from the result. In this case, you undertake a Quick Test. If you hit the Advance number, you succeed. If not, you fail, but nothing especially bad happens. You don't gain Edge or Problem cards from the Outcome of a Quick Test. Although you can spend an Edge to gain an extra die on a Quick Test, the Director will warn you that it carries lower stakes than a full

Challenge and therefore might not be worth it. Although ongoing penalties from Problem cards apply to Quick Tests, you may not discard the Problem card. Quick Tests don't allow for Stunts.

GMs choose Quick Tests for situations where big positive or negative results are either hard to think of, or would take the story in an annoying or fruitless direction. Quick Test Difficulties should start at 8 and go up from there.

If you have trouble thinking of Problems, including Extra Problems,

for a Challenge, that's a sign that you should probably replace it with a Quick Test.

Where the result lacks any whiff of danger or great import, skip even the Quick Test and allow the ability use to succeed automatically.

Sometimes you'll envision a possible Challenge for which you can think of only two Outcomes. As long as there's an Edge or Problem to arise from it, it's still a Challenge, not a Quick Test.

CHALLENGE, QUICK TEST, OR NEITHER?

SITUATION	RESOLUTION METHOD
Both success and failure lead to interesting story developments. Either could bring additional consequences, negative and positive, that might matter later.	Challenge
Both success and failure lead to interesting story developments. Neither inspires compelling additional consequences for later scenes.	Quick Test
Failure would be boring.	Automatic Success

NO SECRET TESTS

On occasion, the Director may be tempted to make a secret Challenge roll on the player's behalf.

The classic example occurs with **Sense Trouble**, a General ability allowing the character to react quickly to approaching danger. A Director might reason that the player should not be tipped off if the character fails to notice something wrong.

In practice, it is almost always more effective to tip the player off by requesting a test, but in the case of failure, to withhold knowledge of what exactly the character didn't spot. Think

of this generalized idea that something has been missed as the roleplaying equivalent of ominous music playing on the soundtrack or an eerily composed shot from overhead. Should the player attempt to have the character act on the sense of unease, all the Director has to do is ask her to justify why it makes sense to do so. If she can, well, it makes sense, so allow it. If not, she'll relent, no harm, no foul.

One-2-One requires this level of transparency, because the player usually has the option to make a sacrifice, either spending an Edge, using

a Stunt, or taking on an Extra Problem, to increase her chance of success.

You may have noted the game is entirely player-facing, meaning the player makes all rolls, and the Director never touches a die. Secret tests would break that principle.

In practice, you can frame most Challenges so that the bad results of a Hold or dire ones of a Setback become immediately apparent anyway: the goons ambush the character, the vampire bat flitting around the house breaks through a window.

FIGHTS

In multiplayer GUMSHOE, fights can provide fun and excitement, without stopping the entire story dead when a player character bites the dust. The survivors mourn their loss and carry on the investigation as the player gets to work creating a new character.

In One-2-One, that won't do. The death of a sole protagonist takes a much greater toll on the story than the demise of one team member. When you set aside the possibility of death as a result, tactical choices lose their impact. So we omit these as well, providing a much more abstracted combat system than multiplayer GUMSHOE — which compared to other RPGs is already plenty abstract.

A fight plays out like any other Challenge, using your **Fighting** or **Shooting** ability. Feel free to describe your Agent's badass combat style – do you rely on a flurry of martial arts blocks and strikes? Are you a brawler, slamming and shoving your opponents? Do you make clever use of your surroundings, grabbing improvised weapons? Or is it still a more low-key, gritty game where one shot can end it all? Describe every individual die roll – rolling a 2 on the first **Fighting** you roll might be contextualized as, "You grab the goon, but he's frightfully strong, and he smashes you through the door" while a roll of a 5 on the second die might be described as, "You use his momentum against him, shoving him so he blindly barrels into the granite table, then you grab the table lamp and wrap the cord around his neck."

FIGHT OUTCOMES

The Director spells out fight results like those of any other Challenge. Each fight may have different consequences, as seen in its description:

ELEVATOR BRAWL
FIGHTING

Advance 7+: You step out of the elevator unruffled, leaving a half-dozen unconscious goons on the floor behind you. You tuck the room key card you looted from Goon #4 into your purse. You can check out the bad guys' room in the scene "Room 1001."

Hold 4-6: There are too many of them to fight in this cramped elevator, so when the doors open you throw yourself out and run like hell. You manage to lose them by darting into a laundry room, but they're looking for you.

Setback 3 or less: There are too many of them and you've got to escape. When the doors open, you fling yourself out of the elevator, race down the corridor, and smash through the window. Gain the Problem "Hasty Exit." You can't return to this hotel again without being spotted, so pick another line of investigation.

Extra Problem: ""The Big Guy's Nose"

Stunt? Yes. (**Athletics**, for acrobatic fighting in the elevator; **Mechanics**, to grab a fire hose and use it as an improvised weapon; **Shooting**, to go loud.)

> ◀ **PROBLEM** ▶
> ## Hasty Exit
> You smashed your way out of the hotel, and now the bad guys are on their guard. You're at -1 die to your next **Surveillance** or **Infiltration** Challenge, then discard this Problem.

> ◀ **PROBLEM** ▶
> ## The Big Guy's Nose
> ### BLOWBACK
> In the course of the fight, you smashed the nose of the biggest henchman. He wants revenge.

NO ONE COULD HAVE SURVIVED THAT

Espionage thrillers involve a lot of guns and murder, which makes losing a fight scene tricky. Early in an investigation, the bad guys might be satisfied with beating the meddling spy to a pulp, but later, it may be tweak suspension of disbelief if the enemies don't go for the lethal option. Some options for serious-but-not-lethal Setbacks:

◆ **Finish Her!** The Director can phrase Challenges so that even a Setback is a win (or, at least, a pyrrhic victory for the player). You're guaranteed to survive the shootout; the dice roll determines whether you take out the Renfield miniboss too, or if your buddy gets mortally wounded instead in the crossfire.

◆ **Captured!** The bad guys knock the hero unconscious and take her back to their lair for interrogation or to feed her to the vampires.

- **Probably Dead!** The player falls into the dark waters of the Thames, or gets thrown off the skyscraper, or the car goes over the side of the mountain. The bad guys assume the player is dead and leave, not knowing that the spy managed to swim to safety/grab onto a window ledge and dangle just out of sight/leap from the car at the last moment before it explodes. The Agent survives, but gets a suitably harsh Continuity Problem as a consequence.

- **Mortally Wounded!** Another option is to hit the player with a lethal Problem – if the player can't Counter that Problem by the end of the adventure, the character dies. A Problem like "Bleeding Out" gives combat Challenges lots of, ah, bite without bringing the story to a premature end. After all, Quincey Morris didn't survive killing Dracula.

GETTING CAPTURED

Getting captured is a time-honored genre habit for the thriller spy, from James Bond to Sydney Bristow. By and large, players absolutely *hate* for their characters to get captured: losing an arm is preferable to losing a few days in the box. Directors should get player buy-in at the beginning of the game: if capture simply isn't an option, then it simply isn't an option. Ignore this text.

If captured by civilian authorities, then the standard protocol is to use **Network** to create a contact who can spring you. You'll likely end up owing this contact a favor, but it's better than rotting in a jail cell.

If you're captured by the conspiracy, that's bad, but here's our GUMSHOE promise: **If you are captured, you will learn something you want to know.** If your Agent is captured by the opposition, you can ask the Director one question about *any* aspect of the opposition. The answer will appear in the session in which you asked it. If at all possible, it will appear in prison with you: a Rolodex on the desk, a computer monitor left on, a confession by a fellow inmate, a conversation overheard, a quick scene played out in the course of your inevitable escape.

And you *will* have a chance to escape. That, too, is time-honored spy thriller tradition. The Director may turn your prison break into a whole session's operation. Or he may just let you show off your skills in a taut combat scene and a suspiciously easy **Infiltration** test or two.

CONTACTS IN FIGHTS

Sometimes, you'll find yourself in the middle of a firefight while in the company of one of your Contacts. As a general rule:

♦ If the Contact has an appropriate General ability (**Shooting**, **Evasion**, etc.), they can take care of themselves and either don't penalize you or assist you, depending on the situation and their attitude towards you. When in doubt, spend a Push to ensure they help out.

♦ If they're a non-combatant, they're in trouble. You have a choice. Either you take a -1 die penalty to protect them, or they're assumed to be collateral damage to whatever extent the GM wishes.

♦ In either case, if you suffer a Setback, your Contact a similar fate.

*For example, Leyla's meeting her hacker Contact Sergei in a hotel room in Prague, when suddenly a knife-wielding conspiracy assassin bursts through the door. Sergei doesn't have **Fighting**, so Leyla has to choose whether or not to protect him (accepting a -1 die penalty if she does). If she doesn't take the penalty, then Sergei gets stabbed no matter what Leyla rolls. If she takes the penalty, then Sergei has a chance of surviving – but her own chances of survival also go down.*

EXTENDED CHALLENGE SEQUENCES

Sometimes, a story demands a longer action sequence that extends beyond a single dice roll. Often, these sequences come at the climax of an operation –it's the knock-down, drag-out fight with a hated villain, it's the final assault on a mountain fortress, it's the final fight with Dracula. Extended fight scenes are built as sequential challenges – one challenge links directly to the next, with Advances and Setbacks representing advantage or disadvantage in the ongoing fight.

The Director should make plenty of Edges and Extra Problems available in an operation that includes an Extended Challenge like this – if a player goes into an Extended Challenge without a solid hand of cards or scope for Stunts, she's in big trouble. Remember, without a break to Take Time and refresh, the player will quickly Deplete her dice pools and have to rely on bonus dice to survive.

Extended Challenges should rarely be longer than two or three rolls.

FIGHT IN THE CHAPEL

FIGHTING

Advance 7+: You wrestle with the vampire. It's like fighting a savage dog, with its snarling teeth inches from your vulnerable neck. With a twist, you manage to push the creature back for an instant, giving you time to grab a jeweled cross from the altar and slam it into the monster's face. It recoils, stumbling into the blizzard outside. Gain a bonus die in the next Challenge, "A Suicide's Grave."

Hold 4-6: The vampire throws you around the chapel with its supernatural strength. Sulfurous smoke hisses from its feet whenever it steps on holy ground, so it leaps from pew to pew, like a monstrous child pretending the floor is lava. You spot a crucifix on the altar and lunge for it, but the vampire's faster. It grabs you and throws you through the doors out into the snowy graveyard. Go to the next Challenge, "A Suicide's Grave."

Setback 3 or less: The vampire grabs you and smashes you through the stone floor, and you both fall into the inky blackness of the crypt. Gain the Problem "Shattered" and go to the next Challenge, "In the Crypt."

Extra Problem: "Bitten."

Stunt: Yes (**Cool** to fight against the terror of its presence; **Filch** to grab that crucifix).

◄ PROBLEM ►

Shattered

SERIOUS INJURY

You've been badly injured – several of your ribs are broken, and you may have fractured your skull. You need Medical Attention as soon as possible.

◄ PROBLEM ►

Bitten

INJURY, SHADOW

The vampire got its fangs into you, and you're feeling woozy.

A SUICIDE'S GRAVE

FIGHTING

Advance 7+: Grabbing an improvised weapon of some sort, you pursue the vampire through the swirling snow, and catch the monster as it tries to crawl into an unmarked grave to escape the rising sun. You cut its head from its shoulders, and the corpse crumbles into dust. It's over.

Hold 4-6: Grabbing an improvised weapon of some sort, you stagger after the vampire through the snowstorm. You swing your weapon, trying to cut the monster's head off – did it turn to mist in the instant before you struck, or did you kill it? You cannot be certain. Gain the Problem "Haunted."

Setback 3 or less: The vampire laughs. "This place is holy ground, yes. But the rest of your world – all that belongs to the Devil and his children." The creature fades into mist and vanishes in the snowstorm. Gain the Problem "Hunted."

Extra Problem: "Frostbite."

Stunt: Yes (**Athletics** or **Evasion** to pursue the monster; **Surveillance** to track it).

IN THE CRYPT

FIGHTING

Advance 7+: In the darkness, your hand falls on something sharp and metal – an old dagger, maybe. You swing it blindly, and it bites home. Gain the Problem "Haunted" and the Edge "Rusted Dagger."

Hold 4-6: You scramble through the crypt, pursued by the vampire. In the darkness, you stumble across a set of stairs, half-choked in dirt and dead roots, and manage to force your way back to the surface. Behind you, you see the monster's red eyes glare at you for a moment, then it vanishes. Icy winds howl around you. Gain the Problem "Hunted."

Setback 3 or less: There's no escape – the vampire's fangs sink into your throat. It's over.

Extra Problem: "Fear of the Dark."

Stunt: Yes (**Cool**; **Sense Trouble**).

PROBLEM

Haunted

CONTINUITY, SHADOW

You'll never be sure if you killed the vampire in that abandoned chapel, and the memory of its red eyes haunts your dreams. Discard if you find proof of the vampire's demise.

PROBLEM

Hunted

CONTINUITY, SHADOW

The vampire escaped, and took its revenge on you. Pick one of your Contacts to be killed by the monster. While you hold this card, you suffer a -1 penalty on all Network tests, as the stench of death clings to you. Discard it if you atone by killing the vampire.

PROBLEM

Frostbite

An unholy will directs this icy wind. This is no natural storm. You've got a -2 penalty on all General/Manual tests until you warm up.

PROBLEM

Rusted Dagger

You don't know who left this old Bowie knife in the crypt, but you're glad you found it.
As long as you hold this weapon, you have a +1 bonus to Cool tests. Discard for an extra die in a Fighting test.

PROBLEM

Fear of the Dark

CONTINUITY, SHADOW

You nearly died in the dark crypt, and now dark places remind you of that traumatizing experience. You're at a -2 penalty to any tests made in darkness. Discard after the next adventure.

CONTACTS

Your **Network** ability means that you can find useful contacts no matter where you are – you can always dig up a local guide, an informant, a bureaucrat who takes bribes, a gangster with criminal connections, a former colleague in the company who'll still take your calls – or maybe an eccentric priest who keeps a cache of guns and sharpened stakes hidden in the belfry of his little church.

NETWORK TESTS

Sometimes, the GM will ask you to make a **Network** test, or you can suggest it.

This is the generic version of a **Network** Challenge that applies in most situations; your Director may create customized Challenges reflecting the unique circumstances of a particular operation.

CONTACT CARDS

Contacts come on cards, listing the Contact's abilities and a brief background sketch. Once you acquire a Contact, keep them in your hand – you can call upon them in future operations in the same region (and some Setbacks may eliminate your existing allies and Contacts).

ABILITIES

Contacts have Investigative abilities, just like you, and these work in the same way as your abilities. An ally can find clues and interpret information for you. Usually, this means you've got to bring the raw data to them: if you don't have **Archaeology**, you can bring the mysterious vampiric idol to a Contact so they can examine it and tell you what it means.

Contacts may also have General abilities, but unless you bring a Contact into the thick of the action (see below), they'll rarely have recourse to use these abilities. If it comes up, you can add their score as bonus dice to yours.

FAVORS

To convince a Contact to follow you into danger, or do something beyond passing on information, you may have to use a Push. If the Contact already owes you a favor, then you get a free Push usable only on that Contact.

Even with a Push, a Contact isn't necessarily going to give you all the help you want. It depends on their own situation and personality – an arms dealer might be willing to sell you unlicensed weapons with a Push, but balk at the prospect of following you into a shootout.

FRIENDS IN LOW PLACES
NETWORK

Penalty: -1 per Heat Problem in your hand (see p. 47).

-4 if you've got the "Angel of Death" Problem.

Advance 7+: You've got a Contact in town, and an associated advantage. Pick one: either the Contact is someone you know and trust, or the Contact owes you a favor from a past encounter (free Push), or you've got blackmail or other leverage over the Contact (free Push), or the Contact is unusually influential, highly placed, or skilled.

Hold 4-6: You've got a regular Contact in town. They'll supply you with information, and may give extra help if you spend a Push.

Setback 3 or less: You've got a Contact in town, but there's a catch.

Pick one: either the Contact hates/mistrusts you (requires an extra Push to get help from this Contact), or you owe the Contact a debt or favor (requires you to balance the scales before the Contact helps you), or getting to the Contact is difficult and challenging (they're in prison/under surveillance/far away).

Extra Problem: Gain one Heat Problem.

Stunt: No.

PROBLEM

Angel of Death
CONTINUITY

You got a Contact killed through your actions, and word has spread. You've got a -4 penalty to **Network** tests while you hold this card. Discard at the end of the *next* operation.

CUMULATIVE PROBLEMS

There are three types of special Problems that work a little differently than other Problem cards. We call these Cumulative Problems, because they build on each other: the more problems of a particular type you have, the tougher things get. These Cumulative Problems are Heat, Injuries, and Shadow.

The number of a particular type of Cumulative Problem card you have is referred to as your Score. So, if you've got three Heat Problems in hand, you've a Heat Score of 3.

- **Heat** measures the attention of the police and other authorities. If you've got a Heat Score, the cops are looking for you. Heat makes it harder to use your **Cover** and **Network** abilities.
- **Injuries** are, obviously enough, the bruises, cuts, and nastier wounds you've picked up along the way. Injuries slow you down and force you to rest.
- **Shadow** measures the baleful influence of supernatural threats. The higher your Shadow Score, the more aware the vampires are of your presence. **Cool** is the key ability when it comes to resisting Shadow.

Each type of Cumulative Problem comes with ways of Countering individual cards to drop your Score back down to a manageable level. So, hiding from the cops or throwing pursuers off your trail drops Heat; resting and getting Medical Attention treats Injuries; finding ways to block vampiric influence like garlic or running water reduces Shadow.

HEAT

Running all over Europe shooting vampires attracts attention from governments, police agencies, and other unsympathetic official observers. *Solo Ops* represents this attention, and the concomitant investigations and pursuits, with Heat cards.

While Heat's primarily used to measure the alarm level of the authorities, you may assume that the conspiracy has plenty of crooked cops, double agents, and bugging devices in its arsenal. As Heat rises, it also becomes easier for the bad guys to find you.

GAINING HEAT

You gain Heat when:

- Things explode – public gunfights, explosions, or fires draw lots of notice.
- People get hurt – especially civilians, police, or public figures. You get more Heat from beating up a journalist than beating up a mugger.
- You commit crimes – breaking into government buildings, hacking into government systems, stealing large amounts of cash or documents.

You also risk gaining Heat when crossing borders or interacting with the authorities while undercover. You'll often have to make a Quick Test of **Cover** when moving from one city to another: if you fail, you gain Heat as your false passport or travel papers come under added scrutiny.

Individual Heat cards vary. Some Heat cards represent the police closing in on you, others reflect the stress of covert operations.

A Heat Score of 1-2 means there's some heightened security, but you're still operating mostly under the radar of the authorities.

A Heat Score of 3-4 means you're actively a person of interest to the authorities, and you need to be careful.

A Heat Score of 5 or more is very high and very bad news. Your name and mugshot may be splashed across every television screen and newspaper in the city and the police are probably combing the streets for you.

◄— PROBLEM —►

Surveillance State

HEAT

Cameras on every street corner, in every store – and you know what facial recognition can do these days. At least, for those who show up on camera...

◄— PROBLEM —►

Closing In

HEAT

You can see it in your mind's eye – the calls going out. The alerts flashed to cell phones, activating kill teams and hunters. They're out for your blood. If you get caught, you won't be going to jail – they'll send you straight to the morgue, or bury you in an unmarked grave.

There's a set of generic Heat cards on p. 259.

EFFECTS OF HEAT

The number of Heat Problems in your hand gets applied as a penalty to **Network** tests, representing the difficulty of finding allies and Contacts when you're bringing trouble with you.

You'll also sometimes be called upon to make **Cover** or **Cool** tests to avoid arrest or stay calm as the pressure mounts. These are usually the result of Taking Time (p. 39).

QUESTIONED BY THE COPS

COOL

Bonus: Automatically advance if you Push **Cop Talk**.

Penalty: -1 per Heat Problem in your hand (see p. 47).

Advance 7+: You spin a very convincing story, and by the end, they're apologizing to you for wasting time. Discard any two Heat Problems.

Hold 4-6: You're questioned for some time, and spend hours sitting in a waiting room, but at the end, they let you go. You're considered to have Taken Time and you can discard one Heat Problem.

Setback 3 or less: They stick you in a waiting room and tell you to stay there. Muffled voices out in the corridor... the ringing of cell phones. Something's not right, you can tell. Someone's selling you out, right now. You've got to get out of here!

Extra Problem: None.

Stunt: No.

PAPERS, PLEASE

COVER

Penalty: -1 per Heat card in your hand (see p. 47).

Advance 7+: The passport control officer at the airport scrutinizes you for several long, long heartbeats – and then hands your papers back to you. ""Enjoy your flight." Discard any one Heat Problem.

Hold 4-6: You get through security, but you have to keep a low profile. Discard any one Mastery Edge in your hand or gain one Heat Problem.

Setback 3 or less: You're pretty sure your passport's been flagged. Gain one Heat Problem.

Extra Problem: None.

Stunt: No.

LOSING HEAT

You can lose Heat by:
- Waiting until the attention dies down. You can Take Time and hide to drop your Heat by one.
- Hiding in a safe place, like a safehouse operated by a Contact, allows you to discard an additional Heat card.
- Crossing international borders (assuming you don't draw more attention at any border checkpoints).
- Getting protection from a well-placed Contact or ally. A Contact who's a police officer, government official or other authority figure could (as a favor) remove some Heat.
- Framing or transferring blame to someone else – like an unlucky conspiracy goon.

INJURY

Over the course of your adventures, expect to get punched, beaten, clawed, burned, shot, thrown through windows, tossed out of moving cars, and to endure many other such injuries. As a highly trained Agent, you can take hits that would bring down an ordinary civilian.

GAINING INJURIES

You gain Injuries as a result of Setbacks in fights and other violent challenges, or as additional Problems. **Each Injury gives a -2 penalty to all Physical rolls as long as you hold the card.**

Some Injuries come with additional penalties, or affect more than just Physical rolls.

◄─── **PROBLEM** ───►

Beaten

INJURY

The Mafioso goons worked you over with a baseball bat. "Stay away from the Hacienda club!" they told you.

◄─── **PROBLEM** ───►

Frostbite

INJURY

You've made it to the Finnish border, but you're suffering badly from exposure to the arctic cold.

There's a big set of generic Injury cards on p. 258.

EFFECTS OF INJURIES

Each Injury gives a -2 to all Physical tests. So, if you're fighting a vampire, and it claws you across the chest, you've got a -2 penalty to all Physical tests for the rest of that fight, and for any subsequent tests as long as you hold those Injury Problems.

Some Injuries have additional penalties to other abilities. For example, if that vampire rakes you across the face instead, then you might pick up a penalty to Social tests.

When you Take Time, you may choose to discard any Injury cards you've picked up, and gain half as many Hurt cards (rounding down). So, if you end a scene with two Injuries, you swap them for one Hurt card. Hurt cards still penalize you, but not as much as Injuries.

Having both Injury and Hurt cards represents the resilience and determination of the action hero – you're temporarily incapacitated by being smashed through a window, or kicked down a flight of stairs, but you're tough enough to quickly recover and most injuries end up being effectively cosmetic damage. (Jason Bourne may be staggered when a bad guy punches him in the throat, but he's not wearing a neck brace for the rest of the movie.) At the same time, you're not immortal, and enough damage will slow you down.

You can end up with multiple Hurt cards in hand; the penalties stack with each other and with Injury cards.

Hurt cards stay in your hand until the end of the operation. If there's an unusually long period of downtime between scenes – a few days at least – then the Director might let you discard some of your Hurt cards.

(Hey! As you round down when working out how many Hurt cards you have to take, try to end with an *odd* number of Injuries if you can.)

If you're getting Medical Attention, you make the Medic roll first, and *then* swap Injuries for Hurt cards (p. 49).

◀━━━━ **PROBLEM** ━━━━▶

Hurt

It's only blood.
Maybe not even your blood.

The accumulation of wounds slows you down. While you hold this card, you're at -1 to all Physical rolls. Discard at the end of the adventure.

SERIOUS INJURIES

Some injuries don't just temporarily slow you down – they're life-threatening. If you've been shot in the stomach or poisoned, then gritting your teeth or taking a quick breather isn't going to get you through this situation. Such Serious Injury needs to be Countered soon by getting Medical Attention, or you'll die.

Other injuries aren't necessarily life-threatening, but can't be shrugged off like most cuts and bruises. They're injuries that require you to slow down and get treatment. You can't exchange these Injuries for Hurt cards automatically – you've got to take some special action to do so, like getting Medical Attention.

Each Serious Injury card describes how to Counter it, and how long you have to live if you don't.

◀━━━━ **PROBLEM** ━━━━▶

Poisoned

SERIOUS INJURY

The vampire snake sank its fangs into your wrist. You're at -2 to all rolls. You have to Counter this Injury before discarding any other Injury cards. If you still hold this card at the end of the mission, you die.

RECOVERING FROM INJURIES

Some Masteries (like "Grit" or "Vodka and Painkillers") let you avoid or shrug off Injuries.

Alternatively, if you've got the Medic ability or (better yet) have someone who can treat your wounds with their Medic dice, roll on the Medical Attention Challenge. This usually requires Taking Time.

You can get the benefits of Medical Attention before swapping Injuries for Hurt. For example, if you finish a Scene with three Injury Problems, and manage to get an Advance on your Medical Attention test, then you walk away unscathed, you lucky devil. You Counter two Injuries on an Advance, and can then discard the last one for free (remember, you round down when exchanging Injuries for Hurt cards). Similarly, if you have two Injuries and score a Hold, you can Counter one and discard the other.

MEDICAL ATTENTION
MEDIC

Penalty: -1 die if you're trying to treat yourself.

Advance 9+: Counter two Injury cards or one Serious Injury card.

Hold 4-8: Counter an Injury card, or turn a Serious Injury into a Hurt Problem.

Setback 3 or less: Turn a Serious Injury into a Hurt Problem.

Extra Problem: None.

Stunt: No.

INJURY EXAMPLE

Khan has a nasty tussle with some goons and ends up with four regular Injuries – "Bruised," "Broken Fingers," "Beaten," and "Hard Impact." Each of these four Injuries gives her a -2 penalty to Physical Challenges, so she's at a crippling -8 to most rolls. She needs to recover.

When she Takes Time to rest, she trades in those four Injuries for two Hurt cards. Now, she's at -2 to all her Physical rolls – still a penalty, but one that's a lot more manageable.

If she'd crawled off to get Medical Attention from a doctor, she might have been able to Counter some of those Injuries instead of trading them in for Hurt.

DUAL-USE PROBLEMS

Some Problems have two keywords. Getting bitten by a vampire might be both a Shadow and an Injury Problem; if the vampire's hunting you with a swarm of mind-controlled rats, that's possibly both Shadow and Heat.

You only need to counter such a card once to remove it from your hand – you could get rid of a Shadow/Injury card by Taking Time and swapping it for a Hurt Problem, or by or you could use an Edge that removes Shadow.

SHADOW

Shadow measures the degree to which the supernatural threat is aware of you. A low Shadow Score means the vampires don't know you're in their city, or can't pin down your location. A high Shadow Score means they know about you, they can smell your blood, and can strike at you with supernatural attacks.

Think of Shadow as Vampire Heat.

GAINING SHADOW

You gain Shadow by:

♦ Encountering supernatural entities
♦ Causing spiritual disturbances that vampires can detect
♦ Damaging or thwarting the conspiracy, causing the vampires to stretch out their power and search for you
♦ Recalling previous encounters with vampires

A Shadow Score of 1-2 means the vampires are dimly aware of you, but aren't exerting themselves to strike at you in the spiritual realm. A Shadow Score of 3-4 means the vampires know you're out there, and may hit you or those around you with supernatural attacks. A Shadow Score of 5+ means the vampires are at your throat, spiritually speaking.

EFFECTS OF SHADOW

The precise effects vary from vampire to vampire (Directors: see *Vampire Powers* on p. 69). One monster might be able enter your dreams to steal your secrets and plant hypnotic suggestions; another might flap down in the shape of an enormous bat and drink the blood of your sleeping Contacts; another vampire might be able to command the weather, and pin you down with

thunderstorms and unnatural fog to keep you trapped.

Your Shadow Score comes into play most often when:

♦ You Take Time: many of the Director's Blowback reactions (p. 89) are only available if your Shadow Score is high enough.
♦ You confront vampires: your Shadow Score gets applied as a penalty when resisting certain mental or spiritual attacks.

A high Shadow Score also incurs bad dreams, ill omens, sinister visions, and other psychic perils as you walk in the shadow of the vampires.

LOSING SHADOW

The best way to get rid of Shadow is to kill the vampire at the heart of darkness, or to flee to another city – either approach allows the player to discard all temporary Shadow Problems. (Especially traumatic or significant contact with vampires may inflict Shadow Problems with the Continuity keyword, giving you a permanent Shadow Score.)

Events in the game may also let you discard Shadow Problems.

SUPPRESSING SHADOW

More commonly, you'll find yourself avoiding Shadow by temporary suppressing your Shadow Score. Different vampires have different supernatural Blocks – spiritual impediments that diminish their ability to strike at you. In the course of your investigations, you may discover these Blocks, and you can then use them to temporarily hide from vampiric attention. For example:

EDGE

Garlic

The smell of garlic repels vampires. If you line every entrance with garlic flowers, suppress your Shadow Score by -2 when Taking Time.

EDGE

Running Water

Vampires can't easily cross running water. Gain a +2 bonus to **Evasion** tests against vampires if you escape across running water, or suppress your Shadow Score by -1 if surrounded by running water.

These blocks only work in the limited circumstances described on the card. Garlic only works to protect your sleeping quarters (or those of your allies) against nocturnal intrusions. Running water can reduce your Shadow Score at any time – but only if you're actually surrounded by running water. So, you can take refuge on an island or meet with an informant on a boat to avoid vampiric spies, but your Shadow Score returns to its usual full value when you no longer have the protection of the river.

Blocks vary from vampire to vampire. One might be especially vulnerable to crucifixes, another to silver, another to ultraviolet light. You must use your Investigative abilities to discover which methods are actually efficacious against the undead, and which are just empty superstition.

DEATH

Your character never dies in mid-story, but can keel over at its the end: succumbing to wounds, shot by gangsters, eaten by vampires, or ending up in an unmarked grave on some desolate hillside in Eastern Europe.

You can also be eliminated in other ways –if you fail to Counter a Problem, you might spend the rest of your life in jail, or fall under the thrall of a vampire, or be forced to go underground and vanish.

Of course, nobody ever completely retires from the Great Game – if you're not dead, then there's a chance your character could come back in a future operation. If you are killed, though, then it's time to create a new operative to take on the next challenge.

IMPROVEMENTS

Assuming your character survived with mind and body intact, at the end of each case, you can add one of the following:

♦ an Investigative ability you lack
♦ a **tick** on a General ability

A tick moves you incrementally toward a rating improvement in a General ability. You gain no more than 1 tick per ability per case. Once you have three ticks in a General ability, you cash them in to improve a rating from 2 to 3.

General abilities may never exceed 3. (If a General ability is diminished by some injury, then two ticks are enough to raise an ability from 1 to 2.)

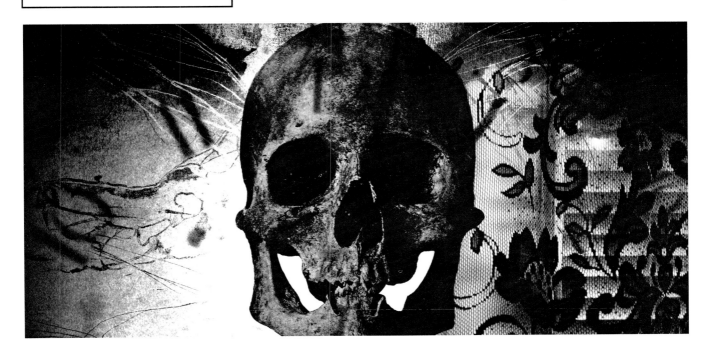

BACKSTAGE EUROPE

Although this section lists the main intelligence actors in Europe, it is far from exhaustive. Some countries (those with primarily domestic intelligence and security concerns) are not listed, and even some agencies in the listed countries are missing, mostly due to space limitations. Hit Wikipedia or elsewhere on the Net to dig deeper for any given country or agency.

BULGARIA

During the Cold War, the First Directorate of the Committee for State Security (KDS) actively cooperated with the KGB, murdering dissidents abroad and famously abetting the attempted assassination of the Pope. Its successor, the **National Intelligence Service (NIS)** performs extraordinary renditions and provides other assistance to CIA anti-terrorist campaigns.

CHINA

China's **Ministry for State Security (MSS)**, colloquially known as the Guóanbù, performs both intelligence and security functions for the Communist regime. In Europe, its activities focus on industrial espionage and monitoring Chinese students and residents abroad. Typical MSS practice is to flood the zone with hundreds or even thousands of short-term, low-level assets gathering a "mosaic" of OSINT and HUMINT to be analyzed in Beijing. The Seventh Bureau of the Bu Er, or (more formally) **Military Intelligence Department (MID)** hosts China's famed cyber intelligence teams of hackers, cryptanalysts, and spyware programmers.

CZECH REPUBLIC

The domestic **Security Information Service (BIS)** monitors political dissidents and foreign threats to the Republic; its foreign counterpart is the **Office for Foreign Relations and Information (ÚZSI)**, which has strong ties to the CIA and other European intelligence agencies. The Czech military intelligence group is referred to as the **VZ (Vojenské zpravodajství)**, and focuses primarily on threats from the east, especially Russia. During the Soviet era, the **Czech State Security (StB)** maintained an oppressive domestic regime with thousands of informants, and scored several notable successes overseas, deploying agents to the United States and even infiltrating the CIA. The StB was disbanded and its officers barred from holding any role in public service (including serving in the successor BIS), a process known as lustration, until the law expired in 2000.

FRANCE

France's security and intelligence apparatus rivals America's for intentional bureaucratic tangles. Broadly speaking, the **Direction Générale de la Sécurité Extérieure (DGSE)** handles foreign intelligence (its clandestine, paramilitary arm is **Division Action**) while the **Direction Centrale du Renseignement Intérieur (DCRI)** serves as the primary domestic security directorate. Both engage in technical and industrial espionage against the U.S. and other nominal allies, as well as more conventional intelligence missions. The **Direction du Renseignement Militaire (DRM)**, the French directorate of military intelligence, concentrates on operational intelligence for the French military; it operates wherever French forces do (currently Bosnia, Libya, and various African states). France's **National Police** (the former Sûreté) generally takes the lead on organized crime investigations, although the intelligence arms often horn in on international cases, and the national customs police **Direction Nationale du Renseignement et des Enquêtes Douanières (DNRED)** has primary jurisdiction over smuggling, cybercrime, and counterfeit money.

GERMANY

With a legacy of totalitarian security forces from the Nazi Gestapo to the Communist Stasi, Germany rigorously delimits its intelligence agencies. Despite this resolution, Germany's **Bundesnachrichtendienst (BND)**, the Federal Intelligence Service, began as a splinter group of Abwehr, SD, and SS operatives recruited by the CIA to spy on the Soviet bloc. The BND takes primacy not only in external intelligence operations (focused on HUMINT and close cooperation with Mossad) but in SIGINT, and in combating organized crime and WMD proliferation. The **Bundesamt für Sicherheit in der Informationstechnik (BSI)**, or Federal Office for Information Technology Security, covers not only government information security, but the information security of the German banking industry. Germany's internal security agency, the **Bundesamt für Verfassungsschutz (BfV)**, or Federal Office for the Protection of the Constitution, limits its remit to counter-espionage and monitoring and infiltrating extremist groups. The elite counter-terrorist special forces unit **GSG 9** is a police agency, not a military unit.

GREAT BRITAIN

The British intelligence apparatus is, for the most part, clearly delineated and quite competent. The Security Service, **MI5**, handles domestic intelligence, counter-espionage, and other threats to the Realm. The Secret Intelligence Service, **MI6**, the fictional home of James Bond and George Smiley, conducts external intelligence operations. Less well-known are Britain's all-source military and security intelligence group **Defence Intelligence** and its SIGINT, cybersecurity, and cryptanalytic arm **GCHQ** (Government Communications Headquarters). In general, British espionage agencies rely more heavily on HUMINT, with networks in some areas of the Middle East going back a century or more. Founded in 1883 to combat Irish terrorism, the **Special Branch** of London's Metropolitan Police is now officially called the **Counter Terrorism Command** or **SO15**. Its mission remains the same: thwart terrorism in London and coordinate police work with MI5 and other intelligence services.

IRAN

Iran's secret police and intelligence organization, **Vezarat-e Ettela'at va Amniyat-e Keshvar (VEVAK)** is also known as VAJA, MISIRI, and MOIS depending on the source. It assassinates dissidents at home and abroad, assists Iran-allied terrorist groups (especially Hezbollah), and monitors expatriate Iranian populations, as well as carrying out more conventional intelligence functions.

ISRAEL

Israel's external intelligence agency, **Mossad,** punches considerably above its weight in the espionage world. Its operations include kidnappings, assassinations of PLO and Hamas leaders, extraordinary renditions of Nazi war criminals, and sabotage of WMD components intended for enemies of Israel. It maintains generally good relations with the BND and MI6, as well as the CIA. Its katsas, or case officers, can draw on hundreds of sayanim, non-Mossad local friendlies (usually Jews) who support Israel. **Shin Bet** (officially called Shabak or the ISA), the Israeli domestic intelligence arm, handles counter-terrorism with the help of the "Duvdevan" and Sayeret Matkal special forces units of the IDF. **Unit 8200** is the Israeli SIGINT and cyberwarfare brigade under the Israeli military intelligence directorate, **Aman**.

ITALY

Italy's intelligence agencies have been reshuffled twice in the last 40 years, following an attempted neo-fascist coup by elements of the military intelligence service (SID) in 1970 and the revelation of massive internal surveillance, intimidation of the press, and black operations against leftist politicians and magistrates by the SID's successor SISIMI in 2007. Currently, Italy's external intelligence agency **AISE**, domestic security agency **AISI**, and information security agency **DIS** operate under (theoretically) strict parliamentary control. Anti-mafia investigations usually fall to the **ROS**, a special operations unit of the **Carabinieri**, Italy's military national police. Their work overlaps with another military police agency, the **Guardia di Finanza**, tasked with combating narcotics and financial crimes.

POLAND

Immediately after the Cold War, Poland reorganized its intelligence services to eliminate the old SB security agency. Continued allegations of corruption, arms smuggling, and malfeasance associated with Soviet-era officials caused a further reshuffling of the civilian agency UOP in 2002 (now split into the **Intelligence Agency (AW)** for external intelligence and the **Internal Security Agency (ABW)** for internal security) and the military intelligence agency WSI in 2006 (now split into a counter-intelligence arm, **SKW**, and an intelligence arm, **SWW**. Polish agencies of all sorts have worked closely with the CIA and NSA in Iraq and elsewhere, starting as early as 1990.

ROMANIA

Romania is another former Communist state with strong intelligence links to the U.S. intelligence community, mostly through its **Foreign Intelligence Service (SIE)**. The **Romanian Intelligence Service (SRI)** is a domestic intelligence service, the successor to the feared Securitate of the Cold War era. Romania's Interior Ministry has its own criminal intelligence service, the **General Directorate for Intelligence and Internal Security (DGIPI)**.

RUSSIA

After the fall of Communism, the new Russian government reorganized the KGB into two agencies. Many old KGB hands simply retired, setting themselves up as fixers and bag men for the newly powerful Russian mafiyas; some of these new gangsters keep powerful connections in their former service. The **Foreign Intelligence Service (SVR)** took over the foreign intelligence portfolio of the old KGB

First Directorate, and rapidly extended its power over Russian foreign policy and development. Every Russian business overseas, especially Gazprom and Aeroflot, provides cover to SVR agents, who engage in assassinations of dissidents, bioweapons espionage and smuggling, and conventional espionage. Even more power fell to the heirs of the KGB Second Directorate, the internal security and counter-espionage agency now known as the **Federal Security Service (FSB)**. The FSB incorporates the border police as well as domestic surveillance, counter-intelligence, counter-terrorism, cyberwarfare, cryptology, and export control functions. It carries out targeted killings of Chechen and other terrorist leaders, and commands two units ("Alfa" and "Banner") of Spetsnaz special forces.

The **Main Intelligence Directorate (GRU)** of the Russian General Staff dwarfs them both. With six times as many spies in the field as the SVR, control of a global SIGINT network (the Sixth Directorate of the GRU operates listening posts in at least 60 Russian embassies, as well as enormous facilities in Cuba and Vietnam), a network of 130 satellites for ELINT and IMINT, and 25,000 Spetsnaz special ops troops under its command, the GRU is probably the single largest, most powerful intelligence organization on the planet. Like the SVR, the GRU carries out targeted killings both at home and abroad, mostly but not exclusively targeting Russian emigres and troublemakers. Many of its agents are "illegals," running networks in host countries with no diplomatic or other government cover.

SWEDEN

Sweden unifies its domestic and foreign intelligence under its **Military Intelligence and Security Service (MUST)**. Within MUST is a specific espionage office, the **Office for Special**

Acquisition **(KSI)**, which works with foreign intelligence agencies, especially the CIA and Shin Bet. In 1973, crusading journalists revealed a secret agency called **IB** within the Swedish armed forces, dedicated to infiltrating Sweden's neighbors (especially Finland), penetrating the Soviet Union, and monitoring radical groups in Sweden. IB has never been dissolved.

TURKEY

The **Milli Istihbarat Teskilati (MIT)** is Turkey's intelligence and security organization. Formerly a military command, it is now over 90% civilian, although it still competes with the Ministry of Interior's domestic intelligence and security office, **KDSM,** on terrorism and internal security operations. The MIT plays a key role in Turkey's post-Cold War expansion of influence into the Middle East and the former Soviet bloc. Formerly, MIT recruited almost exclusively from family members of MIT officers but this is slowly changing.

UKRAINE

Ukraine's **Foreign Intelligence Service (SZRU)** split off the controversial **Security Service of Ukraine (SBU)** in 2005. Scandals, accusations of cronyism (the SBU director owns Ukraine's largest TV network) and botched serial killer investigations have dogged the SBU since Ukrainian independence. More seriously, the SBU may well have attempted to thwart Ukraine's "Orange Revolution" and return the country to the Russian sphere.

UNITED STATES

The U.S. has 16 major elements in its intelligence community, and a dizzying number of ad hoc offices, committees, bureaus, and oversight boards. In addition, almost 2,000 independent contractors do some intelligence work for the U.S. government. It spends about $80 billion a year on everything from satellite launches to bribes for foreign officials; over 100,000 people work directly for some arm of U.S. intelligence. The primary U.S. intelligence actors in Europe are the **Central Intelligence Agency (CIA)**, America's foreign intelligence agency; the **National Security Agency (NSA)**, America's SIGINT, cybersecurity, and cryptanalysis agency; and the **Defense Intelligence Agency (DIA)**, which has increasingly worked around a CIA seen as obstructionist and incompetent by the Pentagon. Other key U.S. intelligence players in Europe include the **Office of Terrorism and Financial Intelligence (OTFI)**, which monitors terrorist finances in European banks; the **Federal Bureau of Investigation (FBI)**, the U.S. domestic intelligence, counter-intelligence, and criminal intelligence agency, which works overseas to combat organized crime, terrorism, and cybercrime; and the **Diplomatic Security Service (DSS)**, the State Department office tasked with counter-intelligence, embassy protection, passport fraud, and international fugitive pursuit.

THE VATICAN

From 1944 until at least 1956, the Vatican's intelligence arm in Eastern Europe was the **National Military Union (NZW)**, an anti-communist Resistance movement in Poland; its successor (if any) is unknown. Various writers have argued that the **Sovereign Military Order of the Knights of Malta (SMOM)**, an international hospital and ambulance service (successors of the Knights Hospitaller), also serves as a Vatican intelligence gathering system tied to the CIA. Others have fingered a theological internal-affairs brotherhood set up by

Pope Pius X called Sodalitium Pianum, the conservative clerical movement Opus Dei, the Congregation for the Defense of the Faith (formerly the Inquisition), or the Pontifical Russian College for evangelism and ministry to Russian Catholics as the "real" Vatican spy service.

INTERNATIONAL ORGANIZATIONS

Despite many well-meaning attempts, there is no truly multinational intelligence, police, or security agency in Europe. Many national bureaus or military services diligently attend inter-agency cooperative meetings; some of these groups even have permanent staff. Existing multinational bodies like NATO, the BIS, or the EU have intelligence committees or counter-terrorism and anti-mafia committees, again with permanent staff analysts. The UNDOC (UN Office on Drugs and Crime) serves as a sort of clearing-house for research; the closest thing to U.N.C.L.E. in the real world is probably the **Budapest Group**, a cooperative OSINT effort of 14 EU countries.

INTERPOL

The International Criminal Police Organization, better known as Interpol, has been in operation since 1923. Originally headquartered in Vienna, it fell under Gestapo control during WWII; since then, its base has moved to Lyon, France. It exists to coordinate police activity and information between its 188 member nations: an American FBI agent in Greece can coordinate with the Interpol liaison in Athens rather than trying to untangle the maze of local jurisdictions. Interpol keeps databases (especially fingerprints and stolen documents) and rap sheets on criminal activity supplied by its member police forces, emphasizing cross-border crime. All that said, there aren't Interpol cops chasing down criminals or making arrests; an Interpol "red notice" merely requests an arrest warrant from the local authorities.

UNDERGROUND EUROPE

Since the fall of the Soviet Union, European organized crime has exploded in power, influence, and wealth. Much of this growth stems from the rise of the Russian Mafiya, and from the sudden opening of the "heroin road" from Central Asia through the Balkans to Central Europe. Increasing European economic and political integration has fed this trend as well; cross-border crime battens on more open cross-border flows of people, goods, and capital. Terrorists interested in funding their activities find ample opportunity for fanatics used to violence in such an environment; the linkage between

terror groups and mafias goes back to the Italian Carbonari in the 1820s.

Intelligence agencies trying to track — or enable — clandestine movement across borders have a natural interest in smugglers of drugs, humans, or weapons. They nurture assets and alliances within criminal groups when they don't actively cooperate with them. The links between the FSB and the Russian mafiyas, or the MSS and the Triads, are well documented; the CIA is far from the only intelligence agency accused of padding its black budget by providing "protection" for drug traffickers. In short, players in the shadow world of underground Europe may be spies, crooks, or terrorists — or all three, depending on who's paying.

TERRORIST GROUPS

Since 9/11, security and police agencies in Western Europe have made over 2,300 arrests for terrorist activity or conspiracy; in 2007 alone, terrorists planned almost 600 attacks (most of them thwarted) in those countries. **ISIS** and its Islamist front groups and allies are headline hogs, but old-school terror groups like the Basque **ETA** in Spain, the Kurdish **PKK** (in Germany and anywhere else Turks live), and **Hezbollah** still set off bombs, or kill and kidnap targets. The Algerian Islamist **GIA** mounted a decade-long bombing campaign in France in the 1990s and it still operates under a lower profile. Old **IRA** bombers train young Macedonians; former **Stasi** paymasters keep their smart phones full of contacts in Italy and Lebanon.

THE RUSSIAN MAFIYA

The "Russian Mafiya" is something of a misnomer. There is no overarching criminal organization linking all of Russia's various criminal societies; rather, there are several thousand independent groups scattered all over Russia and the world that share a common past. The Soviet prison system bred a hardened aristocracy, the *vory v zakone*, or "thieves in law." The *vory* ran criminal gangs all across the USSR from inside the gulag; gangs that included various black-market operations in their smuggling activities. During the Brezhnev era, the Communist Party made a deal with the black marketeers in order to keep a semblance of a civilian economy functioning at all. When the USSR fell, the Party bureaucrats and their black-market contacts kept the system going at home, bringing in mostly KGB officers to provide hard currency and connections in the West, and demobilized Afghan war vets for muscle. The new mafiyas looted the Soviet vaults of diamonds, gold, oil, and anything else that would sell; the KGB set up the deals overseas and took their percentage. Roughly $2 billion per month flowed out of the old USSR into the mafiyas' bank accounts; by now, something like 80% of the banks in Russia are mafiya-owned, and two-thirds of Ukraine's economic activity likewise. The Russian mafiyas used this tsunami of cash (and those Afghan veteran killers) to buy and murder their way into the major criminal enclaves all over Europe, especially the French Riviera.

The various *bratva,* or "brotherhoods," of the Russian mafiyas operate independently, coming together on an ad hoc basis for operations and then dissolving again: a true multicellular network. The biggest player is the **Solntsevskaya Bratva** out of the Solntsevsko neighborhood in Moscow; others include the **Tamborskaya Bratva** in St. Petersburg, the **Podolskaya Bratva,** the **Izmailovskaya Bratva** operating as far afield as Mexico, and the **Tverskaya Bratva**.

THE ITALIAN MAFIAS

America's mafia, **La Cosa Nostra,** descended from Sicilian criminal families who emigrated to the United States. The relatives they left behind still run the **Sicilian Mafia,** trafficking heroin and arms and keeping a thumb on Italian politics and business despite a 30-year anti-mafia campaign by a handful of brave magistrates. A different offshoot of the Sicilian Mafia in Calabria became the **'Ndrangheta,** an extended network of family clans that exploded in power after taking over the cocaine traffic in Europe in the 1990s. The 'Ndrangheta has a lucrative sideline in smuggling nuclear waste for illegal disposal in Third World countries. The **Camorra**

began in Naples in the 18th century as a protection racket for illegal street gamblers; it now controls every aspect of the city and surrounding province. Its famous garbage monopoly pales next to its grip on heroin, prostitution, protection, and racketeering. A loose network of clans, its internecine wars kill around 100 people a year. Other regional mafias control Apulia and the Veneto, like the mafias busily acquiring legitimate businesses in Italy and elsewhere to launder drug profits, with the connivance of local officials. All Italian mafias participate in the immense trade in illicit antiquities and art centered in Italy.

OTHER NATIONAL MAFIAS

An estimate by the national police of the Netherlands tallied around 300 national or ethnic organized crime groups in that country; most of these groups have branches or connections all over cosmopolitan, urbanized Europe. Currently the **Albanian mafia** dominates the heroin routes up through the Balkans from Turkey and the sex trade in Britain, the **Nigerian mafia** controls human trafficking from Africa, the **Bulgarian mafias** are key players in human trafficking from Eastern Europe, the **Naša Stvar** (the Serbian mafia) keeps its hand in human trafficking and arms dealing, and the **Israeli mafia** (non-hierarchical and non-ethnic, including Arabs and Russians) dominates diamond smuggling and ecstasy trafficking, but such roles and domains seldom remain hard and fast for long. The **Union Corse,** for example, once ran the famous "French Connection" in the heroin trade; it has been relegated to second-banana status by the Italian and Russian mobs in the Riviera since the 1990s, and a flood of Afghan heroin has driven the Corsicans' North African connections out of the market. Now, Moroccan gangs run hashish into Europe alongside illegal African immigrants bound for sweatshops

or simply for undocumented labor wherever they can get it.

The Chechen mafia, the **Obshina,** has an enviable reputation for bloody, vengeful violence that allows them to punch above their weight wherever they go in Europe. They do not require actual Chechen descent for membership, although the connections between Chechen warlords and Islamic terrorism make them natural allies of extremist groups in Europe.

OTHER ORGANIZED CRIMINAL GROUPS

The heirs to London's Krays and other East End gangs of the 1960s and 1970s are called the Firms; the **Clerkenwell Firm** in North London remains perilously atop the roost for now.

Various outlaw motorcycle gangs in Northern Europe and Scandinavia — and increasingly in Bosnia and the Balkans — serve as muscle and local drug lords, with sidelines in bank robbery and arms dealing.

The Chinese Triads have had a presence in Western Europe since the 19th century; then as now, their base is extortion of local "Chinatown" businesses and sweatshop labor supply. The **14K** and **Wo Shin Wo** Triads have drug, counterfeit and knockoff consumer goods, and lumber smuggling operations in Britain, France, and the Benelux countries; Triad "snakehead" people-smugglers hook up with Serbian mobsters to ship arms and gems to and from Burma and other interdicted countries. Triads also operate underground casinos and clubs in Europe, both as money laundering operations and as narcotics distribution points.

Japan's **Yakuza** launders money in Europe through Japan's heavy foreign investment there; its local operatives (mostly contract killers and negotiators) work out of Europe's largest Japanese communities, in London and Düsseldorf.

TRADECRAFT

Being a spy means mastering, or at least becoming familiar with, a wide variety of tricks and tactics meant to provide you with a secure, reliable intelligence network and degrade that of your enemy. In the game, some of that tradecraft can be handwaved or subsumed under a single ability use; other tactics and methods lead into or even define whole scenarios.

With all tradecraft techniques, if they provide core clues for an operation then they require no Push from the relevant Investigative ability. If they merely provide additional confirmation, shortcuts, protection, or any other secondary benefit, the Director may rule that a Push is necessary.

COVERT COMMUNICATION

Any spy network is only as good as its communications. Distributed groups following a common ideology can occasionally score one-off victories, but for real coordinated action, a network's cells and strategists need to be able to talk — ideally, without anyone else listening in. If at all possible, networks communicate through **cut-outs,** messengers tasked anonymously for one-time meets or passes, who get details from burner phones, classified ads, or the Internet, and thus can't identify either end of the chain. Sometimes, a face-to-face rendezvous is possible, established either by routine ("Someone will always be at the mausoleum to take a message") or by signal ("Carry a copy of the *Financial Times* to work if you want a meeting and we'll text you the time and place"). But those approaches are risky and labor-intensive; sometimes communication must happen at a remove.

BRUSH PASSES

A brush pass occurs in person between two members of a network. Either or both carry something — a document, a message, an envelope full of bills, a flash drive — and without obviously making contact, brush past each other and exchange it. This might involve actual contact, or a drop somewhere in the other's view: a trash can, a parked car, a bookshelf in the library. A brush pass into (or from) a vehicle is also called a "car toss."

Depending on the specifics, carrying out a brush pass may involve tests of **Driving**, **Filch**, or **Surveillance** (if actively opposed by enemy agents) or merely invoking **Tradecraft** (under normal circumstances). Noticing an opposition brush pass falls under **Tradecraft**. Intercepting a brush pass definitely takes some planning, and possibly a chase.

DEAD DROPS

A dead drop is a way to pass information without ever physically encountering the recipient. One party puts the information somewhere; the second party retrieves it later. Dead drops are usually pre-arranged: "the fifth tree from the north corner of the park" or "the third pew from the back." The dropper usually stashes the information in a non-magnetic container secure from moisture, such as a plasticized mailing envelope, a film canister, or a lipstick tube. Some agencies use hollow plastic or aluminum spikes that can be shoved into the ground with a simple step, and buried by kicking leaves or dirt over them: the retriever goes to a pre-arranged set of GPS coordinates or follows a beacon triggered only by a specific cell phone signal.

Carrying out a dead drop is usually a simple matter of **Tradecraft**, although shedding any shadows on the way to the site (or choosing the right time to retrieve the drop) might require **Surveillance** tests. Noticing an opposition dead drop, likewise.

"**Digital dead drops**" post information somewhere on the immense spaces of the Internet: chatrooms for Hindi singles, fan forums for Peruvian pop starlets, Craigslist Zagreb, or just a seemingly random set of URL numbers. At least one Al-Qaeda group posts its dead drops as drafts to a Gmail mailing list to which all the members have admin privileges: they can read messages that haven't actually been sent anywhere, and thus avoid NSA surveillance of packet-switching nodes. Other document-sharing sites no doubt have similar features. The information may stay up for an hour, a day, or a week before automatically being taken down by a specialized sweep or by the asset handler.

Setting up and concealing a digital dead drop is relatively simple; retrieving information from it takes nothing more than the URL or login and access to any computer for the length of a download. Finding an opposition digital dead drop requires government-level SIGINT capabilities, or (far easier) breaking someone who knows which site to check, or subverting their computer, smart phone, or Internet accounts.

STEGANOGRAPHY

This term, meaning "hidden writing," goes back to the earliest printed books. To escape omnipresent censorship, scholars concealed their text in elaborate codes, anagrams, and allusions: Trithemius concealed his work on codes in a book seemingly about magic! Modern digital steganography hides data inside other data: a picture of someone's grandson, a techno MP3, a piece of freeware, a pirated copy of *Twilight*, when "solved" with the correct algorithm, it rearranges its ones and zeroes into a more significant message, image, or the like.

Cryptography or **Data Recovery** (or both) lets you crack steganography; **Cryptography** lets you construct it.

COVERS AND LEGENDS

To move freely without inviting suspicious observation, spies need cover identities, or "legends." Agents use the **Cover** ability to use pre-existing legends stashed away against just such an emergency.

Breaking an enemy's cover identity usually involves either **Research** or **Traffic Analysis** to turn up weird holes or patterns in their legend and its connections (or lack thereof) with vital statistics and other databases.

CUCKOO'S EGGS

Infiltrating an enemy network, or working yourself close to an enemy, is almost always a long-term action involving any number of Interpersonal abilities, **Human Terrain** (to identify organizational openings or weak spots), and possibly even the odd spot of disguise. Seldom do any of those abilities immediately deliver core clues

in an operation: planting yourself or another Agent as a "cuckoo's egg" infiltrator may, however, set you up to receive core clues or (more likely) to mount an active operation against the target. The GM may handwave the entire social infiltration process with one scene, or make the would-be cuckoo earn prime placement with a few scenes (and possibly even Interpersonal Pushes) spaced out over the course of the session like an episode of *Mission: Impossible* or *Leverage*.

ASSET HANDLING

Rather than infiltrate an enemy network themselves, intelligence operatives often try to recruit assets already in place or who can more easily work themselves into position. Asset recruitment is a three-stage process: identify a likely asset, contact them, and flip them to your side.

Identify: Finding a potential asset might be as easy as picking a picture off the surveillance video, or it might involve **Human Terrain** analysis of the target organization to specify a potentially fruitful subject. **High Society** might supply the name of a jilted girlfriend, **Streetwise** provides hints of restive gang subordinates, or **Traffic Analysis** could give the phone number of someone everyone in the target organization has called in the last month. The Director might offer a range of possibilities, or just feed one "core clue" name to the player.

Contact: Making contact with an asset can happen in any fashion, but usually while the asset is either vulnerable or comfortable: eager and needy, or lulled into false security. Figuring out the right Interpersonal approach to an asset is part of the fun of the spy game; suitable **Research** or previous **Surveillance** can give tips and pointers.

Flip: Turning a contact into an asset is the tricky part. Traditionally, assets flip for one of four MICE: Money, Ideology, Coercion, or Ego. In a normal game, Coercion will be your go-to strategy: figure out something to hold over your asset's head, show him his weakness, and twist. Those three steps can be three nice little scenes in a mini-op that nets you an asset. That said, a GM interested in the changeup will occasionally trail a possible Ego or Ideology flip past you, the latter especially in STAKES games. Of course, an Ideology flip might not stay flipped! A Money flip usually needs excessive resources, but if you can help a capo to rise in the Genoa mafia by wiping out a Corsican rival, that gives a suitable Money-style reward — and the Coercion can come when you threaten to tell the Union Corse that he ordered the hit.

ASSET RUNNING

Once you've got an asset, you can get information from him; you can spend a Push to make him do something risky for you. If you use **Tradecraft**, you can gain information or cooperation covertly (although if your asset is under pressure, you may need to make a **Surveillance** test to avoid blowing his cover). If the Director plants a core clue with your asset, getting that information from him never requires a Push.

The difference between an asset and a **Network** Contact is that assets are always, fundamentally untrustworthy. They know you're manipulating them; **Network** Contacts might be friends, colleagues or just hired to do a job, but you're not exerting leverage over them the same way.

THE YOJIMBO OPTION

Everybody has enemies. Criminals, terrorists, and ambitious corrupt Eurocrats are no exception. One strategy for an indirect attack on a conspiracy target is to recruit the target's competition, pursuers, or resentful victims. This recruitment can also be indirect: attacking your target's rival, and making it look like your target was responsible, is a great way to trigger a blowback aimed at your actual enemies. You might "accidentally" tip off the rival about your target's vulnerable operations — or feed false intel to the rival and lure them into a vampiric ambush as a diversion from your own operation. Or you might openly suggest an alliance with the rival to take down your mutual enemy — how much of your plans (or of the truth) you reveal is, of course, up to you.

ADVERSARY MAPPING

The ongoing goal of intelligence operations is to uncover the opposition's network, facilitating its destruction, rolling up, or isolation. Agents typically conclude a given investigation by updating their adversary map, a speculative org chart identifying the apparent relationships between the members of the vampire conspiracy. Adding one or two names, or a suggestive surveillance photo, to the adversary map, counts as a victory regardless of how the rest of the operation might have gone. By understanding the relationships between your foes, you know where to lean on them, who to expect to respond, and which seemingly innocuous Eurocrat to kidnap for further intel.

PRESSURE

Another good way to weaken an organization — either for its own sake, or to pop loose a potential asset — is to put it under pressure. This can also force the target group to reveal its own assets, its hidden strengths, or its emergency strategies. If, for example, you've tapped the city's cellular network, sudden pressure on a foe can reap a rich harvest of **Traffic Analysis** as everyone in the gang calls their boss for instructions, and then their bosses call key subordinates to coordinate a response.

Pressure can involve a direct attack, an indirect attack on allies or sources of funding, exposure of criminal or terrorist activity to the police or other officials, or any combination or repetition of the above. Pressure can also be "pull," setting up a tempting opportunity and seeing who bites, or egging the target on to overreach.

CAPTURE AND INTERROGATION

When all else fails, there's good old kidnapping. This requires a target (usually identified by **Human Terrain**, **Streetwise**, **Surveillance**, or **Traffic Analysis**), an extraction plan (planning and carrying out a snatch job is usually the meat of a whole session or even a whole operation), and a secure location for interrogation (set up with **Network**, or possibly mapped out with **Urban Survival** and staked out with **Surveillance**). If it works, a grab is an excellent way to get current intel and (if the snatch alerts the opposition) a look at the target group's responses.

The actual interrogation requires an isolated or controlled space and a secure hold on the prisoner. Using the **Interrogation** ability automatically extracts a core clue, if any are available, although it might take hours or even days if the subject is trained or conditioned to resist. (If a subject had a core clue, other Interpersonal abilities can often get it faster without kidnapping.) For intel the Director doesn't deem "core," spends still probably turn up something actionable — a name or two for the adversary

map, for instance — unless the target actually doesn't know anything, thanks to compartmentalization, or vampiric mind-wipes, or the Director running a MIRROR mode switcheroo.

TRUTH SERUM

In the real world, some intelligence agencies use some specific barbiturate cocktails, including scopolamine and sodium thiopental, to assist interrogation. These drugs induce a general sense of well-being, lowered inhibitions, and (under proper guidance by an interrogator) a tendency to rattle off anything and everything on their mind, truthful or not. In effect, "truth serum" acts just like getting someone really, really drunk or high.

In spy thrillers, truth serum works much more reliably; after an injection of "sodium pentothal, the interrogator can pry reliable answers forcibly out of a writhing victim. Real-world Russian defectors claim the FSB uses a flavorless, odorless truth serum called SP-17 that also erases memories of the interrogation.

The **Pharmacy** ability does not cover mixing truth serum from scratch. If the Agent wants truth drugs, she needs to steal them from an agency medical facility or source them with **Network**. Using truth serum speeds up the **Interrogation** ability, assuming someone present has the **Shrink** ability as well.

Needless to say, even a drop of vampire blood entirely counteracts truth serum.

61

THE BUCHAREST RULES

The "Moscow Rules" guided Western agents through Cold War operations in the Soviet bloc. In the thriller world, they're a little staid, so we've replaced them with a few "Bucharest Rules" to get the game going: techniques or concepts to take on board that can help maximize your own fun.

YOU CAN WIN

Yes, this is a game of horror, in which your Agent might well be slaughtered, exsanguinated, or buried in a Slovakian cement factory. That will *definitely* happen if you do nothing, so you might as well do *something*.

Take the initiative: pick the most appealing offense and execute it. Will something horrible happen? Of course it will — it's a horror game! Something horrible will happen no matter what your plan is. At best, you'll find one that requires desperation and daring, and

might still cost you your lives. But no fun whatsoever will happen unless you choose something to do and do it.

So be bold and seize the initiative. Pick the type of terrifying risk you're most able to confront and go after it with both hands. Who knows? Maybe you'll surprise the Director, if not the opposition. As in any game, the Director will allow any halfway credible approach you come up with a good chance of success, and will place nasty obstacles in your way to make your choices more exciting. Pick something quickly, grit your teeth, and send your Agent into that cement factory.

WITH GREAT ABILITY SCORES COMES GREAT RESPONSIBILITY

Nobody wants to watch a movie where James Bond doesn't seduce the girl, or Jason Bourne doesn't beat the crap out of some mooks, or Ethan Hunt doesn't wear that cool face mask. You've got the same responsibility to your audience and to your Director. Look at your Edges and assets, and play to win; and better yet, to a win where you look cool. If you're stuck for an approach or a plan, think about how to use your mastery edges to make what you want to happen, happen.

WHEN STUCK, GET MORE INTEL

If you are legitimately stuck, and not just rejecting perfectly viable courses of action, don't stick close to home hashing over your options. Whenever you get stuck, *get out and gather more information*. Ask yourself what you need to know in order to formulate a plan. Then figure out how to get that information, and go out and get it.

FOLLOW THE MONEY

Nobody works for vampires for their health. Even if the hard core of the conspiracy is bonded in heretical Cathar baptism, somebody has to pay for all the robes and chalices. Hit bagmen, and obvious sources of income like rich scumbags, casinos, or drug rings. Comb financial records to find suspiciously well-off civil servants; find out who *actually* bought that medieval icon or Etruscan tomb amulet. Even if vampires don't cast shadows, their money does.

HUMINT IS KEY

Many players are reluctant to use their Interpersonal abilities, figuring that they can get into less trouble by sticking purely to physical clues, or by downloading data in a well-lit hotel room. This is a disastrous mistake. Talking to assets, witnesses, experts, and informants is by far the best way of gaining intel about the situation. With information, access, and assets, you can find that coveted way in that will set up a kill shot for you.

BUILD YOUR OWN NETWORK

Agents have Networks and the ability to create assets for a reason: to give you the tactical flexibility and strategic depth your enemies already have. Use those qualities to the utmost: think "Who could help me here?" and build, buy, or break that person. In the best-case scenario, you have lots more eyes on the opposition, feeding you lots more intel. In the worst-case (or most cynical) scenario, your network becomes a string of Judas goats: when the vampires take out your assets, they leave more clues for you to follow.

KEEP MOVING FORWARD

Expect to find only one major clue per scene. Although you shouldn't be too quick to abandon a scene for the next one, some Agents make the opposite mistake, returning endlessly to the same few places or witnesses, hoping to scrape more info out of them. If you find a clue that leads you somewhere else — go there! Chances are, once you're there, you'll find another clue, that will in turn lead you to a new scene, with a further clue that takes you to a third scene, and so on. Unsuccessful spies endlessly re-sniff the same ground. Successful ones follow a trail.

REMEMBER, YOU'RE THE BADASS HERE

When you created an Agent, you cast a character — a hero — in a story. A story about a badass who fights vampires. Sure, some people curl up into a ball and whine that vampires don't exist. Those people are called "non-player characters." Or "lunch."

Paralysis is boring. When you create your Agent, or develop her personality during play, think about realistic ways to portray her as proactive and resourceful and dangerous — as, in a word, badass — even in the face of bloody horror.

Players in horror games — and spy games! — often make the mistake of thinking solely about how realistic their responses are. Instead, make interesting choices and then find a way to make them seem plausible. An interesting choice is one that keeps your Agent moving fast, kicking tail, and looking good.

ALWAYS KNOW WHERE THE EXIT IS

Sometimes what you needed to find out is that you can't hit them there. Not yet, anyway. You don't get extra experience points for finishing the dungeon: you can call a mission suddenly gone deadly a "probing raid" or a "reconnaissance in force" and live to fight again another night. Don't count on the Director's kindness to leave your Agent alive: do your part to get her out of the fire. You can count on the Director to give you more clues, more intel, after your Agent runs **Traffic Analysis** on the hornet's nest her near-suicidal assault stirred up, or uses **High Society** to find out which Hungarian financier shows up to the conference with a bodyguard — or a bullet wound — all of a sudden.

RUNNING SOLO OPS

This chapter, addressed to the Director, discusses how to run the game for the player.

THE CORE OF GUMSHOE

GUMSHOE makes a promise to the player: "you will never be stuck without a lead to follow. That lead might send the player into danger; the player might miss the importance of the lead when it's first encountered and have to circle back to an earlier scene; following the lead might incur some cost or danger – but the player will never be completely stymied. As Director, you've got to live up to that promise. The player should always have at least one clear lead to follow (or, better, two or three leads to choose from).

If the player does get stuck, you might:

♦ Review existing leads and ask her to pick one
♦ Point out leads she found but forgot about
♦ Roleplay through a scene with a Contact to nudge the player towards a clue
♦ Suggest there's more to be discovered in a previous scene, or by questioning an informant again

Remind the player that there's always a route forward – although such routes usually lead into danger. If someone's trying to kill you, it's a sign you're on the right track.

PARANOIA MANAGEMENT

One-on-one games are intense, nerve-wracking experiences for both player and Director.

For the player, it's the experience of playing without a net. She's all alone, without backup or allies. In a regular roleplaying game, one player can rely on having another bail her out, either by coming to the rescue if she gets into trouble, or by pointing out the errors in her thinking *before* she rushes into danger. In solo play, there's no eject button and there's no brake – not only is the player solely responsible for all her decisions, but she's also going to bear the brunt of all the consequences.

The player is up against supernatural monsters that are faster and stronger than any human, not to mention a vast conspiracy with a seemingly endless supply of armed goons. To add to the player's fears, the game takes place in an approximation of the modern world and the conspiracy has all the lawyers: shooting guns and setting off bombs draws Heat and the eager attention of counter-terrorism forces. The player is all alone against overwhelming odds, and has to be *subtle* about it too.

Often, the player reacts to this heightened intensity by "turtling" – taking ever more precautions and seeking to put barriers between herself and harm. They never talk to non-player characters without putting on a disguise, and try to do as much investigation remotely through computers or Contacts as possible. They avoid using violence or direct action. The player's personal security routine becomes increasingly elaborate – countermeasures against surveillance, against vampiric subversion, endless worrying about how to avoid the attention of the authorities.

To a degree, this plays right into the genre – the point of playing a game about vampiric espionage is to have fun dodging surveillance and worrying about vampiric subversion in between shooting bad guys. It becomes a problem, though, if the player becomes paralyzed by paranoia or the action slows down to a crawl. In a group game, there's always one player who's gung-ho to charge ahead, so the Director can't spend *too* much time on the group's precautions. In a single-player game, where the player has every reason to be cautious and can monopolize the game time, it's all too easy to enter such a morass.

Some tactics to counteract an excess of caution:

♦ **Let the player be a badass:** The type of badass is up to the player – is Leyla a Bourne-esque invincible warrior, or more of a Smiley-type who's always one step ahead? Either way, she's able to take out or avoid multiple hostiles. Show the player how effective she can be by wrapping a whole gang of bad guys into a single Challenge. For example, if the player's fighting her way up through a building full of conspiracy goons, make the whole encounter a single **Fighting** Challenge, and describe the action with every dice rolled. (*"Okay, there's a trio of guards at the back entrance. What do you roll on your first **Fighting** die? A 5. You take them down without a scratch. Tell me how you do it…"*) Make it clear to the player that while one guy with a gun can still be dangerous, ten guys with guns aren't that much more of a challenge, mechanically speaking.

♦ **Clues reveal weaknesses:** Investigative abilities might reveal weaknesses in the conspiracy's defenses that can be exploited by the player. Offer several lines of attack where you can: **Human Terrain** might spot that one conspiracy gang lord is worried about his standing with his vampire masters, and will try to deal with Khan personally instead of alerting the vampires to her presence so he can boost his standing by eliminating her himself (so she can try drawing him out using herself as bait), while **Architecture** notes the presence of an old sewer line that could be a route into the gang's HQ, and **Streetwise** lets Khan know that one of the gang members frequents a particular bar where she could easily ambush him. Give the player plenty of information *and analysis*. Use phrases like "As an experienced operative, you can tell…" Khan's Investigative abilities don't just give her raw information, they let her draw conclusions and make predictions about what's going on.

♦ **"And after that it's just a chase scene":** Use the vocabulary of cinema, and cut scenes. If the player flees an encounter with bad guys, then you can just move straight onto how she arrives back in her safehouse, or ask her where she hides from her pursuers and then describe how they pass by without finding her. Instead of stopping the player from escaping, or playing through a city-wide hunt, just give the player a Problem card and move onto the next scene. Turn your back on Leyla and she vanishes.

♦ Similarly, don't impede the player's actions, even if Heat or Shadow Scores reach dizzying levels. A player with a high Heat Score might be a wanted criminal, but that shouldn't stop her from moving about in public. The consequences for high Heat or Shadow come in Challenges and Blowback; it may not be realistic for the character who blew up a politician's limo last scene to be able to walk into a government building through the public entrance, but if there's a conflict between tiresomely realistic logic and the needs of the story, let the story win. (It's way more fun to run from the guards *after* the player discovers the clues inside the politician's office, instead of blocking her path from the get-go).

♦ **Reinforce the reward cycle:** *Night's Black Agents* rewards danger with information, and that information points to more danger. Defeating that danger gives more information, which leads to more danger, *ad infinitum* or at least *ad until you slay Dracula*. Whenever possible, give the player extra clues about what's going on as a reward for taking risks. It's even better to give the player information that can be leveraged, either as part of the main story or in a subplot. Show the player that action is always rewarded, even if the dice are against her and she ends up having to take a few Problems too.

PLAYING CARDS

Use cards to highlight important elements of the game. If you want the player to focus on something, put it on a card. Obviously, this applies to Problems and Edges, but you can also do it for Contacts, key locations, and key clues. Putting something on a card effectively adds it to the player's mental to-do list, either as an issue to be dealt with or a resource to be drawn upon. This lets you nudge the player by pointing out seemingly trivial clues that will payoff later on (pipe clues, in the parlance of GUMSHOE).

Don't use cards for clues, Problems, or Edges that pay off immediately. If Khan finds a photograph of a tomb in one scene that leads her to visit that very tomb in the next scene, there's no need to make it a card – the photograph is still at the forefront of the player's mind. However, if you want to plant the clue early in the mystery so the player can uncover its significance much later on (for example, Khan finds the photograph of the tomb among the possessions of a murdered spy in scene one, and after many narrow escapes and monstrous encounters, she discovers that the inscription on the tomb is the password to a conspiracy computer network).

The exception is the three running Scores of impending doom – Injuries/Hurt, Shadow, and Heat. Here, the important thing is the mechanical Score, and the card text is mostly for atmosphere. It doesn't matter if the Heat comes from Khan getting spotted as she flees a murder scene, or from the chaos that ensued in the wake of a shootout at a shopping mall – they're just specific incidents that contribute to the general Heat Score. Use Heat and Shadow cards to represent rising danger. As a veteran operative, Khan can tell when things are safe...

... and when *they're* coming...

Now, it's the opposition's turn.

Why do vampires exist? Where do they come from? What are their powers? How do humans stop them? When did they begin to corrupt Europe – or mankind as a whole? Who do they control? The Director builds his vampires, and their conspiracy, from those answers and choices, and from his imagination and creativity. No two games of **Solo Ops** will have exactly the same vampires, so the player won't know what to expect even if she expects vampires.

Our "default" vampires, the Linea Dracula, are pretty close to the vanilla vampire, but you can customize each member of that bloody family. One vampire might be especially talented at hypnotism, another studied the forbidden arts of necromancy, and a third might focus on raw physical power.

THE LINEA DRACULA

Vampires began when Vlad Tepes, the Impaler, made a pact with Satan while in captivity in Hungary in 1466. He, and his descendants, became vampires of the Linea Dracula: the lineage of the son of the Dragon. Vampires retain human hungers and sins, but do not need to eat, drink, or breathe.

After a century or so, the Linea got out of the habit of having children, especially since children of the Linea became rivals for power. A few vampires retain the ability to sire or bear children with the aid of blasphemous sorcery or advanced reproductive medicine, but the "true" vampire population is mostly static. They can create new vampires by feeding their blood to those on the brink of death, but such "assigns" are less powerful, and cannot turn others; by long habit, the Linea usually only turn their brides or most faithful retainers. Between that habit, a grotesque internecine war in the 16th century, and the devastation of Eastern Europe in 1944, there are probably only 250 full vampires in the world, and approximately 1,000 assigns.

The Linea remains split into two factions: those who follow the returned Vlad Tepes (beheaded in battle in 1476; his head disappeared with the fall of the Ottomans in 1918, and his body vanished from the Bucharest Historical Museum in 1940) and those who follow Count John Dracula (of the "Hungarian" line, from Vlad's second wife Ilona). Rumors of the Impaler's return during WWII restarted the internecine war, as the Transylvanians began a series of blood sacrifices and rituals as offerings to their monstrous ancestor/messiah. Vlad's strength and supporters are in Romania, Russia, and the Balkans in general; the Hungarian line dwells in Western Europe and elsewhere in the world.

Conflict between members of a line is forbidden by custom; vampires of the same faction may snipe at each other, stealing valuable assets and servants, but they may not kill each other. Currently, it's also forbidden for vampires of one line to kill the other – there's a fragile peace between the two clans, and a direct attack from a Hungarian-line vampire on a Transylvanian-line individual (or vice versa) might restart the war. However, both sides are clearly preparing for another conflict.

THE HUNGARIAN LINE

The Hungarian line is better established and has considerably more wealth and influence in the mortal world; they are also considerably more numerous than their cousins. The family has controlled portions of the European banking network for centuries, and has agents in place in the Roman Catholic Church and most major western governments. The vampires are furtive parasites, operating in secret. They don't run the world, but they have access to many, many levers of power and know how to protect their interests.

They pose, usually, as the wealthy elite, flitting from city to city. While they still need to sleep on the soil of their birth, they have a well-established network of smugglers and shipping companies who can discretely transport coffins, provide victims, and dispose of corpses. They may not be comfortable in the modern world, but they have learned to adapt to it and the tools it offers.

Structurally, the Hungarian line operates like a network of loosely connected cells. Each full-blooded vampire has an area of influence, operated by its assigns, Renfields, and other minions – a vampire might control a city, a government department, a corporation, or some other asset. The vampires then trade favors with their kin, exchanging money and power for victims. Different branches of the family work independently, meeting infrequently to consult and plan. The whole line has not been summoned together since the 1950s.

THE TRANSYLVANIAN LINE

They refer to themselves as "the line of Tepes" or the "true line of the Dragon." They harken back to their founder's occult practices, and have more supernatural gifts and unholy servants. The Transylvanian line is also more unified under the original Dracula than their Hungarian-line counterparts; Dracula terrorizes his subjects to ensure their loyalty.

Each vampire rules its own domain, feeding from victims within that territory. Each vampire exerts as much influence as it can within that domain over institutions and groups. The Transylvanian vampires' influence is therefore much more geographically concentrated, but it is more complete within that region. Hungarian-line vampires might have some sway within, say, the French DCSE, and the Parisian government, and the Parisian police, and in some major companies headquartered in Paris. In contrast, a Transylvanian vampire might rule over a minor town in Romania, maintaining sway over every person of importance in that small region.

Vampires of the line of Tepes are cautious, even hidebound. They never leave their lairs without extensive preparation, preferring to dispatch their minions as messengers and agents. Most still act like 15th-century warlords.

POWERS

Blood is the key – the blood is the life. Once a member of the Linea Dracula has fed from a victim, the vampire can exert tremendous psychic influence over its new pawn. The "blooded" victim is compelled to obey the vampire's wishes, and can be commanded at a distance through dreams, post-hypnotic suggestions and other occult means. This influence fades over time, but can be renewed if the vampire encounters the victim again. The vampire does not have to feed from the victim again to refresh the bond, although most of the Linea Dracula establish routines where they visit their key thralls regularly to preserve their loyalty.

Some vampires can even possess enough psychic force to possess their victims, wearing their bodies as disposable shells.

Vampires can hypnotize people they have not fed from, but their ability to do so is much more limited. It is only when they *know* a victim, inside and out, through the taste of blood that their commands become irresistible.

Other gifts common to the line include the power to change shape – into a wolf, a bat, or rat, or into mist – and preternatural senses, strength, and speed. Uncommon talents among the vampires of the Hungarian line are supernatural talents like necromancy, sorcery, and commanding the weather.

WEAKNESSES

Linea Dracula vampires cannot be seen in mirrors or on camera and they cast no shadow.

A stake in the heart paralyzes but does not kill the vampire. Sunlight robs it of most of its powers, but does not destroy it. A vampire in direct sunlight cannot change its shape, or move with preternatural strength and speed, or work its unholy will upon most people. It can, however, still command victims it has fed from, although its control is weaker during the day.

Running water, garlic or rosewood all work as Blocks, preventing the vampire from entering a protected place, but do not injure it. Crucifixes and other holy objects may also work, depending on the vampire's strength of will and the potency of the relic.

Vampires age normally, but can renew their youth by drinking the blood of the innocent.

Full-blooded vampires must sleep on native earth from their homelands, or in places where their unholy connection to the underworld is strong enough to sustain them.

To destroy the vampire, its head must be removed and its body burnt – and even that is not enough to destroy Dracula or one of his more powerful descendants.

ASSIGNS

These are the spouses or cherished servants of the Linea, turned into lesser vampires. Assigns drink blood to sustain themselves, but are still dependent on the unholy life force of their creator, and need to drink vampire blood every so often to be truly sated. Most Linea, therefore, only create a handful of assigns, to avoid having to give up too much of their own blood to satisfy the hungers of their offspring. Dracula himself has only three brides, after all.

Assigns live as long as their creator does, unless destroyed. Some Linea have had the same Assigns for centuries; others create and destroy offspring as needed. In rare cases, assigns have escaped or been driven away without being destroyed, but these unfortunate creatures suffer terribly. They can survive on the thin blood of mortals, but are wracked with a hunger for the blood of their sire, and soon go mad.

An assign who has not died and been reborn returns to humanity upon the death of her sire; no other cure for vampirism is known, although alchemy and magical lore in general might provide one, as might powerful relics like the Holy Grail.

For many Linea, their assigns are a connection to the modern world. Even the youngest full vampire is five centuries old, so they need intermediaries and allies to guide them. Mortal thralls are useful pawns, but lack independent will; sometimes, only an assign will do. Assigns are immune to the psychic influence of their creators, but their loyalty is still guaranteed by their need for fresh tastes of vampire blood.

Unlike their sires, assigns are almost ageless. They do not grow old, but are held fixed as they were when they were created. Sometimes, this even extends to injuries and other physical features – an assign turned into a vampire to save him from a mortal wound on a battlefield might spontaneously bleed from his side, and have his business suits transmute into bloodied chain mail when he draws on his unholy powers.

Assigns cannot successfully create vampires. An assign who drains a victim dry and then feeds them some vampire blood may produce a savage undead beast, but this creation quickly devolves into a witless monster or serial killer.

Powers: Assigns can be almost as strong and fast as their creators, and some have even mastered supernatural talents like shapeshifting or necromancy. They cannot exert the same level of mind control as a full vampire.

Weaknesses: Assigns cast no shadow, but do cast reflections. The reflection shows pain and torment, which is why they still dread mirrors. They do not rise again after being killed by a bane. They perish (or, in certain legends, are freed from bloodlust and have their mortality restored) if their creator is slain.

Sunlight and other Blocks affect assigns more than full vampires: an assign might be repelled by garlic, instead of merely deterred by it, and sunlight confuses them; it can even burn weak assigns.

Unlike full vampires, assigns do not have to sleep on their native soil.

VAMPIRE POWERS

The rules of **Solo Ops** are all player-facing – vampire powers are described in terms of Problems that the player must Counter, and Edges that must be acquired to have a chance of success. For example, if a vampire can only be hurt by unearthly weapons, then the first time the player tries to kill the vampire in a **Fighting** or **Shooting** Challenge, the player gets this Problem:

◄ **PROBLEM** ►

Invulnerable

Your weapons couldn't hurt it. Bullets went through the monster's pale flesh like mist.

VAMPIRE

Ordinary weapons can't hurt this vampire. You need to find something that can.

Later, through the use of Investigative abilities and daring espionage, the player obtains an Edge that overcomes this problem.

EDGE

Meteoric Iron

You uncovered an account of a 12th century knight who wielded a sword of meteoric iron, and used it to kill devils.

VAMPIRE

Vampires are vulnerable to weapons made of unearthly metals, like meteoric iron.

The player might also discover Vampire Problems through investigation.

- **Vampirology:** From your study of vampire lore, you know that the monsters can command the "meaner things" – wolves, bats, rats, and other unpleasant creatures.
- **Reassurance:** She breaks down sobbing, pressing her head into your chest. "It was invisible!" she weeps, "it was there and it wasn't there – like a hole in the world..."
- **Forensic Pathology:** Those scrapes on the hands and knees are post-mortem injuries, and the way the blood pooled... it's as though the corpse got up and walked, or at least stumbled, *after* death. And what about those fibers under the fingernails – they're consistent with attempted strangulation. Could the vampire possess the power to *resurrect* its victims as zombies?
- **Occult Studies:** Consulting the fabled *Le Dragon Noir*, you learn of the unholy sorcerous techniques that only the undead can master.
- **Chemistry:** The residue left in the wreck of the limo is similar to insect chitin, but there are some curious compounds in there that remind you of snake venom. The touch of the creature may be poisonous.

BASIC ABILITIES

Linea Dracula (and vampires in general) are assumed to all have a few basic abilities in common.

- **They're strong:** Even if they don't have full-on superhuman strength, vampires still have considerably greater physical strength than their outward appearance might suggest. Even a small, decrepit vampire has enough physical prowess to wipe the floor with the average opponent, and can overpower the player in a straight-up contest of strength.
- **They're tough:** Normal weapons may be able to hurt a vampire, but they're more resilient than a mere human. One **Shooting** or **Fighting** contest isn't going to kill one – the player needs to *work* to put an end to the undead.
- **They can fight:** Vampires might have claws or fangs, or have the sort of experience with melee weapons that comes only from spending the last few hundred years stabbing people you don't like. Modern vampires might even use guns. In any case, vampires are dangerous in a fight.

You can change things up if you wish – maybe your vampires are fragile and brittle as dried bones until they become young by drinking blood, or your vampires are alien fields of psychic fetor who take on physical form by possessing corpses.

BARRIERS VS. COMPLICATIONS

Some Vampire Problems are insurmountable obstacles that stop the player from successfully completing the mission until that Problem is Countered. For example, if the aim of the operation is to kill a vampire, and the player discovers the vampire's immune to damage, that's a definite Problem. Later, through investigation, the player finds clues suggesting this particular vampire is vulnerable only when standing in the ruins of the castle where it became undead. That knowledge is an Edge that can counter the otherwise impossible Problem – the solution to the mystery is "lure the vampire to the ruins." The Edge is a specific solution to a specific obstacle: it's the answer to a question. They're inextricably bound together.

Other Problems just make it harder for the player to triumph, and other Edges just make it easier. A vampire that can summon a host of bats or is extremely difficult (but not impossible) to injure makes things literally more challenging for the player, but doesn't block progress completely. If the player finds an Edge that helps – say, an ultrasonic whistle that drives the bats away, or a blessed dagger that can cut undead flesh – then that's a boost to the player's chances, but finding such an Edge isn't the only way to overcome such a Problem.

Similarly, some Edges aren't tied to a particular problem. The discovery that a vampire can't cross the shadow of a church spire is an Edge that could be applied in lots of different ways, depending on the circumstances and the creativity of the player. The player could evade a pursuing vampire by ducking into the shadow of a spire, or trap a vampire by hiding searchlights behind key buildings in a city and turning a church-lined square into a prison cell for the dead. A player might even try applying that Edge against seemingly unrelated problems – would placing a mind-controlled victim of the vampire in the shadow of the spire free them from the vampire's influence? If church shadows have power, then is the vampire itself a projection, a corporeal *tulpa* emanating from a buried corpse? Edges without obviously associated Problems reward player creativity and ingenuity, but are also harder for you to work into a coherent narrative.

If you prefer a game of diligent investigation and intricate plotting, then go for tightly bound pairs of Problems and Edges when building your vampires. If, however, you want looser action and more improvisation and creative interpretation, then come up with Problems and Edges without worrying too much about how they'll pair up.

BRINGING OUT THE BIG GUNS

For a suitable sense of dramatic escalation, tie your vampire's nastier abilities to the player's Shadow Score. For example, you might say that your vampire can only use its Possession power if the player has a Shadow of 4 or more. (**Vampirology** gives a sense of the risks associated with a high Shadow Score.) This means the vampire has to use a variety of powers instead of concentrating on one instant-win button, and the player has to take steps to keep her Shadow Score under that threshold of doom.

You can also use this to convey a sense of varying power thresholds among vampires. Your average bloodsucker might only be able to use Control Weather when the player has a Shadow of 3+, but Dracula himself can throw storms around on a whim.

AWARENESS

Vampires might have unnaturally keen senses, or extra senses beyond those possessed by mortals. Maybe they can detect neuro-electrical impulses in muscles and nerves, or can feel the vital energy of living things at a distance. Perhaps vampires can "borrow" the senses of animals they command, seeing through the eyes of rats or wolves, or even through the eyes of those they have fed from in the past. Other vampires might have access to modes of supernatural awareness, and be able to see the skein of fate, know instantly when someone sets foot on their ancestral estates, or tell the grave of a suicide from that of a shriven man.

Awareness Problems threaten the player's ability to sneak around, to postpone a confrontation with the vampire, or to ambush the monster. They're especially terrifying in one-on-one games, as the ability to stay concealed and unexposed often becomes the player's security blanket.

◆ PROBLEM ◆

The Lidless Eye

You can tell that the vampire's watching you. Its attention crawls over the city like an invisible spider.

VAMPIRE

Increase your Shadow Score by 1 as long as you hold this card. This card does not count as a Shadow Problem card.

◆ PROBLEM ◆

Superhuman Senses

It can hear your heartbeats. It can taste your sweat from across the room.

VAMPIRE

Until you Counter this card, you automatically get a Setback on any **Infiltration** Challenges near the vampire.

DRAIN

Feeding on the vitality of victims, especially by drinking blood, is the defining trait of the vampire. Virtually every tale of the undead talks about how they feed on the living. In many vampire stories, vampire bites remain open, obvious oozing sores and easy to spot with almost any ability, although naïve doctors call them insect or animal bites. But in others, vampires can lick the wound closed (or it closes preternaturally rapidly), leaving only minute traces under UV light or close examination. The Director should determine if vampire bites on a living victim are:

- ◆ obvious
- ◆ detectable automatically with **Diagnosis** (or **Forensic Pathology** or **Vampirology**)
- ◆ detectable with a Push of **Diagnosis** (or **Forensic Pathology** or **Vampirology**)
- ◆ detectable with a test of **Medic**, possibly with **Vampirology** also required
- ◆ any of the above, but only by those who have already seen (or been bitten by) a vampire, or exposed to vampire blood, or figured out a foolproof test for vampire bites
- ◆ essentially undetectable

He should make the same determination for blood tests to determine the presence of vampire blood. Are vampire blood cells invisible in a microscope? Does a contaminated victim's blood fluoresce (or combust) under UV light? Does it react explosively to holy water or do the red blood cells flee a tincture of garlic oil? Or perhaps any medical tech notices that there's something wrong with this blood sample: its cells keep dividing like leukemia cells, or T-cell counts are off the charts, or it's obviously inhuman. Maybe vampire contagion mimics (or is a mutant form of, or is carried by) some other disorder — AIDS, porphyria, leukemia, TB, Ebola, or plague — which masks the signs of vampirism to the unwary.

Like detecting vampires (see "The Two-Way Mirror," p. 73), the easier and more convenient the test for vampire victims, the faster and more efficiently the player can narrow down the scope of vampiric influence.

Usually, if the player gets bitten by a vampire, it's game over – unlike a multiplayer game, a solo Agent may not have any allies to rush in and break the unholy embrace by driving the vampire away. Drain problems are more likely to drop up in play when dealing with other victims of the vampire.

◆ PROBLEM ◆

Blood Drain

The vampire drained your blood, becoming younger and stronger with stolen life.

SERIOUS INJURY, SHADOW

◆ PROBLEM ◆

Psychic Vampire

The vampire's drained your vitality. You're exhausted, numb – almost defeated.

VAMPIRE, SHADOW

Until you Counter this card, you can't spend Pushes. If you still have this card at the end of the operation, you lose a die of Cool.

FIELD EFFECTS

In addition to cold spots, reflection-free mirrors, nervous animals, shadows that don't match visible light sources, and other traditional vampire spoor, vampires may cause other weird effects by their mere presence. Tells like this are a great way to subtly signal to the player that vampires are nearby.

Field effects work as penalties to the player that are applied only in the presence of the vampire. The player keeps the Problem card as a reminder that this supernatural danger is something she'll have to deal with the next time she tangles with the undead, but the penalty from "Stifling Air" or "Temporal Distortion" or whatever aura of weirdness surrounds the dead only applies when the vampire is right in front of her.

PROBLEM

Malign Presence

The world suddenly seems darker, colder... deader.

VAMPIRE

Add +2 to your Shadow Score while in the vampire's presence.

PROBLEM

Stifling Air

The vampire's presence is unimaginably foul. You can't breathe.

VAMPIRE

Until you Counter this card, you lose a die from any tests in the vampire's presence.

PROBLEM

Temporal Distortion

The monster flickers and judders, skipping forward in time and space. It's there and not there and suddenly it's right on top of you.

VAMPIRE

Until you Counter this card, any dice that roll an odd number on Challenges in the vampire's presence are discarded.

INFECTION

Being bitten by a vampire may have effects beyond simple blood loss. The creature's fangs might carry a supernatural toxin, or the unholy intimacy established by the bite might allow the vampire to corrupt the victim's soul.

PROBLEM

Domination

It's an addiction. You have a physical need to get bitten again, even though your mind – and soul – recoils in horror.

VAMPIRE

Unless you Counter this card, you'll willingly give yourself to the vampire when you next encounter the creature if your Shadow Score is 4 or more.

PROBLEM

Unclean!

You've been bitten. If you don't cure yourself of this contagion, you'll become one of them!

VAMPIRE

If you still have this card when you die or at the end of the operation, you'll rise from your grave as a vampire.

INVISIBILITY

Vampires might be able to vanish or otherwise occlude themselves from detection. Any vampire invisibility technique might be selective: the monster is invisible to everyone except her target, or to the Agent it is trying to spook into firing, or to schizophrenics, or to prepubescent children. This selectivity might be automatic or deliberate. Animals may be able to sense the presence of the vampire even when invisible.

PROBLEM

Cloak of Darkness

A shroud of icy darkness surrounds the vampire. You've looked into that abyss.

VAMPIRE

Unless you Counter this card by finding a light source that can penetrate the shroud, you cannot use Shooting on the vampire and suffer a 2-die penalty on any Fighting tests with the monster.

PROBLEM

Invisible

The monster cannot be seen when it wishes to vanish.

VAMPIRE

Unless you Counter this card, you'll be unable to defeat the vampire. You have to find a way to see the unseen.

MAGIC

According to Abraham van Helsing, Dracula could command the wind and waves, grow and shrink at will, teleport, create fogs and storms, and "come on moonlight rays as elemental dust." Some of this is not due to Dracula's vampiric nature, but his long training at Scholomance, the Devil's school under Lake Hermannstadt in Transylvania.

Hence, the GM can have vampires that can do *anything*. Any magic should come at a cost to the vampire – spells might involve elaborate rituals, tap some source of power that can be exhausted or sabotaged, or involve bargains or restrictions that the player can later turn on the vampire.

For subtle sorcery, focus on basic folk magics: the Evil Eye, curses and blights, and treasure-finding. Stoker's Dracula went out treasure hunting on

THE TWO-WAY MIRROR

According to Bram Stoker, vampires cannot be seen in mirrors. Stoker played on the superstition that mirrors reflect the soul (which is why breaking them is bad luck) to indicate the soulless condition of Dracula. Since Stoker, vampires have variously been invisible to mirrors, cameras, motion detectors, and electric eyes. In *Ultraviolet,* electronics can't even transmit vampires' voices! An Internet-age version of the myth might have vampires' names or biometric data simply disappear from digital records: only ink and paper can record their existence.

However you decide to riff on this trope, keep in mind that making vampires invisible to anything — mirrors, cameras, ultraviolet light — also creates a reliable vampire test. The same applies to any other vampire characteristic that can be reliably detected at range: low body temperature, variations in local gravity or magnetic field strength, glowing eyes, no shadow, etc. Invisibility to imagery, or extra visibility on specialized imagery, both allow the Agent to identify vampires and hunt them more effectively.

Vampires can counter some of these conditions with heated clothing, zinc oxide sun block, tinted contacts, lead-lined or Faraday-caged limousines, or specialized software. Consider allowing vampires to exert themselves in order to cast a reflection or shadow or otherwise show up in whichever imagery they normally confound, or vice versa. (If you do this, it's only fair to let the Agent see it happen at least once — ideally, right after she's gotten a trifle overconfident about her perfect vampire un-imaging system.) This is also where Renfields come into their glory: as humans, they still respond to everything short of a blood test normally.

But the bottom line is this: in general, any sure test for vampirism, especially one that can be performed at a distance, is a great tactical asset for the Agent. And at the end of the day, rewarding the player for thinking tactically might be more important to the campaign than "realistically" thwarting the Agent with vampiric countermeasures.

St. George's Eve, guided by witch-light; other vampires know how to bottle souls, change the weather, predict deaths, or create magical (or poisonous, or both) food and drink.

For bigger stakes, the demonic vampires of the Romanian line have the magics of Hell at their command: not just communion with demons, but other dire ritual sorceries. Hell is also very big on treasure-finding, along with magical flight, scrying enemies, and building unholy structures. Later damned vampires (especially in comic books) have a wide variety of balefire blasts, astral projections, telekinetic punches, divination abilities, and rituals to remove vampiric weaknesses at their disposal.

PROBLEM
Command Weather

The vampire can call up storms and bad weather at will. Howling snowstorms surrounds its lair.

VAMPIRE

You need to Push **Outdoor Survival** to approach the vampire's castle.

PROBLEM
Sorcery

The vampire has all the powers of Hell at their command.

VAMPIRE

Until you find a way to Counter or defend yourself against the vampire's sorcery, you have no chance of fighting the monster.

MENTAL ATTACKS

Vampires might be able to intrude into the dreams of their victims (or their hunters), send terrifying visions to drive their foes insane, psychically compel action from a distance, emit pheromones to trigger a prey's flight response, or blast enemies with bolts of magical will or psychic malice. Resisting mental attacks calls for a **Cool** Challenge in most circumstances, and it's usually possible to counter such attacks by discovering the appropriate Block (see p. 78).

PROBLEM
Basilisk Gaze

The vampire's red gaze hit you like a physical blow, almost knocking you unconscious. How can you fight something that can wound with a glance?

VAMPIRE

You're shaken – ignore any dice that roll a 6 in a test. Discard this card once you've Taken Time to recover, or when you've ignored four dice.

PROBLEM
Nightmares

The visions fill your sleep, and are bleeding into the waking world. Every time you close your eyes, you see those horrors again.

VAMPIRE

You've got a penalty to **Cool** tests equal to your Shadow Score. If you still have this card at the end of the operation, you'll go insane. Counter by killing or blocking the vampire.

MOVEMENT

Vampire movement depends on the vampire's form and nature. Vampires might be physically superior to humans, being both faster and more agile, or they might be restricted by their corpse-like nature, and be bloated, stiff, brittle, or shambling-zombie slow. Alternatively, they might move in a bizarre, inhuman fashion – scuttling like insects, slipping from shadow to shadow without passing through the intervening space, riding on moonbeams, or oozing bonelessly through cracks.

Most forms of supernatural movement, though, don't need to be modeled as Problems. Only turn Movement powers into Problem cards when the vampire's powers present an otherwise insurmountable obstacle to the players' plans.

PROBLEM
Apportation

The vampire can enter and leave a place at will, materializing out of thin air. If you're going to kill it – hell, if you're ever going to sleep soundly again – you need to find a way to stop the vampire from teleporting like that.

VAMPIRE

PROBLEM
Turn To Mist

The vampire dissolves into greyish mist before your eyes, and seeps out through a crack in the wall. You'll need to find a way to stop the monster from escaping in future.

VAMPIRE

NECROMANCY

Necromancy usually happens "off-screen," but Agents might watch it happen in horrified silence, learn of it by interrogating vampire cultists, or capture evidence of the practice by means of a cunningly placed bug. Necromancy could also be used to set up subplots and extra Problems, especially involving disposable Contacts.

PROBLEM
A Stolen Soul

You saw the vampire kiss Georgios on the lips, and drag Georgios' soul right out of his corpse. He spat it into a bottle – you've got to rescue your friend's soul.

VAMPIRE, CONTINUITY

If you fail to rescue Georgios' soul by the end of the mission, gain the Problem "Haunted."

PROBLEM
Haunted

Vengeful and malicious ghosts assail you, hampering your actions.

VAMPIRE, CONTINUITY

The first time you roll a natural 1 on a Challenge where an Extra Problem is available, you get that Problem (but don't get an extra die). Put this Problem aside until the next operation. Counter by exorcism.

POSSESSION

Vampires can completely take control of a human body, looking out through its eyes and operating its limbs. Vampires might be able to possess anyone they make eye contact with, anyone they have previously possessed, anyone they have fed on, or anyone who carries their blood. They may be able to possess a puppet at a distance (usually only after possessing once in person). The vampire's original body might continue to act normally, or lay torpid and empty.

Possession is more fun in GUMSHOE One-2-One than in regular roleplaying games. In a multiplayer game, the possessed player is not only robbed of control but they have to sit there helpless while the other players continue to play around them. In a single-player game, the period of possession can be elided over ("you wake up with blood on your hands and no memory of the night before") or turned into a ghastly, tense narrative ("helpless, you find yourself picking up the knife and advancing towards the old professor"). The player might be able to break free of possession with a Push or a **Cool** test; blocking possession requires discovering the corresponding Block (p. 78).

PROBLEM
Fugue

You don't know what just happened. There's a gap in your memory, but you suspect you did something awful.

VAMPIRE, CONTINUITY

One of your Contacts no longer trusts you. Choose which Contact you betrayed.

REGENERATION

Even when you can do damage to a vampire, its unnatural flesh heals and regenerates. A powerful vampire can even regenerate from its own ashes, if exposed to enough blood. This makes it very hard to kill a vampire without explosives or banes. In some cases, a vampire only regenerates after being killed again. A dead vampire can be revived by any number of expedients: necromancy, moonlight, blood, striking the corpse, removing the stake from the body, or otherwise disturbing any anti-vampire precautions. Other vampires might be effectively immune to damage. In any case, the player needs to find a way to actually hurt the vampire in order to Counter this Problem.

PROBLEM
True Death

You've killed the vampire – for now. You know that it'll rise again in three days. You've got three days to find a way to keep it in the ground forever.

VAMPIRE, CONTINUITY

If you cannot Counter this card, the vampire rises and continues to plague you.

SHAPESHIFTING

Minor changes to a vampire's form – growing fangs, for example – are too small-scale to be considered a Problem. It's only if the vampire cannot be defeated until the Agent discovers a way to counter the monster's shapeshifting that you need to break out the cards.

PROBLEM
Distortion

You couldn'++++t look directly at the creature – it was a maddening, scintillating fractal of dark lines and flickering shadows. How do you kill something that only partially exists in this reality?

VAMPIRE

Until you Counter this card, you cannot slay the vampire.

PROBLEM
Wolf-shape

The vampire took on the shape of a wolf, its wounds closing and vanishing beneath fur and muscle.

VAMPIRE

Until you Counter this card, you'll be unable to defeat the vampire with conventional weapons.

SUMMONING

Vampires can summon assistance from dark and hateful powers, or from the low and crawling beings of the night. As a general rule, summoning something more powerful than the vampire (a demon lord, an alien mothership) takes a ritual lasting several minutes, summoning something less powerful than the vampire (a swarm of rats, a ghoul) takes a command lasting a few seconds.

A vampire might summon:

♦ thugs or an escape helicopter or inbred clansmen, summoned telepathically
♦ nearby corpses as zombies
♦ those he has fed on, or who share his blood
♦ monstrous servitors
♦ demon lords or lesser imps
♦ wolves, rats, flies, or other fell creatures

Response time to a vampire summoning is very rapid, or even immediate, unless the Agent takes precautions to isolate the combat space. On his home ground, any vampire who can summon assistance has such assistance pre-positioned and ready to go. Vampires automatically command the obedience of any summoned aid except demons, who can get surly.

PROBLEM
Swarms of Rats

Rats! Thousands of rats! You'd get torn to bits if you plunged into that hideous swarm.

VAMPIRE++++

If you can't Counter this Problem, you'll have to force your way through the rat swarm when you next face the vampire.

PROBLEM
Trained Ratters

You obtained these specially trained dogs from an eccentric breeder in England.

VAMPIRE

Discard to counter the vampire's summoned rats, or for +1 die in a suitable **Conceal** or **Fighting** Challenge where you can sic your small but vicious dogs on an enemy.

PROBLEM
Victims of the Vampire

There's a human wall of spellbound victims between you and the vampire. How does it exert such hypnotic control over all those people?

VAMPIRE

Either find a way to Counter this Problem, or you'll have to kill innocent people on your way to the vampire.

VENOM

Some vampires inject venom with their bite. This venom might be a hallucinogen, clouding the victim's memory of the attack, or an aesthetic or opiate that makes the bite painless or pleasurable. Venom attacks are more likely to yield clues (discovered through **Diagnosis**, **Forensic Pathology**, or **Pharmacy**) than full-on problems, but there are exceptions like:

PROBLEM
Running Out of Time

You've got to find a cure for this toxin quickly.

VAMPIRE

Put a mark on this card every time you Take Time, to a maximum of four marks. You've got a -1 penalty to all Challenges for each mark on this card. If you still have this Problem at the end of the operation, you die.

VOICE

Vampires might be able to hypnotize or compel with sepulchral infrasonics or by speaking in the secret pre-Adamic tongue of the dead, or have the power to shriek like a bat to shatter glass and stun enemies.

PROBLEM
Language Contagion

You heard it speak, and now you've been infected by the vampire's alien language. It's becoming harder and harder to SPEAK NORMALLY.

VAMPIRE, CONTINUITY

Until you Counter this problem, you'll have to spend an extra Push whenever you make an Interpersonal Push. If you still have this Problem at the end of the operation, you'll go insane.

WEAKNESSES

These are traits of the vampire that can be discovered and weaponized by the player. Some weaknesses are commonly known (sunlight, garlic, crucifixes) – but these might be superstitions that have no effect on your vampires. Other weaknesses are secret and have to be discovered through investigation and observation – maybe a vampire's powers are connected to the presence of death and decay, so it's more powerful in graveyards, morgues, and hospitals, but powerless in a sterile, lifeless cleanroom or on an airplane. Anything that the player can use to even the odds against the undead can be an Edge.

BANES

A bane is something that Counters a vampire Problem preventing the vampire from being injured or slain. Most banes come from vampire folklore; some come from fiction and film. Some banes are already weapons (silver bullets, beheading by sword, stake to the heart) or act as environmental hazards (sunlight) while others must be "weaponized" by the Agent (garlic, holy water).

Some banes can only be employed in a single obvious way – if vampires are vulnerable to blessed silver bullets, then there is an obvious, already extant, common and highly effective method for using bullets to injure someone. Other banes are open to interpretation and creative weaponization by the player – if ultraviolet light is a weakness, then that might lead to anything from "I break the windows so the sunlight can get in" to "Screw guns! I'm going to use **Preparedness** to get a really high-powered ultraviolet flashlight" to the tactical uses of tanning beds as a method for executing staked vampires.

SUNLIGHT

Folkloric vampires attacked at night because that is when evil spirits were up and around, not because they had any particular aversion to the sun. Indeed, Polish and Russian vampires hunted from noon to midnight. In the 19th century, fictional vampires from Coleridge's Geraldine to Stoker's Dracula walk about in the sunlight all the time, although Le Fanu's Carmilla prefers to sleep late into the afternoon. Stoker's Dracula cannot use any of his vampire powers in daylight, including his preternatural strength.

Vampires smoldering and disintegrating in the sun comes from the movies: specifically, from *Nosferatu* (1922) and *The Return of the Vampire* (1943). Anne Rice's vampires catch fire in the sunlight thanks to their combustible blood and the vampires on *Ultraviolet* actually explode in the sun. It's up to you whether the effects of sunlight are supernatural (in which case, you need genuine sunlight) or grounded in some physiological or psychological reaction (opening up the possibility of using artificial sources of ultraviolet light). There's even a fun middle ground (only "true" sunlight has any real effect on a vampire, but a 500-year-old medieval warlord might still instinctively recoil from the heat and ultraviolet light of a UV lamp that feels like sunshine).

Herewith, a menu of possible sunlight effects:

- nothing
- prevents use of all vampire powers or all powers except strength
- effect is prevented if vampire touches their native soil
- prevents vampire from regenerating damage, especially including damage from sunlight
- must be shining on vampire in order for something else to kill them
- turns vampire to dust when the vampire is mortally wounded
- turns vampire into a corpse; night or darkness or moonlight revives them
- does damage based on exposure, like fire
- does damage based on intensity: the brighter and more direct the sunlight, the more damage
- damage it does can never be healed or regenerated
- explodes vampire

If only the ultraviolet light in sunlight kills vampires, polarized glass (as in tinted windows) or a high SPF sunscreen might protect them. With some tweaking, these effects might apply to any bane.

Vampire banes from various sources include:

- beheading
- crucifix, holy wafer, or other holy symbol or sacred object (burns like red-hot metal for -1 damage; +0 damage to the face)
- dead human's blood (injected or accidentally ingested)
- death of the vampire creator or sire
- drowning (in holy water or otherwise)
- enchanted or blessed blades (to the heart, throat, or anywhere)
- exorcism
- fire
- garlic: treat a cloud of aerosolized allicin as tear gas
- holy water
- iron (meteoric, "cold," or other)
- killers from a specific lineage or magical tradition; killers born with a birth caul; dhampirs
- lightning
- needles, spikes, or impaling weapons in general
- sacred bullet fired into the coffin (in Romani lore; mentioned in *Dracula*)
- severed spinal cord
- silver
- stake to the heart
- sunlight (see box, p. 77)
- ultraviolet light
- vampire antivenom, blood thinners
- wood (or only one specific wood: ash, aspen, blackthorn, hawthorn, linden, maple, mulberry, peach, rowan, white oak, willow, or yew)

EDGE

The Angel's Sword

It looks like a battered, rusty blade, still oddly warm to the touch.

VAMPIRE

This weapon can injure the vampire in any form.

EDGE

Ultraviolet Light

You saw the vampire recoil from ultraviolet light.

VAMPIRE

Discard for a bonus die in any contest with the vampire where you can shine UV light on the monster.

EDGE

Rosewood Stake

If you drive a stake of polished rosewood into the monster's heart, it'll paralyze the creature.

VAMPIRE

Discard to stake a defeated or sleeping vampire. You can try using it in a **Fighting** contest; if you do so, you're at -2 dice, but stake your foe on an Advance.

BLOCKS

This is something that blocks the passage, attack, or influence of a vampire. The vampire may be unable to pass through a Block, or be injured or depleted if it forces its way through. The major benefit of most Blocks is that they temporarily suppress the player's Shadow Score as long as she's within the protective aegis of the Block.

Vampire Blocks from various sources include:

- aloe vera
- blood of a black dog
- broom across or behind the door
- cigarette smoke
- crucifix, icon, or other holy symbol
- garlic
- hawthorn
- holly
- incense (consecrated)
- juniper
- neem tree leaves
- no invitation to enter the room
- peach wood
- rowan
- running water (usually open water like rivers, not water pipes)
- salt
- shoes turned backward
- sticky (glutinous) rice
- wild rose (or fresh flowers in general)
- wolfsbane

EDGE

Fresh Garlic

The vampire can't abide the smell of this herb.

VAMPIRE

Suppress your Shadow Score by 2 next time you Take Time.

EDGE

Running Water

You know the vampire can't cross running water.

VAMPIRE

You get an extra Evasion die on all Challenges involving the vampire when you can cross running water.

DREADS

Dreads are things the vampire hates and fears instinctively. The vampire cannot easily move towards the subject of its dread, and will try to destroy or otherwise rid itself of the potent object as its first action. Vampires also dread many banes (fire, sunlight) and blocks (garlic, hawthorn, wild rose).

Vampire dreads from various sources include:

- bright light of all kinds
- cats
- chicken eggs
- churches, or consecrated ground in general
- crucifix, icon, or other holy symbol
- dogs
- hemlock
- mirrors
- wormwood

A requirement is an action (or sometimes a material) necessary for the vampire's continued survival. Usually, drinking blood is such a requirement. If the vampire fails to obtain what it needs, it grows weaker and more desperate.

Vampire requirements from various sources include:

- cocktail of vampire drugs
- drink blood
- drink vampire blood
- exposure to moonlight (or light of a specific star, or cosmic radiation undamped by sunlight)
- possession of vampire artifact
- repeated magical ritual, demonic oath, etc.
- return to place of origin (original crypt or grave, meteor landing site, demonic crossroads)
- sex
- sleep in grave earth each night
- sleep in their native soil each night

VAMPIRE VARIANTS

If it sucks life energy, lurks in the shadows, and treats humanity as cattle, it's a vampire. Your vampires should superficially resemble the classic bloodsucker from folklore, but as the player digs deeper into the mystery, they may find something very different behind the myth. This section discusses how to create variant vampires. As a starting point for design, consider the following four general types of vampires: alien, damned, mutant, and supernatural.

These are not mutually exclusive by any means: a mutant vampire virus could have come from outer space or from Hell; all supernatural phenomena might be fundamentally demonic or, following Lovecraft, fundamentally misunderstood alien science. Is the "astral vampire" a supernatural being, or a paraphysical one? Especially in modern fiction, vampires can partake of all four types: evil infected humans who follow alien physical laws that eerily resemble vampire folklore. Much of the fun of postmodern horror comes from blurring these boundaries, and the Director should feel free to do so. Nevertheless, much of the thrill of Gothic horror comes from playing into the tropes and stereotypes of the genre, so the Director shouldn't necessarily discard the default version or traditional answer for a given vampire.

SANGUINARY CONSIDERATIONS

Even before you begin to build your vampires mechanically, take some time to consider the phenomenon of vampirism in your campaign. What kinds of stories do vampires highlight? What do they make possible or impossible? Your campaign vastly alters if there is only one true vampire in the world working through a horde of Renfields, instead of six enormous vampire clans tracing their descent back to ancient Dacia wrangling over their own internal politics.

ORIGIN

Although the type of vampire you use covers the more general question of vampire origins, the specifics also matter. Where in the world do vampires originate, and when did they emerge? If they emerged millennia ago, why haven't they taken over completely yet? If they only recently began awakening (from hibernation, or from nowhere), why now? One common reason for vampires' sudden activity: humanity suddenly poses a threat that needs to be broken. Perhaps human technology finally makes vampire slayers truly deadly, or human pollution threatens the vampires' food supply, or some human agency (the NSA, the Vatican, the FSB) has suddenly uncovered the vampire conspiracy. Vampirism might be caused by performing a certain recently translated ritual, or by touching a recently unearthed artifact (or meteorite), or by some environmental effect with a very long periodicity: a comet, the blossoming of some rare Balkan plant, or the position of the sun against certain stars.

Do vampires infect the living to create new undead? Are new vampires created using some sort of ritual, like an unholy baptism or resurrection, or are they reanimated using weird science? Maybe vampirism is genetic, and you need to have the right gene sequence (perhaps the right bloodline) to come back from the dead? Alternatively, the population of vampires could be static – they're the immortal crew of a crashed alien starship, or they're the members of a cult who successfully invoked a demon, or they're the knights who sacked a particular temple in the Holy Land during the Crusades and were cursed by God. In this case, every time the player kills a vampire, she's one step closer to putting an end to the monsters forever.

SPREAD

How far have vampires spread? This question is related to the size and scope of the vampire conspiracy, but not inextricably so: you could have a single clutch of eight alien vampires still living in the meteor crater in Poland where they landed 5,000 years ago whose servants have infiltrated the whole world. It's more closely related to how often and how prolifically vampires reproduce. If everyone bitten by a vampire automatically rises again, then vampires spread globally after only a few generations. If vampirism is harder to acquire or propagate, then it might still be restricted to one bloodline, one cult, or one vampire, even after millennia.

NUMBERS

How many vampires are there? In general, the more powerful the vampire, the fewer of them there should be. As a hard upper limit, a stable predator-prey ratio (assuming that virtually all missing persons and unsolved murders are actually vampire killings) equates to 1 vampire per 2,000 humans: about 4,000 vampires in London. A more likely upper limit derives from predator behavior patterns; assuming vampires hunt like wolves, an urban area (rich hunting ground) supports 1 vampire per 60 sq km: about 40 vampires in London.

VARIATIONS AND DIVISIONS

How many types of vampires are there? Are they all bloodlines of a common ancestor, or are they rival species competing for the ecological niche of human predator? While the default vampire conspiracy assumes only one kind of vampire, and only one conspiracy, you can make the underlying typologies and politics as complex as you think the player can stand. One warning: players can usually handle a maximum of five factors in any setting, and only keep track of about three of those at once. If you have rival vampire conspiracies, think hard about limiting the number to three main bloodlines and two lesser sources for "rogue vampires" or one-off weird horrors.

LIFE AND DEATH

Vampires, traditionally, are things between death and life, feeding on life to stave off death. From this basic myth come scores of variations: most vampires feed on blood, but others feed on spinal fluid, breath, sex, emotions (anger, fear, lust), memories, youth,

feces, food, or psychic power. Of all these, blood just plain works best thanks to centuries of fiction and millennia of symbolic weight; even if your vampire feeds on will force or souls, consider using blood as the medium or host for the meal.

Are vampires truly dead? Do they breathe, emit body heat, circulate blood, heal, feel emotions, react to toxins, excrete, have sex, notice the passage of time, sleep, dream? Can they return from the dead, even if beheaded or burnt, if something goes wrong (or right)? The general unlife cycle of your vampires will drive their plans, their housing arrangements, and their feeding patterns: does a vampire gangster keep women around as a larder, a status symbol, a harem, or all three?

HUMANITY

Many vampires were once human, before they rose from the dead, signed a pact with Satan, were bitten, were infected, or what have you. To what extent are they still human? Do they retain their human memories and desires? Human loyalties and hatreds? Can they pass as human, or do they depend on magic, or psionics, or heavy coats and hoodies to move around the city? These questions provide motivations for the conspiracy, and some constraints on its resources.

CURE

Besides beheading or a stake to the heart, is there a cure for vampirism? Specifically, one that returns vampires to a human, living state? Searching for such a cure may be the personal narrative arc of the Agent, or the overarching goal of the whole campaign. Most stories — folklore and fiction alike — don't provide any such option, but some hold out hope if the victim has not yet truly died and risen again as a vampire.

MONSTERS

Vampires aren't the only members of the supernatural crew. There are other horrors lurking in the shadows. Some of these are servants or creations of the vampires; others might be encountered while hunting vampires.

DEMONS

Save the fire-and-brimstone horned monsters for the end of a campaign; demons are more likely to manifest as suave fallen angels in sharp suits, aggressive monstrous animals, swarms of insects, or as recurring patterns of malign coincidence – you know when a demon is present when everyone in the casino simultaneously loses their game of chance, or when cars crash all around you. (Once is chance, twice is coincidence, three times is a demon.) Demons might be fallen angels, evil spirits, or emanations from a botched first attempt at creating the universe or they could be the ghosts of long-dead sorcerers or maybe they're the collective psychic self-loathing of humanity.

Build demons much like you'd build a vampire, picking Edges and Problems, but focus on malign influences and spooky weirdness more than physical attacks. Demons are even less bound by reality than vampires, which can make them frustrating enemies to deal with for the player, so either keep their presence subtle and low-key or else give the player clear clues on how to strike back at them.

Demons might possess their victims, perhaps inhabiting a gang boss, or hit the player with horrific supernatural attacks like plagues of insects, hallucinations, curses, nightmares, or surreal warping of space-time.

ESCAPING THE POSSESSED GANG

"My name is Legion," they hiss in unison, "for I am many."
As one, they charge towards you, howling like wild beasts.

EVASION

Advance 7+: You fight your way clear of them and escape into the alleyways of the medina. You spot them trying to find a way out, and notice something odd – they always move in twos or threes, never alone. Gain the Edge "The Nature of the Beast."

Hold 4-6: You escape into the medina, not daring to look back as you crash through the crowded alleyways and markets. You think you're probably clear of them, but you can't be sure – anyone could be part of that demon host!

Setback 3 or less: You wake up in a cellar, alone. Your shoulder hurts. Gain the Problem "Mark of the Beast."

Extra Problem: "Disturbance in the Medina."

Stunt: Yes (**Fighting** to throw a punch or two; **Cover** or **Conceal** to hide in the crowds).

PROBLEM

Disturbance in the Medina

There are signs and portents all over the old town tonight. Unexplained fires, bad dreams, outbreaks of violence. The demons are loose, and everything's riled up.

HEAT

PROBLEM

Mark of the Beast

You've got an occult symbol freshly tattooed on your shoulder. It hurts like hell...

SHADOW

PROBLEM

Nature of the Beast

Where two or three gather in my name, there I am with them.

VAMPIRE

The demon can only possess groups of its minions, not individuals. If you can get a gang member alone, the demon can't possess them.

EXORCISING THE DEMON

COOL

Bonus: +2 if you Push **Occult Studies**.

Penalty: -1 per Shadow Problem.

Advance 7+: You chant the ritual from the ancient grimoire while frantically etching the rune of banishing onto a 9mm round. You chamber the round and fire into the darkness. You hear something shriek – and vanish. The demon's gone.

Hold 4-6: Invisible icy hands claw at your arm, your throat. The demon's trying to stop you from banishing it. As you chamber the holy bullet, it grabs hold of your hands, wrestling you for control of the gun. There's no other option – you know where the demon is right now, it's under your skin. You cover the muzzle with one hand and pull the trigger. Through the pain and shock of shooting yourself, you hear the demon wail as it plunges back to Hell. Gain the Problem "Stigmata for Spies."

Setback 3 or less: The demon seizes control of you. It speaks in your own voice, using your own mouth, your throat. "This world is mine now. Your weapons cannot harm me." You can't stop it from hurling the pistol with its precious holy bullet into the dark waters of the Tiber. You'll have to find another way to defeat this monster.

Extra Problem: "Plagued."

Stunt: No.

PROBLEM

Plagued

You're cursed. Insects and other vermin infest any place where you rest for more than a few hours.

SHADOW

You can Counter this card by passing the curse onto a Contact. Discard that Contact.

PROBLEM

Stigmata for Spies

You shot your own hand, and now you're missing two fingers. At least the demon's gone for good.

CONTINUITY, INJURY

You're at -1 to **Cover** Challenges. You're also at -1 to all Manual Challenges in the next operation. After that, the penalty to Manual Challenges no longer applies but you must keep this card.

GHOSTS

If vampires are a metaphor for a spy's fear of subversion and infiltration by the enemy, ghosts are regrets, the memories of dead friends, of relationships destroyed and lives half-lived in the shadows. Vampires exist on the threshold between life and death, and their presence stirs up the death, agitating ghosts into wakefulness. Alternatively, a vampire might deliberately call up a ghost with necromancy, either to interrogate the shade or use it as a supernatural sentry or surveillance device. A technologically adept spy plants hidden microphones and motion-activated cameras; an ancient vampire whistles up the dead and binds them to bone fetishes to serve his undying will.

As knots of psychic energy, violent emotion, and fragmentary memory imprinted on the world, ghosts have no physical presence. They can't be fought, but can be laid to rest or driven away with an effort of will.

FINDING THE BODY

There's the corpse of one of the vampire's victims hidden somewhere in this house, and until it gets a proper burial, the ghost cannot rest.

CONCEAL

Bonus: +2 if you Push **Architecture**.

Advance 7+: You find the body, concealed beneath the floorboards. You break open the floor, gather the bones and bits of flesh into a body bag, and inter the remains in a hastily dug grave in the garden. Maybe that'll be enough. You may discard the Problem "EVP."

Hold 4-6: You can find the body, but it'll take all night. If you want to Take Time, you can automatically Advance but do not gain a bonus Push. Otherwise, you have to leave the old house without putting the ghost to rest.

Setback 3 or less: As you search the upper floor of the house, the rotten boards give way beneath you and you plunge down into the cellar. It's full of rats, thousands of the beasts. You're bitten several times before you can struggle free. In the distance, you hear hollow mocking laughter. Gain the Problem "Bitten by Rats."

Extra Problem: "The Smell of Death."

Stunt: No.

> ### PROBLEM
> #### EVP
> *You've been cursed with a ghost. Every time you listen to a recording or live audio feed, you can hear terrifying voices whispering in the static, making it impossible to eavesdrop.*
>
> **SHADOW**
>
> While you hold this card, you cannot Push **Electronic Surveillance**.

> ### PROBLEM
> #### Bitten by Rats
> *The brutes took chunks out of your hands and forearms.*
> *You're going to need a rabies shot.*
>
> **INJURY**

> ### PROBLEM
> #### The Smell of Death
> *The musty, rotten smell of that old house clings to your clothes.*
> *You've got to change.*
>
> You can't make Interpersonal Pushes while you hold this card. Counter by freshening up.

GHOULS

Technically, a ghoul is anyone who eats corpses, although the word comes from a desert demon of Arabic legend, the *ghul*. That demon ate human flesh and drank blood, often taking the shape of a beautiful woman to lure fresher meat. Famously strong and fast, a ghul would resurrect itself after being struck a second blow. In ***Solo Ops***, ghouls tap into the Lovecraft conception of the creature, casting them as cannibalistic subterranean monsters who might infest a vampire's crypt or castle dungeon.

NAVIGATING THE CATACOMBS

If you can sneak through the catacombs, you can enter the gallery undetected.

INFILTRATION

Bonus: +2 if you Push **Urban Survival** or **Archaeology**.

Advance 7+: Either you're lucky, and you make it through the tunnels without running into a ghoul pack, or you're able to escape the monsters and find your way into the basement of the gallery. Gain the Edge "Covert Entry."

Hold 4-6: The ghouls pin you down in the tunnels. Make an Evasion Quick Test (8+): if you Advance on this test, you make it into the basement of the gallery. If you fail, you've got to flee the catacombs.

Setback 3 or less: The ghouls trap you in a dead end. Describe how you fight your way clear, but gain the Problem "Clawed."

Extra Problem: You get lost in the catacombs; this counts as Taking Time.

Stunt: Yes (**Fighting**; **Evasion**).

> ### PROBLEM
> #### Clawed
> *The ghouls tore shreds out of your back as you fled.*
>
> **INJURY**

Covert Entry

You've found the one unwatched route into the conspiracy meeting.

You've got +1 dice on all Challenges in the gallery, as long as you remain undetected. Discard if discovered. If you leave the gallery and you've still got this card, it becomes a free Push.

RENFIELDS

In a sidelong tribute to Dwight Frye's unhinged performance in the 1931 *Dracula,* people forget that in Stoker's novel Renfield was a homicidal maniac, a dangerous killer. In **Solo Ops**, any human servant of the vampires is a "Renfield," and is also likely to be a dangerous killer. Like Renfield in the novel, these assets are promised "life," and usually have a drop or two of vampire blood in their veins to seal the bargain and grant them some level of supernatural power.

Renfields have enhanced strength and speed at the very least, and may also have a lesser version of some other power possessed by their master. Downsides: they're dependent on the gift of blood to maintain their abilities, and unlike vampires, they still age. Becoming a Renfield is the first step towards becoming an assign – but a vampire can sustain far more Renfields than it can have assigns, so competition within the ranks of the conspiracy can turn bloody unless the ruling vampire keeps the minions in check.

As they're human, Renfields aren't subject to the supernatural taboos and limits that restrict vampires. They can chow down on garlic while sunbathing and don't need to be invited in. Spotting them is a function of Investigative abilities and **Surveillance**, not to mention **Sense Trouble** tests.

SLUGERI

Slugeri (singular Sluger) is how traditionally minded Linea Dracula vampires refer to their chosen mortal servants. The term is an old Slavic one, meaning a noble who provides meat for the prince's larder. Outsiders call these servants Renfields (p. 84); modernists of the Hungarian line prefer the term Knight or Agent, or just use the euphemism "blessing" – as in, "she has my blessing." A Sluger must drink vampire blood once a month or so to maintain their strength; in exchange, the Sluger ensures its master's larder is always full of victims.

Only a fraction of the vampires' minions are Renfields; just as a vampire can only maintain two or three assigns, the burden of feeding more than a dozen Slugeri is hard to bear.

Assigns can create their own Renfields, but only the oldest and strongest assigns can sustain more than one Slugeri.

THE HITMAN

You're being followed. You know that a fiend doth close behind you tread – you spotted him on the Rue De Rivoli ten minutes ago, and you've led him a merry chase through Les Halles. Now it's a game of cat and mouse: one of you is going to die in an alleyway tonight.

SURVEILLANCE

Bonus: +2 if you Push **Urban Survival** or **Streetwise**.

Advance 7+: You watch him pass you by in the reflection of a shop window. Once you're on his tail, you try to ambush him, to take him down from behind, but he's too strong. He slams you into the wall – and you shoot him at point-blank range, muffling the gunshot with his body. He slumps down, shot through the heart. You'd better run before the *gendarmes* find you.

Hold 4-6: You follow him through the streets, listening to him mutter to himself about the Master, about how they'll all pay, all suffer. Other passers-by give him a wide berth, avoiding trouble. You have to hang back to avoid being spotted as the crowds thin out.

You turn a corner and he's gone. Vanished – and then he jumps down on you, knocking you to the ground. He was clinging to the wall above you like a spider. His limbs, too, like a spider's – human arms shouldn't bend that way. He stabs at you, bites you, smashes his forehead into your face. It's you or him – you have to shoot him in full view of several witnesses. Gain the Problems "It Was Self-Defense" and "Renfield Ambush," then choose if you want to wait for the authorities or run like hell with an **Evasion** test.

Setback 3 or less: He's gone. You lose him in the crowds. You guess he's out there, somewhere nearby, watching you. He could be right behind you. Gain the Problem "Stalker."

Extra Problem: None.

Stunt: Yes (Cover, Evasion).

PROBLEM

It Was Self-Defense

*You killed a Renfield
in public and on camera.*

HEAT, CONTINUITY

This card counts as +2 Heat
in France and +1 Heat in the
Eurozone. Counter it by clearing
your name or destroying the
security camera recordings.

Renfield Ambush

*"The blood is the life", he shrieked as
he beat you, "the blood is the life!"*

SERIOUS INJURY

Stalker

The Renfield is still out there.

BLOWBACK

Next time you Take Time, remind
the GM you've got this card.
Counter by finding a way to hide
your tracks.

CONSPIRACIES

Standing between the player and the vampires is the conspiracy, a network of minions, criminals, spies, corporations, and other servants. Discovering the size and shape of the conspiracy, tracing those connections between apparently disparate groups, and working out how to bring the whole monstrous edifice down is up to the player.

There's always a vampire at the top of the conspiracy. There may be more vampires, or other supernatural monsters, at lower levels in the organization, but most of the vampire's minions are human. Some serve willingly, some have been bribed or paid, and others have been compelled to serve through threats, blackmail, or other leverage. Most, though, are unaware that they're working for inhuman monsters.

How big is the conspiracy? Start with your vampires. How long have they been around? If they've been around since time immemorial, then the innermost layers of the conspiracy might be ancient religions, mystery cults, and secret societies. If they've only been around for a few hundred years, then the vampires might be connected to a specific bloodline, kingdom, or other polity.

Next, consider what the vampires want and need. What are their goals, and what tools might they seek to

accomplish them? If the vampires are interested only in securing a ready supply of victims, then they might want to secure control over human trafficking routes and criminal gangs, as well as politicians and journalists who could threaten or expose their feeding grounds. If they want to set off volcanic eruptions that will cloak the whole planet in a dust shroud of darkness, blocking out the sun and letting them walk outside freely, then they might target military units, governments with access to nuclear weapons, geologists, and other scientists. If they want to open a portal to Hell, then the vampires might seek to control religious figures, academics, fringe cults, and the like.

If the vampires have any supernatural assets, these also slot into the conspiracy. These might be other supernatural creatures, artifacts, places of power (forbidden castles, hidden temples, alien spacecraft), or associated groups, like a circle of seers whose powers are activated by ingesting vampire blood. Adding too many supernatural elements diminishes the real-world espionage appeal of the game, but some suitably disturbing weirdness adds spice to the usual cavalcade of trench-coated spies, gangsters, and corporate shells.

Not every part of the conspiracy is necessarily connected to the vampires

or their ultimate goals. An ancient conspiracy might have vestigial organs – forgotten, hollow cults that still worship vampires, crumbling banking houses and inbred families, or groups that were once important but have lost their strategic value (controlling the state's Communist party might have served the vampires well in the 1940s, but now it's a useless remnant). Other parts of the conspiracy might be disposal appendages, or ready sources of income. A vampiric cult that seeks to seize control of Transylvania might end up indirectly controlling heroin shipments across the Black Sea, because it took over a criminal network with connections all over the region. The vampires' ultimate goals have nothing to do with the heroin, but it's important to their minions, and money is as fungible as blood.

You don't need to plot the whole conspiracy at the start of the game; each operation can map a little more of it. It is a good idea to have at least a sense of how the player might get from the initial trembling contact with the conspiratorial web to the vampire in the middle, and to note down some key parts of the conspiracy that the player will encounter along the way so you can foreshadow threats to come. In a mystery, the investigator often gets clues that seem meaningless or irrelevant at the time, but actually relate to elements that crop up later in the plot. For example, if your vampires were created by an outbreak of a mysterious plague in a small village in Hungary hundreds of years ago, then a high-level node in the conspiracy might be the aristocrat Czako family of landowners (who owned the village, and were taken over by the vampires shortly after the disease victims rose from their graves). During early operations, the GM could drop mention of the Czakos – maybe the player runs into a scion of the family at a swanky art gallery (**High Society**) or the Czakos could show up in a list of investors in some conspiracy front company. None of these clues should, individually, be strong enough to prompt the player to dig deeper into the Czakos, but this foreshadowing pays off by making the game seem more coherent when the player finally does reach that node. Similarly, you can hit the player with unexpected threats by having the conspiracy bring in an asset that has hitherto gone unnoticed – while investigating the Czako family, the player's kidnapped by French special forces working for an entirely different branch of the conspiracy.

THERE'S NO I IN THE PYRAMID

Devotees of the multiplayer *Night's Black Agents* rules will doubtless recall that book explicitly calls for a pyramidal conspiracy map, gloriously dubbed the Conspyramid. Why the change?

One of the great virtues of the Conspyramid is that you've got multiple low-level entry vectors to the conspiracy, which means any player character in a group can take the lead in tackling the investigation and end up in the same place. The team's ex-GRU gun runner can get the group embroiled in a plot to take out occult terrorists in the Urals; the team's bagman could bring them into an investigation into a cryptic hedge fund in London. Later in the campaign, the team's hacker uncovers a mysterious psy-ops project. All three nodes lead to other nodes that eventually join up later on – the Conspyramid is broad enough to cover the backstories and specialist interests of a half-dozen or more player characters.

In a single-player *Solo Ops* game, you don't *need* such a broad conspiracy. You can still use one, if you want a vast and sinister vampiric illuminati who have their claws in everything, but a short, focused game can benefit from a small, focused conspiracy. Go for a more intimate, backstabby family of murderous vampires.

BLOWBACK

Blowback, in intelligence jargon, is the repercussions, retaliations, and unintended consequences that follow from covert activity. In game terms, it's the actions of the bad guys in response to the player's moves.

The form Blowback takes depends on the assets and pawns available to the conspiracy. If the conspiracy's local minions are, say, a cell of human traffickers, then they might strike back at the player by trying to murder her, kidnapping Contacts or loved ones, trying to abduct the player, trailing one of their victims as a lure so they can ambush her, or outsourcing the retribution to their own criminal contacts. If the conspiracy's assets in town are concealed as a financial services corporation, then the Blowback might involve freezing the player's assets, hiring private detectives and investigators, or bribing local authorities to increase Heat. Supernatural assets like Renfields or lamiae open up other forms of retaliation for the conspiracy.

Blowback puts added obstacles in the way of the player. Depending on circumstances, Blowback can entail anything from "the player's put under surveillance by the police and has to sneak away" to "a hit team of assassin Renfields kick down the door."

You check for Blowback whenever the player Takes Time. There are three possible triggers for Blowback:

- **Heat:** The authorities consider the player to be a dangerous criminal and hunt for her.
- **Shadow:** Supernatural threats from vampires and the conspiracy.
- **Blowback Problems:** Some Challenges can give problems that only show up to bite the player after some time has passed.

List Blowback scenes together with their trigger conditions separately to the other scenes in your operation, and drop them in as needed when the player takes time.

For example, your menu of possible Blowback options might be:

TRIGGER	BLOWBACK	SUMMARY
Heat 2+	"Detective Waldek Wants a Word"	Waldek warns the player about drawing too much attention; optionally, gives clue pointing at gasworks club
Heat 3+	"Waldek's Sting"	Waldek contacts the player and offers to meet; it's a trap (**Evasion** Challenge)
Shadow 1+	"Thing at the Window"	The player's woken by something rapping and bumping at the window of wherever she's staying; if they don't abandon the safehouse, give her the problem "Made"
Shadow 3+	"Freezing Fog"	Unnaturally icy fog blankets the city; everyone's got a -2 penalty to **Driving** and Athletics rolls
Shadow 4+ & Problem "Made"	"Freezing Attack"	Sorcerous frost besieges the safehouse; how does the player avoid freezing to death in the teeth of a personalized blizzard?
Problem "Broke The Big Guy's Nose"	"The Big Guy Wants Revenge"	**Fighting** Challenge if the player is staying at Jurgen's flat; otherwise, Jurgen gets beaten up and has to be reassured with an Interpersonal Push
Problem "Jurgen's Debt"	"The Big Guy Wants Revenge"	As above, but can be bought off with cash instead
If Jurgen's Dead...	"Dreams and Regrets"	Bad guys call up Jurgen's ghost to locate player's safehouse; may lead into "Freezing Attack"

If several Blowback scenes have met their triggers, pick the most interesting or dramatically suitable one; don't drown the player in multiple simultaneous Blowback consequences.

FRAMING BLOWBACK SCENES

With any Blowback, you've got two options.

You can use the Blowback to liven up the downtime when the player Takes Time. For example, the player takes a Serious Injury and retreats back to her hotel room to sew up the wounds left by the vampire's claws. You describe how she disinfects and treats her injuries, then collapses onto the bed to rest. Normally, you'd then ask the player what she does the next morning when she wakes up – but instead, you describe how she's woken in the middle of the night by two guys with guns kicking the door down. Having Blowback scenes happen when the player Takes Time adds to the paranoia and pressure of the game; there's no rest for the spy.

Alternatively, you can work the consequences of Blowback into other scenes in the operation. The player might get a good night's sleep after treating her injuries – but the next day, when she's interrogating a witness, the two guys with guns show up, and what you'd planned as a quiet scene of interpersonal dramatics turns into a gunfight and chase sequence. Combining Blowback with pre-planned scenes makes the game seem more spontaneous and organic; the player's actions cause ripples that affect everything around her.

CLUES AND BLOWBACK

While Blowback is primarily a threat to the player, not a boon, you can drop clues in Blowback Scenes for the player to find with the right Investigative abilities. Once the player survives the attack by those hired goons with guns, a little **Interrogation** or **Streetwise** lets the player find out who hired them. After the player survives the death curse laid upon her by the vampire sorcerer, some **Research** or **Occult Studies** lets her discover that this form of magic relies on conducting power-gathering rituals on certain unholy nights of the year – and why, it's Walpurgisnacht tomorrow night, giving the player a clue that the vampire's plans are time-sensitive and hence vulnerable to well-timed disruption.

HEAT AND BLOWBACK

Heat measures how alarmed the local police, intelligence, and counter-terrorism forces are by recent events. The player gains Heat by public displays of violence and carnage – shootings, explosions, arson, murder, grand theft, anything that causes terror and an increased security presence on the streets.

The player's actions aren't the only thing to cause Heat – if the conspiracy or other criminal elements cause havoc in the city, and the player is nearby when that happens, then that's a Heat Problem too.

A Heat Score of 1-2 means the player is mostly below the radar of the authorities; the police may be circulating a grainy security photograph, or want to bring her in for questioning, but alarm bells aren't ringing yet.

A Heat Score of 3-4 implies an increased security presence on the streets, armed guards at key locations, and an active operation to crack down on criminal elements. This level of Heat makes the sort of career criminals that the player relies on – informants, arms dealers, burglars, hackers, smugglers – decide to take a vacation or lie low until the fuss dies down.

A Heat Score of 5+ means the player is a primary target for law enforcement.

Too much emphasis on Heat makes the player feel trapped; the game's not fun if you "realistically" respond to every action scene with overwhelming counter-terrorist operations. Too little, and the game becomes a cartoon, no longer connected to the real world. The sweet spot is two or three Heat Blowback scenes per operation – one low-Heat "the cops are paying attention" scene to remind the player to keep a low profile, and one mid-level Heat scene to raise tension.

Heat also penalizes **Cover** and **Network** rolls, which is its primary function in the game.

SAMPLE HEAT BLOWBACK

Heat 1-2:

◆ **Too Hot For My Blood:** One of the player's Contacts gets nervous and has to be reassured.

◆ **Friendly Advice:** A law enforcement officer known to the player offers a warning to lie low.

◆ **Just a Bystander:** The player is stopped on the street and questioned as a potential witness. A successful **Cool** test and/or the use of Interpersonal abilities can avoid further suspicion.

◆ **Ring of Steel:** Increased security presence means the player needs to make a **Cover** test to visit embassies, police stations, and other sensitive places.

◆ **Forensics:** The player discovers the police are investigating a previous scene; is there any physical evidence left behind?

◆ **She's the One:** Some ambitious young detective gets a hunch that the player is important, and starts investigating her outside his normal duties, becoming a recurring thorn in the player's side.

Heat 3-4:

◆ **Wanted for Questioning:** A Contact is arrested. Is their relationship with the player strong enough that they'll lie for her?

◆ **Frame Agent:** The conspiracy frames the Agent for some crime, in whatever fashion seems believable. Agents with amnesia like Leyla Khan are *perfect* for this. With the police already looking for a threat, this puts the Agent front and center.

◆ **Matching the Description:** The GM calls for random **Cover** tests in the middle of other scenes: fail, and you're spotted by a cop who's looking for someone who matches your description.

◆ **Javert:** A veteran detective's assigned to look into the case, and pursues the player across Europe on an Interpol warrant. This becomes a Continuity Problem that the player has to Counter or it'll keep coming back in future operations.

◆ **All Your Sins Remembered:** The player's arrested, and has to talk her way out. Older Heat episodes may get dredged up and if Heat gets too high, the only option may be breaking out. (See "Getting Captured," p. 42.)

◆ **Make It Look Like a Suicide:** The player's arrested, but the cops in the station are conspiracy double agents and intend to murder her.

◆ **APB on Dracula:** Police investigations threaten to uncover something they can't handle; the player has to get ahead of the cops while avoiding their notice.

◆ **Bad Timing:** The police show up at exactly the wrong moment in a future scene. Possible examples: the player's about to break into a church to recover the relic in the crypt when a cop car drives by; SWAT teams show up in the middle of another fight scene; the police do a sweep of the airport just as the player is trying to sneak out using a false passport.

◆ **I Have Information:** A Contact betrays the player, informing on her to the police. In this case, the Contact is willing to work with the police to get the player arrested.

Heat 5+

◆ **Dragnet:** Contacts of the player are arrested and questioned.

◆ **Manhunt:** There's a city-wide manhunt for the player, with a dedicated investigative team.

◆ **License to Kill:** The GM calls for random **Cover** tests in the middle of other scenes: fail, and the cops try to shoot you on sight.

◆ **Wetwork:** The player's former employer (MI6, in the case of Leyla Khan) tries to clean up the potential embarrassment by quietly eliminating their former asset.

Inspector Waithe

Waithe of Interpol is on your case.

HEAT, CONTINUITY

When your Heat reaches 2, this Problem becomes active, raising your Heat by 1. Counter by killing Waithe or convincing him of your innocence.

SHADOW AND BLOWBACK

Shadow measures how aware the supernatural elements of the conspiracy are of the player's presence. It's like vibrations in a spider's web: step on the wrong grave, leave a taste of your blood behind, open the wrong crypt, and the vampires sense an unexpected presence in their city.

(When we say "vampire" in this section, read "supernatural threat connected with the conspiracy": it might be a vampire, a necromancer, a circle of bound ghosts, a demon. Whatever ghoulish assets the conspiracy has available get alerted by rising Shadow.)

A Shadow Score of 1-2 means the vampire knows something's out there, but doesn't necessarily know who or where. Low-level Shadow responses are typically investigative and probing.

A Shadow Score of 3-4 means the vampire knows that the player is trespassing in the city, but isn't yet willing to put forward its full strength. Mid-level Shadow Blowback is indirect and subtle; it impedes the player and strips away their support network instead of attacking them directly.

A Shadow Score of 5+ opens the door to full-on vampire attacks.

SAMPLE SHADOW BLOWBACK

Shadow 1-2:

◆ **Shadow Agent:** The vampire sends a supernatural minion to watch the Agent. It might send rats or bats to scurry after the player, or a ghost to eavesdrop on it, or just search for the Agent in bat form itself. Unless the player keeps under cover – perhaps with **Infiltration** or **Sense Trouble** tests – the vampire learns valuable intel about its prey.

◆ **Shadow Contact:** One of the player's contacts is stalked through supernatural means, and complains about it to the player. Time to put **Reassurance** to good use.

◆ **Probing Attack:** The vampire uses mind control (or money, which amounts to the same thing) to send some low-level thugs after the player. The goal here isn't to seriously injure or threaten the player; it's to give the vampire a chance to observe the player in action and – if possible – get a taste of her blood.

◆ **Bad Dreams:** The player's cursed with bad dreams of the vampire when she rests. There may be clues buried in this psychic link between hunter and hunted that the player can discover with Investigative abilities.

◆ **Threaten Safety:** The vampire strikes at the player's safehouse, hitting it with an unpleasant but low-grade supernatural attack – a plague of insects, a poltergeist, blood running down the walls, unnatural chills, or something similar. Alternatively, the vampire might attack a resource used by the player: fell voices jamming radio links, or packs of wild dogs on the streets frequented by the hunter.

Shadow 3-4+:

◆ **Devour Contact:** The vampire kills one of the player's Contacts and dumps the body. It might leave the body on waste ground, or on the doorstep of the character's safehouse. There may be useful clues on the remains if the player can examine it before the authorities claim it.

◆ **Feral Vampire:** The vampire spawns a lesser supernatural monster and sets it loose. The goal is to flush the player out of hiding by sowing chaos and forcing the player to expend effort putting the monster down.

◆ **Haunt:** The vampire strikes at the player (or a Contact) with a non-physical supernatural threat like a ghost or demon (or a shadowy vampire in mist form), with the aim of driving the player insane or weakening her without any physical risk to the vampire.

◆ **Double:** The vampire flips one of the player's Contacts, either through mind control, bribery, blackmail, threats, or other means. The Contact's orders are to lure the player into an ambush but failing that, the vampire interrogates the Contact to learn as much as possible about the player's abilities and intentions.

◆ **Blatant Supernatural Attack:** The vampire puts forth its power in a way that's obvious to those who know what signs to look for. It might shut the city down with an unnatural storm, call up a host of ghosts and rattle the cages of every cemetery in the city, or drive every sensitive soul into a frenzy of bloody worship of the Master.

Shadow 5+:

◆ **Hunt:** The vampire goes hunting for the player. Unless the player wants a fight with the vampire under the worst possible conditions, the player had better stay undetected.

◆ **Turn:** The vampire turns one of the player's Contacts into a Renfield or even a full-on vampire (or kills the Contact and calls up the resulting ghost), and then sends the supernatural killer after the player.

- **Psychic Assault:** The vampire besieges the player with nightmares or psychic assaults, trying to drive the player mad or take control of her. A successful **Cool** test allows the player to retain control, but the best thing to do is to suppress Shadow as quickly as possible.

BLOWBACK PROBLEMS

The longer the player survives, the more grudges and debts she builds up. If a player does something that warrants later Blowback, give her a Blowback Problem card.

If the player can counter or otherwise deal with the Problem card before the blowback hits, that's one less thing to worry about. A canny spy might be able to cut a deal or cover her tracks before the repercussions hit.

Use Blowback Problems to develop complications related to subplots, especially ones connected to Contacts.

OPERATIONS

The default **Solo Ops** campaign is a series of operations against increasingly dangerous foes that build on one another, as the player shoots her way up through the conspiracy to get to the vampires. You can kick things off with an introductory adventure (like *Never Say Dead*, p. 123) where the player discovers the existence of vampires and becomes marked for death by the conspiracy, or just jump right into the middle of the action by assuming that the player and the conspiracy are already locked into a life-or-death struggle in the shadows and running from there.

Each operation after that introductory baptism of blood is an investigation into some aspect or node of the conspiracy; completing that investigation and exposing or destroying the conspiracy activity yields more clues that point to other nodes of the conspiracy. Along the way, the player maps the structure of the conspiracy, discovers the true nature of vampirism, and develops sources and methods to enable her to kill the dead. Rinse and repeat until one side or the other dies. Investigation leads to danger leads to more information, which leads to investigation and the start of the cycle again.

Take a look at a mid-campaign operation like *No Grave for Traitors*, and mimic its structure for your own **Solo Ops** operations.

THE HOOK

Start with the hook that gets the player involved. Ideally, this will be a clue from a previous operation. It might equally be a tip-off from an agency or trusted Contact, a rumor or news report that suggests conspiracy activity, or a plea for help from some victim of the vampires. If you're using Leyla Khan as your protagonist, then she can recall a fragmented memory of her time as an agent of the conspiracy. Arouse the player's interest with an interesting and evocative hook, and give her an obvious place to start her investigation.

Depending on your tastes and those of your player, you might want to start off in the middle of the action, or begin at some remove and let the player cautiously approach the hook.

Allow the hook to inform the ensuing storyline. The hook sets the mood and tone for the whole operation – if you kick off with a body of an accountant washing up on the riverbank in London, then most of the operation is going to take place in England: it's going to be relatively low-key and investigative, there's a vibe of seedy corruption, dark money, and murder by night – and a body in the river instantly brings up questions of running water. Was the victim trying to evade a vampire by crossing the river? If so, what went wrong?

WHAT'S GOING ON?

Once you have your hook, work out what's tied to the other end. What conspiracy elements are present? Who are their victims? Who are they hiding from? Who's compromised? Figure out the situation before the player gets involved. It may help to write out a list of potential cast members and map their relationships. It's also useful to do background research and planning – look at maps of the region, Google "<CITY NAME> + vampires/murders/crime/occult", brainstorm some evocative locations and set-piece action sequences. Think like a movie producer, and bring along your internal script writer, your fight choreographer, your location scout...

What happened before the player got involved? For especially involved backstories, organize the information by writing out a timeline of events.

What *would have* happened if the player had not interceded? What do the conspiracy hope to achieve here?

CREATING STARTING PROBLEMS

Optionally, give your Agent an introductory Problem, like the four given in the opener for *"No Grave for Traitors."*

If you've already run at least one scenario for your player, the Agent probably has some lingering Problems still in hand. In that case, write an introduction that connects the most salient of those Problems to the assignment given in the first scene.

If you need a new starting Problem, create three or four of them to give the player a sense of control over the character's story arc. Some players prefer to invent their own, and are good at it. Whenever you can offload narrative tasks onto the player, seize the opportunity. Write Problems you create in a general manner, allowing the player to customize them with specific detail when you play the scene out.

INTRODUCTORY SCENE

The introductory scene delivers the hook to the player, and gives a starting point for investigation. Use it to establish time, place, and mood. If it's a player-driven operation (*"I'm going to follow up on the dying nun's confession, and investigate the monastery in Budapest"*), then your intro scene is the first time their efforts turn up a clue or run into difficulty. If this is a reactive mission, in response to a hook assigned to the player or a plea for aid, then the introductory scene might be meeting a Contact or receiving a request for aid.

In any case, the introductory scene needs at least one **core clue** leading out from it.

ANATOMY OF A SCENE

Scenes in published GUMSHOE scenarios start with header entries to help the GM quickly spot their purpose and place in the flow of the operation.

The Scene Type header entry shows the GM the scene's purpose.

An **Introduction** scene starts the operation. If the player initiated the operation, it states the goal of the operation (*"Find out what the vampires are doing in Budapest, and destroy their assets and organization in the city"*) and introduces an initial line of investigation. If the player's reacting to something the enemy has done (*"Someone killed my buddy and left his bloodless corpse on the roof of the embassy as a warning"*), then the introduction gets the player involved in the mystery and suggests a starting point (*"His husband begged me to investigate the killing; I'll start by finding out what he knew"*). It also contains the elements of a core scene:

A **core scene** provides information that is essential to the operation – there's information here that the player *must* obtain. If the player fails to use the right Investigative ability, then the GM might:

- Require the player to return to this scene again later on (*"Okay, I'll head back to the nightclub and force Ivanescu to talk with **Intimidation**"*)
- Get the clue to the player in some other way (*"**Flirting** with Ivanescu's girlfriend, you learn..."*)
- Warn the player that there's more to be uncovered here (*"Your instincts tell you Ivanescu knows more than he's saying. How do you get it out of him?"*)
- Give the player the clue anyway. (*"As an experienced Agent, trained in **Interrogation**, you can tell Ivanescu is concealing something. You press him, and he reveals..."*)

Alternate scenes cover possibilities that aren't core to the investigation, but are still likely courses of action for the player. Alternate scenes may provide a way for the player to get to the final reveal without playing through some core scenes, or give information or advantages that will help the player survive the ultimate confrontation. Discovering the location of a vampire's lair is core information; finding out in advance that this particular vampire is only vulnerable if you incant a secret Etruscan prayer might be found in an alternate scene.

A **climax** is the final confrontation of the operation. Operations can have multiple alternate climaxes – for example, if there's an earlier challenge where the vampire tries to escape the player's snare, then you might have two possible climax scenes – one where the player successfully traps the monster, and one where the vampire breaks free and the player must chase the creature down.

The **Aftermath** wraps up the story. The fates of any surviving characters are discussed, the effects of any Problems or Edges with the Continuity keyword get resolved, and the player obtains clues pointing to the next level of the conspiracy.

Blowback scenes describe the antagonists taking action against the player, or what happens when certain Problem cards come home to roost. Blowback happens in response to the player deciding to Take Time, so these scenes aren't directly linked to the rest of the operation and therefore are listed at the end for ease of reference. When the player Takes Time, flip to the end of the adventure and select your torture weapon.

LEAD-INS

This header entry lists other scenes that might precede this one when you play out the operation.

LEAD-OUTS

This entry lists other scenes its core clues might prompt the Agent to go to next.

Think of Lead-Ins and Lead-Outs as bookmarks. When running the game, they orient you in relationship to the other scenes. More crucially, when designing the scenario, they remind you to create options for the player. When every scene has only one Lead-In or Lead-Out, you've created a linear storyline that can only unfold in one way. When a scene can be reached, and followed up on, in a number of ways, your player has meaningful choices to make.

A few scenes with only one Lead-Out are fine, as the multiple Lead-Outs in other scenes allow the Agent to pick up another thread of the investigation.

BODY TEXT

It's up to you how much detail you want to go into for each scene. Some Directors work best with brief scribbled notes whose cryptic scrawl only makes sense to themselves. Others write up their plans in detail, mimicking the style of the operations in this book. Often, you'll find yourself going into detail on the initial scenes in the adventure, and leave the later scenes as bare skeletons to be fleshed out later on.

Within a scene, deal with its basic elements in whatever order you prefer.

Find a quick, evocative way to evoke the setting of each scene. Conjure a mood with details of location and, where applicable, background characters. Lean on stock tropes from the espionage and vampire-horror genres: gothic castles, isolated hillside villages in Eastern Europe, run-down apartments, government offices, diplomats in expensive hotels. These days, you can also call up images and web pages on any part of the world in an instant; if your game is set in Bucharest, you can zoom in on Google Street View and get a feel for the real-world back streets, then overlay that with the grime and paranoia of the clandestine, occult world of the vampires.

CHARACTERS

If the scene involves one or more key characters, then note one or two descriptive features, and a memorable quirk that you can act out when portraying that individual. A vampire thrall might twitch and slap at invisible bugs, or stare hungrily at the player's throat. A suave diplomat might have a glass of wine in hand, or speak with a notably measured and considered tone. Also note the character's agenda – what do they want? What will they reveal, and what will they attempt to hide? Don't try to script things too closely in advance – the player *will* surprise you. Note down the clues and the most likely ways you anticipate them coming to light, but be prepared to improvise. When writing compelling details into a supporting character's backstory, see to it that the player has some way of discovering or somehow interacting with that material. When you are caught up in the flow of adventure creation, this need can be surprisingly easy to forget.

Sometimes, to convey motivation, you have to include facts the witness would never intentionally reveal. Do so sparingly.

Avoid scenes that require the Agent to talk to more than one major character at a time. Portraying multiple supporting characters simultaneously as a GM will usually prove taxing for you and confusing for the player.

LOCATIONS

If the scene doesn't revolve around a character, then note down entrances and exits, possible threats or security systems, and a few evocative details about the place. Location-based scenes often include a number of physical challenges – sneaking into the laboratory, scaling the castle wall, beating up the guards at the prison camp; for these, see "Building Challenges," below. Note, however, that the more time the player has to scope out and prepare, the more likely it is that she'll be able to bypass such challenges by taking an unexpected route. A player under pressure of time might run straight into the crypt and have to fight the zombies; a player with time to plan can research the history of the crypt, bribe a city clerk to provide accurate plans of the underground area, sneak into the sewers that run under the graveyard, borrow a drill and snake-cam from an old military contact to spy on the zombies, and then plant explosives to collapse the section of the tomb where they slumber.

CLUES

After setting out the context of the character and locale, segue into the **clues** the Agent will seek in your scene. A bullet-point format for the clues, core and otherwise, enables you to find them quickly during play. Make sure you flag any core clues as such, to ensure you don't miss them in the hurly-burly of play.

When writing up operations, it helps to note which Investigative ability yields a clue, so you know how the player might get that information. For example: *Art History* reveals she wears a *heavy gold ring with an ornate sigil on it – the symbol of a dragon.* Of course, that's not necessarily the only way to get that intel. The player might use **Notice** (*"Is there anything unusual about her?"*) or **Streetwise** (*"Can I tell if she's part of a gang or clique or anything like that?"*) or **Flirting** (*"I'll chat with her and buy her a drink: do I learn anything?"*).

CLUE DELIVERY

Some are obvious: the player gets them without having to do anything or use any Investigative abilities. Clues like can be discovered by anyone, not just a veteran investigator like the player, so use them when the player is the first person to investigate a situation.

- A folder of documents on a table can be picked up and read by anyone.
- You don't need **Forensic Pathology** to realize that the guy lying slumped on the desk was shot in the back of the head.
- If you follow the rival spy to an abandoned factory, it's clear that there's something worth checking out in there.

Other clues can be spotted without any effort on the part of the Agent, because she's an experienced spy. You can either give these clues straight to the player, or wait until she uses the appropriate Investigative ability.

Clues like this are great for suggesting lines of investigation and opening up possibilities the player might have missed.

- Your expertise in **Criminology** identifies his tattoos as Russian prison tattoos.
- She's clearly lying about what she saw – you barely need **Bullshit Detector** to pick up on her nervousness.
- Your knowledge of **History** means you recognize the guy in the tweed jacket who's boring everyone at the cocktail party by lecturing them about the Ottoman dynasty. He's an expert on the life of Countess Bathory...

Some clues require some action or effort from the player, but it's just a question of asking the right questions or applying the right specialist training. Most clues should fall into this category – it shows off the Agent's talents, and explains why the player is the only one who can tackle this operation.

- She mentions a few people who've visited the gallery recently, and with your knowledge of **High Society** you know they're all associates of the Hungarian cultural attaché.
- A quick search of the room with **Architecture** confirms that there must be a false wall there – the room's six feet shorter than the corridor outside.
- You flash him an old SIS recognition code with **Tradecraft** from across the room. After a few minutes, he leaves and signals for you to follow him.

Finally, there are clues that require considerable time, effort, and legwork on the part of the Agent. Clues like this might be a montage sequence if the operation were a movie; they're great for gluing apparently unrelated parts of the conspiracy together, as you can handwave over how exactly the Agent worked out the information.

- With **Traffic Analysis**, you're able to cross-reference the movements of the shipping company's trucks, and you're sure they're making unscheduled detours somewhere near Tbilisi.
- You spend several hours working through the shell company's records with **Accounting**, following the money.
- It takes you several days to run through the chemical analysis of the drug sample, but you discover that the active ingredient is found only in a rare flower from the Amazon...

CLUE TYPES

A core scene must have at least one **core clue** pointing to the next core scene. This chain of core clues is the spine of the mystery; its existence ensures that the player is never stymied or stalled without anything to do next. A scene can have multiple core clues, offering different lines of inquiry or action to the player. Core clues should always be flagged in some way in your notes to ensure you remember to get them to the player.

A clue leading to an alternate scene is, unsurprisingly, an **alternate clue**.

An alternate scene might lead directly to no other scene. Or it might provide a secondary Lead-In to a core scene.

A **pipe clue** becomes significant only when combined with another piece of information gathered separately. (The name references screenwriting jargon, where the insertion of exposition that becomes relevant later in the narrative is referred to as "laying pipe." The term likens the careful arrangement of narrative information to the work performed by a plumber in building a house). Pipe clues are a form of foreshadowing; the importance of the dead man's rubber-soled shoes only becomes clear when the Agent discovers she's hunting an electrical vampire. Often, pipe clues get delivered in the form of clue cards, to remind the player that this information is important, but not immediately relevant.

A **leveraged clue** prompts a witness to spill his guts after being presented with another clue uncovered earlier. It is usually accompanied by the use of an Interpersonal ability, like **Intimidation** or **Reassurance**.

USING CONTACTS

The player has access to Contacts who have Investigative abilities and insight that she does not. Be careful of attaching core clues to information that the player can only obtain through a Contact – the player will usually have to go visit or call up the source, which may be difficult in the heat of action. For example, if a Contact is the only one with the **Archaeology** ability, then don't have a core clue that requires the player to use **Archaeology** to follow the vampire into a hidden dungeon during a chase scene. ("*You sprint after the vampire as it races through the graveyard, and then – detouring only to drive back to the airport, fly back to London, drive to Oxford, collect Professor Wrexal, drive back to Heathrow, fly back to Prague, drive back to the graveyard, and ask the Professor to examine the tombs to discover which one bears the sigil of the Skelezy family – you kick open the door of the tomb and plunge into the darkness.*")

Contacts work best for background research, or for chewing on clues that that take time to work out. For example, if the player steals a thumb drive full of data from a conspiracy hideout, then she can give it to a source with **Data Recovery** to examine in the background while the player pursues other leads.

Telecommunications can allow a Contact to be called on remotely ("*Actually, thinking about it, you just phone the professor and stream a live video of the graveyard so he can spot the right tomb with* **Archaeology**..."), but this isn't always reliable.

USING PUSHES

In addition to clues, note places where a player can use a Push to elicit more information or gain an advantage or Edge.

Possible benefits for using a Push include:

♦ Getting maximum effect out of an Interpersonal ability.

> "*The gangster tells you where the drug shipment's arriving if you* **Interrogate** *him. If you push* **Interrogation**, *he's so scared that he also tells you about the sea monster that guards it.*"

♦ Getting information faster.

> "*It'll take you all day to go through these files with* **Law**. *You'll have to Take Time unless you want to spend a Push to do it faster.*"

♦ Getting an added benefit.

> "*You can find your way to the hideout with* **Urban Survival** *– and if you spend a Push, you can also discard one Heat Problem.*"

♦ Tweak the story a little.

> "*With* **Human Terrain**, *you recognize the little token as a souvenir from the monastery of St. Michel. If you spend a Push, then we'll say that you spent time in that monastery a few years ago, and have a trusted friend there, Brother Angelos.*"

♦ Convincing a Contact to help you or do you a favor.

> "*Professor Wrexal will identify the tomb for free, as that's a clue – but if you want him to accompany you into the tomb to help you open the coffin, and stand watch while you cut off the woman's head and fill her mouth with garlic, that'll require a Push.*"

Note down places where you see a possible Push; the player will suggest more during play. ("*Can I spend a Push to...*")

INSERTING CHALLENGES

Along with clues, scenes may also include Challenges. When planning your adventures, think about most likely way the player might approach a situation, and write up a Challenge to test the player's luck and courage. Be prepared, though, for the player to do the unexpected and approach the situation in ways you haven't anticipated. Master the art of adapting existing challenges, or building new ones on the fly.

BUILDING CHALLENGES

Challenges are the action scenes in your movie, adding suspense and uncertainty to your narrative. They give the player the feeling that their narrative is not predetermined, and therefore special. The version of *Never Say Dead* you play out will be your own unique variant on the experience, one shared in absolute detail by no one else. The variations that make it yours arise from the player's choices, and also from the unpredictability of die results, which player choices can influence but not control.

Even when running published adventures, the GM should expect to improvise Challenges in response to player choices that were not anticipated by the scenario writer.

Some Challenges are full-scale branches in the story. If the player succeeds, she gets one set of subsequent scenes; if she fails, she gets another set entirely. An Advance means the player shoots the cult leader, causing the rest of the vampire cultists to flee in terror. A Hold means the player is able to make a shooting retreat, using suppressive fire to hold back the mob, but the cult leader gets away. A Setback means the player is overrun and captured. Each branch goes to a wholly different next scene.

Such branches are a lot of work and it's perfectly acceptable to have Challenges lead to the same place in the story, but put the player in different circumstances. Imagine if the player is trying to sneak into a terrorist-held compound in the mountains. On an Advance, the player sneaks in, picking up an Edge or some other advantage. On a Hold, the player gets in, but only just avoids detection. On a Setback, the player is caught – or maybe the player sneaks in, but at a cost.

Where you see only two promising story directions, one a good result and the other bad, drop the Hold result, so that the hero can either Advance or suffer a Setback.

If you're familiar with improvisation techniques, you could think of Advances, Holds, and Setbacks in terms of "yes, and..." and "no, but..." If success is certain, and the only question is how well the Agent succeeds, then an Advance is "yes, and..." while a Hold means "yes" and a Setback is "yes, but..." Can the elite spy eliminate a lone guard with a silent take-down? "Yes, and you find a bunch of keys on the guard's belt." "Yes, the guard's unconscious." "Yes, but you had to kill him, and now you've got blood on your hands."

If success is only a possibility, then the Outcomes might be "yes, and…" "yes," and "no," or "yes," "no," and "no, and…" A Hold is always a middle ground between extremes.

SETTING THRESHOLDS

Though it has numbers in it, the process of assigning numbers to the three Outcome thresholds is an art rather than a science, involving more creative craft than formulaic arithmetic. Keep these guidelines in mind as you proceed.

"You Don't Know Who You're Dealing With": Minimal risk to the Agent – a chance to show off and refill some Pushes.

Action Sequence Single Shot: Use only as part of a sequence where the player's using the same ability multiple times; think of this as one shot in a rapid-fire action scene.

Advantage: Player: The player's done something clever to tilt the odds in her favor before entering the Challenge.

Average Day at the Edge: The average Challenge for a super-spy. The player's got a roughly 40% chance of an Advance, and about a 15% chance of

a Setback (assuming no Bonus, Extra Problem, Stunt, or other modifiers).

Risky Situation: The odds are still in the player's favor, but there's a noticeable chance of failure.

Desperate Times: The player's up against significant opposition, but can still probably pull through with a Stunt and some luck.

A Lucky Break? The Agent's likely to Hold, but can go for a bigger reward with a lucky roll/Extra Problem/Stunt.

Really Tough Challenge: The only way to win is to pull out all the stops.

Climactic Fight: You're dead unless you've assembled the allies, tools, and Edges you need.

CHALLENGE TYPE	ADVANCE	HOLD	SETBACK
"You Don't Know Who You're Dealing With"	5+	3-4	2
Action Sequence Single Shot	6+	4-5	2-3
Advantage: Player	7+	4-6	2-3
Average Day at the Edge	8+	4-7	2-3
Risky Situation	9+	6-8	2-5
Desperate Times	11+	7-10	2-6
A Lucky Break?	10+	4-9	2-3
Really Tough Challenge*	12+	9-11	2-7
Climactic Fight*	13+	9-12	2-8

*Make sure you have an Extra Problem or Stunt available at the very least, and ideally the player should be able to pick up a hand of Edges before encountering this Challenge.

CARDS ON THE TABLE?

Not every Advance needs to produce an Edge card; not every Setback or even Extra Problem has to be associated with a full-fledged Problem card. Sometimes, the Outcome of a Challenge is so immediate that you can just narrate the results to the player. For example, if the result of an Advance on an **Evasion** Challenge is "you get away cleanly," then that doesn't need to go on a card.

Use cards when:

◆ It's a major story element that you want to emphasize by having a physical reminder of it on the table.
◆ The effects of the Edge or Problem won't immediately manifest in the story.
◆ It's something the player has control over – either it's an Edge that the player can choose to spend at some later point, or a Problem that the player has to Counter by taking some action.

(We say "cards," but they don't have to be physical cards. You could equally use Post-Its, bullet points on a shared document, notes on a corkboard, text messages…)

STUNTS

Stunts are an opportunity for cinematic action and player creativity. They let the player use all their talents and resources by drawing on abilities other than the one being tested. Spies are inherently transgressive – they look like ordinary people, but they unexpectedly do extraordinary things – and Stunts reflect that.

In Stunts, the player describes *intent*, not execution. The player might say "Oh, I whip out my gun and shoot both the Renfields dead," but you should take that as a declaration of the character's intended action, not the actual result. Factor in not only the player's intent, but also the dice rolls themselves, the possible Outcomes of the Challenge, and the Problems and Edges you've got to hand when you finally describe how events turn out. You can always discuss staging and "fight choreography" with the player as you decide on what really happens in the end.

For example, the player says "Oh, Leyla whips out her gun and shoots both the Renfields dead," but rolls a 1 on the Fighting die she got from the Stunt. She's still getting a Setback so you describe how one of the Renfields kicks the gun out of her hand. The player then decides to take the Extra Problem "Messy Exit," which raises her Heat, and rolls on the die she got from the Extra Problem, bringing her up to a Hold. You modify the description – Leyla shoots one Renfield, who stumbles backwards through the window and falls onto the street below, attracting plenty of attention. The other Renfield wrestles the gun off Leyla, who then flees out the broken window and over the balcony, escaping as per the Hold result in the Challenge.

When a player Stunts, she uses dice from one ability to reinforce another. Make that risky – look for ways to hit the player with Challenges that rely on abilities she's already depleted in this encounter, which encourages her to use unexpected combinations of skills. For example, if a player used Athletics to Stunt in an Evasion Challenge, then have some bad guys flee across the rooftops. "How are you going to follow them? You've depleted your Evasion or Athletics – you've no chance on this next Challenge with only one die. I guess you could take this lovely Extra Problem card and hope you roll high..." Instead, the player uses Driving as a Stunt, stealing a car, and driving at high speed through the crowded streets, trying to cut the targets off as they flee across the city.

Stunts also offer the player a chance to score extra Pushes, rewarding descriptive flair with enhanced investigative opportunities.

No-Stunt Challenges: Not every challenge needs to permit Stunts. Some abilities lend themselves to improv better than others ("I acrobatically use my Athletics to parkour down the wall, vault into the coffee shop, dive into my seat, and then casually meet my contact – can I stunt this Network roll?"); at other times, you want to keep a tight lid on difficulties or don't want to slow the action to allow the player to consider which ability they want to tap.

Suggested Abilities: In published scenarios, we suggest which abilities might fit a challenge. These are always only suggestions – go with whatever the player comes up with.

STUNTS AND SPECIFIC ABILITIES

Stunts are a place in the game where the player gets to add color to the narrative, coming up with her own clever descriptions and tactics in action scenes. The role of the GM here is to support the player, and work her ideas into the scene's final resolution.

Some General abilities really lend themselves to Stunts. Athletics, for example, can play a part in any action scene. Reward the player for jumping off balconies, running up walls, and using the terrain. A fight that bounces from alleyway to dumpster to fire escape to crashing through a skylight is way more interesting than two combatants trading blows on the ground. Other abilities, like Driving, are far more likely to be the primary ability in a Challenge instead of being used to augment another ability.

Notes on specific abilities:

Athletics: When setting the scene, give the player plenty of furniture and other obstacles to parkour over or jump onto. As most *Solo Ops* fight scenes are one-against-many, give the player ways to isolate her foes or take them on one at a time. Athletics is one of the most common go-to abilities for Stunts; to avoid your Challenges turning into wuxia movie scenes where every problem involves improbable aerial action, mix in plenty of Athletics Challenges that penalize the player for relying too much on Athletics stunts.

Conceal: Conceal is good for Stunts that involve the player using deception or stealth ("I hide by spread-eagling myself against the ceiling!") or grabbing unexpected items ("When he throws me against the kitchen counter, I grab a knife from the drawer and conceal it up my sleeve!").

STUNTS AND SPECIFIC ABILITIES (CONTINUED)

Cool: Cool works for Stunts against supernatural threats; if a foe relies on the sheer terror of its unnatural presence, the player can distinguish herself from lesser mortals by showing no fear in the face of the vampire.

Evasion: Evasion covers dodging and ducking, but can also be used to temporarily escape a fight scene. The player might use Evasion to flee the assassin who's invaded her safehouse, and ambush her foe as he follows her out the window.

Fighting: Fighting can be dropped into almost any other Challenge for a sudden flurry of violence. For example, in an Infiltration Challenge where the player's trying to sneak into a military base, a Fighting stunt could be described in terms of the player silently taking down a guard without raising the alarm.

Filch: Like Conceal, Filch lets the player grab items from her surroundings and use them as part of a Stunt ("I've got your gun!"). You could also use Filch to describe the player winning by "losing" a conflict – the player fails to sneak into the military base, but manages to grab the passcard from one of the guards to the armory as she's being escorted out.

Mechanics: Mechanics Stunts include using machines and devices in the vicinity as part of a Stunt. Bond chasing an escaping bad guy by stealing a bulldozer in *Casino Royale* is an example of a Mechanics Stunt in an Evasion Challenge; for that matter, so is hitting a bad guy with the door of a fridge.

Preparedness: Preparedness Stunts work like regular Preparedness, but involve the player unexpectedly producing some item or weapon. Keep previously established continuity in mind: if the player was searched before entering the nightclub, then it's unreasonable to use Preparedness to produce a knife as part of a Fighting Stunt. (On the other hand, if the player visited the club earlier, she could have stashed a knife within easy reach, knowing the bad guys would turn on her.)

Sense Trouble: Sense Trouble's used to avoid nasty surprises, and to read a situation with the paranoid eye of a veteran operative. A Sense Trouble stunt is usually framed as the player anticipating the intentions of the enemy and bursting into action. For example, the GM might initially frame a Challenge as "the bad guys jump on top of you and try to wrestle you down," but Stunting Sense Trouble to add to Fighting reframes it as "one of them tries to jump on you, but you kick him in the knee before he can move, so now you've only got one to deal with."

Shooting: A Shooting Stunt doesn't have to involve actually discharging a firearm. The player could get the bonus die in a Fighting contest by describing how she draws a gun, only for her enemy to knock it out of her hand. Similarly, she could get the bonus die by describing how her foe flees or surrenders when she manages to get to the gun she had concealed under the table...

FRAMING CHALLENGES

Be flexible when describing Challenges. Take the text as written in a prepared operation as a starting point, not a fixed script.

Some Challenges are obviously standalone. You only want to make one roll to see if the player's Cover passes muster when bluffing her way into a military base, or if the player's Medic is good enough to treat that poisoned knife wound. Other challenges could be framed as a montage or an action sequence.

An action sequence consists of a series of linked Challenges, each one testing a different ability. Breaking into a safehouse, for example, might involve Athletics to climb up the wall, Infiltration to get past the alarms, Fighting to take down a guard, and Evasion to flee when the alarm is raised. That's four Challenges, each of which might generate unique Edges and Problems. Action sequences like that are great for the set-piece action sequence or high-stakes finale of an operation – if breaking into that safehouse is the most important thing the player does in this story, then it warrants a full-fledged action sequence.

Equally, you could frame the break-in as a single Challenge of Infiltration, and let the player use a Stunt to bring in whichever other ability appeals. Boiling it down to a single roll is faster and simpler, but also less immersive; use montages for less important action scene that aren't as central to the operation.

DESIGNING EDGES

Edges are quanta of luck, skill, or leveraged information the player can use to navigate the story. Edges give the player a jolt of positive accomplishment. Receiving one feels good; so does spending it, and so does hanging onto it. In the game design business we call this a win-win-win.

An Edge starts with an evocative title and descriptive text that indicates its relevance and encourages the player to feel an emotional up note.

Edges come in several different flavors:

- A bonus to multiple Challenges, either when a particular condition is met (+2 when sneaking around Budapest) or for a limited time (+2 to your next two Shooting challenges)
- A bonus to an entire category of General abilities (Physical, Mental, Manual, Social)
- A bonus die on a Challenge (and remember, if the player has any dice left over from the primary ability when she scores an Advance, she gets a free Push)
- A free Push in a particular situation (*"You know this city like the back of your hand. Discard this Edge for a free Push of Architecture, Cop Talk, Human Terrain, Streetwise, or Urban Survival while in Prague."*)
- A free Push when dealing with a particular character or faction
- A free Push for a particular type of Investigative ability, usually Interpersonal
- The ability to Counter a type of Problem
- A general description of some advantage, giving the player scope for creativity (*"The priest blessed you."*)

Just as all Challenges are not of equal intensity, not all Edges need provide the same degree of benefit. It is more fun to receive a number of Edges that grant similar but slightly variant benefits

than many duplicates of the same one.

If you tie an Edge card to a particular element of the current operation, then also consider giving it a second clause that's less potent but is more generally useful, like the Edge "Blackmail on Kristof," below.

As with any other element of Challenge design, give yourself license to deviate from the general principles when presented with a compelling special case.

◄■■■■ **PROBLEM** ■■■■►

Blackmail on Kristof

Kristof's been stealing from the conspiracy, and you've got the ledgers to prove it. You've got leverage.

Before Kristof's meeting with the vampire, you may discard this Edge to threaten Kristof with exposure and force him into compliance.
Alternatively, at any time, discard this Edge to empty his Swiss account for the Edge "Suitcase Full of Cash."

◄■■■■ **PROBLEM** ■■■■►

Suitcase Full of Cash
CONTINUITY

You've stolen a fortune from the conspiracy. As long as you have this card, you've got plenty of petty cash. Discard this vcard to make a large purchase.

◄■■■■ **PROBLEM** ■■■■►

The Traitor
CLUE

You found a recording of Alec Trevallion selling you out to the conspiracy. Spend for a free Interpersonal Push when you confront Trevallion.

CONTINUITY CARDS

Where an Edge or Problem sets up a story situation that would break fictional credibility if it were ignored in future scenarios, mark it as a Continuity card by placing a sub-header to that effect under the title.

Unlike other Edges and Problems, the player does not discard Continuity cards at the end of a scenario.

If you are only running one scenario, you can safely ignore the Continuity tag.

CLUE CARDS

If a piece of information is really important, but isn't going to pay off for some time, make it an Edge (or a Problem, if you want to make the player apprehensive about what they may find). Keep in mind two things:

- Make sure there's a way for the player to get the clue that doesn't rely on rolling dice. GUMSHOE promises there's always a way to solve the mystery, regardless of the player's luck with the dice.
- Ensure the player doesn't discard the Clue card before it pays off.
- A Clue card can also have mechanical effects.

DESIGNING PROBLEMS

Problems make the player feel threatened, or force them to overcome adversity. They can be repercussions for failure ("*You try to stab the vampire, but it smashes the stake and breaks your hand*") or justifications for the player succeeding despite a bad roll ("*You manage to escape the pack of wolves by scaling a tree, but one of them claws your leg as you climb*").

In any scenario, you'll need about twice as many Problems as Edges. Most Challenges allow the player to take on an Extra Problem in exchange for an extra die roll. Customize Problems to the operation and Challenges associated with them, instead of relying on generic Problems. (That said, it's a good idea to have a few generic ones on hand in case you need to improvise a Challenge on the fly – there's a selection of generic Problems on p. 258).

Start with a few lines of flavor text, reinforcing the themes of horror and paranoia, and also suggest the sorts of story developments the player might try to introduce in order to Counter them. Requiring the player to Take Time is always a good fallback, as it opens up the possibility of some nice Blowback.

Common types of Problem include:

Consequences: These describe a development in the story without putting it in terms of explicit mechanical effects. Both GM and player can suggest ways that these consequences might come into play, allowing for more improvisation and creative interpretation in the course of play. Too many freeform consequences make the game feel flimsy and unfocused; save consequences for when you can't see another problem type that's an obvious fit, or when a situation is so fluid that you can't predict how it's likely to turn out. For example, if you've got a scene where the player's trying to persuade a crime

boss to switch sides, the consequences could be "You owe the boss a favor in return," "The boss' goons beat you up," "You're allowed to leave, but you're not welcome here again, and can't use Interpersonal Pushes on members of the crime syndicate," or any of a dozen other possible Outcomes.

Blowback: Blowback Problems warn the player that trouble's on the way (see *Blowback*, p. 86). If the player can get rid of this Problem before the trouble hits, then the blowback's averted. Usually, this means the player must be cautious of Taking Time while holding a Blowback Problem.

Injuries: The Agent's wounded. In action thrillers, the protagonist can usually survive any number of kicks, punches, cuts, and bruises, but getting shot or stabbed is much more serious (literally – Serious Injuries require the player to Take Time for Medical Attention). Reserve potentially crippling injuries for the most significant or climactic Challenges.

Injuries are a special category of Problem, so include the Injury keyword on any Injury cards.

In GUMSHOE One-2-One, the player doesn't have hit points or a Health Score. The penalties from Injury cards may stack, but a player may hold any number of Injury cards and keep going. Injury only threatens death if the Injury card specifically says this (see *Dooms*, below).

Heat: Heat (p. 46) represents mounting tension – the police closing in, the conspiracy mustering its forces, the player's growing paranoia. Like Injury, Heat is a keyword and has mechanical meaning (it penalizes Cover and Network tests).

Individual Heat Problems usually don't come with an explicit added penalty – they're purely flavor text describing the tightening noose of the authorities or the conspiracy. If it's appropriate to the story, of course, a Heat Problem could have other consequences, such as preventing a player from using Interpersonal Pushes (criminals won't talk to you while the police are on your tail).

Every so often, run a Heat Challenge like those on p. 116, where the number of Heat cards in the player's hand affects the difficulty.

Heat can be countered by Taking Time to discard Heat, moving from city to city, or by developments in the story ("*You convince the chief of police that you're the innocent victim of circumstances; discard a Heat Problem.*").

Shadow: Shadow (p. 50) measures the growing awareness of the player's presence on the part of the vampire; it's the supernatural equivalent of Heat, and forces the player to employ occult countermeasures like garlic to avoid Blowback. Rising Shadow can also impel the player to learn more about the particular supernatural threat in this operation.

Shadow Problems are a good avenue for the GM to add spooky atmosphere, as they boil down to "creepy signs and portents implying the presence of vampires."

Trust: Problems can degrade the relationship between the player and her Contacts. For one-shot Contacts who show up in only one operation, then a Problem might make them suspicious until it's Countered. ("*Miheva knows you murdered her brother. Counter this by providing proof he was a vampire.*") Problems that affect the player's long-term relationship with recurring Contacts are usually phrased as impending dooms. ("*If you've still got this Problem at the end of the operation, Rathclyde loses faith in you.*")

Penalties: A penalty makes it harder for the player to succeed in tests. A penalty is usually a -2 modifier applied to one (or more!) of the categories of General abilities:

♦ **Physical:** Most injuries penalize physical abilities; it's hard to run, climb, or fight when you've been hurt. Drugs or restraints (manacles) also impair Physical ability tests.

♦ **Manual:** Injuries to the hands or eyes are the usual cause of Manual ability penalties.

♦ **Mental:** Shock, mental trauma, emotional distress, or exhaustion can hit Mental abilities.

◆ **Social:** Social abilities might be penalized by shock or emotional damage, but they can also be impaired by cosmetic problems. It's hard to blend in using Cover when you're wearing blood-stained clothing.

For a bigger penalty, remove one of the dice from a player's ability.

Levies: Levies require the player to spend an extra Push in a particular situation. Usually, this refers to Interpersonal Pushes and applies to a particular individual or group – if Dr. Tollen doesn't trust you, you might have to spend an extra Push when trying to persuade her with **Reassurance** to let you see her notes on blood diseases. Levies can apply to any Investigative ability, though – for example, if **Cryptography** is needed to decode an ancient book and the book gets damaged, it could impose a **Cryptography** levy to get the information.

Blocks: Blocking Problems prevent the player from taking a particular action until the Problem's resolved. They can be nuisances that prevent the player from tackling bigger issues, like an Injury card (*"Blood in your eyes"*) that imposes no penalty to tests, but has to be Countered before any other Injuries can be removed. They can be more serious complications that restrict the player's actions – for example, if the player's been disarmed, then she can't make Shooting tests until she obtains a gun.

Dooms: Doom Problems shape the ending of the story, usually in a negative way. If the player's still holding the card at the end of the operation, bad things happen. Dooms can result in death (*"You've been poisoned – if you haven't found a cure by the end of the operation, you're dead"*) or other terrible consequences (*"The vampire has kidnapped Lena, and will turn her into an undead unless you stop him"*). Dooms should always describe how to Counter them.

Most Serious Injuries are Dooms.

IMPROVISATION

The GUMSHOE One-2-One system uses cards, Challenges, and highly detailed scenarios to offload as much cognitive work as possible from the Director. However, we can't anticipate everything, and players always go in unexpected directions. If the player goes go off-piste, here's how to keep the game running smoothly.

Loop Back When You Can: Look for ways to get back to your pre-prepared material as smoothly as possible. If you expected the player to sneak into the nightclub and covertly interrogate the gang boss, and the player instead follows the gang boss to his apartment, just move the interrogation scene to the apartment instead.

Reskin Challenges: Take a look at the Problems and Edges associated with a Challenge, and see if they can easily be repurposed. For example, if sneaking into the nightclub with an Advance gives the Edge "Party Animal," but a Setback results in a brief brawl with the bouncer and the Injury "Bruised," then you could easily replace that Cover test with a Surveillance test, and reskin the Setback as the Agent slipping off a rooftop and getting bruised that way instead. The Edge isn't as obviously germane, so replace it with some other benefit instead (like a free Push that can only be used when interrogating the gang boss).

Keep the pre-printed cards in mind when reskinning a Challenge, or creating a new Challenge entirely. Only create new cards when you have to. If there's a way to use an existing card, do so.

Remember, also, that an Advance or Setback doesn't necessarily require an associated Edge or Problem. You can keep things moving by handing out conditional Pushes, refreshes, or bonus dice.

Create New Cards: Most types of Problems can easily be created on the fly. Injury, Shadow, or Heat cards don't need added mechanics or rules. Blowback Problems are effectively a note to yourself as Director to throw in trouble the next time the player Takes Time. The one sort of Problem that requires thought are plot-related Problems and complications – only create one of these if you have an idea of how the complication might be resolved later in the game.

Edges require a little more thought. Often, you can use Edges to nudge the player towards a particular course of action. If you want the player to go to a nightclub, then an Edge that gives a bonus in social situations can prompt the player to seek out social challenges...

Continuity is Your Friend: When in doubt, write "Continuity" on a card and work out how it all fits together *after* the game. Both the espionage and vampire-horror genres are full of mysteries, ambiguities, and delayed revelations. The confusing plot hole in session one of your game can become the mystery to be investigated in session four...

CONTACTS AND PATRONS

In a game where the player is mostly alone against a vast conspiracy, meetings with Contacts are one of the few times when the player can talk about their suspicions and fears, plan future moves, and seek insight on their situation. Contacts come in two flavors – established allies who recur from operation to operation, and transient Contacts who are only in play for a single operation. Let Contacts drift between these categories according to the choices of the player. If the player needs an occult expert, does she call up Fr. Loretti from "Never Say Die" (p. 149) or does she seek out some new Contact who can offer a different perspective on the supernatural?

There are also Patrons – organizations or influential allies who may be well disposed towards the player, but are not as tractable as a Contact. It's up to you as game master to play all three types of character.

PLAYING CONTACTS

The usual advice applies – come up with two or three verbal or behavioral quirks so you can memorably portray the Contact, avoid scenes where you've got to play two or more characters talking to one another (if a Contact does tag along with the player, then always let the player take the lead in conversations, or just narrate when the Contact talks to other characters instead of playing through the whole dialogue: *Rathclyde greets the lawyer, and the two quickly discuss mutual friends from Cambridge and the latest government scandal before Rathclyde explains your particular problems. The lawyer turns to you and says...*).

You also need to keep the Contact's knowledge and agenda in mind when playing, and maintain a strict firewall between what the Contact knows and thinks, and what's really going on. Make sure you don't give the player too much help, or worse yet, start solving the mystery for her. The player is the protagonist, and it's always up to her to decide what to do next. The Contact can offer advice, suggest options the player may have overlooked, and help clarify information, but cannot replace the player in any way (either in solving the mystery, or in tackling Challenges).

FAVORS

With a Push, the player can ask a Contact for assistance. A Contact can never be the one to solve the whole mystery, but the player can use the right Contact to bypass a Challenge, or at the very least grant some extra dice. Bringing along a buddy might give an extra Surveillance die in a stakeout, or set explosives for the player instead of requiring a Mechanics test, but a Contact can't be the one to sneak into a vampire lair or take out the bad guys in a firefight.

Depending on your style of play, you may include scenes where the player remotely "walks" a Contact through an action scene, or have Contacts do exciting things offscreen in support of the player. Some players even enjoy playing the chess-master, directing and manipulating their own Agents in a clandestine conflict against an unseen foe. The important thing is to avoid games where the player is a bystander, stuck listening to the heroic exploits of the GM's own darling characters.

BETRAYAL

Betrayal is the flipside of trust. It can be a devastating blow when a Contact betrays the player to the conspiracy, but it's a key trope of the espionage genre. The source might have been working for the bad guys all along, or be blackmailed or coerced into turning on the player, or fall under the hypnotic influence of a vampire. Betrayal can be a planned twist in the story, the result of Blowback (p. 86) or the consequence of the player's actions.

Possible betrayals:
- Leading the player into a trap
- Deliberately lying to the player (**Bullshit Detector** works, but only if the player actively uses it)
- Inviting a vampire into the player's safehouse
- Destroying evidence or vital equipment
- Passing on information about the player to the conspiracy
- Removing counter-vampire protections
- Eliminating or betraying other Contacts
- Reporting the player to the authorities (increasing Heat)
- Removing the player's anti-Shadow precautions

PATRONS

Patrons are larger organizations (intelligence agencies like the CIA, SIS, GRU, governments, corporations, private foundations, religious orders) or influential and well-informed individuals who know about vampires and the conspiracy, and use the player as their weapon in the shadow war against these enemies. Patrons give assignments to the player ("*go investigate this weird murder in Sicily*") and provide support and funding. They don't give information or help with the investigation unless pushed – they prefer, for their own reasons, to keep the player at arm's length.

Depending on your campaign setup, the player may start with an associated Patron, or pick one up in play.

It's possible for a Contact to be associated with a Patron, and even for the Contact and Patron to have radically different views of the player. For example, the player might be held in suspicion by the CIA, but have a Contact in the agency who believes in the vampire-hunting cause. Similarly, the Catholic Church might be neutral towards the player, but the enigmatic monsignor who handles the Church's secret inquisition might think the player is an unwanted interloper and be suspicious towards her.

SAMPLE CHALLENGES

One Challenge per General ability, plus commentary on how those abilities are likely to crop up in play. There's lots more advice on constructing Challenges and tests, and connecting them to a plot, on p. 94.

ATHLETICS

Athletics covers all manner of physical Stunts and defying danger. It's jumping, climbing, falling, chasing. It's heart-pounding action, not subtle intrusion – if you're sneaking up the side of a building, you're using Infiltration, not Athletics. Failing an Athletics Challenge usually results in an Injury or getting blocked by an obstacle.

GRAB THE LAST PARACHUTE

The plane's falling out of the sky, there's only one parachute – and you don't think the Spetsnaz assassin is interested in sharing it with you.

ATHLETICS

Advance 7+: You half-stumble, half-fall through the tumbling aircraft and grab the last parachute. The assassin's eyes widen in terror as you hurl yourself out into the infinite blue of the sky. The chute blossoms above you, and you fall gently to earth within half a mile of the original landing site.

Hold 4-6: You manage to grab the chute, but the assassin hurls himself out of the plane and wrestles with you. You fight him off and send him plummeting to his death, but you end up landing well off-course. You've got a twenty-mile trek through Siberian forests to get to the landing site.

Setback 3 or less: You're too slow – the assassin grabs the parachute and bails out first! With no other option, you throw yourself out of the plane and manage to catch up with him. The fight is brief and bloody, but in the end, you find yourself clinging to a dead man as the parachute carries you both to earth. It's a bad landing and you're more than a dozen miles away from the landing site, but at least you're alive. Gain the Problem "The Assassin's Last Words."

Extra Problem: "Bad Landing."

Stunt: Yes (**Fighting** to grab the parachute en route; **Preparedness** for your own spare chute).

PROBLEM

The Assassin's Last Words

In the instant before the life went out of his eyes, he said "Nebesnyy d'yavol" – sky devil. Was he cursing you as he died, or was there something else up there with you, drawn by bloodshed at 20,000 feet?

SHADOW

You've attracted the attention of supernatural forces. You dare not fly again until you find a way to Counter this.

PROBLEM

Bad Landing

You landed awkwardly, and twisted your ankle. It's not broken, but it slows you down.

INJURY

CONCEAL

Conceal's for hiding objects or people – and for hiding hidden things.

If finding the Labov Dossier were a core clue, then you could either dispense with this Challenge entirely, or give the player the clue regardless of the result (in which case, the roll would determine if the player finds the dossier without any problems, not whether or not she finds it at all).

SEARCHING THE HOTEL ROOM

You know that you've only got a few minutes before the police arrive, but you've got to find the documents that Nikolai hid in his hotel room.

CONCEAL

Advance 7+: You hastily turn the place over, searching every likely hiding spot. You unscrew an air vent, and there you find the dossier. Gain the Edge "The Labov Dossier."

Hold 4-6: Damn! You look everywhere, but can't find the dossier. With seconds to spare before the police arrive, you slip out of the hotel room and walk calmly down the corridor to the back stairs.

Setback 3 or less: As you search the hotel room, the door bursts open. It's the police! Detective Swierz can't be dissuaded this time – they're going to bring you down to the station for a full interrogation.

Extra Problem: "Fingerprints."

Stunt: Yes (**Disguise** to grab a bellhop's uniform and walk right through the police cordon; **Evasion** to escape in a thrilling chase).

EDGE

The Labov Dossier

Nikolai Labov's notes on the connections between the Warsaw drug rings and the vampires make a lot of wild guesses, but there's some good intel in here.

Discard for a free Push of **Criminology**, **Streetwise**, or **Traffic Analysis** when dealing with the Warsaw cartel, or else give the dossier to Detective Swierz and she'll owe you a favor.

PROBLEM

Fingerprints

You wiped down almost everything, but you still left a partial print on one door handle. If the police find it, it'll cause more trouble for you.

HEAT

COOL

Cool is used to stay in control, in both stressful situations and in the face of supernatural compulsion.

This Challenge plays with the formula; an Advance is a clear victory, but a Hold gives the player a slim chance of eking out a victory at a cost. The Problem "The Lamia's Claws" is both an Injury and Shadow Problem, giving the player a double penalty.

LURE OF THE LAMIA

"You want me," she insists, pressing herself against you. With a twist, she shucks off her jeans like a snake sheds its skin. Her breath is hot on your neck, and it's intoxicating. She's intoxicating, irresistible...

COOL

Advance 7+: You push her away, and see her for what she really is, now that she's dropped her veil of illusion. Human from the waist up, but her lower body is that of a writhing snake. You grab your gun and shoot her three times – the bullets don't kill her, but she flees, slithering out the window and vanishing into the night. You won't be fooled by her illusions again. Gain the Edge "Clear-Sighted."

Hold 4-6: The two of you fall onto the bed, caught in the coils of passion – and then, suddenly, she's got a snake's tail instead of legs, and it's wrapped around your throat! She's strangling you! Gain the Problem "The Lamia's Claws" and make a Quick **Fighting** Test to break free. On an Advance (4+), you also Advance on this Challenge. Otherwise, you suffer a Setback, but don't gain the Problem "Under Her Spell."

Setback 3 or less: You fall unconscious. Gain the Problem "Under Her Spell" and go to the scene "Kidnapped."

Extra Problem: "The Lamia's Claws."

Stunt: No.

EDGE

Clear-Sighted

You saw the true horror that the lamia keeps concealed beneath the veil of magic. You won't be fooled again.

Discard for a free Push of Bullshit Detector, or a bonus die on a Conceal or Sense Trouble test.

PROBLEM

The Claws of the Lamia

Her nails scrape your back, your neck – and then she laps at the blood. Now, she's in your head, your veins, calling to you.

INJURY, SHADOW

Keep this card as a Shadow Problem even if it's no longer operative as an Injury.

PROBLEM

Under Her Spell

You'll do anything she asks. You'll die for her.

CONTINUITY

Whenever the lamia makes a request of you, you've got to make a Quick Cool Test (8+) to resist. If you've still got this card at the end of the operation, you'll be in her thrall forever.

COVER

The various results – get straight in on an Advance, sneak in through an unpleasant route on a Hold, or have to bluff your way in on a Setback – could each lead to different Challenges, but they could equally just color the description of how the player enters the next location. Not every consequence has have mechanics and cards attached to it; emotional weight is sometimes just as important.

DISGUISED AS A GUARD

*Keep your head down. Act like you belong on this missile testing base.
Just keep walking... and then one of the officers calls you over.*

COVER

Advance 7+: He points towards a jeep. "General Niyalov's driver is sick," and he mimes drinking from a bottle, "and I can't spare any of my men. Drop whatever you're doing and bring the general up to the main assembly building, immediately!" It's a stroke of luck – you get waved past security thanks to Niyalov's presence and can drive right into the cavernous assembly building.

Hold 4-6: You manage to get a good look at the tight security around the assembly building. You spot a potential route in – there's an outflow pipe carrying chemical waste that opens onto the canal that runs through the base, so you can sneak in that way.

Setback 3 or less: One of the officers stops you. "I haven't seen you here before –what's your name? Who's your commander? Show me your papers." You don't have good answers to any of these questions – what do you do? Try and bluff, or turn and run?

Extra Problem: "They Found the Body."

Stunt: Yes (Cool).

PROBLEM

They Found the Body

When you mugged that soldier for his uniform, you hid his unconscious body in a ditch. Looks like they found him, and now they've sounded the alarm.

You'll have to fight or sneak your way out of the base after the next scene.

DRIVING

This is an example of an extended action sequence with multiple connected challenges. Remember that the player's Driving won't refresh between "Paris Car Chase" and "Final Chase" or "Wrong Way, No Turning Back" – the only way for the player to get through this sequence is by using Stunts and Extra Problems.

PARIS CAR CHASE

If the vampire cultists get away with that suitcase, it's all over. You steal a car and take off in hot pursuit.

DRIVING

Bonus: +2 if you Push Urban Survival, +2 if you've got the Edge "Borrowed Aston Martin."

Advance 7+: The first cultist car goes off a bridge into the Seine. You sideswipe the second into a traffic island on the Rue de Rivoli. Now, you do a handbrake turn around the Arc de Triomphe and close on the final car down the straight of the Avenue Charles de Gaulle. Go to the Challenge "Final Chase."

Hold 4-6: You take out one of the cultist cars, but the second blocks your route. To get around him, you end up driving the wrong way across the quays, facing oncoming high-speed traffic. Go to the Challenge "Wrong Way, No Turning Back."

Setback 3 or less: The two cultist cars block your path, and you smash into them. Go to the Challenge "Sudden Stop."

Extra Problem: "Police Chase."

Stunt: Yes (**Mechanics** to push the engine; **Shooting** to take our pursuing vehicles; **Cool** to play chicken).

◄ PROBLEM ►

Police Chase

The gendarmerie of Paris are in hot pursuit.

HEAT
If you have two or more copies of this card, then you must make a Quick Driving Test (Advance: 3 + the number of copies of this card in hand) to escape. Otherwise, you must abandon your car and Take Time to lose your pursuers in the alleyways. Discard one copy of this card at the end of each scene.

FINAL CHASE

One car left, and now it's just a question of speed.

DRIVING

Bonus: +2 if you Push **Urban Survival**.

Advance 7+: You make it look easy. A nudge sends the other car spinning out of control until it slams into a concrete crash barrier. The passenger door opens, and Cesar flops out, bloody and broken, with the suitcase still clutched in his hand. You grab it and drive off, vanishing into the Parisian traffic. Discard one Heat Problem.

Hold 4-6: You knock the other car off the road, and manage to grab the suitcase, but the police are in hot pursuit. Gain the Problem "Police Chase."

Setback 3 or less: There's no other option – you have to deliberately crash into the last cultist car in order to bring them down. Gain the Problem "Extreme Ways."

Extra Problem: "Police Chase."

Stunt: Yes (**Mechanics** to push the engine; **Shooting** to take our pursuing vehicles; **Cool** to play chicken; **Filch** to grab the suitcase).

WRONG WAY, NO TURNING BACK

DRIVING

Bonus: Burn your luck – gain +1 per Edge discarded.

Advance 7+: You weave through traffic, swerving around crashing cars and other obstacles, and emerge hot on the tail of the last car. Gain the Edge "Short Cut" and go to the Challenge "Final Chase."

Hold 4-6: You make it through the barrage of oncoming cars, suffering several near misses. Go to the Challenge "Final Chase."

Setback 3 or less: You nearly make it, but one of the cultist cars sideswipes you into the path of an oncoming truck. You manage to swerve out of the way, but smash into a wall. Go to the Challenge "Sudden Stop."

Extra Problem: "Near Miss."

Stunt: Yes (**Mechanics** to push the engine; **Shooting** to take out pursuing vehicles; **Cool** to play chicken).

SUDDEN STOP

You emerge, stunned and bloody, from the wreckage of your own car – and then duck down behind the wreck, as the cultists open fire. You've got to get out of this ambush quickly if you're going to chase down that suitcase.

FIGHTING

Advance 7+: You vault over one car, kicking the cultist in the face and grabbing his car keys in mid-air. You slip behind the wheel of one of their cars and put the pedal through the floor. Go to the Challenge "Final Chase."

Hold 4-6: You dodge and duck behind obstacles, taking out the bad guys one by one, until you're close enough to grab a car and get the hell out of there. Go to the Challenge "Final Chase," but you can't achieve better than a Hold there.

Setback 3 or less: You charge forward, slamming into the nearest cultist. You grab him and use him as a human shield – but some of his buddies fire away. One bullet punches through him and into you. Gain the Problem "Wounded" and go to the Challenge "Final Chase," but you can't achieve better than a Hold there.

Extra Problem: "Police Chase."

Stunt: Yes (**Evasion; Shooting; Driving**).

◀ PROBLEM ▶

Wounded

You've been shot in the side. Probably not lethal, but definitely painful.

INJURY

EVASION

Always get the player to describe how Pushing an Investigative ability helps in a challenge; what does it actually look like?

THE WOLVES OF BUCHAREST

A street gang under Dracula's command is at your heels.
You've got to vanish into the crowds and find a way to lose your pursuers.

EVASION

Bonus: +2 if you Push **Urban Survival**.

Penalty: -1 if you're holding 3 or more Heat Problems.

Advance 7+: You lure the last of your pursuers into an alleyway, and take him down with a sucker punch. You grab his mobile phone as you vanish. Gain the Edge "Stolen Phone."

Hold 4-6: You pull every trick out of the tradecraft manual – hopping on a train going in the opposite direction, disguising yourself, blending into crowds, taking unexpected routes – and you finally manage to lose your pursuers. You've wasted a lot of time, though – it's nearly dusk, and you don't want to be on these streets after dark.

Setback 3 or less: You make it back to your safehouse – but when you look out the window, you see a pale face on the alleyway across the street. One of them followed you back here, and as you watch, more of them show up, like a pack of wolves gathering on your doorstep. You don't have long before they storm the house.

Extra Problem: "Out for Blood."

Stunt: Yes (**Filch** to grab the phone; **Cover** to hide; **Athletics** for parkour).

EDGE

Stolen Phone

You borrowed the phone of one of the gangsters working for Dracula.

If you've got **Data Recovery** or **Electronic Surveillance**, discard this for a free Push of **Traffic Analysis** or any Interpersonal ability when dealing with the gang.

PROBLEM

Out for Blood

You hear the gang members howling with inhuman voices as they chase you. They're animals, and they want you dead.

BLOWBACK

Counter by finding a way to throw the gang off your trail.

111

FIGHTING

The free Push when interacting with Karavelov could be made into an Edge, but the assumption here is that the player will immediately interrogate the mobster.

ENTER FREELY AND OF YOUR OWN WILL (OR ELSE...)

You need to snatch a diplomat named Karavelov. He's coming out of a nightclub in ten seconds, and you need to grab him and wrestle him into your car. He's here in 3...2...

FIGHTING

Advance 7+: Textbook. You tase Karavelov's bodyguard, grab the diplomat by the arm, and fling him into the passenger seat. He's clearly terrified. You get a free Push that can be spent on **Interrogation** or **Intimidation** when dealing with Karavelov.

Hold 4-6: You tase his bodyguard, but Karavelov tries to run for it. You catch him, but you attract the attention of a pair of nightclub bouncers. You escape, but you'd better watch out if you come back this way again.

Setback 3 or less: Karavelov's bodyguard spots you, and knocks the taser out of your hand. You skirmish in the alleyway. He goes down when you slam his head into a dumpster, but Karavelov's gone. Gain the Problem "Loose Ends."

Extra Problem: "Caught on Camera."

Stunt: Yes (**Shooting** for gunplay; **Cover** to hide among the crowd; **Sense Trouble** to spot the bodyguard).

PROBLEM

Loose Ends

Karavelov's in the wind – if he makes contact with his embassy or his conspiracy allies, you're in trouble. You've got to find him soon.

BLOWBACK

Counter by finding Karavelov.

PROBLEM

Caught on Camera

There were security cameras outside the nightclub, and they may have seen you. You may need to clean things up.

HEAT

If you hold 2 or more Heat Problems, then the cops start digging deeper, and this card becomes an additional Heat Problem. Counter it by erasing the nightclub's servers.

FILCH

PLANTING THE BUG

*With a glass of champagne in one hand, you drift through the party.
You need the passcard that Von Rorich keeps in his wallet,
and the only way to get it is to steal it.*

FILCH

Advance 7+: You spot your moment – Von Rorich's talking to a beautiful woman, and he's distracted. You brush against him and slip the wallet out of his jacket pocket. Without looking at the cards, you run your fingers over them until you find the embossed logo of the bank, then flick that card into your palm. You're looking for an opportunity to put the wallet back when the woman spills her drink on Von Rorich's suit. He splutters and removes his jacket, dabbing at the red wine stain with a napkin. In the confusion, you can easily return the wallet without being seen.

The woman raises her glass and nods at you. Who is she, and why did she help you? Gain the Edge "A Mysterious Friend."

Setback 3 or less: You grab the wallet when he's not looking and quickly search through it. The passcard's missing! There's an empty slot in the wallet's card holder… and suddenly you remember Von Rorich talking to a woman at the party. She was laughing, flirting; she put her hand on his chest, inside his *jacket*. She stole the card first!

And just as you come to that realization, one of Von Rorich's security guards spots the stolen wallet in your hand. You've been set up! Gain the Problem "Framed!" and now you've got to flee the party.

Extra Problem: Von Rorich's the center of attention, so you've got to wait a long time before you spot an opening. This counts as Taking Time.

Stunt: Yes (**Cover** to blend into the party; **Sense Trouble** to spot the mysterious woman).

A Mysterious Friend
CLUE

The woman from the party at Von Rorich's helped you steal the passcard. Who is she and what does she want from you?

◄ **PROBLEM** ►

Framed
BLOWBACK

Von Rorich thinks you stole his passcard. You know it was taken by the mysterious woman from the party. You've got to find her and that card.

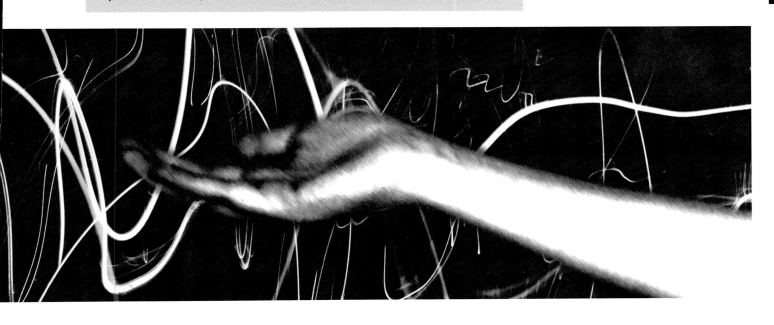

BREAKING INTO THE CASTLE

The people in the valley below insisted this castle is a ruin and that no one's lived here since before the war, and you suspect they're right – no one has lived here in a very long time. But still, you tread quietly, so as not to wake the dead...

INFILTRATION

Advance 7+: You have to use your lockpicks to get through a few padlocked doors – fresh scratches on the locks, too, where someone fumbled with a key, suggesting that there have been recent visitors before you. After a short search, you find a door that opens onto a staircase that goes down into what smells like a crypt.

You spot a flaky, pink-grey residue along the edges of the door-frame. Someone once tried to seal this door with some sort of putty. Intrigued, you put a little of the putty into a sample bag for later analysis. Gain the Edge "I Brought It from Amsterdam."

Hold 4-6: You have to use your lockpicks to get through a few padlocked doors – fresh scratches on the locks, too, where someone fumbled with a key, suggesting that there have been recent visitors before you. After a short search, you find a door that opens onto a staircase that goes down into what smells like a crypt.

Setback 3 or less: You come to a padlocked door. Fresh scratches on the lock suggests that someone fumbled with a key implying that there have been recent visitors before you. You kneel down to pick it, and your lockpick snaps in the mechanism, jamming it. If you want to move forward, you'll have to kick this door down, making a lot of noise.

Extra Problem: "Swarms of Bats."

Stunt: Yes (**Conceal** to find a hidden door; **Athletics** to climb the sheer cliff).

EDGE

I Brought It from Amsterdam
CLUE

You took a sample of the substance used to seal the vampire's crypt from the castle.

Take Time to analyze it with **Chemistry** or **Vampirology** to discover more about it.

PROBLEM

Swarms of Bats

Your intrusion into the castle disturbs the thousands of bats who nest in the ruined towers. They swirl around the mountain peak, chittering angrily at you.

SHADOW

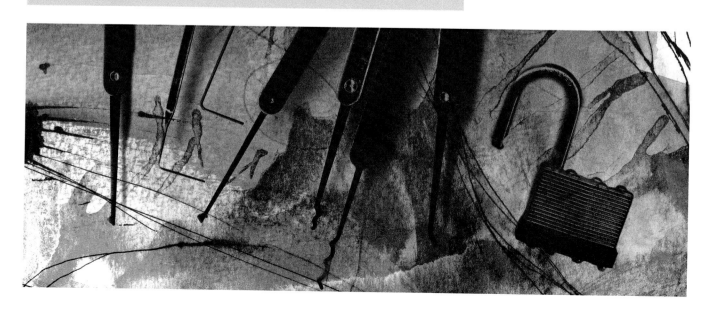

MECHANICS

REPAIRING THE ENGINE

You managed to put the Cessna down on the salt flats safely, and you think you can take off again if you can fix the engine. Otherwise, it's a long, long walk out of this desert – and if they sabotaged your engine, then you don't know if you can trust the water supply, either.

MECHANICS

Advance 7+: You find the fuel line that the saboteur cut and patch it, then check over the rest of the engine. Everything's in order, and you can take off again without problems.

Hold 4-6: Most of the fuel's gone. You patch the leak, and you think you have enough left to make it to Zâbol, but it'll be very tight – you'll have to make a Quick Piloting Test to glide it home without injury. If you fail, gain "Rough Landing."

Setback 3 or less: It's no good – the fuel pump's irreparable. You've got no choice but to walk out of here. Gain the Problem "The Merciless Desert of Dasht-e Kavir."

Extra Problem: "Rough Landing."

Stunt: Yes (**Preparedness** for spare parts and tools).

◄ PROBLEM ►

The Merciless Desert of Dasht-e Kavir

The sun beats down on you, and the salty dust clogs your mouth. You may die out here.

Push **Outdoor Survival**, or you're at -1 dice until you Take Time to Counter this card. Either way, it takes you several days to cross the desert and Zâbol.

◄ PROBLEM ►

Rough Landing

You can walk away from it, but it's not a good one.

INJURY

Any tests involving the Cessna are at -2 until you Take Time to repair it.

MEDIC

TREATING THE VAMPIRE'S VICTIM

The ragged wounds on her throat tell you all you need to know: a vampire's drained her dry. She needs a transfusion and you need to close those wounds, stat!

MEDIC

Bonus: +2 if you Push **Diagnose** or **Vampirology**.

Advance 7+: It's touch and go for a while, but you keep her alive, and her signs are stable when the paramedics arrive. Retain Hopkins' Contact card.

Hold 4-6: You do your best, but she's lost too much blood, and she slips away from you. She's gone. Discard her Contact card.

Setback 3 or less: You try, but you can't hold onto her. She's dead. The paramedics rush in and take custody of the body. Gain Problem "Blood on Her Lips."

Extra Problem: "Run Ragged."

Stunt: Yes (**Preparedness** to have a medical kit in your car).

◄ PROBLEM ►

Blood on Her Lips

Was it her blood that flecked her lips, or had he given her the baptism of blood? You won't be able to rest easy until you're sure that Hopkins won't rise again as undead.

BLOWBACK

Counter by ensuring that Hopkins can't return as a vampire.

NETWORK

This is an example of a Challenge that's best described as a montage sequence, where the player spends days or weeks scouring Europe for a quarry.

THE ELUSIVE HUNGARIAN

You need to track down the mysterious Hungarian, an investment banker and antiquarian who knows a thing or two about vampires. Unfortunately, he's infamously paranoid.

NETWORK

Bonus: +2 if you Push **High Society** or **Tradecraft**.

Penalty: -1 per Heat or Shadow Problem.

Advance 7+: You manage to make contact with the Hungarian, and track him down to an eye-wateringly expensive restaurant in Zurich. He agrees to help you – for now. Gain the Hungarian's Contact card.

Hold 4-6: You can't locate him in person, but through a mutual friend you manage to get a brief phone call with him. "You have questions," he says, "I have a modicum of answers."

Setback 3 or less: The Hungarian is, as far as you can figure, a ghost or a myth. You'll have to go to Transylvania without the Vambery papers.

Extra Problem: "In the Hungarian's Debt."

Stunt: No.

◄ PROBLEM ►

In the Hungarian's Debt

"I am comfortably wealthy," he says, "but money is not the only form of recompense. At some point in the future, I will ask a favor of you – you must promise, here and now, that you will grant it."

CONTINUITY

PREPAREDNESS

Problems like "Limited Luggage Allowance" let the GM tamp down on excessive use of this potent ability, while still letting the player pull off Stunts.

STOP THE ESCAPING HELICOPTER

Carlyle's getting away on that helicopter. Time to bring him down – if you remembered to pack a little insurance...

PREPAREDNESS

Advance 7+: Why, yes, you *do* have a rocket launcher. No more Carlyle.

Hold 4-6: By the time you get things set up, the helicopter's nearly out of range. You've got to make a Difficulty 7 **Shooting** Quick Test to hit. If you pass, Advance; if you fail, it's a Setback.

Setback 3 or less: Carlyle gets away – for now. He'll be back, and now he knows you're willing to kill him. Gain Problem "Carlyle's Revenge."

Extra Problem: "Limited Luggage Allowance."

Stunt: Yes (**Athletics** to get line of sight; **Conceal** to have stashed the launcher safely).

PROBLEM

Carlyle's Revenge

Maybe not today, maybe not tomorrow – but soon, one of you is going to die.

CONTINUITY, BLOWBACK

PROBLEM

Limited Luggage Allowance

-2 to your next **Preparedness** test, then discard.

SENSE TROUBLE

THROUGH THE ABANDONED CITY

You pursue the Renfield through the snowy, empty streets of Pripyat. Enemies could be behind any corner.

SENSE TROUBLE

Bonus: +2 if you Push **Urban Survival**.

Advance 7+: After a tense hunt, you spot your quarry climbing onto a rooftop. He's planning to ambush you, but you've got the opportunity now to turn the tables. You sneak up behind him and put your gun to the back of his head. He surrenders.

Hold 4-6: You spot the sniper an instant before he fires, and you throw yourself to the ground just in time. His shot misses, but now you're pinned down. What do you do now?

Setback 3 or less: You've been hit! You're knocked sprawling as a shot rings out. Gain the Problem "Down in the Dead City."

Extra Problem: "Ghosts of Pripyat."

Stunt: Yes (**Infiltration** to stay hidden; **Surveillance**, to watch the streets).

PROBLEM

Down in the Dead City
SERIOUS INJURY

You've been shot. If you don't get Medical Attention by the end of this operation, you'll die.

PROBLEM

Ghosts of Pripyat

As you explore the deserted city, you hear voices whispering at the edge of hearing, glimpse faces in the dust when you blink. Something's stirred up the ghosts of this city...

SHADOW

SHOOTING

Forcing the player to choose between protecting allies and having a full **Shooting** pool is a quick way to model having to shield a non-combatant in a firefight.

BLOOD UNDER THE BRIDGE

You've been ambushed by conspiracy assassins under the Pont Alexandre III Bridge in Paris. You've got to fight your way out.

SHOOTING

Bonus: +2 if you Push **Military Science**.
Penalty: -1 die if you've got any Contacts with you that you've got to protect.

Advance 7+: A literal advance – you march towards the ambushers, snapping off deadly accurate shots from your SMG whenever any of them pop their heads out of cover. Their boss, Le Croiz, tries to get away, but a burst of fire from your gun takes out his engine. Choose – either grab Le Croiz to question him, or gain the Edge "Terror of the Night."

Hold 4-6: You fall back, snapping off bursts from your gun that force the attackers to retreat. You can escape unharmed.

Setback 3 or less: They've got you pinned down, and you suspect they're trying to force you into the sewer tunnel. You can either take a hit, or else flee into the sewers. If you take the hit, gain the Problem "Shot in the Leg."

Extra Problem: "Paris Heat."

Stunt: Yes (**Sense Trouble**; **Evasion**).

118

EDGE

Terror of the Night

You turned their ambush back on them. The conspiracy's terrified of you.

Discard for a free Push or a +2 bonus in any Challenge against mortal foes in Paris.

PROBLEM

Shot in the Leg

You've been hit, and you're limping badly.

INJURY

While you hold this card, you can't Stunt with **Evasion** or **Athletics**.

PROBLEM

Paris Heat

The violent ambush drew police attention.

HEAT

SURVEILLANCE

GRAVEYARD VIGIL

You suspect there's a vampire lurking in this graveyard.
Can you spot it before it spots you?

SURVEILLANCE

Bonus: +2 if you Push **Archaeology** or **Vampirology**.

Penalty: -1 per Shadow Problem.

Advance 7+: After a chilly night spent camped in a church steeple, you spot a shadowy figure slipping into a crypt. She shrinks down, passing through the gap between door and lintel that's no wider than a knife's breadth. Vampire. Gain the Edge "No Hiding Place."

Hold 4-6: You watch the graveyard all night. Bats circle your hiding place in the steeple, and there's an unnatural chill in the air. Gain the Problem "Breath of the Vampire."

Setback 3 or less: As above, but you've been spotted. Gain the Problem "Stalked."

Extra Problem: None.

Stunt: No.

No Hiding Place

You've found the vampire's hidden coffin. You can either destroy it while she's absent, or risk trying to kill her while she sleeps by day.

Breath of the Vampire

An unholy miasma hangs over the graveyard, and the fog curls in shapes that remind you of grasping hands. Even as you leave, the unnatural cold clings to you like the smell of death.

SHADOW

Stalked

The vampire spotted you while you watched the graveyard. You're being followed.

BLOWBACK

Counter by finding a way to lose your tail.

THE HUNTRESS

Leyla Khan hunts vampires.

The life of a spy is always ambiguous. There are always lacunae, contradictions, hints of buried tragedy. The past is erased to make a blank slate on which false histories can be written.

Rewind. Go back. Trace the patterns.

Born in Beirut, the daughter of a British diplomat and a Lebanese academic. She grew up in Lebanon, then moved to the United Kingdom in her mid-teens. From an early age, it was clear that her life had a singular velocity; she excelled both academically and athletically, always driven to be the best. Even the untimely death of her father in a car accident failed to slow her down, although she did lose most of the friends she'd made as her grief made her redouble her focus on her studies. She attended Cambridge University, studying history and politics. Her tutor recommended her to MI6 recruiters, and she joined the Secret Intelligence Service four years after graduation.

After a few years, she was assigned to the Cairo station as an asset handler, under cover as an embassy attaché. She shuttled between Cairo, Prague, and London, tracing the movements of dark money and terrorist suspects across Europe. She made contacts all over the continent, and was seen as a high flyer within MI6. She made enemies, too, who envied her career or mistrusted her.

And then... Then *they* found her. The vampires. She remembers them as nightmare figures, pale horrors with lips stained red. They got inside her head, changed her memories, made her their puppet. Their agent.

And as the scars on her neck prove, even their victim.

She can only guess at what she did for them. She suspects she did terrible things; she has flashes of memories of breaking people, stealing secrets, committing bloody murder. It's like remembering a nightmare. She can only guess at what she's done over the last five years.

She was the thrall of a particular savage vampire named Jovitzo, an undead warlord who's one of the conspiracy's enforcers. She was Jovitzo's emissary and troubleshooter in his various criminal enterprises across Europe, but the details are vague.

Give the player Leyla's character sheet on p. 268.

CONVENIENT AMNESIA

Leyla remembers little of the last few years. She knows that she was forced to serve a vampire, and that she did terrible things in his service – but she doesn't recall what those things were, or what secrets she discovered, until some external factor jogs her memory. In game terms, this convenient *Bourne*-style amnesia lets the Director pass necessary information to the player ("you remember that guy – he's a banker working for the conspiracy") to move the plot along, while still keeping the game challenging and exciting ("you don't know where the money's coming from – you'll need to find a way to eavesdrop on the banker, or else kidnap and interrogate him").

KHAN'S "BLESSING"

Given her former rank in the conspiracy, it's likely that Khan was once a Sluger, a blooded servant of a vampire (p. 84). She drank the tainted blood of Jovitzo, and obtained supernatural powers of strength and speed. Presumably, this taint and its associated supernatural powers were washed away by the Rosewater Potion in *Never Say Dead* (p. 123), however, you may want to attribute part of Khan's resilience and strength to some lingering effects of this unholy gift.

If, in desperation, Khan draws on these gifts to perform some act of inhuman strength or speed, that's worth a permanent Shadow Problem.

KEY QUESTIONS

Key questions to answer about your version of Leyla:

- **Does she want back in, or does she blame MI6?** Leyla knows she was an MI6 officer before the vampires got to her. Now, she's burned – but does she want back in, or does she suspect that someone in the service betrayed her to the vampires?
- **Is everything from that missing time tainted?** While Leyla's memories of her time in the vampires' thrall are fragmented and hazy, she can recall a little. Is everything she recalls flavored with blood and ashes, or are there parts of her second shadow life that she wants to keep? Who was she when she was under the spell of the vampire?
- **Has she made contact with her family?** Do they know she's still alive? Was she in contact with them while she was Jovitzo's thrall? Are they potential Contacts? Potential victims? Can she go home again?
- **What's her moral reference point?** Leyla believes she can redeem herself – how? What convinces her that she can be saved? Is her goal revenge or redemption? What kept her together after trauma that would have shattered anyone else's sanity?

THE OPERATIONS

This book contains three sample operations for Leyla Khan.

- *Never Say Dead* (p. 123) is Khan's origin story. The action begins when she wakes up, having broken free of Jovitzo's control. Over the course of the operation, she's got to stay ahead of Jovitzo's hunters, rescue her would-be rescuers, and escape both Jovitzo and his rival, the Hungarian-line vampire Carlyle.

By the end of that mission, she's either:

- On the run from the vampires, knowing that she's still vulnerable to falling back under their control
- On the run, but armed with knowledge of a treatment, the "Rosewater Potion, that temporarily blocks vampire control. The catch – making the potion requires vampire blood, so she'll need to hunt and destroy vampires to stay free. If she survives, she may eventually earn the Sykoran Crucifix in a future mission that will give her more reliable protection.
- On the run, but in possession of the Sykoran Crucifix, which means that Rostami has confirmed Khan as the chosen weapon of the mysterious vampire hunting cabal.

The other two scenarios can be played in any order.

- *No Grave for Traitors* (p. 167) pits Khan against one of Carlyle's minions in a race to find the ghostly castle of a slumbering Romanian-line vampire.
- *The Deniable Woman* (p. 213) sends Khan to Moscow on behalf of MI6, searching for a missing spy. Her quest leads her to another attempt to recover a sleeping vampire and the legacy of a Soviet-era bioweapons program.

CONTINUING KHAN'S STORY

All three operations have plenty of loose ends and plot hooks for a Director to use in future tales. Some questions for you to consider as you craft your own operations...

- How much influence does Carlyle have in London? Has he compromised MI6? Why is he obsessed with capturing Khan? How can Khan defeat him?
- Who was Baron Vordenburg, the 19th-century vampire hunter? What became of him?
- Who was Johannes Sykora, the mysterious 16th-century alchemist who created the Rosewater Potion and the Sykoran Crucifix? How did he discover a way to thwart the occult powers of the vampires?
- Who are the vampire hunters connected with Madame Rostami? Is she the last of a small cabal, or part of a larger organization? Why have they chosen Khan as their weapon?
- What happened to Khan's family? Could they fill in her missing memories? Was she in contact with them while under Jovitzo's control? Did her former master kidnap or eliminate them?
- Why are the slumbering Romanian vampires stirring now? Has Dracula returned?

NEVER SAY DEAD

In her first mission, Leyla Khan wakes up in a hospital bed in Budapest with a gap in her memory and a bullet in her chest.
Can she escape the hunters on her trail and find out what's going on?

BACKSTORY

For the last three years, Khan's been the thrall of a vampire named Jovitzo. The monster controlled her mind and stole her life. It made her into his spy, his fixer – his assassin.

Enemies of the vampiric conspiracy – a small cell of vampire hunters, former spies and occult investigators – managed to make contact with Khan and were able to temporarily suppress Jovitzo's psychic influence using a potion. During her brief periods of free will, she was able to plan her escape from the conspiracy. The hunters warned her that while they could break Jovitzo's control, the effects would be traumatic, and that she would lose most of her memories of the last three years. Freedom, Khan decided, was worth the risk.

To break her free, the hunters supplied her with a dose of the Rosewater Potion, an alchemical elixir that temporarily disrupted the vampire's hold on her. The hunters have possession of a second relic, the Sykoran Crucifix that provides ongoing protection from vampiric influence to the wearer. The plan is for Khan to escape her captors, get clear of Jovitzo's minions, and then rendezvous with the hunters to receive the crucifix. Protecting the relic is of paramount importance to the hunters – they can try again with some other vampiric thrall like Khan, but they only have one crucifix.

Last night, Khan took the Rosewater Potion and escaped from one of Jovitzo's safehouses, a ski lodge outside Esztergom, with the intent of stealing a car, picking up her cached supplies (*The Cache*, p. 134) and rendezvousing with the vampire hunters at their safehouse.

Unfortunately, her would-be rescuers were already compromised by another vampire, a rival of Jovitzo named Carlyle. This rival vampire covets Khan, and tried to purchase her from Jovitzo. When Jovitzo refused, Carlyle decided to teach the weaker vampire a lesson by taking his prized toy away from him. When Khan broke free of Jovitzo's control, shattering her mind, Carlyle's agents eliminated most of the extraction team. Their plan is to masquerade as the vampire hunters until Khan is clear of Jovitzo's forces, and then deliver her to Carlyle. The scheme is designed to humiliate Jovitzo while still keeping Carlyle's hands clean – the other vampire will have no proof that Carlyle robbed his slave away.

Khan made into the cover of the forest, but Jovitzo, circling overhead in the form of a bat, commanded her to return. The strain of defying Jovitzo's psychic command nearly broke Khan, and left her disorientated. She made it to the main road at the base of the mountain before collapsing; fortunately, she was picked up by a passing police officer and brought to this little hospital.

OVERVIEW

To successfully complete the operation, Khan must:

♦ Evade Jovitzo's forces as they try to recapture her

♦ Evade Carlyle's forces as they try to capture her by posing as the hunters

♦ Make contact with the scattered hunters

♦ Acquire either the formula for the Rosewater Potion or the Sykoran Crucifix

♦ Escape Budapest

If she plays her cards right, she may be able to take down Jovitzo.

CAST LIST

The key characters in the operation:

THE VAMPIRES AND THEIR MINIONS

♦ **Jovitzo:** Khan's former master, Jovitzo's a vampire of the Romanian line, the old line. He's a monster, a 15th-century warlord preserved into the present day. He has little understanding of the modern world, but makes up for this with supernatural force and sheer savagery. He relies on his Slugeri, like Khan and John Sinclair, to be his interpreters and agents in dealing with outsiders.

Play Jovitzo as a feral brute. His attitudes and mindset were forged in the 15th century, and becoming a demonic serial killing monster has not improved him in the slightest.

♦ **John Sinclair:** Another of Jovitzo's Slugeri, on a par with Leyla Khan. Like her, he was recruited out of the British security establishment – 'she's former special forces. Sinclair runs Jovitzo's criminal operations in Budapest, and is in charge of the effort to recapture Khan once she goes missing.

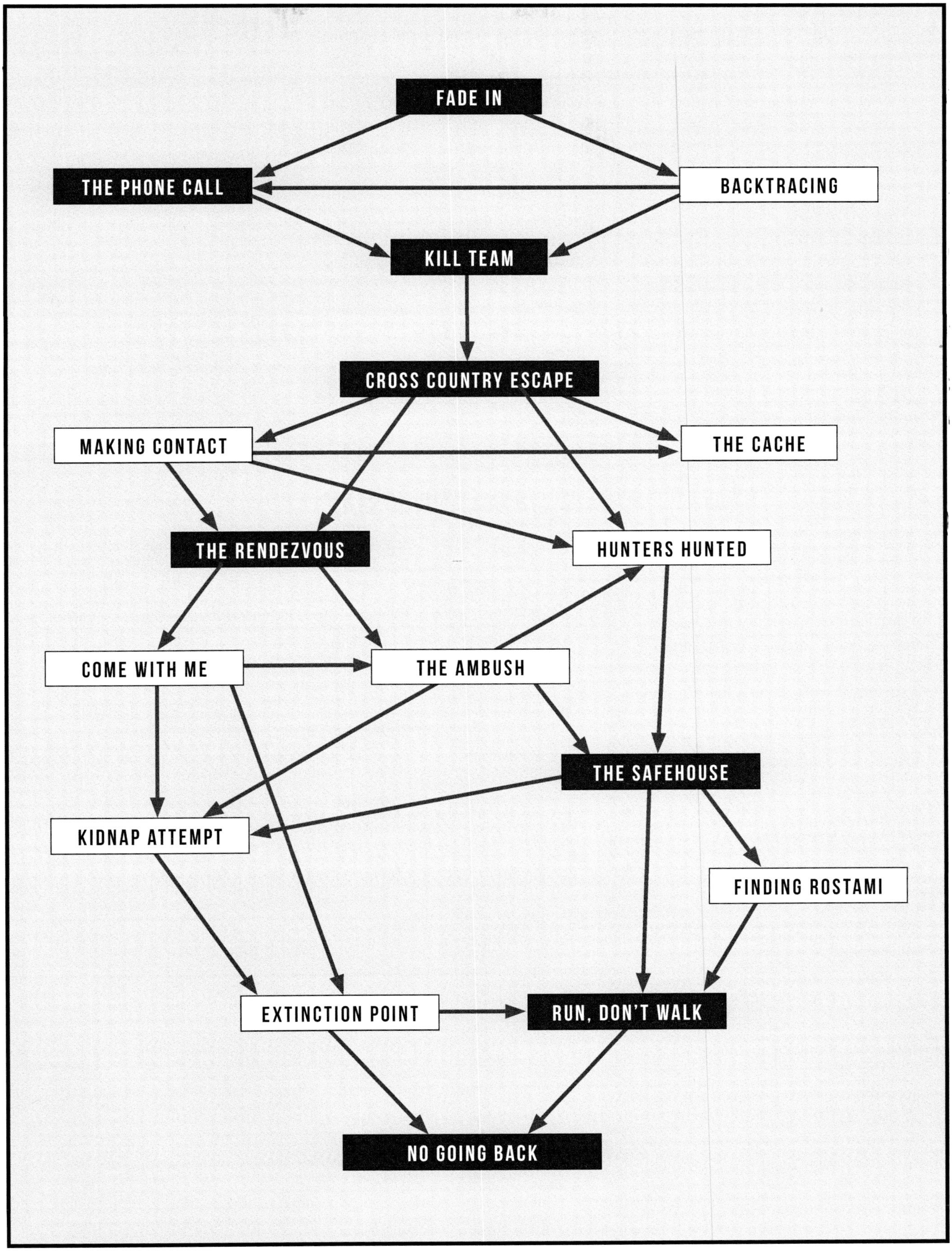
FADE IN
THE PHONE CALL
BACKTRACING
KILL TEAM
CROSS COUNTRY ESCAPE
MAKING CONTACT
THE CACHE
THE RENDEZVOUS
HUNTERS HUNTED
COME WITH ME
THE AMBUSH
THE SAFEHOUSE
KIDNAP ATTEMPT
FINDING ROSTAMI
EXTINCTION POINT
RUN, DON'T WALK
NO GOING BACK

- **Dr. Vertag:** A crooked doctor who does no-questions-asked medical procedures and treatments for Sinclair's men – he patches up bullet wounds, ensures that a cause of death other than "complete exsanguination" shows up on a death certificate and the like. At the start of the operation, Khan wakes up in his hospital.
- **Carlyle:** Jovitzo's rival Carlyle doesn't appear physically in this operation, but he's a constant presence. Carlyle's a much younger vampire of the Hungarian line; while he was born in the 18th century, he's much more adapted to the present day. Sleek and suave, he poses as a wealthy financier. He doesn't need his minions to deal with the modern world, so he recruits agents for their specialized skills instead – he has a retinue of assassins, spies, and other "useful" operatives, and Khan will be the jewel of his collection.
- **Marina Stokovitch:** One of Carlyle's Renfields, sent to secure Khan for her master. She discovered the plot to free Khan from Jovitzo, and took advantage of it by raiding the hunter's safehouse. She's on the verge of insanity – she doesn't know it, but Carlyle wants to replace her with Khan, swapping out a cracked blade for a keener, stronger one.

THE VAMPIRE SLAYERS

- **Dr. Hulier:** A biochemist, Hulier was the last of the three hunters to be recruited, and this is his first real experience with the clandestine world. He managed to recreate the long-lost Rosewater Potion from alchemical notes provided by Fr. Loretti; he hoped that would be the extent of his involvement, but the other two convinced him to accompany them to Budapest to help extract Khan. Nervous and easily led.
- **Fr. Loretti:** A Catholic priest in his mid-70s, Loretti has retired to Rome where he is a part-time curator and consultant in the Vatican library. Madame Rostami has called upon his aid many times in the past; she put him on the trail of the Rosewater Potion and the Sykoran Crucifix. Loretti believes that this operation is the last act of his life, but it will all be worth it if he can redeem Khan.
- **Madame Rostami:** A mysterious vampire hunter and occult expert, Rostami has been fighting against the conspiracy for the last two decades. She's extremely paranoid, and takes elaborate precautions to avoid falling under the sway of the undead.

OTHERS

- **Nurse Halmi:** A nurse in Dr. Vertag's hospital, Halmi is the first person Khan encounters after waking. Halmi has no idea that Vertag's in league with criminal gangs – or vampires.
- **Grigor:** A farmer living outside Budapest. His son Piotr was part of the conspiracy, and got killed by the vampires. Later, Khan hid a cache of supplies in his barn.
- **Sam Eczes:** A fixer and informant; one of Khan's few reliable allies in Budapest.

THE ROSTAMI CONNECTION

One of the three vampire hunters escaped Stokovitch's betrayal, and is now on the loose in Budapest, and she's got the vital Sykoran Crucifix. Rostami's goal is to make contact with Khan and give her the crucifix, freeing her permanently from the control of the vampires.

Rostami's attempt to make contact with Khan is a floating scene that can be dropped in at any point in the latter half of the mission.

- If the player goes to *The Rendezvous* first and then *The Safehouse*, run *Finding Rostami* after *The Safehouse* (Rostami's watching the safehouse).
- If the player goes to the safehouse first, run *Finding Rostami* after Khan visits the Cave Church in *The Rendezvous*.
- If the player gets into a dead end or no-win situation, you can have Rostami show up to rescue her.
- Alternatively, you can have Rostami follow Khan in *Kidnap Attempt*, or just have her call Khan's cell phone once she's sure that Khan is still a free agent.

While Rostami desperately wants to get the crucifix to Khan, she also wants to keep the relic out of the hands of vampires. Khan isn't the only servant of the vampires that needs saving.

Use Rostami's appearance to modulate the player's emotional response to the events so far. If the player's feeling defeated and lost, then Rostami can be played as a source of hope – she's not alone, she has allies who haven't been compromised by vampires. On the other hand, if the player's kicking ass and enjoying the thrill out of outwitting her pursuers, then position Rostami as a complication that raises the difficulty – now, Khan's got to stay ahead of the bad guys *and* get the crucifix from Rostami.

FADE IN

Scene Type: Introduction
Lead-Outs: The Phone Call,
Backtracing

The smell of disinfectant, the sound of low, muffled voices in the corridor outside, scratchy hospital sheets... Leyla wakes up in a small, private hospital room. She's got an intravenous drip in one arm, and she's got a dressing on a wound on her side (a bullet wound, from the feel of it, although she'd need to ask someone with **Forensic Pathology** to be certain), but appears otherwise uninjured.

Give the player Problem 1, "Beaten Up." Remind the player that she can get rid of the card by Taking Time here and resting. If she does, run *Backtracing*.

There's no one else in the room, although there is a call bell.

◆ The voices outside are speaking Hungarian. A woman – a nurse, maybe – says that "the hiker" is still unconscious, and that Dr. Vertag will examine her soon.

Outside, through the window, she can see a mountain valley: there's a small town near the hospital, and beyond it are thickly forested hills and mountains. It's late afternoon; the descending sun sends long shadows creeping across the hillsides like crawling fingers. Something about the sight tells Leyla that she's in Hungary.

SEARCHING THE ROOM

Hauling herself out of bed (remind the player that she needs to Take Time to get rid of that pesky Problem card), Leyla can quickly search the little hotel room. She's dressed in a hospital gown, but hanging in a wardrobe are more suitable clothes – mostly hiking gear. A wealthy tourist, who got lost through the woods and hills?

◆ **Notice:** Her shirt has been recently resewn, and there are scratches and missing teeth on the zipper of the jacket. Something – a big animal? – attacked her.

◆ The clothing is all new, but not brand-new, and is a little scuffed and stained.

◆ It's all in her size. The pockets, though, are empty.

At the foot of the wardrobe, next to a pair of hiking boots, is a small backpack. Inside there's another change of clothes, and a mobile phone (core clue).

◆ **Tradecraft:** Cheaply bought disposable burner phone. No numbers, no text messages.

◆ The phone is locked with a six-digit passcode, but Khan recalls the number instantly.

◆ The phone has an electronic note on it. It gives the address of a church in Budapest. See *The Phone Call* if the player examines the phone or tries calling the number. The address is Edge 1, The Church.

Give the player Problem 2, "Running on Empty."

THE NURSE

After a few minutes (or if the player tries to leave, or presses the call button), a young woman in a nurse's uniform arrives. She tuts if Leyla is out of bed, and encourages her to lie down and relax. She starts off talking in Hungarian (if Leyla pretends not to speak Hungarian, the nurse tries what little English and German she can muster with the help of her smartphone). The nurse introduces herself as Magdalena Halmi, and insists that Leyla wait for Dr. Vertag to examine her before exerting herself. Halmi explains the following:

◆ The local police found Leyla by the side of the road last night, and brought her to the hospital. She was unconscious.

◆ They learned her name from her passport, which Halmi claims is in Leyla's backpack. If it's discovered to be missing, Halmi guesses that Dr. Vertag took it to check on her status with the police. **Bullshit Detector** confirms that the nurse is telling the truth, as far as she understands it – she's not trying to hide anything from Khan.

◆ Halmi tells Khan that she's in a private hospital in Esztergom, about fifty kilometers outside Budapest. The police assumed she was a hiker in the hills who got lost and confused – is that so, asks Halmi, watching Leyla carefully. She's probing for the real story about how Leyla arrived here. (Halmi's assumption is that there's more to the situation than is immediately apparent – drugs, maybe, or was she thrown out of a car after an argument?)

BAD MEMORIES

When a cloud passes in front of the sun, or at some other suitably dramatic moment, give Leyla Problem 3, "The Dark Call," and call for a **Cool** test from Leyla.

Advance 9+: You're assailed by a flood of confusing memories. The bitter taste of blood, running through the woods, something swooping down from above, shrieking. With an effort of will, you fight it off – gain Edge 2, "No Turning Back."

Hold 4-8: You're beset by strange, fragmented images of pain and darkness, but manage to ride out the flashback. You're left chilled and shaking, but unhurt.

Setback 3 or less: There's something out there in the darkness, calling to you. You feel an overwhelming compulsion to *obey*, to heed this terrible command from your *master*. Gain Problem 4, "Sleepwalking."

Extra Problem: You lose your hold on sanity for a moment, and the shadows around you seem all too real. Describe how you overreacted violently and disturbed everyone around you, and gain Problem 5, "We Should Sedate Her." Run *Backtracing* even if the player doesn't Take Time.

Stunt: No.

RECRUITING HALMI

The innocent nurse could be convinced to help Khan when things get dangerous. If Khan wants to turn Halmi into a Contact, she needs to do *two* of the following:

◆ Push a suitable Interpersonal ability, like **Reassurance**, and roleplay out how she wins Halmi's trust.
◆ Expose Dr. Vertag's treachery in *Backtracing*.
◆ Protect Halmi during *Kill Team* (p. 130).
◆ Make *another* Interpersonal Push during *Cross Country Escape* (p. 133) to persuade Halmi to flee with her.
◆ If recruited, give the player Halmi's Contact card.

THE PHONE CALL

Scene Type: Core
Lead-Ins: Fade In
Lead-Outs: Kill Team

If Khan hasn't found the burner phone in her bag yet, she's alerted to its presence when it starts ringing. When she answers, though (or checks voicemail), all she hears is thumps, grunts, and heavy breathing – it sounds like two people fighting for possession of the handset. Then there's a gunshot, and the phone goes dead. A few seconds later, it chimes as a text message arrives. "THEYRE AFTER YOU. GET TO CHURCH ASAP."

Searching the phone turns up the one other text message: a message listing the address of a church in Budapest. If the player doesn't have it already, gain Edge 1, "The Church."

CALLING BACK

There's no answer if Khan tries calling back.

Electronic Surveillance could trace the other phone – if Khan had access to the cell phone network computers, or some highly specialized equipment, neither of which are available right now.

THEY'RE HERE

If Khan hasn't Taken Time, then she's got a few minutes to get moving before the *Kill Team* arrives. She sees a trio of black cars coming down the road towards the hospital, moving at speed.

If she Took Time already, then she hears the squeal of brakes as the cars pull up outside the hospital and the *Kill Team* goons pile out. Run *Kill Team* immediately.

If the player doesn't have it already, give Problem 2, "Running on Empty."

HOW MUCH DOES KHAN REMEMBER?

Khan's memories are conveniently vague. She knows that she's in danger, and that there's something horrible out there looking for her, but that's all. As Director, you should feed the player extra information as needed to keep the game going smoothly. If the player's too trusting of Vertag, or doesn't run when the kill team show up, feed her cues in the form of recovered memories. If the player hides or hesitates, remind her that she's got a clue pointing to the church in Budapest.

BACKTRACING

Scene Type: Alternate
Lead-Ins: Fade In
Lead-Outs: The Phone Call, Kill Team

The doctor overseeing Khan's case is Dr. Herman Vertag. He's crooked, and in league with the conspiracy – he's treated some of their members in the past, when they needed to falsify medical records or avoid attracting the attention of the police. When Khan showed up in his hospital, Vertag called his contacts in the conspiracy and was ordered to keep Khan there until their kill team arrived.

Vertag enters the adventure if:
- Khan Takes Time (he comes in to examine/sedate her).
- Khan goes looking for Vertag to recover her belongings or to question him.
- Khan causes a disturbance (say, because of Problem 5, "We Should Sedate Her" or Problem 4, "Sleepwalking").
- You want to throw in an extra Problem on the way out of the hospital.

DOCTOR VERTAG

Vertag is an ambling, bear-like man with a bushy beard and sleepy eyes. He gives the appearance of gentleness, but it's disguise, not anything genuine – he's quietly greedy and ambitious, an easy mark for the conspiracy. When Khan ended up in his care, he removed her personal belongings from her bag and drugged her to keep her unconscious. His plan is to keep sedating her until the kill team shows up.

Vertag's account of events mirrors that of Nurse Halmi – Khan was found unconscious on the road, the police brought her here, and he took her passport so he could contact her family. **Bullshit Detector** goes off like a siren; it's the way he keeps shuffling closer, like he's only talking until he can get his syringe full of Propofol to Khan's IV line. Time for a **Sense Trouble** challenge! Substitute **Fighting** if Khan's up and moving when she confronts Vertag.

VERTAG'S NEEDLE

SENSE TROUBLE

Advance 7+: You grab Vertag's hand as he jabs the needle towards you, and disarm him (describe how). Gain either Edge 3 "Time for Some Answers" or Edge 4, "Syringe Full of Propofol."

Hold 4-6: You knock the syringe out of the doctor's hand, preventing him from sedating you.

Setback 3 or less: Vertag lunges at you with the syringe. You manage to deflect him, but he slams you into a wall. Gain Problem 6, "Slammed."

Stunt: Yes (**Fighting** to grab the syringe with brute force; **Filch** to snatch it).

Taking out Vertag isn't hard – have the player describe how Khan subdues him. Segue into *Kill Team* once she's dealt with Vertag by having the bad guys arrive outside the hospital (or run *The Phone Call* first if you haven't played through that scene already).

Khan's stolen property is concealed in Vertag's office down the corridor from her private room. She can either force Vertag to hand it over, or find with **Notice**. Inside his desk drawer is a small wad of cash (mostly euros, some dollars), her (illegal and unlicensed) handgun and a few spare clips, and a few other non-specific bits and pieces (which will get defined later on through the use of **Preparedness** – enough to counter Problem 2, "Running on Empty.")

If compelled to talk (with an **Intimidation** Push), Vertag admits the following:

♦ He's worked with a criminal group before – patching up injured members, off-the-books medical procedures and the like. He doesn't know who they are, but his main contact there is a man called Sinclair. When Khan hears that name, give her Edge 4, "Memories of Sinclair."

♦ When Khan ended up here, he called Sinclair, and was ordered to keep Khan prisoner until Sinclair arrived. Sinclair's coming here now.

♦ He doesn't know anything about vampires or the supernatural, although he's seen things he can't explain – patients dying of blood loss after multiple transfusions, strange chills and whispering shadows in the hallways, break-ins at the morgue.

KILL TEAM

Scene Type: Core
Lead-Ins: The Phone Call,
Backtracing
Lead-Outs: Cross Country Escape

The situation – Khan's in a small private hospital, and there are three cars' worth of bad guys outside.

The hospital is four stories tall, and Khan's on the top floor. It's early evening, so the hospital's getting ready for the night shift. There aren't many other patients (mostly older patients recuperating, or younger wealthy patients in for cosmetic or other elective procedures), and a few staff members and visitors.

The bad guys – led by John Sinclair – are here to recapture Leyla Khan, and to kill her if they can't. They believe that she's still unconscious and sedated upstairs, and all they need to do is walk in, grab her, and walk out again. Four goons head upstairs to collect Khan, another four secure the obvious exits from the hospital, and the rest (including Sinclair) wait in their cars with the engines running.

Urban Survival gives the best exit route – get down to the ground floor, escape out the lightly guarded service entrance, and steal a car. In game terms, that's a series of linked Challenges – an **Evasion** Challenge to escape pursuers, a **Fighting** Challenge to fight past the guys at the door, and a **Mechanics** Challenge to hotwire a car. Adapt the order of the Challenges to reflect the player's decisions. An aggressive player might want to take down some of the goons so she can interrogate them or steal their car; a cautious player might prefer to use **Infiltration** to sneak through the hospital without being seen, and then **Filch** the keys to an ambulance.

If Khan wants to take Nurse Halmi with her, then that's a -1 die penalty to any Challenge where Khan has to keep Halmi safe.

GETTING OUT OF THE HOSPITAL

EVASION

Bonus: If you haven't Taken Time yet, you can use **Infiltration** dice as **Evasion** dice in this Challenge.

Advance 9+: You make it down to the exit without being spotted. You've got a bonus die on your next Challenge in this sequence.

Hold 4-8: You make it down to the exit without being spotted, but they're searching the hospital for you.

Setback 3 or less: "She's here! She's here!" Shit. They're right on top of you. You've got a one-die penalty on your next Challenge in this sequence as a bunch of bad guys join the fray.

Extra Problem: Problem 7, "Still Woozy."

Stunt: Yes (**Athletics** to leap down a stairwell; **Fighting** to sucker-punch a guard; **Cover** or **Filch** to grab a white coat and disguise yourself as a doctor).

BACKDOOR GOON FIGHT

FIGHTING

If you've got a gun, you can take him out with a gunshot and automatically Hold, but you gain Problem 8, "Messy Exit."

Advance 9+: You beat the crap out of the goon guarding the back door. Pick one – either you overhear him reporting in via radio, and recognize the voice on the other end to gain Edge 5, "Memories of Sinclair," or else you grab him and can interrogate him.

Hold 4-8: You have a knock-down fight in the hospital's service entrance, amid the dumpster bins and cleaning equipment. At the end, the goons are unconscious at your feet, and you're limping towards the exit.

Setback 3 or less: Making it into the car park isn't an option – your only chance is scramble over the fence at the back of the hospital and try escaping cross country. Gain Problem 9, "Alone in the Dark."

Extra Problem: Problem 10, "Bruised."

Stunt: Yes (**Athletics** for some dramatic jumping; **Mechanics** to clobber him with an improvised weapon; **Infiltration** to take him by surprise).

STEALING A CAR
MECHANICS

If you've turned Halmi into a Contact, then an Interpersonal Push lets you persuade her to drive you out of the hospital and automatically Advance. Alternatively, if you've **Filched** the keys to an ambulance or pushed Vertag into handing over his car, you automatically Hold.

Bonus: If the player has the "Grand Theft Auto" Mastery, it's an automatic Advance.

Advance 9+: You quickly identify an unlocked car, slide into the driver's seat, and hotwire it. You make it as far as the side gate of the car park before they spot you. You gun the engine and catch one of the other cars with a glancing blow, sending it into a spin while you race out onto the main road. In your rear-view mirror you catch a glimpse of a familiar face – gain Edge 5, "Memories of Sinclair." If you already have that Edge, gain Edge 6, "Momentum."

Hold 4-8: You manage to steal a car and get clear of the hospital, but the bad guys are in hot pursuit. You can lose them on the road, but they'll be close behind all the way to Budapest.

Setback 3 or less: You're trying to hotwire a car when more bad guys show up. Bullets shatter the windshield, forcing you to duck, scramble out a side door, and vanish into the woods. Gain Problem 9, "Alone in the Dark."

Extra Problem: None.

Stunt: Yes (**Filch**; **Driving**).

RUNNING ACTION SCENES

When playing though thriller challenges like these, the key to making a compelling experience for the player is to marry description to the dice rolls. First, review the Challenge's possible Outcomes: what happens on an Advance? On a Hold? On a Setback? Then have the player roll the dice *one at a time*, and use the roll's result and the possible Outcomes as a guide. Describe the results of additional dice garnered through Edges, Extra Problems, or Stunts as surprising reversals.

For example, in "Getting Out of the Hospital," the possible Outcomes are (Advance) sneaking out without being seen, (Hold) escaping, but bad guys are close behind or (Setback) bad guys attack Khan and it's a fight scene. The player rolls her first **Evasion** die and it's a 2 – not a great result, and on track for a Setback. You describe how Khan's moving through the hospital when she sees an elevator door open, disgorging a trio of bad guys. She manages to duck down behind a desk to hide, but they'll find her in a few seconds – what does she do? The player rolls her second **Evasion** die, and gets... a 1. Still in Setback territory. The player describes how Khan sneaks around the desk and makes it to a stairwell, but there are more bad guys coming up the stairs – she's trapped!

The player considers her options. There's that Extra Problem on offer, but that might be a long-term drag on her chances. She goes for a Stunt instead, and uses two **Athletics** dice to get a single **Evasion** die. Khan jumps from bannister to bannister down the stairs, parkouring down the stairwell past the shocked goons. That bonus die rolls a 3 – enough to get her into Hold, but not Advance.

The player agrees to take the Extra Problem, and describes how Khan stumbles at the bottom of the stairwell, suddenly dizzy and nauseous. The hospital spins around her; the shouts of the bad guys are momentarily drowned out by the rushing noise of blood in her ears as she begins to black out. To focus, she smashes the glass and sounds a fire alarm. Panicked staff and patients pour into the stairwell, slowing the bad guys down and giving her a chance to vanish into the maze of corridors and small rooms in the hospital basement. She rolls a 5 on her final die, earning an Advance in the end.

CAR CHASE
DRIVING

Advance 9+: You knock one of the pursuing cars off the road into a tree. Gain Edge 7, "Attrition."

Hold 4-8: You manage to lose your pursuers on the twisting back roads. You're clear of them – for now.

Setback 3 or less: One of the cars chasing you smashes into the back of your vehicle, nearly forcing you off the road. You manage to break free, but your rear axle's damaged. This car isn't going to last much longer – you'll need to dump it and Take Time to get to Budapest.

Extra Problem: None.

Stunt: Yes (**Shooting** to take out tires; **Mechanics** to push engine).

I'VE GOT A BAD FEELING ABOUT THIS
SENSE TROUBLE

Penalty: -1 per Shadow Problem.

Advance 10+: You spot a shape circling overhead – a tremendous bat. The wound in your side suddenly aches. The monster's out there, looking for you. You don't know why you do it, but you twist the wheel hard, heading down a side road. The moonlight glimmers off a small stream, and you bring the car to a sudden halt in the middle of the bridge over the water. Surrounded by flowing water... and the bat wheels overhead without stopping, then vanishes into the clouds. Gain Edge 8, "Flowing Water."

Hold 4-9: You spot a shape circling overhead – a tremendous bat – and know instinctively that it's something immensely dangerous. You need to get out of sight, *now*. Either dump the car and hide in the forest, gaining Problem 12, "Pursued into the Woods," or else gain Problem 4, "Sleepwalking."

Setback 3 or less: The thing in the sky suddenly wheels and dives, vanishing behind the treeline. You feel cold phantasmal fingers run over your skin, and shiver. Gain Problem 4, "Sleepwalking."

Extra Problem: Problem 12, "Shaken."

Stunt: No.

CROSS COUNTRY ESCAPE

Scene Type: Core
Lead-Ins: Kill Team
Lead-Outs: The Rendezvous, The Cache, Making Contact, Hunters Hunted

By this point, Khan's escaped from the hospital. It's less than an hour's drive to Budapest from the hospital in Esztergom, but it's already twilight when she escapes, so night falls en route. If the bad guys are right behind her, then run the optional *Car Chase* Challenge.

The kill team sent to the hospital isn't the only danger out there. Khan's former master, Jovitzo, is also abroad tonight, in the form of a gigantic bat.

Run "Attack of the Bat" at a suitably shocking moment. Before that, though, give Khan a moment to catch her breath. The drive to Budapest is a good time to take stock.

TAKE A BREATH

Her primary lead – her current core clue – is the address of the church in Budapest, Edge 1, "The Church." Heading there is covered in *The Rendezvous*.

Other possible routes of investigation:

♦ If she's got Edge 5, "Memories of Sinclair," then she can try confronting her former ally at his apartment in Budapest. That's covered in *Hunters Hunted*, p. 146.

♦ Suggest to the player that she could use her **Network** ability to recall a relatively dependable ally in Budapest she could rely on. For that, see *Making Contact*, p. 136.

♦ Offer a trade – if the player takes Problem 12, "Shaken," then she has a sudden memory-flash – she planted a cache of weapons and documents in an old farm outbuilding near here. She can collect these buried supplies in *The Cache*. (If the player has the Preparedness Mastery card "Cache," then she gets that benefit for free without having to take "Shaken.")

Use the night drive to Budapest as a chance to let the player roleplay a little. How does Khan feel? Her memories of the last three years aren't so much incomplete as exploded, like a bomb went off in her mind and everything's got psychic shrapnel embedded in it. The sight of the car headlights reflecting off a puddle reminds her of a pool of blood on the floor of a sauna in Hamburg – whose blood? Why Hamburg? What was she doing there? The answers might be there, somewhere in her head, but all connections and context are lost.

Is she still the person she was last night? The person she was three years ago? She can't really tell.

If Khan's accompanied by Nurse Halmi/Vertag with a gun to his head/ some other unfortunate who got dragged into it, use that character to prompt the player with questions. What does Khan want? What does she expect to find at the church? Who called her? What happened to her?

If Khan's on her own, then ask the player to reflect on Khan's inner emotions. How does she feel now?

ATTACK OF THE BAT

Just as the player relaxes, hit her with this **Driving** Challenge. Jovitzo's goal here is to stop his prized plaything from escaping, not to recapture her personally. He won't shapeshift out of his giant bat form.

▰▰▰▰▰▰

THE CACHE

Scene Type: Alternate
Lead-Ins: Cross Country Escape, Making Contact
Lead-Outs: Making Contact

If Khan recalls it, she buried a cache of supplies in the countryside near Budapest. The cache is hidden in the barn of an old farmhouse; she bribed the farmer to let her conceal the supplies there. The old farmer, Grigor, is a widower in his 70s; the farm is a tumbledown ruin for the most part, surrounded by crumbling outbuildings and empty fields. He still keeps plenty of chickens and pigs – and a pair of aging but still fierce wolfhounds. The dogs recognize Khan's scent if she

approaches the farm openly, and won't attack as long as she doesn't provoke them by heading straight to the barn. (Alternatively, **Outdoor Survival** lets her sneak past them without being scented.)

TALKING TO GRIGOR

The old man is obviously nervous when talking to Khan. He wears a crucifix on a silver chain around his neck, and is careful to take it out and hang it over his heart when she arrives. He's clearly used to dealing in her old identity as a minion of the vampires; she can play on that with **Intimidation** and force his compliance, or **Reassure** him that she's not who she used to be. In either case, Grigor can reveal the following:

♦ His son Piotr got involved with "your people" many years ago. Grigor nearly disowned him, but he loved the boy and wanted to make sure that he could always return home.

♦ Piotr's new friends used the farm for their illegal activities. They'd hide things here, and strangers would collect them. Drugs, he assumes. He knew better than to ask questions. There are old stories about what happens to those who cross… *them.*

♦ Over time, Piotr came to the farm less and less, but the strangers kept coming. Not many – two or three a year, maybe. Khan was one of them. She was colder then… something has changed about her.

♦ He hasn't heard from Piotr in over a year. He thinks his son must be dead. He didn't come to his wife's funeral, but that was six years ago.

♦ Two weeks ago, she came to the farm in the dead of night. It wasn't the usual arrangement; she was in a hurry, and told him not to say that she'd been there to anyone. There was a strange smell on her breath – like roses – and she looked unwell.

▰▰▰▰▰▰▰▰▰▰

BAT OUT OF HELL

A dark shape swoops out of the sky. You glimpse leathery wings, claws, and glowing red eyes, and then it's right on top of you.

DRIVING

Penalty: -1 per Shadow Problem.

Advance 9+: You swerve around the creature and drive the pedal through the floor. Nothing in your rear-view mirror – but the bastard's a vampire, so you dodge hard to the right, and the bat-thing swoops past you again, barely missing. It shrieks in frustration, then flaps hard and climbs back into the sky. It's gone for now.

Hold 4-8: The bat-thing rakes the side of your car. You manage to keep the car on the road, but it tears deep rents in the doors and smashes the windows. You can get to the outskirts of Budapest, but then you've got to dump this car and find a different mode of transport.

Setback 3 or less: The bat-thing slams into your car, knocking you off the road. You fight for control, but it's too late, and you smash head-on into a concrete bollard. You black out for an instant as you slam into the steering wheel. Gain Problem 14, "Car Crash."

Extra Problem: If there's anyone else in the car, then the vampire bat pulls them out through the broken window and flies off into the night. Gain Problem 15, "Abducted." Otherwise, gain Problem 16, "Clawed."

Stunt: Yes (**Cool** to resist the vampire's influence; **Shooting** to drive it away).

♦ On that last visit, there was a man with her; Grigor's dogs didn't like him, and he stayed in his expensive car instead of following Khan into the barn. He recalls Khan referring to him as "Eczes." Give the player Edge 9, "Memories of Eczes."

If invited into the rundown little farmhouse, full of broken furniture and dusty memories, Khan spots a photograph of Piotr above the fireplace. It triggers a flashback in her – give her Edge 10, "Memories of Piotr."

With a suitable Interpersonal Push, Khan can make Grigor into a Contact and obtain some basic assistance from him. He can provide Medical Attention (**Notice** spots a well-stocked first aid box), or offer the loan of his rusty but still functional old Suzuki Swift. He's also got a well-maintained pair of shotguns, and his dogs will see off any intruders.

SUPPLIES

Hidden in the barn in a shallow grave is a bundle wrapped in a waterproof plastic sheet. Inside is:

♦ A handgun and several clips of ammunition.

♦ A sheaf of passports – different names, but all with Khan's picture.

♦ Cash, in various currencies and denominations.

♦ Medical supplies, including painkillers.

♦ Some other non-specific gear for use with Preparedness.

♦ A rugged thermos flask.

♦ A photograph – very, very old, dating back to the 1920s. It's damaged and faded, but Khan can still make out the image of a crucifix of some sort.

The supplies are enough to Counter Problem 2, "Running on Empty."

THE FLASK

The flask contains a clear liquid that smells strongly of rosewater, but tastes acrid and horrible. It's a potion that blocks vampiric influence for a short period, provided by the vampire slayers who helped rescue Khan from Jovitzo's control. The flask is more than half-empty. Give the player Edge 11, "The Rosewater Flask."

There's a sticker on the side of the flask, which looks like it was once a tracking barcode, of the sort used in medical laboratories; it's partially torn, but a string of digits and the letters "HUL" can be read (foreshadowing Dr. Hulier in *The Rendezvous*, p. 138).

THE CRUCIFIX

A close examination of the photograph discovers the following:

♦ The crucifix looks to be made of metal (probably silver). It's finely made; definitely an antique.

♦ There's what appears to be a glass vial built into the crucifix. There's something in the glass, but the photograph isn't detailed enough to determine what it is.

♦ The crucifix rests on a cushion. The photograph looks staged, like a museum exhibit.

Khan lacks relevant Investigative abilities (**Art History**, **History**, **Occult Studies**) to discover more about the crucifix. She'll need to use her **Network** ability to find an expert to consult with; if she does so, see *Making Contact*.

— APPROACH WITH CAUTION —

If the player tries to gather info in Budapest before heading to a particular location, or tries a stealthy approach, run this scene. Only run "Approach with Caution" once; if the player tries a cautious approach again, improvise your own Challenge based on this sequence, offering the chance to acquire extra information at the risk of some other danger (perhaps drawn from the list of Blowback, p. 159).

MEAN STREETS OF BUDAPEST
SURVEILLANCE

Bonus: +2 if you Push **Streetwise**.

Penalty: -1 per Heat card in your hand.

Advance 9+: You spot several familiar faces on the streets – men working for Jovitzo the vampire, probably coordinated by his lieutenant Sinclair. You manage to stay out of sight for now, but the noose is tightening. Gain Edge 5, "Memories of Sinclair" or Edge 6, "Momentum," your choice.

Hold 4-8: You can sense a tension in the city; dark forces are abroad tonight. Right now, though, you seem to be under their radar.

Setback 3 or less: You manage to stay out of trouble, but the danger's getting closer. Problem 26, "Dragnet."

Extra Problem: Problem 28, "Something in the Sky."

Stunt: Yes (**Conceal** to hide from surveillance).

MAKING CONTACT

Scene Type: Alternate
Lead-Ins: Cross-Country Escape,
The Cache
Lead-Outs: The Rendezvous, The
Cache, Hunters Hunted

As she approaches Budapest, Khan finds she recalls the city intimately. She's spent months here. She knows all its streets and hidden places. She knows how to survive here, how to move about without being seen.

She knows people here. Most of those memories feel like they're covered in glass, as if it was a different person who experienced them, but there are a few where she still recalls some human connection. Sam Eczes is one of those; he's a crook and informant, always involved in one dodgy deal or another, but at least he's utterly and unrepentantly human. He might be a useful ally to approach.

Locating Eczes requires a **Network** test.

SAM ECZES

Sam Eczes is in his mid-40s; he still acts and dresses like he's a shark, young and predatory, but his suits aren't as sharp as they used to be, and his face is fatter and redder than it once was. He smokes furiously, and has the habit of jabbing the lit end of the cigarette towards people when making a point.

He's known Khan for several years; he was an informant of hers back when she was working for MI6, and continued in this capacity when she became a thrall of the vampires. He may have noticed a shift in her behavior when the vampires took control of her mind, but Eczes is nothing if not morally flexible as long as there's easy money to be made.

FINDING SAM ECZES
NETWORK

Bonus: +2 if you've got Edge 9, "Memories of Eczes."

Penalty: -1 per Heat card in your hand.

Advance 7+: You track Eczes down in his favorite bar, a swanky cocktail place. Describe how you get him out of trouble by arriving at just the right moment, then gain him as a Contact and have a free Push when dealing with him.

Hold 4-6: You find Eczes' phone number and track him down. He looks warily at you, like he knows you're bringing trouble to him. Gain him as a Contact.

Setback 3 or less: Eczes has gone to ground. You can find him, but it means Taking Time to chase up leads and other mutual contacts. If you do Take Time, gain him as a Contact.

Extra Problem: Gain Problem 17, "Hunted."

Stunt: No.

When interacting with Eczes, ask the player if she wants to reveal that she's no longer under the vampire's control, or if she wants to pretend that nothing's changed. Eczes works with her either way.

If she needs help, an Interpersonal Push is enough to convince Eczes to take Khan back to his apartment (he's been flirting with her for years, to no avail, and at this point it's more of a running joke than anything else).

Questioning him get the following information:

♦ He's known Khan for years. She first showed up asking about... what was his name, that banker who was laundering money for the Turkish mob? Ack, no matter, he turned up dead in a hotel room in Dubai long ago.

♦ He knows that Khan was... associated with the British government, and that her... association later changed to another group. Throughout, he continued to be of use to her, passing on this and that – little rumors, little secrets.

♦ A few weeks ago, he noticed her acting oddly. There were all sorts of rumors in the underworld of some sort of power shift, of some individuals rising in stature while others were about to be thrown down. Everyone was on edge, as though the city could sense the tension. He knew better than to ask questions, but he could tell there was some sort of strife between Khan and another of her associates, a Mr.... Sinclair, isn't it? That Englishman with the shiny head and the unpleasant attitude.

◊ Give Khan Edge 4, "Memories of Sinclair." This can lead into *Hunters Hunted,* p. 146.

♦ Around the same time, in his... professional capacity, he saw huge transfers of money through anonymous, discrete channels.

◊ If Khan asks about this, give her Edge 12, "The Eczes Papers."

♦ Two weeks ago, she asked him to drive her out to some filthy little farm in the middle of nowhere. He's no spy, but she was trying to avoid being followed, which is why she took his car instead of driving herself. He recalls the address of the farm (it's where *The Cache*, p. 134, is).

DR. GILBAN

If Khan found the cache, then she may wish to learn more about the photograph of the crucifix. She could do her own digging with **Research**, but that would take time, and it's always more interesting to play a clue-finding scene as a conversation instead of the GM reading out text. The expert Khan finds with **Network** is Dr. Gilban, an antiquarian and dealer in rare religious artifacts.

Unless the player wants to make a Push, Gilban isn't a full-fledged Contact – his role in the adventure is just to satisfy the player's curiosity about the photo and foreshadow the importance of the crucifix.

Gilban tells Leyla:

♦ He's heard of the crucifix in the photo; it's a religious relic made in Prague, in the 16th century, by an alchemist named Sykora.

♦ As far as he knows, the crucifix ended up in some Vatican museum.

♦ According to legend, Sykora was murdered after he discovered the fountain of eternal youth.

FINDING DR. GILBAN
NETWORK

Penalty: -1 per Heat card in your hand.

Advance 9+: You find a reputable dealer in antiques named Dr. Gilban, and he's willing to help you.

Hold 4-8: You find a dealer in antiques named Dr. Gilban, but he's suspicious and brusque. You'll need to make an Interpersonal Push of some sort to get information out of him.

Setback 3 or less: You find a dealer in antiques named Dr. Gilban, but he's suspicious and brusque. You'll need to make an Interpersonal Push of some sort to get information out of him. Also, Gilban's on Sinclair's payroll, and reports his contact with Khan once she leaves his little shop; throw an episode of Blowback at the player after this scene.

Extra Problem: None.

Stunt: No.

THE RENDEZVOUS

Scene Type: Core
Lead-Ins: Cross Country Escape
Lead-Outs: The Ambush, Come With Me

— NO LEVERAGE —

If Khan's already been to *The Safehouse*, then she knows that Stokovitch is lying to Hulier – Fr. Loretti is already dead. If she wishes, she can remove Stovovitch's hold over Hulier by revealing that he can't save Loretti even if he betrays Khan.

The rendezvous point given in Khan's phone is that of a famous church in the heart of Budapest, the Gellért Hill Cave – an underground chapel in a cave network on the banks of the Danube. The church was used as a field hospital during the Second World War, and sealed up during the Soviet occupation; today, it's back under the control of the Pauline monks who first established it.

In the original plan, Khan was supposed to come here after escaping Jovitzo's control with the Rosewater Potion; the slayers and their Pauline allies would then help her disappear and bring her to safety. Now that the original extraction plan has been subverted by Carlyle's forces, they intend to wait here for her, then bring her to Carlyle instead of to safety.

The huge iron gate at the front of the church is locked (assuming Khan arrives after dark; if she waits until daytime, the church has a few tourists wandering around), but there's someone waiting behind the gate with a key. He's an old grey-bearded monk, Brother Adolpho – one of the Pauline monks who tend to the chapel, not one of the vampire slayers. He knows that they deal with supernatural matters, but has no knowledge of vampires or the conspiracy. All he knows is that a woman matching Khan's description will come to the church tonight, possibly in confusion or distress.

As Khan enters the church, she feels a momentary sense of relief. Give her Edge 18, "Holy Ground."

When he sees Khan, he beckons her over and unlocks the gate. "This way," he tells her, "your friends are waiting." He shows her through a small side door in the chapel, closing it hastily behind him, and gestures to a heavy jacket hanging on a peg.

If Khan hesitates, Adolpho tries to reassure her; he was warned that she might be confused. "Upstairs. Mr. Hulier is waiting for. You know him, yes?" (Khan has no memories of a "Hulier," other than a sudden memory-flash of him pressing the Rosewater Flask (p. 135) into her hands). If she flees, segue right into *The Ambush*, p. 141.

The monk leads Khan through several more tunnels carved into the hillside, lit by old electrical lights screwed into the ceiling, then shows her into a small room, oddly homey in this underground catacomb. There's a battered old couch, a few rickety chairs, a once-elegant table, and several paintings and icons depicting Christian saints. Waiting there is a middle-aged man, thin and nervous, with thick glasses.

DR. JEAN HULIER

Hulier's one of the trio of would-be vampire slayers who helped rescue Khan. Now, he's under the thumb of Carlyle's agent Stokovitch. The assassin has captured the other two slayers, and will execute them if he betrays her. His instructions are to bring Khan out through the caves to Stokovitch. He's wearing a wire, so she can listen in on the conversation from outside the monastery.

Put yourself in Hulier's place for a moment before running this scene. You tried to be a hero, you tried to fight the vampires, and you even found a way to free the vampires' victims from their unholy brainwashing. The first time you tried to use this new method, though, it all went horribly wrong, and now your friends will die if you don't deliver Khan into Stokovitch's clutches.

If the player stalls for too long in this conversation, move onto *The Ambush*, p. 141. Otherwise, if the player follows Hulier out through the caves to Stokovitch, run *Come With Me*, p. 140.

Hulier greets Khan and says they only have a few minutes before they need to move. No doubt she has questions – the aftereffects of "absolution" must be very confusing. He reveals the following.

- His name is Jean Hulier; he's a biochemist.
- There are dark forces – the *Linea Dracul* – who have reigned from the shadows throughout the centuries, and he is part of a small group of people who oppose these monsters.
- Khan fell under the sway of one of these monsters, a vampire named Jovitzo. Vampires can mesmerize victims, force them to obey – and if they make you drink their blood, you become one of their creatures, bound to them. That's what happened to Khan; Jovitzo coveted her talents as a spy and turned her into his servant.
- Hulier and his friends discovered a way to undo this unholy baptism, to free a victim of the vampires from

their control. They chose Khan because they thought she would be best able to survive the process, and to fight back against the vampires once they freed her.

♦ Hulier's role was recreating a medieval alchemical formula that could break the spell. He believes that Fr. Loretti dug the formula up in the archive; he doesn't know how the others found Khan.

  o Offer an opportunity to Push **Bullshit Detector** at this point; if the player agrees, mention that she thinks that Hulier is being especially evasive on this point. There's something else he's not mentioning here, something he's trying to hide – not from Khan, but from someone else. Someone's listening in. The player can then use **Electronic Surveillance** to spot that Hulier's wearing a wire.

♦ Hulier's allies in this are Fr. Loretti, a priest, and Rostami, an occult expert.

♦ The plan is to extract Khan from Budapest before Jovitzo's minions recapture her. Hulier has... friends who are coming soon to bring her to the airport, once they are sure they are clear of any pursuers. They have a way to protect her from the vampires.

♦ If they are separated, Khan must go to the private airfield at Tököl. Give the player Problem 18, "The Extraction Point."

Throughout the conversation, play Hulier as nervous and jittery; let the player see that he's under duress.

If the player picks up on what's going on, offer a **Cool** Challenge if she wants to try bluffing through the conversation without alerting whoever's listening in. If she doesn't, move onto *Come With Me*.

♦ **Tradecraft (core clue):** Hulier reveals the location of *The Safehouse* (p. 149) if given a pen and paper or some other way of communicating covertly. Give the player Edge 13, "The Safehouse."

KEEP TALKING AND NOBODY DIES

Hulier's wearing a wire. Someone's listening in.

COOL

Bonus: +2 if you Push **Reassurance**.

Advance 7+: You keep Hulier calm, and keep your own voice under control. No one suspects a thing. Gain Edge 14, "Impending Sucker Punch" and move onto *Come With Me*.

Hold 4-6: You keep Hulier talking, but you can tell he's losing it – and so can whoever's on the other end of that wire. Move onto *Come With Me*.

Setback 3 or less: Hulier snaps. He tears off the wire and shouts, *"It's a trap! They got Loretti!"* Gain Problem 19, "Sitting Ducks."

Extra Problem: None.

Stunt: No.

SAVING HULIER

The most likely fate for Hulier is that he gets killed in a shootout, either by Stokovitch or by Jovitzo's minions when they attack the church in *The Ambush* (p. 141). If the player's absolutely determined to keep Hulier alive, and is willing to take a -1 die penalty in any Challenges in order to protect him, then give the player Hulier's Contact card. After escaping, Hulier can give Khan the location of the safehouse (p. 149), tell her about Rostami and the Sykoran Crucifix (*Finding Rostami*, p. 152).

COME WITH ME

Scene Type: Alternate
Lead-Ins: The Rendezvous
Lead-Outs: The Ambush, Kidnap Attempt

Stokovitch waits in the deeper caves, outside the church section. Extensive caves and catacombs run underneath Budapest, and connect to various underground cellars, tunnels, and sewers. Stokovitch remained outside the monastery to avoid stepping foot on holy ground.

There are two ways this scene might play out:

◆ If Khan doesn't suspect Stokovitch is trying to capture her, or if Khan's playing along, run with "A Friend in Dark Places." This crosses over with the events of *The Ambush*.

◆ If Stokovitch's ploy has failed, run "Murder in the Dark."

A FRIEND IN DARK PLACES

Stokovitch is a gaunt, stern-faced woman, dressed in dark clothes. She's got an earpiece in one ear; her close-cropped hair makes it easy to spot. Unlike Hulier, she's armed and is clearly comfortably with firearms. Stokovitch portrays herself as one of the slayers. "Come with me," she tells Khan, and leads her and Hulier through a maze of tunnels.

If asked, Stokovitch claims to be a former investigative journalist turned vampire slayer, and that she'll explain more once they're out of these caves.

◆ **Urban Survival:** Stokovitch must have excellent night vision; these caves are very dimly lit, and she's not carrying a flashlight.

As they hurry through the caves, they hear shouts and running feet behind

them. Stokovitch curses, exclaiming that it's Jovitzo's men, here to recapture Khan. She urges Khan to start shooting, and fires several deadly accurate shots herself at the pursuing forces.

Run the Challenge "Cave Shootout" at this point, remembering to add the bonus die for having Stokovitch on side. Regardless of how that Challenge turns out, Stokovitch leads Khan out to another exit from the cave network, bringing her to a maintenance door that opens into a narrow alleyway. There's a van waiting there, engine running, with a man behind the wheel. Lying on the ground nearby is one of the goons from the hospital, unconscious or dead – he was sent to watch this exit from the cave

network and grab Khan if she emerged, but the van driver took him out.

The driver throws the door open. "Get in," urges Stokovitch.

Move onto *Kidnap Attempt*.

MURDER IN THE DARK

If Stokovitch knows that her scheme to trap Khan has failed, then she goes to plan B – offer Khan an ultimatum, and then try to kill her if she refuses.

When Khan emerges from the Hill Cave Church into the tunnels, Stokovitch blinds her with a powerful flashlight. From the darkness, she implores Khan to listen:

◆ She introduces herself as Marina Stokovitch.
◆ Stokovitch and Khan are sisters in the blood. They both serve immortal masters.
◆ Her master Carlyle sent Stokovitch to capture her. She'd hoped to bring Khan peacefully, but that may not be possible now.
◆ So, Khan has a choice. Jovitzo's men – the ones she escaped at the hospital – are coming to recapture her. If Khan waits for them, they'll drag her back to her vampire master, and if she's *lucky*, he'll kill her for trying to escape.
◆ Her only other option is to come with Stokovitch, right now, and escape Hungary.

From the church behind her, Khan hears shouts and gunfire; the forces hunting her are closing in. She has only a moment to decide before it's time to segue into *The Ambush* (p. 141).

If Khan goes with Stokovitch now, switch to "A Friend in Dark Places."

If Khan refuses, Stokovitch spits a curse. "We could have been immortal brides, you and I!" She fires down the tunnel at Khan, then flees. Khan has a chance to dodge the hail of bullets.

After shooting at Khan, Stokovitch flees to her waiting escape van. If Khan pursues (after escaping *The Ambush*), she might be able to trace the van to the airport (*Extraction Point*).

◤◤◤◤◤◤
THE AMBUSH

Scene Type: Core
Lead-Ins: The Rendezvous
Lead-Outs: Kidnap Attempt,
Hunters Hunted, The Safehouse

Having failed to recapture Khan at the hospital, Jovitzo's forces under the command of Sinclair follow her to the Hill Cave Church. Just like at the hospital, they show up in a swarm of black cars. Most park outside the main entrance; another car circles around to watch the nearest underground exit. They know the tunnels under the city very well, and can guess at Khan's likely escape routes.

If Khan came to the church by day, and there are still tourists in the chapel, then the bad guys take a subtle approach; they sent in half-a-dozen goons, accompanied by two crooked police officers who work for

the vampires. The cops approach the monks and explain they're looking for an escaped criminal (Khan); if the monks give her up, or stall, then the goons start kicking doors in.

If Khan arrived at night, then the bad guys don't have to be so subtle. They still bring the crooked cops, but they're a lot more willing to wave guns at monks.

Either way, a short time after Khan arrives at the rendezvous, the bad guys follow her in. You can run this scene:

◆ While Khan's talking to Hulier
◆ When Khan's in the tunnels with Stokovitch
◆ When Khan tries to leave the church

Optionally, you can also set up *Finding Rostami* (p. 152) now – Khan spots a figure across the church looking up at her, and then folding a scrap of paper and sliding it into one of the charity boxes for donations of loose change. Khan can recover the note from this dead drop later in the mission and make contact with the third hunter. Spotting this with **Tradecraft** is a core clue.

SITUATIONAL AWARENESS

Two key facts

◆ There are two possible ways out. If she goes through the tunnels, it'll be a nasty running gun battle (run the "Cave Shootout" Challenge). They'll have no compunction about using lethal force when no one's watching. If she tries to leave the way she came, she may be able to sneak out, but it'll be tricky (run the "Through the Shadows" Challenge). She can try shooting her way out through the church, but she'll be exposed to fire from multiple attackers *and* there's potential for lots of civilian casualties – it's a bad plan (see "Church Shootout").
◆ There's no sign of Sinclair. Either he's outside somewhere coordinating the whole operation

---

▰▰▰▰▰▰▰▰▰
JEALOUSY ISSUES

Stokovitch sprays a hail of bullets down the tunnel towards you.

EVASION

Bonus: If you've got Edge 14, "Impending Sucker Punch,", you've got a bonus die in this challenge.

Advance 9+: You duck back into the church and hide. Stokovitch's gunfire attracts the attention of the hunters pursuing you. Gain Edge 6, "Momentum."

Hold 6-8: You're forced to take cover behind a rocky wall as bullets ricochet around you. Stokovitch vanishes in the chaos, and now you've got bad guys coming close behind you.

Setback 5 or less: You're hit! Gain Problem 20, "Bleeding Out."

Extra Problem: Problem 21, "Lights Out."

Stunt: Yes (**Shooting** to fire back; **Conceal** to hide).

– or he's not here, which means there's something else going on tonight, something that's even more important than capturing Khan.

CAVE SHOOTOUT

Sinclair's men are on your heels. You've got to shoot your way out of these caves.

SHOOTING

Bonus: Bonus die if you're working with Stokovitch.

Advance 11+: In these narrow corridors, it's a killing field. They can't get close to you. Gain either Edge 6, "Momentum," or Edge 7, "Attrition," as you escape the caves.

Hold 7-10: They're close behind you, but you lay down a hail of suppressive fire, forcing them to drop back. You take the opportunity to run like hell.

Setback 6 or less: You stumble out of the caves, clutching your side. Gain Problem 20, "Bleeding Out."

Extra Problem: Problem 22, "Blue Lights on the Danube."

Stunt: Yes (**Athletics**; **Evasion**).

THROUGH THE SHADOWS

The shadowy nooks and corners of the monastery provide plenty of hiding places. Maybe you can sneak out of here without being seen.

INFILTRATION

Advance 9+: You sneak out of the monastery like a ghost, and vanish into the streets of Budapest without being seen. Describe how you evade the bad guys.

Hold 6-8: You manage to make it out of the monastery, but you're spotted outside. Go to the Challenge "Run Like Hell."

Setback 5 or less: You're spotted. There's no way out of this without bloodshed. Pick your poison – "Cave Shootout" or "Church Shootout."

Extra Problem: You've got to dart across open ground – you'll be at -4 to the next Challenge in this sequence.

Stunt: Yes (**Evasion** to run like hell; **Fighting** to silently mug a goon; **Athletics** for acrobatic climbing).

CHURCH SHOOTOUT

This is going to be horribly messy.

SHOOTING

Advance 11+: It's a ballet of gunfire. They never expected you to turn on them, and they fall back, giving you a chance to escape the church. Gain Problem 22, "Blue Lights on the Danube," Edge 15, "Angel of Judgement" and go to the "Run Like Hell" Challenge.

Hold 7-10: You make down to the floor of the church, snapping shots at your foes from behind the cover of pews and icons. The floor's slick with blood. Gain Problem 22, "Blue Lights on the Danube," Problem 23, "Out of Ammo" and go to the "Run Like Hell" Challenge.

Setback 6 or less: You're hit! Gain Problem 20, "Bleeding Out." And now the bad news – as you're lying there on the floor of the church, strong hands grab you and drag you into the shadows. Gain Problem 24 "Captured" and go to the scene *Kidnap Attempt* as Stokovitch grabs you.

Extra Problem: Problem 25, "Collateral Damage."

Stunt: Yes (**Evasion** to dodge; **Infiltration** to get into a good firing position; **Preparedness** for a grenade).

RUN LIKE HELL

You've made it out of the church, but you've still got to vanish before you're recaptured.

EVASION

Advance 9+: They're right on your heels – and then they turn a corner, and you're gone. Describe how you disappeared, and gain Edge 6, "Momentum."

Hold 4-8: You've got only one change to escape – and that's over the parapet. You dive into the black waters of the Danube. Bullets cut through the water around you, but you manage to swim clear and hide beneath the stanchions of the Liberty Bridge.

Setback 3 or less: You think you're clear of your pursuers, when a black van comes out of nowhere and knocks you down. Gain Problem 24, "Captured" and go to the scene *Kidnap Attempt*.

Extra Problem: Problem 22, "Blue Lights on the Danube."

Stunt: Yes (**Athletics** for parkour; **Driving** to steal a car or moped and escape).

KNOW YOUR ENEMY

The city's crawling with Sinclair's agents and hunters. You can pick them out of the crowd by the way they move, the way they scan the crowds. They're looking for you – but you've got the upper hand. Follow them, and you'll find out what they want.

SURVEILLANCE

Bonus: +2 if you Push **Urban Survival** or **Streetwise**.

Advance 11+: You're able to follow your pursuers without being seen. Gain Edge 16, "Lie of the Land," and clues pointing towards either Sinclair's apartment (*Hunters Hunted*, p. 146) or an anonymous house in the city (*The Safehouse*, p. 149).

Hold 7-10: By the skin of your teeth, you manage to keep your pursuers in sight while staying hidden. You get a glimpse of them vanishing into a building. It's either Sinclair's apartment (*Hunters Hunted*, p. 146) or an anonymous house in the city (*The Safehouse*, p. 149).

Setback 6 or less: Suddenly, police cars flood the street with blue light. You've been spotted. You manage to get off the street, but they're on your trail. Gain Problem 26, "Dragnet."

Extra Problem: Problem 27, "Something in the Sky."

Stunt: Yes (**Cover** to disguise yourself; **Driving** to tail using a stolen car; **Conceal** to hide).

If Khan escapes, then most of her pursuers keep sweeping the streets around the church for her (**Cop Talk** or **Streetwise**: it's clear that the bad guys are working with the Budapest street cops, but *not* the counterterrorist TEK special forces), but two groups head off across the city.

If Khan has Edge 13, "The Safehouse," she can head there (*The Safehouse*, p. 149).

If she's got Edge 5, "Memories of Sinclair," she can try visiting Sinclair's home (*Hunters Hunted*, p. 146).

Alternatively, she can try using **Surveillance** to track her pursuers (the "Know Your Enemy" Challenge in the sidebar). She could look for an ally (*Making Contact*, p. 136).

KIDNAP ATTEMPT

Scene Type: Alternate
Lead-Ins: The Ambush
Lead-Outs: The Safehouse, Extraction Point

Stokovitch's mission is to extract Khan and bring her to the airport. Her plan is to lure Khan to the cave church, playing along with the slayers' original scheme to free Khan from the vampire's control. If she can, she'll trick Khan into accompanying her into the van and drive her to the airport (*Extraction Point*, p. 154).

Here's how this plays out if Hulier's with Khan:

- If Khan complies and gets into the van, then they take off at speed, racing through the streets. Hulier stares out the window in growing panic as he realizes that they're not going to rescue the other hunter, Loretti. He cracks after a few minutes, shouting "It's a trap! He's dead! He's dead" and throwing himself at Stokovitch. She shoots him in the face; his blood splatters Khan.

- If Khan refuses to get in or hesitates, then Stokovitch shoots Hulier and drags Khan into the van at gunpoint.

If Hulier's not with her, and Khan gets in, then describe the van racing through the streets of Budapest.

TURNING THE TABLES

Even if Khan manages to get the jump on Stokovitch, she's still in the back of a van that's racing at high speed towards the airport at Tököl. If she's got Problem 29, "Unsafe at Any Speed," then the van's about to crash – she can have a brief interaction with Stokovitch

KIDNAP ATTEMPT

Stokovitch grins at you, and her teeth gleam.
"You too will be a bride of my master," she hisses, as the van races through the dark streets of Budapest. You've got to get out of here – but you can feel the inhuman strength in her grip. This isn't going to be easy.

FIGHTING

Bonus: If you've got Edge 13, "Impending Sucker Punch," you've got a bonus die in this Challenge.

Advance 11+: You slam your elbow into Stokovitch's face, stunning her. You grab her gun. She flings you against the roof of the van, but you hold on to the firearm – and she might be inhumanly strong, but she's not bulletproof. Go to "Turning the Tables," p. 144.

Hold 7-10: You wait until the van takes a sharp corner, throwing Stokovitch off balance, and then leap at her. You wrestle for the gun – it goes off, twice, shattering the windows of the van. She's incredibly – inhumanly – strong, and forces the gun out of your grip. You throw yourself out the door of the van, slamming into the road at high speed, but you're out and alive. Gain Problem 27, "Roadkill."

Setback 6 or less: You try to struggle, but it's too late. Someone grabs you from behind and everything goes dark. Gain Problem 24, "Captured" and move onto *Extraction Point.*

Extra Problem: Problem 29, "Unsafe at Any Speed."

Stunt: Yes (**Filch** for the element of surprise; **Shooting** to grab the gun).

before the collision, or sacrifice that opportunity in order to stabilize the hurtling vehicle and avoid a crash. Otherwise, she gets to interrogate Stokovitch, and then demand that they let her out (alternatively, Khan can execute Stokovitch and the driver if she wants to clean up loose ends).

Stokovitch admits the following at gunpoint:

- She's like Khan. They both serve immortal masters. Stokovitch's master is Carlyle, and he wishes to have Khan as his servant – perhaps even one of his immortal brides, if she proves worthy of eternity.
- Khan was a thrall of the vampire Jovitzo.
- There's no escape once you've undergone the baptism of blood. Khan may have temporarily broken free of her master's influence, but she'll fall back under his spell. Hulier

and the others are fools – they thought they could free Khan from her bond to Jovitzo, but the vampire will reclaim her soon.

◊ **Bullshit Detector:** Stokovitch *really* wants to believe that, but she might be lying to herself. There's a little too much force in her denial.

- Khan can't be free – but she can change masters. Jovitzo is a monstrous brute, and he will not forgive her attempt at escape. Carlyle is a far more powerful and noble vampire. Join Stokovitch, and they shall be blood sisters under Carlyle!
- Waiting at the airport is a plane that will take them out of Budapest. They have to get out of Jovitzo's reach – if he finds them, he'll kill Stokovitch and suborn Khan. She won't be able to fight it; her only hope is to find shelter with Carlyle.

With **Intimidation**, she admits:

♦ Carlyle's agents discovered the plan by the slayers (Hulier, Loretti, Rostami). Stokovitch hijacked their plan – they originally intended to smuggle her out through the church, too, but Stokovitch captured Loretti and forced Hulier to lie to Khan.

♦ The third hunter, Rostami, escaped. Stokovitch doesn't think she'll get far.

♦ She gives the location of *The Safehouse*, p. 149 (core clue).

♦ She insists that her plan to escape Budapest is the only viable one; if Khan remains in the city, or tries to escape on her own, then Jovitzo will certainly find her.

If Khan agrees to go with Stokovitch, then move onto *Extraction Point*, p. 154. If the van crashes or if Khan flees into the night, then she needs to work out another way to escape Jovitzo's domain.

Run this challenge if the player picks up Problem 29, "Unsafe at Any Speed."
The Problem remains as a Heat card even if the van doesn't crash.

VAN CRASH

Stokovitch's black van careens through heavy traffic along the Rákóczi Bridge,
pursued by a police car – and then it clips a car and goes into a spin.

ATHLETICS

Advance 10+: The van smashes through the railings and plunges into the dark flowing waters of the Danube. You wrestle free and swim out through a broken window, dragging yourself onto the bank near an industrial estate. Gain Edge 14, "Survivor."

Hold 4–9: The van smashes into an obstacle and crashes violently. You're mostly unhurt – the driver's unconscious, maybe dead. You stumble out and vanish into the night. There's no sign of Stokovitch.

Setback 3 or less: The van crashes head-on, and you're thrown through the windshield. Gain Problem 30, "Crash Victim."

Extra Problem: Problem 31, "Person of Interest."

Stunt: Yes (**Driving** to steer the van).

◤◤◤◤◤◤ HUNTERS HUNTED

Scene Type: Alternate
Lead-Ins: Kill Team, Making Contact
Lead-Outs: The Safehouse

Sinclair – Jovitzo's man in Budapest, Khan's local counterpart – has an apartment in the center of the city. If Khan has Edge 5, "Memories of Sinclair," then she recalls not only its address, but also spending time there: Sinclair uses the apartment as a safehouse for other servants of their vampiric monster, Jovitzo. She can also guess (**Tradecraft**) that if Sinclair's men are searching the city for her, Sinclair will be running the hunt from the apartment.

The apartment is in a rough part of the city; it's luxurious inside, but the exterior is run-down and unpromising.

SURVEILLANCE

Watching the apartment (no need for a **Surveillance** test) spots the following:

♦ If Khan came here right after arriving in town, then she sees Sinclair arrive in the company of the survivors from the raid on the hospital.

♦ Some of those goons leave shortly afterwards; Khan can trail them to *The Safehouse* (p. 149) if she wishes.

♦ Later, more of them head out to the Cave Church to carry out *The Ambush* (p. 141).

♦ If the player doesn't have it already, give the player Problem 28, "Something in the Sky," as she spots something – a gigantic bat, perhaps – fly out of the apartment and flap up towards the clouds. The sight of this creature warrants a **Cool** test.

NOCTURNAL VISITORS

As the dark-winged thing circles the building, you feel a horrible call towards the monster.

COOL

Bonus: If the player pushes **Notice**, Khan spots a church across from the building. Give her Edge 17, "Holy Ground."

Penalty: -1 per Shadow Problem.

Advance 9+: You dig deep and find the steel in your soul. That monster isn't going to reclaim you. Your mouth tastes of rosewater and ashes. Gain Edge 2, "No Going Back."

Hold 4-8: You fight the vampire's hypnotic compulsion. For an instant, you want to step out onto the street and reveal yourself to the creature; describe how you overcome that unnatural urge.

Setback 3 or less: You desperately fight the urge to reveal yourself to the vampire. It seems to sense your presence, and banks around the building as if searching for you. You've got to get out of here! Choose another lead to follow, or retreat and Take Time before returning to this location.

Extra Problem: You spot two men leaving Sinclair's building, and they look like plainclothes cops to you. Gain Problem 26, "Dragnet."

Stunt: No.

BREAKING INTO THE APARTMENT

Sinclair's apartment building is clearly being used as the base of operations for the manhunt targeting you. Getting in isn't going to be easy.

INFILTRATION

Bonus: Edge 7, "Attrition," definitely applies here.

Advance 9+: You make it into Sinclair's apartment, and you can interrogate him. Describe how you got the drop on him.

Hold 6-8: You make it into the apartment, but Sinclair's waiting for you with a gun in his hand. Gain Problem 32, "The Drop."

Setback 5 or less: You're discovered as you try to sneak in, and things get messy. Gain Problem 32, "The Drop," and Problem 33, "Bloody Carnage."

Extra Problem: Problem 34, "A Trail to Follow."

Stunt: Yes (**Shooting** or **Fighting** to take out the guards; **Cover** to blend in).

The apartment is luxurious, but impersonal. There are a few photographs and other memorabilia of Sinclair's time in the military, but nothing of his time since Jovitzo recruited him.

QUESTIONING SINCLAIR

There are two ways this scene could play out: either the player's got the drop on Sinclair and he's at Khan's mercy, or he's got the drop on her and she has to talk her way out. If the player doesn't have a Push to spend on Sinclair and has Problem 32, "The Drop," then depending on how the conversation plays out, you may end up running the Challenge "Going for the Gun," p. 148. Make a mark on the card for Problem 32 whenever the player throws Sinclair off-balance, either through good roleplaying or Interpersonal Pushes. The more marks, the better the player's chances of surviving this conversation unscathed.

Playing Sinclair: Play Sinclair as a foil for Khan based on the player's portrayal of her. If Khan's tough-as-nails, then play Sinclair as more roguish and humorous. If she's a suave spy, he's a blunt instrument. If she's confused and unsure of what's going on, then play him as a fanatic who's dedicated to Jovitzo's service; if she's sure she hates vampires, then play Sinclair as a reasonable man who points out that it's better to serve in Hell than die in some alleyway, and that working for Jovitzo is her only hope of survival.

Sinclair's Objectives: Sinclair's goal in this encounter is to convince Khan to return to Jovitzo. He's still in the thrall of their vampiric master; he believes that she's been drugged or compromised by a rival vampire, and that all she needs to do is sit down, relax, and let him summon the master. **Bullshit Detector** suggests he's telling the truth to a degree; he doesn't want to

kill Khan, although he would prefer to see her dead than free or in the service of another vampire.

Q&A: If Problem 32, "The Drop" is in play, then Sinclair answers Khan's questions in the hopes of convincing her to surrender. If she's got the drop on him, then she can use **Intimidation** to get answers out of him.

Sinclair will reveal the following information freely:
- He and Khan both serve the same master – Lord Jovitzo.
- Their vampiric lord uses them as his spies, enforcers, and troubleshooters. If they serve well, they will be rewarded with immortality. (**Bullshit Detector:** his words ring a little hollow here – he's not sure himself that Jovitzo will ever really grant him eternal life).
- Jovitzo recruited Khan, spiriting her away from MI6 and convincing her to join his retinue
- There are other, rival, vampires out there. Jovitzo is not the most urbane or pleasant master, but you know where you stand with him. Other vampires are liars.
- Enemies of Jovitzo poisoned Khan. She's hallucinating; she can't trust her own judgement.
- Jovitzo sent Sinclair to recover her. If she returns to him freely and of her own will, Jovitzo will forgive her. If she resists... she will be punished.

If pressed, Sinclair adds:

♦ Jovitzo blesses his servants with the sacrament of blood, and the poison somehow broke this sacrament. If Khan returns, the master can bless her again.

♦ He knows that Khan was secretly working with the poisoners, and she was trying to escape Jovitzo. He hasn't revealed this to Jovitzo – the master would be furious if he knew that his favorite servant was trying to escape from him. Out of respect for their friendship, Sinclair says he's willing to keep Khan's secret – if she returns willingly. (**Bullshit Detector:** he's lying. Either it's a trap, or else maybe he's planning to blackmail Khan by holding the threat of Jovitzo's wrath over her. In any case, friendship had little to do with it.)

An **Intimidation** Push gets the following extra clues:

♦ Sinclair's men are on the trail of the poisoners. They have a safehouse here in Budapest where they plotted to extract Khan from Jovitzo's clutches. There's no point going there – he's already sent a team to hit the safehouse. All of Khan's foolish co-conspirators are dead – her only hope is returning to Jovitzo's service.

♦ He suspects that one of Jovitzo's rivals is active in Budapest. Vampires are forbidden, by ancient compact, to attack each other directly, but they can take advantage of weaknesses and strike at a rival's servants. With Khan missing and Jovitzo's own forces focused on recovering her, Jovitzo's very, very vulnerable tonight.

SHARING FREEDOM

If Khan has Edge 11, "The Rosewater Flask" and forces or convinces Sinclair to drink the elixir, it temporarily blocks Jovitzo's control over him. If she does that, he vomits up blood and collapses, and after a few minutes, hauls himself upright. He confesses that he's not strong enough to do what Khan's doing – the elixir has given him a moment's respite, but he can feel Jovitzo's shadow falling across his mind again. Khan's doing the right thing by running, and he'll buy her a little time.

If it's in play, remove Problem 32, "The Drop," and gain Edge 19, "Who Dares Wins."

Sinclair urges Khan to leave; once she's clear, he summons Jovitzo to his apartment before shooting himself. As Jovitzo's distracted, Khan may discard any one Shadow Problem other than Problem 3, "The Dark Call."

ENDING THE CONVERSATION

There are three ways this conversation ends:

♦ Through roleplaying and interpersonal Pushes, the player convinces Sinclair to let her go, or otherwise prevents Sinclair from trying to stop Khan escaping.

♦ The player uses the Rosewater Flask (see "Sharing Freedom" sidebar).

♦ Most likely (and certain if Problem 32, "The Drop" is in play), Sinclair tries to shoot Khan to keep her from escaping. If he's got the drop on her, she has a chance to grab his gun; if she's got the drop on him, he tries grabbing hers.

GOING FOR THE GUN
FIGHTING

You and Sinclair both go for the gun. Only one of you is walking out of here.

Penalty: -4 if Problem 32, "The Drop" is in play; reduce this penalty by 1 per mark on the Problem card.

Advance 9+: You grab the gun from Sinclair, and you've got a choice. You can either shoot him dead, here and now – or you can just knock him out. If you choose the latter, gain Edge 20, "Merciful" and Problem 35, "Unfinished Business."

Hold 6-8: You wrestle the gun away from Sinclair, and it goes off. He collapses to the floor, dead.

Setback 5 or less: You and Sinclair have a vicious wrestling match across the apartment as you fight for control of the gun. You kill him, but get badly hurt in the process. Gain Problem 36, "Shot by Sinclair."

Extra Problem: Problem 34, "A Trail to Follow."

Stunt: Yes (**Shooting; Sense Trouble**).

CLUES IN THE APARTMENT

A quick search of the apartment turns up the following:

♦ A cache of weapons and other equipment, enough to get rid of Problem 2, "Running on Empty" or Problem 22, "Out of Ammo."

♦ **Notice:** There's a cache of photographs – surveillance shots using a long-range lens. They show Khan and another man, Eczes, meeting in a bar. Gain Edge 9, "Eczes," if the player doesn't have it already.

♦ **Electronic Surveillance:** There's a radio on one desk – encrypted, military-grade – that Sinclair uses to communicate with his field teams. Eavesdropping gives the location of Edge 13, "The Safehouse" and Pushing **Electronic Surveillance** gives the player Edge 6, "Momentum."

THE SAFEHOUSE

> **Scene Type: Alternate**
> **Lead-Ins: The Rendezvous, Hunters Hunted**
> **Lead-Outs: Run, Don't Walk, Finding Rostami**

The safehouse operated by the three vampire hunters is located in a disused furniture store on the outskirts of the city; the ground floor of the building is full of old tables and dining room chairs, shrouded in dust covers, while the three hunters used the offices upstairs as a makeshift hiding place with cot beds and cached supplies. The kitchen's been converted into an ad hoc chemistry lab where Hulier brewed the Rosewater Potion used to free Khan. There are also (**Vampirology**) signs that the building had been warded against vampires, although Stokovitch removed these protections when she arrived. Traces remain: a lingering smell of garlic, cross-marks scratched into the windowpanes, nails driven into doors that once held hawthorn sprigs.

Here's where they planned how to make contact with Khan, and where they prepared the Rosewater Flask they gave her to free her from Jovitzo's control.

Now, the safehouse is compromised. The only remaining member of the trio is the old priest, Fr. Loretti, and he's being held hostage to ensure Dr. Hulier cooperates as they attempt to capture Khan (see *The Rendezvous*, p. 138). Watching over Loretti are two of Stokovitch's mercenaries.

Ways this scene could play out:

♦ If Khan arrives here before *The Rendezvous*, p. 138, then she has a chance to rescue Loretti from his captors. In this case, the mercenaries try to stall Khan in the hopes of salvaging their mission.

♦ More likely, Khan shows up just as Sinclair's men raid the safehouse, and gets caught in the middle of the firefight between the two groups of vampire minions.

♦ Option three – if Khan shows up here later in the mission, then the raid on the safehouse is over and it's crawling with police. In this case, she may get grabbed by the mercenaries as she watches the site.

THE MERCENARIES

The two mercs – Stefan and Jozsua – in the safehouse aren't expecting trouble. They're criminals hired by Stokovitch to babysit her hostages. They don't know anything about the supernatural or vampires; as far as they know, Stokovitch is running some sort of extortion scheme. Their job is to sit on Fr. Loretti and wait for a call from Stokovitch. As long as Loretti's got a gun pointed at his head, they're assured that Hulier will cooperate.

FR. LORETTI

Fr. Loretti is his late 70s; he recently retired from his post in the Vatican archives, and stole the Sykoran Crucifix from the treasury there once Rostami convinced him of its true value. He's been filled with a new energy and purpose since discovering the existence of vampires. He knows he's too old to fight them; he sees Khan's redemption as his legacy. He's not afraid to die if it ensures that she's freed from the control of the vampires and becomes a hunter.

SNEAKING INTO THE SAFEHOUSE

Khan only has the opportunity to sneak into the safehouse quietly if she arrives *before* Jovitzo's men.

WALKING INTO THE SAFEHOUSE

If Khan arrives at the safehouse and just knocks on the door, the mercenaries try to deflect her, and tell her that she should wait here until their boss Stokovitch arrives. A **Bullshit Detector** Push picks up that they're lying. If the player does linger here, then adapt the events of *Come With Me* (p. 140): Stokovitch arrives at the safehouse, tries to convince Khan to accompany her to the airport, and then Jovitzo's strike team shows up and everything goes to hell.

On the other hand, if the player does see through the mercenaries' clumsy attempt at deception, then she's got a chance to take them out when their guard is down.

SNEAKING INTO THE SAFEHOUSE
INFILTRATION

Bonus: +2 if the player Pushes **Urban Survival**.

Advance 7+: You sneak into the safehouse. Two guys, holding one prisoner, an old man. The only question is, do you want to kill the two guards or just knock them out? Gain Fr. Loretti as a Contact.

Hold 4-6: You sneak in, and take out one of the guards, but the other puts a bullet in their prisoner before you can stop him. Fr. Loretti's dying.

Setback 3 or less: As you're sneaking in, you hear cars pull up outside. Two cars; several men in each vehicle. The crackle of radios; the click of safeties on guns. Just like the hospital. Run the Challenge "Gunfight at the Safehouse" immediately, but you've got the advantage of a hiding place.

Extra Problem: There's a booby trap rigged to the window of the safehouse. You get to make a **Mechanics** roll to disarm it. On a 5+, you quickly counter the trap. On a 4 or less, either take a Setback on this Challenge or take Problem 37, "Grenade."

Stunt: Yes (**Athletics** for climbing; **Fighting** to take down the guards quietly).

SUCKER PUNCH
FIGHTING

Bonus: +2 if the player Pushes **Reassurance** or **Negotiation**.

Advance 9+: Describe how you convince them you've bought their story and aren't a threat – then describe how you take them out. Gain Fr. Loretti as a Contact.

Hold 6-8: Shit – just as you're about to tackle them, you hear cars draw up outside. Run the Challenge "Gunfight at the Safehouse."

Setback 5 or less: They didn't trust you either. One of them distracts you, and the other guy sucker punches you. You're knocked out; gain Problem 24, "Captured," then run the Challenge "Gunfight at the Safehouse."

Extra Problem: None.

Stunt: Yes (**Cover**).

THE SHOOTOUT

Alternatively, if Khan arrives later and Sinclair's already sent a strike team to the safehouse...

GUNFIGHT AT THE SAFEHOUSE
SHOOTING

The safehouse is a trap. As soon as Sinclair's men walk in the door, the house fills with smoke from gas grenades. Gunshots light up the quiet street, turning the lower floor of the safehouse into a killing ground. Which side are you on?

Bonus: +2 if Khan's hidden.

Advance 11+: You take advantage of the confusion to storm the building. Upstairs, you find an old man imprisoned in one of the rooms, handcuffed to a radiator. He's been shot – he's dying – but he's still conscious.

Hold 7-10: As above, but gain Problem 38, "Safehouse Shootout."

Setback 6 or less: You're caught and pinned down in the crossfire. Making it into the safehouse isn't an option – you've got to run, and leave whatever secrets were there behind. Gain Problem 38, "Safehouse Shootout," and flee.

Extra Problem: Problem 39, "Caught in the Crossfire."

Stunt: Yes (**Infiltration**; **Fighting**).

AFTER THE ACTION

If the player shows up here *after* the strike team, then the safehouse is surrounded by cops. Khan spots several corpses in body bags; as she watches, another corpse – that of an old priest – is brought down from upstairs. **Cop Talk** gets an update on what happened here: it looks to have been a shootout between two criminal gangs. A Push of **Cop Talk** and a convincing cover story (or **Infiltration** test) lets Khan upstairs to take a look around the crime scene.

LORETTI'S TALE

If rescued – or, more likely, if found bleeding to death – the old priest wheezes out his tale. He desperately wants Khan to escape Jovitzo's clutches; of the three hunters, he's the one who has the greatest belief that she can be redeemed. (Hulier is in over his head and just wants out; Rostami is the most experienced of the three hunters, and hence the most cautious and is more willing to cut her losses and abandon Khan if the situation seems hopeless.)

He reveals:

♦ He was contacted by a woman, a vampire hunter, named Rostami, who asked him to obtain certain items from the Vatican archives: an alchemical manuscript confiscated from a heretic in Prague, and a relic called the Sykoran Crucifix.

♦ He demanded to know the purpose of Rostami's request, and she initiated him into the terrible secret of the underworld: vampires exist.

♦ If he were a younger man, why, he would have fought them! Driven those fiends back into Hell – but alas, he is old. Still, he did what he could. He joined with Rostami in seeking a way to strike back at them.

♦ The alchemical manuscript described a way to break the vampire's unholy spell, but this formula relies on vampire blood, and offers only temporary relief. Rostami believed that the crucifix made by the same alchemist could permanently block the vampire's influence.

♦ They recruited a chemist, Hulier, to recreate the formula and make the Rosewater Potion.

♦ Rostami picked Khan as their best target; if freed from the vampire's control, Khan could be their ideal weapon against the undead. She knows their operations, and she has the skills to strike against them.

♦ They managed to contact Khan and gave her the Rosewater Potion to temporarily free her. They intended to rendezvous once she came to Budapest and give her the crucifix to seal the psychic wound and protect her from the vampires.

♦ He doesn't know how they were discovered, but the plan went awry. A woman named Stokovitch raided their safehouse. Rostami escaped with the crucifix, but Hulier and Loretti were captured, and she forced Hulier to betray Khan.

♦ Rostami is out there, somewhere. Maybe she has fled – and if she's gone, then Khan may be doomed, for without the crucifix, how can she resist falling back into the damnable abyss of the vampire's control? He has to believe that Rostami is out there, waiting to make contact with Khan. Find her, before the vampires find you!

Run this scene at any point in the latter half of the adventure. There are four possible entry vectors:

♦ If Khan learns of Rostami's existence, she may seek her out. She can track Rostami down with **Streetwise** or **Tradecraft**; she knows that Rostami is following Khan and trying to make contact with her, so if she lurks around key sites like the Cave Church or the safehouse, she'll eventually spot her. (If you want to raise tension, you can declare that this means Taking Time to scour the city, or call for another roll on the "Mean Streets of Budapest" Challenge on p. 135).

♦ Rostami might initiate the contact by brushing past Khan on the street and passing her a note, or – once she's seen Khan fighting Sinclair's men and so is convinced that Khan hasn't fallen back under Jovitzo's control – calling Khan's cell phone if it's still operational. Either way, she tells Khan to meet her on Gubacsi Bridge over the Danube.

♦ If Khan gets into serious trouble – say, she picks up a Problem like 30, "Crash Victim" or 36, "Shot by Sinclair," then Rostami can swoop in to rescue her.

♦ Finally, Rostami might show up just before you move into the final scene in *Extraction Point*, having tailed Khan to the airport.

MADAME ROSTAMI, I PRESUME

Rostami's lived in the shadow of vampires for her whole life. Her family comes from a region of Romania where the old precautions are still observed, where people know to hide indoors on unholy nights of the year, and to hang garlic from windows and to bolt the doors when the wind blows down from the mountains. For a time, after the Revolution in '89, she worked with certain government groups who knew about the undead, offering her expertise and her counsel. She got burned – they turned on her, and she suspects the pale hand of the dead behind her fall from grace. For more than a decade now, she's been invisible, hiding from the vampires and the corrupt authorities. She still tries to thwart the machinations of the undead when she can, but she's become cautious to the point of paranoia.

She knows how the vampires operate; how they recruit talented mortals as agents and proxies. In this modern age, the vampires, too, must hide. These are not the old times, when no one dared question the strange behavior of the *boyar* in the old castle. No, the vampires have to conceal themselves from the government, from the media, from investigation and discovery, and so more and more they rely on their mortal servants.

Rostami believes that this dependence could be their undoing. She's the one who came up with the plan to break Khan free of Jovitzo's control.

She took a great risk in recruiting Fr. Loretti and Hulier, and a greater one in contacting Khan and convincing her to take the Rosewater Potion. Now, with her plan in disarray, she's unsure about her next move. The Sykoran Crucifix is a treasure of great power. It could protect Khan from falling back under the control of the vampires – but she's not sure if Khan can be saved at this point. If they'd managed to extract Khan safely, if they'd been able to spirit her away undetected, then Rostami would have happily handed over the crucifix. Now, with both Jovitzo and Carlyle chasing Khan, Rostami fears that if she entrusts Khan with the relic, it'll fall into the hands of one vampire or the other.

MEETING ROSTAMI

You could pass Rostami on the street a hundred times and not notice her. She'd walk on by, head bowed, swathed in a heavy coat with a shawl over her greying hair, infinitely forgettable. It's only when you see her eyes that you might remember her; her eyes are cold as a Siberian winter, pale and harsh.

When Khan meets her, she gets a flash of memory; she's met Rostami before, more than once. There's a memory of questioning Rostami, interrogating her... hurting her. It was a prison cell in Prague; they'd captured Rostami when she tried to break into one of Jovitzo's crypts. Rostami escaped, somehow. The vampire was furious, threatening to tear Khan's throat open, to drain her dry. Another memory – months later, encountering

Rostami on a bridge like this one, half the world away. The bittersweet taste of the Rosewater Potion as she hands Khan a cup...

That flood of memories is worth a free Push, to underline the importance of Rostami.

THE CONVERSATION

When playing Rostami, your first priority is to protect yourself. She knows that anyone could be a minion of the vampires, anyone could be compromised. Survival is her primary objective.

Rostami efficiently explains the following:

♦ She gave Khan the Rosewater Potion that temporarily broke her free of Jovitzo's influence.

♦ Making the potion requires vampire blood; Rostami doesn't have any more. The little she had was used to make the potion, and that sample was centuries old. If Khan's going to stay free, she'll have to learn how to make the potion and hunt vampires to fuel it. She can give Khan the formula.

♦ Without the potion, Khan will become vulnerable to Jovitzo's control, or to the influence of other vampires in his lineage. The ones who made him will also be able to exert control over her.

♦ If asked about the Sykoran Crucifix, Rostami admits that she has the relic, and that's a more potent form of protection. The potion is a stopgap; the crucifix is the real deal.

♦ Entrusting the crucifix to Khan now is too much of a risk; the vampires are on her trail. Rostami has an escape route out of Budapest, but she doesn't dare bring Khan with her now. She wants Khan to draw the attention of the vampires away; if Khan survives, and remains free, then Rostami will find her again and

give her the crucifix but she's got to prove herself worthy of it first.

♦ So, Rostami concludes, Khan has a choice: throw herself into the line of fire, distract the vampires, and if she survives, she might earn redemption. Or she can flee, now, without the protection of the crucifix, and risk both their lives.

The player, of course, may have a different view of her available options. She could:

♦ Use **Negotiation** to persuade Rostami to entrust her with the crucifix now. What does she offer in return? Some possible options: she could promise to infiltrate the conspiracy and feed intel to Rostami and her allies, or to use the protection offered by the crucifix to get close enough to a vampire to kill the monster.

♦ Use **Intimidation** to force Rostami to hand over the crucifix at gunpoint.

♦ If Khan's rescued Loretti and/ or Hulier, then Rostami might be convinced to hand over the crucifix in gratitude. Alternatively, if they're both dead, then Khan could argue that Rostami shares some responsibility for their deaths, and that entrusting Khan with the relic would justify their sacrifice.

♦ Try using **Reassurance** to assure Rostami that Khan's free of vampiric influence.

WEARING THE CRUCIFIX

If Khan obtains the crucifix and wears it, the metal burns her skin, scarring her. Rostami explains that this is a sign that she's still tainted by the vampire's unholy baptism of blood. Only when she's fully free of the curse, only when she redeems herself, will she be free of that scar.

THE NEXT MOVE

Regardless of how the conversation with Khan goes, Rostami vanishes after meeting her. The old hunter has her own escape route of Budapest, and even if she's convinced that Khan has been reliably turned against the vampires, Rostami still doesn't want to multiply her own risk by leaving with her. Khan's on her own.

Khan needs to get out of Budapest; what route does she choose?

THE SYKORAN CRUCIFIX

The relic is a small, ornate silver crucifix, hanging from a cord of black leather. The figure of the crucified Christ can be removed, revealing a small cylindrical recess that contains a tiny stoppered vial. The substance in the glass vial is still viscous; it appears to be black, although it turns reddish if held up to strong light. It might be blood – but if the seal on the vial is broken, the power of the crucifix is broken.

The crucifix's potency may not depend on the faith of the wearer; it was made by the mysterious alchemist Sykora in the Court of Rudolph of Prague, and contains a variant of the Rosewater Potion. As long as Khan has the crucifix, she can use Edge 21, "The Sykoran Crucifix."

EXTRACTION POINT

Scene Type: Core
Lead-Ins: Kidnap Attempt
Lead-Outs: Run, Don't Walk, No Going Back

Stokovitch has a plane waiting at Budapest's small Tököl airfield; Tököl isn't open to the public, but is used for some military and commercial flights, and a bribe in the right pocket let Stokovitch's jet land there. Her plan is to bring Khan here and fly her to London, where she can be initiated into the service of Stokovitch's vampire master Carlyle.

Stokovitch becomes increasingly animated and talkative as they approach the airport, enthusiastically telling Khan about how she too will be able to serve the master, how she'll be free of Jovitzo's barbaric tyranny and instead be part of the great work. Carlyle, she claims, has a vision for the future; he's the immortal architect of the future.

As they arrive at the airport, Stokovitch's van pulls into a side building near the main terminal. Stokovitch gets out, leaving her driver Marius to watch over Khan. Outside, Khan hears Stokovitch arguing with one of the airport staff; it sounds like her contact is demanding more money. (Mention a Heat Problem or two that Khan's picked up along the way to justify the delay; for example, if Khan's got Problem 25, "Collateral Damage," then the airport guard might grumble that the police are looking for the terrorists, and if he falsifies records to let Stokovitch fly out, he risks getting into trouble.)

This delay gives Khan a chance to act. (Alternatively, Rostami could show up here and shoot the driver – see *Finding Rostami*, p. 152).

If Khan's free to act, then taking out the driver isn't that hard. If she's got Problem 24, "Captured," it's a bit more challenging.

ESCAPING THE VAN
FIGHTING

Penalty: -1 die if Khan's got Problem 24, "Captured."

Advance 9+: Describe how you take the driver out silently. You can either vanish and escape the airport (go to *Run, Don't Walk*, or try to take out Stokovitch. Either way, you've got a +1 die bonus to your next Challenge.

Hold 4-8: You take out the driver, but Stokovitch shows up at the worst possible moment. Run the Challenge "We Could Have Been Sisters."

Setback 3 or less: You're interrupted when Stokovitch returns. She grabs you with inhumanly strong hands and drags you towards the waiting plane. Gain Problem 24, "Captured," if you don't have it already.

Extra Problem: Problem 40, "Stabbed."

Stunt: No.

Alternatively, if Khan stays put, then Stokovitch returns shortly and leads her out onto the runway. The sky fills with angry grey clouds, and the rising wind has a cold edge to it. The small Learjet rocks back and forth in the wind as Stokovitch hustles Khan towards it. Both women can tell that there's something up there, circling the air field. Jovitzo is following them...

FIGHTING STOKOVITCH

If Khan tries to take down Stokovitch, then it's a **Fighting** Challenge. Stokovitch is a Renfield, and has supernatural strength, making this a brutal brawl.

WE COULD HAVE BEEN SISTERS

This is your last chance to escape Stokovitch's clutches.

FIGHTING

Penalty: -1 die if Khan's got Problem 24, "Captured."

Advance 11+: Stokovitch is stronger and faster than you are – but she's holding back. Her master told her to keep you alive; you're under no such compunction. Describe how you take her down, then you've got a chance to escape in her plane. You automatically Advance on the "Leaving Budapest" Challenge (p. 157).

Hold 7-10: You aren't able to kill her, but you're able to hurt her enough to slip free, and vanish into the shadows. She hesitates for an instant, torn between her desire to capture you and her fear of encountering Jovitzo directly – then she makes her choice, and runs towards the waiting plane. Gain Problem 48, "Stokovitch Survived."

Setback 6 or less: She's terrifyingly strong, and you're no match for her. She slams you against the wall, then lifts you with one hand. "You could have had this," she hisses, eyes gleaming red. "We could have been brides of the master." And then a huge bat swoops down, shrieking, and Stokovitch recoils in horror. She sprints towards the waiting plane, leaving you at Jovitzo's mercy. Gain Problem 41, "Nowhere to Hide."

Extra Problem: Problem 42, "Stokovitch Kicked Your Ass."

Stunt: Yes (**Filch** to grab Stokovitch's gun; **Shooting** to shoot at her; **Infiltration** to hide amid the shadows of the airfield).

PLAYING IT COOL

Khan's other alternative is to play along with Stokovitch, pretending to go along with the extraction before betraying her and escaping on the plane.

PLAYING IT COOL

You're not going to give in; you're not going to trade one vampire master for another. But you need to make Stokovitch believe you will.

COOL

Penalty: -1 per Shadow Problem.

Advance 9+: It all works beautifully – you convince Stokovitch that you're on her side, that you're committed to joining her at her master's side. She relaxes – and that's a mistake. She may be inhumanly strong and fast, but she still lets her guard down, and that's all the opening you need. Go to the Challenge "Leaving Budapest" and you automatically Advance.

Hold 6-8: Stokovitch keeps watching you, never letting her guard down. She sits opposite you with a gun in her hand. "Soon, we will be sisters, united in the blood of the master," she whispers, "but until then, I cannot trust you." As the plane takes off, you glimpse something moving outside. Run the Challenge "No Escape."

Setback 5 or less: Stokovitch doesn't trust you in the slightest, and searches you as you get on the plane. Discard Edge 11, "The Rosewater Flask" or Edge 21, "The Sykoran Crucifix" – or resist by fighting back, and run the Challenge "We Could Have Been Sisters."

Extra Problem: None.

Stunt: No.

ON THE PLANE

As the plane takes off, Khan spots a dark shape flitting across the runway towards the plane – a huge bat. A sudden gust of wind slams into the side of the jet. The engines scream in protest as the pilot fights to take off. The bat hammers against the windscreen, cracking the tempered glass. Jovitzo's not letting Khan go.

The bat-thing breaks through. One taloned wing sweeps across the cockpit, hooking onto the pilot's face and ripping it to shreds. Stokovitch shoots wildly at the monster as the plane spins out of control. Khan has a brief window to leap forward and take control of the plane.

RUN, DON'T WALK

Scene Type: Core
Lead-Ins: The Safehouse, Finding Rostami, Extraction Point
Lead-Outs: No Going Back

As long as Khan remains in Budapest, she's in Jovitzo's territory and she'll never be safe. She has to escape.

NO ESCAPE
DRIVING

Bonus: +1 die if Stokovitch is on board – her presence distracts Jovitzo briefly before he kills her.

Penalty: -1 die if Khan's got Problem 24, "Captured."

Advance 11+: You manage to seize control of the plane when the pilot's killed. Jovitzo snarls and screams at you in his bat-form, but he can't touch you now, and the wind whips him away. The plane won't fly for long, but it's enough for you to automatically Advance on the "Leaving Budapest" Challenge (p. 157).

Hold 7-10: You aren't able to keep the plane in the air for long, but at least it's a landing you can walk away from. Stokovitch, on the other hand, won't be walking anywhere again. As you stumble away from the wreckage, darkness closes around you. Jovitzo has found you. Go to *No Going Back*, p. 157.

Setback 6 or less: It's a bad, bad landing. Gain Problem 42, "Sole Survivor."

Extra Problem: None.

Stunt: Yes (**Athletics**; **Cool**; **Mechanics**).

The hunters' original extraction route is gone. Stokovitch has a plane waiting at the Tököl airport (*Extraction Point*), which is one way out. Alternatively, Khan can try escaping on her own: she's got the connections and the experience to evade detection.

If she hasn't found a way to guard herself from psychic influence, or at least get her Shadow Score down, then warn her that crossing out of Jovitzo's domain is going to be the moment of peak peril. Her former master wants to recapture her; even with the protection of the Rosewater Potion, breaking free from him the first time nearly broke her and she ended up in hospital. This time, it's going to be even harder.

LEAVING BUDAPEST

Ask the player how she intends to leave Budapest undetected. She can't risk just driving out – Jovitzo's minions are watching the roads, and that bat-thing is still out there in the sky. There are many other options – use **Cover** to conjure a false identity and fly out, **Network** to have some ally smuggle her out, **Infiltration** to sneak out on a train or public transport that the vampire wouldn't dare attack. She could even turn herself over to the British Embassy and get her old colleagues in MI6 to exfiltrate her. (They will, of course, have a great number of awkward questions for her...)

NO GOING BACK

Scene Type: Finale
Lead-Ins: Run, Don't Walk

The final scene in the adventure is Khan's last confrontation with Jovitzo. The vampire doesn't confront her directly; instead, he attempts to use his psychic hold over her. She's tasted his blood; he's woven a powerful web of

The Challenge below assumes that Khan's using **Cover** to escape through Budapest's main commercial airport at Ferihegy. If she takes another route, adapt the Challenge to fit.

LEAVING BUDAPEST
COVER

Bonus: +2 if you Push **Streetwise**.

Penalty: -1 per Heat Problem, -1 per Shadow Problem.

Advance 11+: You slip through the ring of iron that Jovitzo threw around Budapest. Every heartbeat's taking you further away from your former captor, away from the vampire that enslaved you for so long. You can feel his rage in the howling winds, in the fury of the storm that surrounds you. Go to the Challenge "...And of Your Own Will," and gain a bonus die.

Hold 7-10: You make it out of Budapest – but as you leave, you see *him*. Jovitzo, your vampire master. He stares at you, his eyes blazing with fury. Go to the Challenge "...And of Your Own Will."

Setback 6 or less: You're not getting out of this city without a fight. Sinclair's hunters have found you. Go to the Challenge "Blood on the Threshold."

Extra Problem: Problem 44, "Psychic Assault."

Stunt: Yes (**Cover** for a false ID; **Infiltration** to sneak past guards).

If Khan's unable to dodge Sinclair's hunters, run "Blood on the Threshold." Sinclair's men will try to grab Khan unobtrusively by ambushing her on the street, or have bribed security staff at the airport escort her to a "holding area" where they can grab her. Optionally, swap **Shooting** for **Fighting** as the primary ability.

BLOOD ON THE THRESHOLD
SHOOTING

Sinclair's men have found you, and are between you and freedom.
You've got to fight your way out.

Bonus: +1 die if you discard Edge 6, "Momentum."

Penalty: -1 die if you're trying to bring anyone with you, like a Contact.

Advance 11+: Describe how you battle your way clear of this last obstacle – and then run the Challenge "...And of Your Own Will." You gain a bonus die for that Challenge.

Hold 7-10: You make it out alive, but only barely. Gain Problem 45, "A Bloody Mess" – and then run the Challenge "...And of Your Own Will."

Setback 6 or less: There's no way to survive this. Unless you've got an ace up your sleeve (a Mastery Edge, or maybe one of your Contacts can buy you time to escape by sacrificing themselves), you die here, gunned down by your former subordinates. Sinclair will take your place at the right hand of the vampire, but at least you died free. (If you do find a way to escape, treat this result as a Hold instead.)

Extra Problem: Problem 46, "High-Profile Incident."

Stunt: Yes.

enchantment around her. She can break free if her will is strong enough, but it won't be safe.

Describe Jovitzo's appearance as an intrusion of the unnatural. If Khan's flying out of Budapest, then he might appear in the form of a gigantic bat, riding on the winds of a magical storm that he's conjured out of his fury. If she's driving out, then she might be distracted by a flash of lightning – and then, suddenly, the vampire is right there in the car with her, grabbing the wheel. It's a hallucination, but it feels all too real.

If Khan has the Rosewater Potion or the Sykoran Crucifix, now's the time to use them.

Even after escaping Jovitzo, Khan's not free of her former master. He's still out there, ready to be used as a villain later in the campaign. Alternatively, if the player is willing to risk her new-found freedom and her life, and she can get close enough to Jovitzo just as she breaks free of him, she can gamble on one last **Fighting** Challenge.

AND OF YOUR OWN WILL...

COOL

The voice of the vampire thunders through your blood. YOU ARE MINE! YOU CANNOT GO! If you give in, you're doomed. If you fight, you may go mad.

Penalty: -1 per Shadow Problem.

Advance 11+: Your blood burns – literally – as you fight against the taint of Jovitzo's poison. The pain is intolerable, unbearable – but it's worth it when you feel him recoil in shock and terror as you break free.

Hold 7-10: The strain's too much, and you fall unconscious. Your brain feels like it's on fire. The vampire can't hold you, not anymore, but he lopes through your mind like a savage wolf, tearing and rending your memories. Gain Problem 47, "Burnt Renfield."

Setback 6 or less: You don't want to obey. You don't want to do this – but you can't resist. The vampire draws you in, draining your willpower like blood draining from a ruptured artery, a mortal wound. You're still alive, for now, but he strips away everything that makes you a person, as opposed to the thrall of a monster. It's over.

Extra Problem: None.

Stunt: No.

KILLING JOVITZO

FIGHTING

The vampire staggers, shocked by the strength of your will. Now, in this one instant, he's vulnerable.

Advance 11+: You spring forward and slash Jovitzo's throat with a knife. His skin's hard as iron, but you put every ounce of strength behind that blow, and his black blood spills out in a torrent. He chokes and topples backwards, and you strike again, driving the knife into his withered heart. He's dead.

Hold 7-10: You slash at Jovitzo, cutting his throat. His eyes burn with fury, but he can't speak, only gurgle and choke on his own blood. He melts away, vanishing before your eyes. He's not dead, but he's mortally wounded – and you know that a wounded vampire is like a lame wolf. The rest of them will sense his weakness and turn on him. He's a dead man walking. The question is, can you outlast him?

Setback 6 or less: You spring at Jovitzo, slashing at his throat – but he's grabbing at you, biting you. You take him down, but at the cost of your own life. At the end, he lies there, your knife in his heart, and you watch coldly as the weight of centuries catches up on him, and he withers. You're dying too – you can feel your pulse slowing as you bleed out, and the world's going dark – and then you hear his voice, echoing in your mind as if from a great distance. "Drink of me, child," he whispers, "take of the last of my strength, and become immortal..."

Do you die, or become a thing like the monster you just destroyed? Either way, your mortal life ends here...

Extra Problem: None.

Stunt: Yes (**Athletics** to dramatically take the vampire down; **Preparedness** for that hold-out stake).

AFTERMATH

Khan's alive.

She's not free. Even if Jovitzo's dead, she's still walking around with a gaping psychic wound. Her mind's still bleeding, and another vampire could smell that wound, enthrall her again. The conspiracy won't let her go.

Maybe she's got access to the Rosewater Potion, and can protect herself by killing vampires for their blood.

Maybe, if she fights back hard enough, she can earn the Sykoran Crucifix and be safe as long as she holds that relic.

Maybe, if she doesn't give up, she can hunt them all down.

More prosaically, if Stokovitch or Sinclair are still alive, give the player the appropriate Problems (Problem 35, "Unfinished Business," or Problem 48, "Stokovitch Survived".)

BLOWBACK

ANY TIME AFTER LEAVING HOSPITAL

♦ Khan spots a car idling on the road – it's some of Sinclair's men, searching for her. Ask the player how Khan evades or eliminates this potential ambush, then pick the appropriate General ability. On an 8+, gain Edge 6, "Momentum." On a 7 or less, gain Problem 17, "Hunted."

♦ Khan spots something moving in the sky. Call for a **Sense Trouble** roll: on a 7 or less, gain Problem 11, "On Dark Wings."

ANYTIME IN BUDAPEST

♦ Khan spots her face on a television screen – she's been reported as a missing person. Call for a **Cover** test; on an 8+, she can stay hidden. On a 7 or less, gain Problem 26, "Dragnet."

KHAN HAS PROBLEM 4, "SLEEPWALKING"

♦ Khan sleepwalks to Sinclair's apartment; the next scene is *Hunters Hunted*

♦ (Only if this is near the end of the scenario) Khan sleepwalks into Jovitzo's clutches – run *No Going Back* as the next scene.

Heat Score 2+

♦ Khan spots some police officers nearby, and they're clearly looking for someone – they're stopping vehicles, questioning people on the street, going door to door. How does she evade them?

♦ Sinclair sends some of his men to find and question Sam Eczes. If Khan's going to make sure of him, she'll need to Push **Reassurance** or **Intimidation** to ensure his co-operation.

HEAT SCORE 4+

♦ Two police officers spot Khan and attempt to detain her. How does she evade them? If she escapes, gain Problem 31, "Person of Interest" otherwise, she's arrested and put in the back of a police car. Stokovitch's van drives the police car off the road and grabs Khan. Gain Problem 30, "Crash Victim," and Problem 24, "Captured."

SHADOW SCORE 2+

♦ Khan has a flashback or nightmare – she remembers drinking a potion. It tasted of roses, but it burned like strong liquor, and then her stomach twisted like she'd been stabbed. She's at -1 **Cool** die for the next scene.

♦ Rats on the city streets seem to be watching Khan. Add her Shadow Score to her Heat Score for the next scene.

SHADOW SCORE 4+

♦ Gain Problem 4, "Sleepwalking."

PROBLEMS

PROBLEM 1

Beaten Up

INJURY

You don't know what happened to you, but it hurt.

PROBLEM 2

Running on Empty

You don't have any equipment or personal possessions. No gun, no money, no cards, no passport. While you have this Problem, you can't make **Preparedness** or **Shooting** tests. Counter by finding a cache of equipment, a safehouse, or a friend who can shelter you until you restock.

PROBLEM 3

The Dark Call

VAMPIRE

Something still has a hold on your free will, and you know that you won't be able to resist if it gets its claws into your soul again. If you haven't Countered this Problem by the end of the mission, you'll become his thrall again. Counter by finding a way to block your former master's influence, escaping his reach – or by killing the monster.

PROBLEM 4

Sleepwalking

BLOWBACK, SHADOW

Something's calling you to go out into the darkness. You can resist with an effort of will, but the next time you rest, something bad may happen. Discard this card and remind the GM when you next sleep. If you end up with multiple versions of this card, the consequences get worse. Counter by having someone watch you when you sleep or suppressing your Shadow Score to 0.

PROBLEM 5

We Should Sedate Her

The doctors and staff at the hospital think you're dangerously unstable, and intend to sedate you. Counter with a **Reassurance** Push, or by escaping their clutches.

PROBLEM 6

Slammed

INJURY

You've had the breath knocked out of you.

PROBLEM 7

Still Woozy

You're still dizzy and disorientated. For the rest of this scene, reroll any dice that come up 6s. (You can keep a 6 if you reroll a die and it still loves you.) Counter if you take drastic action to focus yourself.

PROBLEM 8

Messy Exit

HEAT

You shot someone when escaping from the hospital. That'll bring attention from the cops – and you're sure that *they* have corrupted the Hungarian police. You can't afford a run-in with the authorities.

PROBLEM 9

Alone in the Dark

You've been forced to flee across country, and the bad guys are on your heels. Describe how you Take Time and get back on the road to Counter this card. Once you do, exchange it for Problem 11, "On Dark Wings."

PROBLEM 10

Bruised

INJURY

You think you may have cracked a rib in that last fight.

PROBLEM 11

On Dark Wings

SHADOW

The sun sets, and you're plunged back into darkness as you scramble through the forest. You think you glimpse a pale face amid the trees, but it's only moonlight... isn't it? Your head's spinning. Something circles above you, a dark shape against dark clouds. You're being hunted.

PROBLEM 12

Shaken

Your head feels shattered. Fragments of memory, glimpses of previous missions, snatches of voices, the taste of blood run through your brain. You're close to breaking – you've a -1 penalty to **Cool** tests while you hold this card. Counter either by confiding in someone or finding some other way to take the edge off.

PROBLEM 13

Pursued into the Woods

You had to hide in the woods to dodge the monster pursuing you. You're wet, cold, and exhausted. You've got a -1 to Physical tests until you Take Time to rest and recuperate. When you do, discard this card.

PROBLEM 14

Car Crash

INJURY

You crashed your car on the way to Budapest.

PROBLEM 15

Abducted

If you've got a Contact card, hand it over to the GM. That Contact was abducted by the vampire bat. Were they eaten? Turned? Are they still a prisoner of the vampires?

PROBLEM 16

Clawed

INJURY

The vampire ripped a chunk out of your arm, and you're bleeding badly.

PROBLEM 17

Hunted

HEAT

There are too many eyes in this city, too many people asking questions about you. You're being hunted.

PROBLEM 18

The Extraction Point

CLUE

What's waiting for you at the airfield at Tököl? You've got to go there to find the answer.

PROBLEM 19

Sitting Ducks

Hulier just warned anyone who's listening that you're coming. If you try to exit through the back of the cave, you'll be an easy target for any shooters.

PROBLEM 20

Bleeding Out

SERIOUS INJURY

You've been shot. If you've still got this Problem at the end of the operation, you'll die.

PROBLEM 21

Lights Out

Stokovitch shot out the lights, plunging the tunnel into darkness. You're at -2 to any Challenges in the caves that rely on being able to see what's going on.

PROBLEM 22

Blue Lights on the Danube

HEAT

A shootout at a historical church in the heart of Budapest? Within minutes, the streets are going to be full of TEK counter-terror cops. Better run.

PROBLEM 23

Out of Ammo

You're out of bullets. You can't use **Shooting** until you Counter this card by obtaining a replacement weapon or more ammunition.

PROBLEM 24

Captured

You've been captured by Stokovitch and whoever she's working for. Your hands are restrained. You're at -1 die to any **Physical** or **Manual** challenges until you break free.

PROBLEM 25

Collateral Damage

HEAT, CONTINUITY

The terrorist attack on the historic Hill Cave Church will be the headline item on news reports around the world, and you're Person of Interest #1. You can't remove this Heat Problem in this adventure or the next one.

PROBLEM 26

Dragnet

HEAT

Jovitzo's men are definitely working with the Budapest cops. They're searching the city for you.

PROBLEM 27

Roadkill

INJURY

You exited a moving vehicle at high speed.

PROBLEM 28

Something in the Sky

SHADOW

There's something circling over the high. You can't see it, but you can tell it's there, prowling like a drone beyond the clouds. A giant bat...

PROBLEM 29

Unsafe at Any Speed

HEAT

The driver of the van tried to grab you when you attacked Stokovitch, and now the van's going the wrong way down a one-way street. It's drawing a lot of attention and is about to crash.

PROBLEM 30

Crash Victim

INJURY

That hurt. You're covered in bruises and broken glass.

PROBLEM 31

Person of Interest

HEAT

You were spotted by the police as you escaped.

PROBLEM 32

The Drop

Place this Problem on the table in front of you. Sinclair was waiting for you, and now he's got a gun pointed at you. You've got to find a way to get him to drop his guard. Every time you spend an Interpersonal Push in conversation with Sinclair, put a mark on this card.

PROBLEM 33

Bloody Carnage

INJURY

You fought your way past Sinclair's guards, but didn't get through unscathed. You've been punched, battered, and shot at, and everything hurts.

PROBLEM 34

A Trail to Follow

HEAT

The conspiracy's still looking for you, and now they know you were at Sinclair's apartment.

PROBLEM 35

Unfinished Business

CONTINUITY

You spared Sinclair's life, but he's still in the thrall of the vampire Jovitzo. If you still have this card at the end of the adventure, then Sinclair will try to hunt you down in the future.

PROBLEM 36

Shot by Sinclair

SERIOUS INJURY

Sinclair's shot you. You need Medical Attention, or you'll die by the end of this adventure.

PROBLEM 37

Grenade

INJURY

You were way too close when that booby trap went off, and now your ears are ringing. In addition to the normal -2, you've got to discard any dice that roll 1s or 2s for the rest of the scene.

PROBLEM 38

Safehouse Shootout

HEAT

Sinclair's men may have started this firefight, but you're the one who walked away, and the police will be after you.

PROBLEM 39

Caught in the Crossfire

INJURY

You had the devil's luck to survive. Still, you were grazed by several shots, and you're bleeding badly.

PROBLEM 40

Stabbed

INJURY

Stokovitch's driver had a knife hidden in his jacket. You're bleeding badly, but you don't think any organs were perforated.

162

PROBLEM 42

Nowhere to Hide

SHADOW

You can't see Jovitzo, but he's up there somewhere, riding on the storm winds like a vengeful god.

PROBLEM 43

Stokovitch Kicked Your Ass

INJURY

She did, though. No question about it.

PROBLEM 44

Sole Survivor

SERIOUS INJURY

You've broken your arm and several ribs. You're at -2 dice to all **Physical** Challenges until you get Medical Attention.

PROBLEM 45

Psychic Assault

Your skull feels like it's cracking under the strain as Jovitzo tries to call you back to him. You've got a penalty equal to your Shadow Score to all Challenges as long as you hold this card. Counter by suppressing your Shadow Score.

PROBLEM 46

A Bloody Mess

SERIOUS INJURY

You've been beaten to a bloody pulp. You're still alive, but only barely. You're at -2 to all rolls until you get Medical Attention, and you start the next operation with a Hurt card.

PROBLEM 47

High-Profile Incident

HEAT, CONTINUITY

Things got loud and messy in your exit from Budapest. You can't get rid of this Heat Problem until after the next operation.

PROBLEM 48

Burnt Renfield

CONTINUITY, SHADOW

You were able to resist Jovitzo's psychic command, but at terrible cost. You start any future operations with only two Pushes instead of three. Counter by killing Jovitzo.

PROBLEM 49

Stokovitch Survived

CONTINUITY

The crazy Renfield Stokovitch is still alive – and still wants to capture you for her master Carlyle, in London. Counter by killing Stokovitch or Carlyle.

EDGES

EDGE 1

The Church

CLUE

Your phone has the address of a church in Budapest. Your memories are still like broken glass, but you're sure there are answers there.

EDGE 2

No Going Back

You've escaped from a nightmare. A monster had you in its thrall, and you're not going back. You'd sooner die. Discard for a bonus die on any test involving escaping the monster's clutches.

EDGE 3

Time for Some Answers

You're determined to find out what's going on, and if that means hurting people until they answer you, so be it. Discard for a free Push of **Intimidation** when questioning a defeated enemy.

EDGE 4

Syringe Full of Propofol

It's a potent and quick-acting sedative. Before any **Fighting** Challenge, you may make a Quick **Filch** Test (4+). If you succeed, discard this card to automatically advance in the **Fighting** Challenge. Only works on humans.

EDGE 5

Memories of Sinclair

A flash of memory – John Sinclair. Ex-SAS. You were friends – both former British clandestine ops, both exiles, both thralls of the vampires. Sinclair, smiling as he cut the throat of a prisoner. And another memory – Sinclair's address in Budapest. Discard this card for a Push or an extra die when facing off against John Sinclair.

EDGE 6

Momentum

You're one step ahead of your pursuers, and that gives you the advantage. Discard this card for an extra die on any **Physical** Challenge, or to Take Time in Budapest without risking blowback.

EDGE 7

Attrition

Every guy you take out now is one enemy you don't need to fight later. Discard this card and describe how you take advantage of the enemy's depleted numbers to gain an extra die or a Push when dealing with the bad guys.

EDGE 8

Flowing Water

CONTINUITY

You remember that flowing water is a barrier to vampiric influence. It's hard for them to sense you when you're surrounded by water, and it's hard for them to cross rivers or seas. Suppress your Shadow Score by 1 when surrounded by running water.

EDGE 9

Eczes

You recall a potential ally in Budapest – a gambler and crook named Eczes. He was your contact, not a servant of the vampires... as far as you know. It could be good to see a friendly face. Discard for a +2 bonus to a **Network** roll to contact Eczes, or for a free Interpersonal Push when dealing with him.

EDGE 10

Memories of Piotr

A flash of recollection – you were in a hotel room. There was a man there – pale, red eyes, screaming in fury at Piotr. He picked Piotr up with one hand and smashed him against the doorframe, over and over. You tried to intervene, but the man – the *vampire* – just glared at you, and it was as though you turned to stone. You remember the monster's name now: Jovitzo. Discard for a free Push when dealing with a friend of Piotr, or a bonus die on a **Cool** Challenge against the vampire.

EDGE 11

The Rosewater Flask

This elixir blocks vampiric mental influence – for a brief time. There's enough left in the flask for one drink; this allows the imbiber to resist vampiric influence and automatically Hold on **Cool** checks for a scene.

EDGE 12

The Eczes Papers

CONTINUITY

You've gotten hold of some financial records that might contain clues about the structure of the conspiracy. You don't have time to go through them now.

EDGE 13

The Safehouse

CLUE

You've got the address of a safehouse – but you don't know if it's still safe. There may be answers there.

EDGE 14

Impending Sucker Punch

You know that this is a setup, that Hulier's under duress. Discard this card for a bonus die in any Challenge while in the caves.

EDGE 15

Angel of Judgement

You took on a dozen bad guys in a gunfight, and walked out alive. Discard this card to gain a Shooting Mastery card of your choice.

EDGE 16

Lie of the Land

You've scoped out the target building and know the escape routes. Discard to automatically Advance on an **Evasion** test to escape, or to push **Architecture** or **Urban Survival** in Budapest.

EDGE 17

Iron Will

You're not going to break or bend. Discard for +2 dice in any Cool Challenge.

EDGE 18

Holy Ground

CONTINUITY

Vampires dread sacred places. Suppress your Shadow Score by 1 while in such places.

EDGE 19

Who Dares Wins

Sinclair gave you some help – a piece of equipment, a secret, a promise of assistance – before he committed suicide. At any point before the end of this adventure, you may discard this card to reveal what aid he gave you, or to gain +2 **Preparedness** dice.

EDGE 20

Merciful

You didn't kill Sinclair when you had the chance, and that act of mercy lightens your soul. Discard this card for an extra **Cool** die, or to suppress your Shadow Score by 2 for one scene.

EDGE 21

The Sykoran Crucifix

CONTINUITY

This relic guards you against the vampires' psychic influence. Once per mission, gain +2 **Cool** dice for any one Challenge.

CONTACTS

CONTACT 1

Magdalena Halmi, Nurse

Innocent and clueless about vampires, Magdalena was the first person you met when you woke up.

Diagnosis, Pharmacy, Reassurance.

Drive 1, Medic 2

CONTACT 2

Grigor, Farmer

His son Piotr was part of the conspiracy, and forced Grigor to allow his farm to be used as a waystation and cache for smuggled goods.

Outdoor Survival, Streetwise.
Shooting 1, Medic 1, Preparedness 1.

CONTACT 3

Sam Eczes, Fixer

Sleazy and crooked, but Eczes has plenty of underworld connections that aren't tied to the vampires.

Accounting, Forgery, Streetwise.
Surveillance 1

CONTACT 4

Hulier, Biochemist

He's recreated a medieval alchemical formula that temporarily blocks vampiric influence. Making more is going to be tricky – vampire blood is one of the components. After nearly dying in Budapest, Hulier wants to return to his old life and put the supernatural world behind him, but you saved his life and he owes you.

Chemistry, Forensic Pathology, Pharmacy.

Mechanics 1, Medic 2.

CONTACT 5

Fr. Loretti, Vatican Archivist

The elderly priest works in the Vatican archives. He's a committed foe of the vampires, but too old and frail to be of use in the field.

Human Terrain, Occult, Research, Vampirology.

CONTACT 6

Madame Rostami

A mysterious vampire hunter, keeper of the Sykoran Crucifix.

Occult, Streetwise, Vampirology.

Network 2, Preparedness 2.

NO GRAVE FOR TRAITORS

What devil or what witch was ever so great as Attila, whose blood is in these veins?

Ambition is a dangerous thing when dealing with vampires. The Linea Dracula are descended from Dracula himself; all other lineages and titles are nothing compared to that august claim. They may raise up a few assigns as spouses or adopted children, but only those of the blood are the true secret masters of the world.

For an ambitious mortal, this barrier is intolerable. Anthony Hollister was an ambitious political fixer and entrepreneur before he was drawn into the service of the vampire Carlyle. For years, he willingly served his vampiric master, enthralled both by Carlyle's hypnotic presence but also by the prospect of immortality. Over time, he learned that no matter how well he served, no matter how much

he helped Carlyle rise in the ranks of the Hungarian branch of the Linea, Hollister would always be barred from the upper echelons of those secret masters because of, effectively, an accident of birth.

Poisoned by his ambition, Hollister has embarked on a scheme to break this barrier. If only a true member of the Linea can rule, then Hollister will *control* a member of the Linea. His current master, Carlyle, is a young and dangerous vampire, comfortable with the modern world and wary of manipulation or betrayal by his servants; if Hollister tried to scheme against Carlyle (and even if Carlyle's psychic sway over him would permit it), he knows he would fail. Carlyle is

too clever and paranoid to fall under the control of a mortal.

What about a member of the other branch of the Linea, the Romanian line? A creature like Jovitzo, a savage with the mentality of a medieval warlord who's spent most of the last five centuries terrorizing the unfortunate peasants who lived within a bat's flight of his crumbling castle? Jovitzo's dependent on his servants (as Leyla Khan knows all too well), but he's got even more potent supernatural gifts than a Hungarian-line vampire, and has an already-established support network of agents and minions.

Hollister needs the impossible – a vampire that's both very, very old and brand new.

He thinks he's found it.

BACKSTORY

Back in the late 1870s, a small band of Russian mercenaries – fleeing the carnage of the Russo-Turkish war – camped in a ruined castle. There, they discovered buried treasure. They fell to quarrelling over the gold, and several of them were killed in the ensuing fray. The survivors escaped back to Russia carrying their stolen gold.

That's the cover story.

The mercenaries were actually hunters, working with a scholar named Vordenburg. They knew that a vampire, Count Kobori of the Romanian line, dwelt in the castle. With Vordenburg's aid, they were able to destroy the vampire – at least temporarily. The castle fell out of reality, becoming a thing of shadow, out of phase with the world we know. Trapped in the void, the vampire slumbered.

Nine months ago, an archaeological dig headed by Professor Jerik camped near the remains of the castle. Kobori

was able to psychically contact Jerik, and turned him into a thrall. Jerik ended up in London, where Hollister found him. The two formed an unlikely alliance.

Both want to reawaken Kobori. Jerik's completely in Kobori's thrall and wishes only to serve his master, but Hollister's plan is to keep Kobori weak and dependent, ensuring that he remains in control. In order to get to the castle, though, they need a key stolen from the castle by the Russians in the 1870s. That key is now part of a trove of art that's about to be auctioned in London.

Hollister doesn't have the resources to purchase the key himself. His vampire master Carlyle is fantastically wealthy, but Hollister can't risk stealing money, as it would attract unwanted attention. In order to get the money, he's going to betray one of Carlyle's minions, a drug smuggler called Calatrava, to a rival

drug lord named Behar. In exchange for Calatrava's death and control of Calatrava's distribution network, Behar will secretly give Hollister the money he needs to obtain the key and resurrect Count Kobori.

OVERVIEW

To successfully complete the operation, Khan must:

◆ Follow the money from Spain to London
◆ Infiltrate the auction house and discover who's behind the purchase of the Kastantev collection
◆ Escape Hollister's attempt to eliminate her in London
◆ Pursue Hollister and Jerik to Transylvania
◆ Enter the nightmarish castle of Kobori
◆ Stop anyone from reawakening Count Kobori

CAST LIST

IN SPAIN

Francesca Curtis: conspiracy messenger on her way to a meeting with Calatrava.

Calatrava: Spanish drug lord and minion of Carlyle. Hollister's arranged to have him eliminated so Behar can seize his territory and distribution network.

IN MOROCCO

Behar: Moroccan rival of Calatrava; his money will fund Hollister's purchase of the Kastantev collection.

IN LONDON

Carlyle: Hungarian-line vampire, now based in London.

Anthony Hollister: Mortal servant of Carlyle. He plans to swap Carlyle for a more pliant vampiric master.

Nestor Kastantev: Russian rich kid, in London to sell off a collection of antiques. One of his ancestors was a Russian soldier who accompanied Baron Vordenburg into the castle of Kobori. The key to Kobori's castle is hidden in a secret compartment in a bookcase in this collection.

Jerik: An archaeologist who went looking for Kobori's castle. Without the key, he was unable to find it, but he fell under the psychic thrall of the sleeping vampire and is now obsessed with resurrecting his master. He knows he needs the key from the Kastantev collection.

Carmen Vidraru: A student of Jerik's who accompanied him on his dig in Romania; she came to London looking for signs of her former teacher.

Dr. Susan Graves: A historian and writer employed by Cornet's auction house to evaluate items; she reviewed the Kastantev collection.

IN ROMANIA

Count Kobori: A Romanian-line vampire, incapacitated but not killed by vampire hunters in the late 19th century. He was an accomplished sorcerer, and his castle was swept away into some timeless netherworld when he was defeated. The castle – and the vampire – can only be reached by means of a magical key.

Baron Vordenburg: 19th-century vampire hunter.

ENTRY VECTORS

The operation begins with Khan tracking Francesca Curtis, a messenger and go-between employed by the conspiracy. Curtis is connected to the Hungarian branch of the Linea Dracula; officially, she's an investment analyst for a small private bank in London. In practice, she handles *sub rosa* money transfers for conspiracy elements. As far as Khan knows, Curtis is largely unaware of the supernatural aspects of her employers, and may not even be aware she's working for vampires.

There are several possible entry vectors for this mission:

- If Khan has the Edge "The Eczes Papers" from *Never Say Dead* or "Financial Irregularities" from *The Deniable Woman*, then those notes identify Curtis as a conspiracy bag-carrier who would be a good source of intelligence.
- **Traffic Analysis** picks up conspiracy chatter about some potential new operation in the Mediterranean region; if Curtis has left her usual haunts in London and come to Spain, following her may turn up some valuable clues.
- Looking into the history of Baron Vordenburg after *The Deniable Woman* could bring Khan into this mystery mid-way through, skipping the initial Spanish action sequence.
- Interrogating low-level conspiracy minions might also identify Curtis as a target.
- If Khan rescued any of the vampire hunters in *Never Say Dead* (Hulier, Fr. Loretti, or Rostami), then any one of them might identify Curtis as someone who was looking into the same sources that led them to the Rosewater Potion (Hollister sent her to look into the matter).
- It could be simple coincidence – while fleeing Romania, Khan spots Curtis in an airport, and starts following her.

STARTING PROBLEMS

Optionally, offer the four Starting Problems to the player and ask her to pick whichever one best reflects Khan's current situation, or pick the most apt Problem yourself and give it to the player. If you've already played through *Never Say Dead* or another Leyla Khan adventure, and your player already has a hand full of ongoing Problems, you don't need to add another.

1. **Building Bridges. Starting Problem.** You need allies and reliable sources; that means rebuilding your connection to MI6. You need to end this operation in MI6's good graces.

2. **Shelter in a Storm. Starting Problem.** The conspiracy's closing in on you – you need to lie low out of your usual haunts, or lose some of the monsters on your trail. If you don't find a way to counter this problem, gain Problem 5, "At Your Throat."

3. **Out of Blood. Starting Problem.** You've exhausted the last of the Rosewater Potion. You need more vampire blood to make more of your protective elixir.

4. **Voice Message. Starting Problem.** A few days ago, you got a brief and confused message from Harry Coleman. He's MI6, you worked with him when you were in the service. Moscow desk. He sounds terrified, drunk. He said you were right, said that he needed to talk to you – but he didn't leave any way to contact him. Discard this for a free Interpersonal Push when dealing with Harry. While you hold this card, you've got a -1 penalty to any **Cool** tests.

NOTE ON TIMING

Some scenes in this operation have deliberately loose chronology. Curtis waits in Girona for "a few days," and the timing of the key lot in the auction is similarly "in the next week or so." Instead of forcing you to keep track of a timetable, we've left things vague. You should still keep close track of time in your game, but let the player set the pace. Some players like the careful weaving of a web of surveillance and intrigue that plays out over time; others want to use every available minute and would prefer to kick a door down instead of waiting. The adventure works just as well if Khan stalks her prey for a week in Girona, or if the whole operation is a madcap three-day thrill bender.

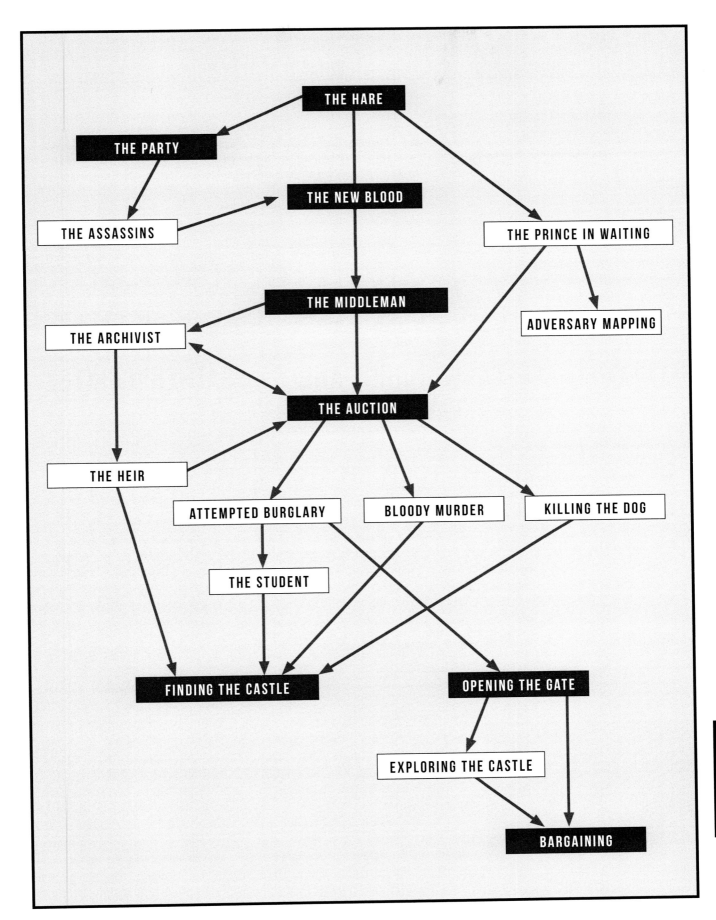

THE HARE

Scene Type: Introduction
Lead-Outs: The Party, The New Blood, The Prince in Waiting

Girona, Spain. The ancient city is a popular tourist destination; the medieval walls and churches draw visitors here, as do the galleries and cafés. Khan's here, tracking a conspiracy asset named Francesca Curtis.

Curtis is staying in the Hotel Historic, a small high-end hotel in the center of the city. To an outside observer, it might look like she's here on vacation, as she's acting like a tourist – going to see the sights, dining out, relaxing by the pool... but **Notice** spots that every day, she checks at reception for a delivery. She's waiting for something or someone.

- **Tradecraft** suggests that there's some degree of deniability involved here; whatever Curtis is doing, she's being kept in the dark about the bigger picture. She may be here purely as a courier, and she'll hand-deliver the parcel when it arrives.

So, what's the player's approach? Just wait and watch until something happens? Try to break into Curtis' hotel room? Grab Curtis and interrogate her? Take advantage of the fact that Curtis doesn't know Khan, and befriend her? Try to steal the delivery when it arrives?

Let the player drive this earlier investigation.

WHAT'S REALLY GOING ON?

As far as Curtis knows, she's in Girona as a courtesy to the drug kingpin Calatrava. She's waiting for some documents to be sent from London; she'll then bring them to Calatrava for his signature, as part of a scheme to launder his heroin money through London real estate purchases. Calatrava's very, very paranoid about his enemies, so he keeps his location hidden. Curtis' contact with Calatrava's operation is through a younger criminal, his nephew Luciano; once she gets the documents, Luciano will bring her to meet his uncle, and not until then.

The real story: Hollister, the villain of the piece, has tipped off Calatrava's rival Behar about Curtis' mission. Behar's men are watching the hotel; as soon as Luciano brings Curtis to Calatrava, they'll follow and assassinate the kingpin.

WATCHING AND WAITING

With **Tradecraft**, Khan builds up an impression of Curtis' routine. Each morning, she makes a phone call from her room that seems to irritate her (she's calling Hollister, impatient at the delay in getting the papers she needs). She then spends the afternoon wandering the city. In the evenings, she sometimes meets with a young Spanish man (**Criminology:** Khan doesn't know the man, but from his associates and the way he throws cash about, she'd guess he's connected to the drug trade; **Streetwise** gets his name, Luciano, and rumors that he's the nephew of Calatrava). It's clear from watching them that Curtis dislikes Luciano, but is maintaining an icy professionalism, whereas Luciano appears to have taken this as a challenge to his seductive wiles.

Call for a **Surveillance** Challenge to spot the danger.

If Khan keeps watching (**Tradecraft** core clue), then after two days, Curtis gets the delivery she's been waiting for, meets up with Luciano, and the two of them head off to *The Party* (p. 174).

GATHERING INTEL

The following information can be obtained through background research, observation, talking to contacts and maybe a little burglary.

- **Accounting** or **High Society:** Curtis claims she's here to assist a client who wants to buy property in London. That could be a cover for money laundering, or even genuine business, but it doesn't explain why she's waiting around in Girona. Why not go straight to the client – unless there's something more going on. Finding out who her client is, and the cause of the delay may both be important.

- **Charm** or **Reassurance:** Talking to the hotel staff reveals that Curtis is waiting for the delivery of a package, and they really hope it turns up soon, as she complains bitterly every morning when it doesn't arrive.

- **Criminology** or **Streetwise:** Some of Curtis' associates in Girona are connected to the Calatrava crime network. A Push of **Criminology** gets some extra background on the Calatravas; they're a well-established ring, dealing primarily

Bonus: +2 if you Push **Streetwise** or **Urban Survival**.

Advance 7+: Not only do you keep an eye on Curtis, but you also spot the guys watching her. She's being followed – at least four men, Moroccans, professional, watching the hotel and tracking her. You manage to get a good look at the faces of all four. Gain Edge 1, "Who Are These Guys?"

Hold 4-6: You're pretty sure that someone's following Curtis – you've seen that guy on the moped too many times tonight for it to be a coincidence. But when you try to get closer, he drives off at high speed.

Setback 3 or less: You're pretty sure that someone's following Curtis – you've seen that guy on the moped too many times tonight for it to be a coincidence. But when you try to get closer, he drives off at high speed – and you glimpse someone else, too, watching you and then vanishing into the crowd. There's a sick feeling in your stomach that tells you you've been made. Gain Problem 7, "Spotted."

Extra Problem: Problem 8, "Sympathy for Curtis."

Stunt: Yes (**Cover** to disguise yourself).

---

in heroin and other opiates, run by the notorious paranoid and evasive Pablo Calatrava.

- **Accounting** plus a Quick Test of **Filch** or **Infiltration** (6+): If Khan gets hold of the hotel records, she can trace the credit card used to pay for Curtis' stay in the Hotel Historic. Her trip's being paid for by Hollister Consulting, a small London firm that Khan hasn't heard of before. If she checks out Hollister Consulting in London, it leads to *The Prince in Waiting* (p. 184).

- Failing the test means Khan's spotted, and may gain a Heat Problem if she can't talk her way out.

- Similarly, an **Infiltration** Quick Test (6+) plus **Electronic Surveillance** lets Khan break into Curtis' hotel room and bug the place. She could plant a hidden camera and microphone, letting her eavesdrop when Curtis phones up Hollister in the morning and shouts at him for delaying the "Calatrava papers," or a tracking device that lets Khan follow Curtis to *The Party* (p. 174).

QUESTIONING CURTIS

If approached socially – say, by posing as another tourist – then Curtis is superficially friendly but inwardly guarded and careful not to give anything away. **Charm/High Society/Reassurance** plus a description of *how* the player is wheedling information out of Curtis gets some added intel:

- Curtis is frustrated because the London office she's working with has apparently fouled up the paperwork. She was supposed to be here only for a day or two, but now she's stuck waiting for the delivery of the contracts. Now, it's not like she minds sitting around in a pricy hotel in a historic town on someone else's expense account, but it's still annoying.

- The nephew of the client – Luciano – is a creep who keeps hitting on her.

Offer the player a free Push in exchange for Problem 8, "Sympathy for Curtis."

A Push of a suitable Interpersonal ability could convince Curtis to bring Khan along as a friend/shield against Luciano when she finally gets invited to *The Party* (p. 174). Give her Edge 2, "Party Invitation."

Alternatively, Khan could easily grab and interrogate Curtis, either posing as police (**Cop Talk**) or just threatening her (**Intimidation**). Curtis protests, arguing that she's done nothing wrong, and demanding to be released. She denies any connections to organized crime – in fact, she's never even *met* Pablo Calatrava and doesn't know where he is (**Bullshit Detector** agrees; in fact, the amount of venom she puts into that denial suggests that she's frustrated that she doesn't know where this Calatrava is, implying that she's waiting to make contact with him).

If Khan maintains a good relationship with Curtis, and saves her life at the party, there's a chance of *Flipping Curtis* – see the sidebar on p. 179.

THE PARCEL

The parcel is a slim folder of legal papers that gets delivered to the hotel on the morning before *The Party* (p. 174). If Khan gets a look at it, either by stealing it from hotel reception or from Curtis, she learns the following:

- It's for the purchase of some property in London (luxury apartments in a new development), and mentions "Hollister Consulting" as one of the parties involved. If Khan follows up on that in London, see *The Prince in Waiting* (p. 184).

- **Accounting:** It's got the smell of a suspicious front for money laundering, but there's nothing immediately incriminating.

- One section does catch Khan's eye: it looks like there was a change about the payment schedule. One of the spreadsheet printouts in the back of the folder describes the client sending a considerable sum of money to London via a Swiss account immediately, which would certainly have raised alarm bells with financial watchdogs. Someone was very, very eager to get the money to London. Normally, one would assume that it's the client who's pushing to get the money into the laundromat, but in this case, there are signs suggesting it was the *broker*, the person who'd be taking the most risk.

(If Khan steals the folder, another copy arrives within a few hours, sent by express courier. The delay was to ensure that Behar got his assassins in place to eliminate Calatrava, and had nothing to do with the paperwork.)

After the folder shows up at the hotel, Curtis collects it and makes contact with Luciano. He tells her that he's meeting his uncle tonight, and that she should accompany him to a party in a private villa where she can see Calatrava and sign the paperwork. Business before pleasure, he leers.

It's a core clue (**Notice**) to spot Curtis leaving with Luciano.

THE PARTY

Scene Type: Core
Lead-Ins: The Hare
Lead-Outs: The Assassins

Luciano drives Curtis out into the countryside along roads that wind up into the foothills of the Pyrenees. He drives fast, and he's got a sports car – unless Khan has a similar vehicle, she'll have trouble keeping up. (If Khan's got Edge 2, "Party Invitation" and is in the car with Curtis, she can still make the **Sense Trouble** Challenge, but Luciano ignores her if she claims to have spotted a tail.)

Call for a **Sense Trouble** Challenge on the drive.

The destination is a private villa owned by a Catalan industrialist, Bernat Puy; it's clear that there's a celebration of some sort here tonight. As Khan approaches, she can hear loud music and revelry. Judging from the cars parked in the villa's courtyard, and the caliber of the guests, it's a private event for the wealthy and famous. There's limited private security – enough to keep gatecrashers and paparazzi away, nothing especially serious.

A push of **High Society** can get Khan past the bouncers and into the villa; alternatively, she can sneak in with a **Cover** or **Infiltration** Quick Test (8+); if she fails, gain Problem 11, "Party Crasher." (The "trouble" referred to on the card is a fistfight with the bouncers if discovered before *The Assassins*, or a Heat Problem afterwards).

The crowd at the villa is a mix of wealthy tourists, crooks, and raucous partygoers; there's dancing and cocktails around the pool, sex and drugs in the rooms upstairs. DJs blast dance music through the night. Khan can also sense business being done on the fringes of the party – older men making deals and smoking cigars as they watch the girls dancing in the disco lights.

Luciano spends a few minutes trying to ply Curtis with drinks; when that fails, he shows her over to his uncle's coterie of friends.

PABLO CALATRAVA

The drug boss has a private salon in the back of the villa; he's staying here secretly as a guest of Bernat Puy. If Khan's here with Curtis, she can get into an anteroom where a pair of bodyguards watch her closely, but she can still eavesdrop. Otherwise, she'll need to sneak into a room near the salon in order to listen.

Listening to Calatrava's conversation with his buddies gets the following information:

- The main topic of conversation is what to do about "the African," a rival drug distributor called Behar. From listening in (and using **Criminology**), Khan gets the impression that Behar is aggressively pushing in on Calatrava's territory and distribution routes, and that Calatrava's subordinates are looking to their boss to come to some arrangement or truce.
  - ◊ A **Criminology** Push or a use of **Network** could get Khan a meeting with Behar; see *The New Blood*, p. 179.

- Calatrava sneers at the suggestion of compromise. Behar, he insists, will perish for his insolence. He thinks he is fighting one war, but he knows nothing about how the world truly works. They must wait until the dark of the moon, maybe a little longer, but the matter is in hand. **Vampirology** or **Bullshit Detector** suggests that Calatrava's referencing the supernatural; he may have vampiric allies that will deal with the threat from Behar.

- Reassured by this, the conversation turns to other matters. When Curtis enters, they talk about the London property deal, and it's clear that

SPOTTING THE TAIL

SENSE TROUBLE

Bonus: +2 if you've got Edge 1, "Who Are These Guys?"

Advance 9+: There's a car following Luciano and Curtis – the same one you spotted in town earlier. They haven't spotted you. If you want to follow them instead, you can. (See *The Assassins*, p. 176). If you haven't already, gain Edge 1, "Who Are These Guys?"

Hold 6-8: You spot another car following Luciano and Curtis, the same one you spotted in town earlier. They take a turning down a side road shortly before Luciano arrives at his destination. Gain Edge 3, "En Garde."

Setback 5 or less: As you follow Luciano, a car suddenly blinds you with a flash of its headlights, and you nearly lose control. If you don't have it already, gain Problem 7, "Spotted." If you have it already, go to the Challenge "Sideswipe."

Extra Problem: None.

Stunt: Yes (**Driving**; **Surveillance**).

SIDESWIPE

Those guys are trying to force you off the road – and down a suddenly steep cliff!

DRIVING

Advance 11+: You maintain control of your vehicle as it spins. You manage to both avoid an accident, but also get it back on the road quickly enough to follow the bastards who just tried to murder you. If you want to track them down instead of going after Luciano and Curtis, you can (see *The Assassins*, p. 176).

Hold 7-10: You're knocked off the road, but wrestle the car to a stop before you go over the cliff. Your attackers have vanished into the night, and you'll need to hurry and get back to the road to catch Luciano and Curtis.

GETTING CLOSE TO CALATRAVA

INFILTRATION

Advance 9+: You find an excellent hiding place in the bedroom just above Calatrava's salon. You can hear everything, and have a good view of all approaches. Gain Edge 3, "En Garde."

Hold 4-8: You find a hiding place outside the window, where you can listen to Calatrava's conversation with Curtis. Describe how it's awkward or perilous.

Setback 3 or less: Oh, lovely. Now one of Calatrava's guards is trying to kill you, and you have to silence them before they raise the alarm. Make a Quick **Fighting** Test (8+); if you fail, gain Problem 12, "Bathroom Brawl."

Extra Problem: None.

Stunt: Yes (**Athletics**, **Conceal**, or **Cover** to sneak in; **Preparedness** for a directional microphone or other bugging equipment).

Setback 6 or less: You bail out of the car as it plunges over the edge, and manage to grab onto a branch before you follow it into the darkness. Gain Problem 9, "Car Crash Survivor."

Extra Problem: Problem 10, "Need a Ride."

Stunt: Yes (**Shooting**; **Mechanics**).

Calatrava is furious with Hollister. The "little shit" tried to squeeze money out of Calatrava up front – feh, the Englishman has no respect, none at all.

◊ **Criminology** or **Vampirology:** Vampires have the advantage of *patience*; they're immortal, after all. While Khan knows they are often savage and impatient when it comes to insults or immediate gratification, they know how to wait when it comes to strategic matters, especially business deals. The conspiracy's core investments pay out over decades and centuries. If someone's trying for short-term financial gain, it's always a mortal.

♦ One of Calatrava's associates suggests threatening Hollister, but Calatrava quashes that idea instantly. Hollister, he says, "is close to power," and cannot be harmed, no matter how much Calatrava might like to punish the brat.

GATHERING INTEL

If Khan hangs back and waits, segue into *The Assassins* (p. 176).

Khan can get more information on Hollister, either by questioning Calatrava (**Charm**) or by searching Calatrava's room for papers and correspondence (**Accounting**). In either case, she'll need to make a Quick Test (9+ against **Cover** in the former case, **Conceal** in the latter).

If the **Cover** test fails, then Calatrava grows suspicious of Khan, and when the attack starts he and his men will assume that she's one of Behar's agents. If it succeeds, then Calatrava's relaxed enough now that he's finally signed the papers Curtis brought that he's willing to be a little indiscreet when talking to Khan.

If the **Conceal** test fails, then Khan's spotted as she searches the room; treat it as if she'd just had a Setback on

"Getting Close to Calatrava." (If she's already got Problem 12, "Bathroom Brawl," then give her another Injury and *another* dead/unconscious guy in the bathroom.) If she succeeds, she finds the Necrophone (see sidebar, p. 179) hidden in a suitcase in Calatrava's room. In either case, there's enough information to point at *The Prince in Waiting* (p. 184) in London.

At a suitably dramatic moment, move into *The Assassins*.

◤◤◤◤◤
THE ASSASSINS

Scene Type: Core
Lead-Ins: The Party
Lead-Outs: The New Blood, The Prince in Waiting

Behar's assassins followed Curtis to the party, and now they're going to try to kill Calatrava. It's a four-man kill team. Two are at the party, having infiltrated as guests just like Khan. A third's the getaway driver, and is waiting a short distance down the road with the engine running. The fourth man has a sniper rifle with a night-vision scope, and has taken up position on the hillside overlooking the villa. All four have short-range radios and earpieces to stay in constant communication.

The two assassins who've infiltrated the party intend to kill Calatrava quietly. If they can ambush the old man when he goes to the bathroom, or catch him alone in his room and shoot him, that's ideal. If that fails, they're going to stage an explosion. When their charges go off, they're gambling that Calatrava's men will try to get their boss to a car to get him away from the villa (Calatrava's a wanted gang boss, and won't want to hang around waiting for the ensuing police investigation). When Calatrava leaves the shelter of the villa, the sniper will take him out from a distance as he crosses to his car.

While Curtis isn't the main target of the assassins, Khan may assume that they're after her, and it's not entirely

incorrect – the assassins have no compunction about killing Curtis to clean up loose ends.

Khan's the wild card in all this; she may be able to stop the assassins. Possible ways this could play out:

♦ If she's at the party, then if she Pushes **Notice** or **Tradecraft**, she spots that one of the guests is wearing an earpiece and scanning the crowd as if looking for a target. Run the Challenge "Takedown.".

♦ If she's with Calatrava, then she's present when one of the assassins tries to ambush the old gangster. Again, run "Takedown."

♦ If she's got Problem 7, "Spotted," then Khan herself is a target of the assassins. Run the Challenge "You're a Target."

♦ Alternatively, if Khan doesn't get involved in the initial attack, then Calatrava survives the first assassination attempt. He tries to retrieve the Necrophone from his room upstairs, but when the assassins set off an explosion, his bodyguards grab him and hustle him out into the courtyard, where Khan can, if she wishes, get involved in the Challenge "Dodging the Sniper."

(It's also perfectly valid, if somewhat cynical, for Khan to lurk in the shadows and watch the assassination play out. She can then grab one of the assassins or search Calatrava's room in the ensuing chaos.)

If he survives the first assassination attempt, Khan has the opportunity to get close to Calatrava. Assuming he doesn't think that she's another assassin here to kill him, she can try to get him to safety when the sniper starts shooting. Saving Calatrava's life puts him in her debt.

Calatrava refuses to leave without first retrieving the Necrophone from upstairs. Khan can drag him out, or take the added risk of fetching the occult device.

The sniper's got a powerful rifle, and while the medieval villa has thick walls, there are plenty of windows and he's got a good angle to shoot at Calatrava's rooms. Dodging the sniper means ducking from cover to cover on the way out to the car.

YOU'RE A TARGET
SENSE TROUBLE

Advance 9+: You spot one of the Moroccans – the guys who were following Curtis in Girona – trying to sneak up on you at the party. Describe how you take him down quietly. You can either sneak out of the party and question him, or just dump his body and go searching for the rest of his team – the radio traffic on his earpiece suggests there's another two or three hostiles out there. You've a bonus die on the "Takedown" Challenge if you take the latter route.

Hold 4-8: Do you want the good news or the bad news? The good news is that you're not dead, and your would-be assassin is down. The bad news is that your cover is completely blown, as you took him down in full view of the rest of the party. And now things are – literally – exploding. Either cut your losses and run like hell, or go to the "Dodging the Sniper" Challenge.

Setback 3 or less: As above, but the assassin was faster than you expected, and you've been shot in the side. Gain Problem 13, "Through and Through."

Extra Problem: Problem 14, "Red Dot."

Stunt: Yes (**Surveillance** to watch the crowd; **Fighting** or **Shooting** to take down the assassin).

TAKEDOWN
SURVEILLANCE

Advance 9+: Scanning the crowd at the party, you spot the assassins converging on Calatrava. Describe how you take them down quietly and efficiently, then decide if you want to grab one for questioning, or if you want to confront Calatrava.

Hold 6-8: You intercept one of the assassins; turns out, he's got a bomb. Gain Problem 15, "Shock and Awe," and go to the Challenge "Dodging the Sniper."

Setback 5 or less: You intercept one of the assassins, but it turns out there was a second bogey out there in the crowd. You see a knot of bodyguards converge on Calatrava, but you can tell the old man is dead. Time to exfiltrate with your prisoner.

Extra Problem: Problem 14, "Red Dot."

Stunt: Yes (**Fighting** or **Shooting** to take down the assassin; **Athletics** to get into position).

DODGING THE SNIPER
EVASION

Penalty: -1 die if you're protecting Calatrava or Curtis, -2 if you're carrying the Necrophone, -2 per "Red Dot" Problem.

Advance 11+: The sniper frantically snaps off a series of shots, trying to bring you down. Wood and stone explode around you as armor-piercing bullets slice through the villa. You stay low and keep moving, and make it to the safety of the back exit, ignoring the screams and panic on the far side of the building. This party's over. If you were protecting someone, gain Edge 4, "Indebted." Otherwise, gain Edge 5, "Drawing Fire."

Hold 7-10: You nearly make it. You get out of the villa as bullets cut through the air around you, but the sniper's last shot hits home. If you were protecting someone, you've got a time for a brief conversation before they slip away. If you're on your own, gain Problem 15, "Down."

Setback 6 or less: As above, but if you were protecting someone, they got killed instantly and there's no time for interrogation.

Extra Problem: Problem 16, "Loose End."

Stunt: Yes (**Athletics** for acrobatics; **Sense Trouble** to anticipate the direction of fire).

- **Curtis:** Saving Curtis' life is enough to push her into Contact status. She's willing to help Khan against the conspiracy, although for now she believes that they're dealing with a criminal organization, not a supernatural threat.
- **The Assassins:** Questioning a captured assassin with **Interrogation** points to *The New Blood*. The two assassins who were sent into the party are Abdel and Mehdi; their getaway drive is Roger and the sniper is Hachim.

CAPTURED

If Khan gets captured by the Calatravas, then Luciano's assigned the job of questioning her and disposing of the body. He hides Khan's unconscious form in the trunk of his car and drives down to the shore, intending to make it look like she was a tourist who slipped and drowned in the Mediterranean. Let the player describe how Khan turns the tables on him and escapes, at the cost of Problem 18, "The Luciano Situation."

AFTER THE ATTACK

Once the dust settles and the assassins flee, what's left?

Leaving the party is everyone's first priority. Calatrava and some of his associates are wanted criminals, and Khan presumably wants to avoid the attention of the authorities too. The partygoers scatter even as police cars race up the mountain roads, lights blazing.

- **Calatrava:** Even if Khan saved his life, Calatrava's still a murderous drug lord. She can force some answers out of him with an **Interrogation** Push, or trade favors with **Negotiation**. Calatrava knows that he's working, ultimately, for vampires. He's seen the undead,

but his usual contact with his vampiric supervisors is a man in London named Hollister (*The Prince in Waiting*, p. 184). If he hasn't already, he reveals that Hollister tried to pressure him for money; he doesn't know why Hollister (or the vampires) would suddenly need an infusion of cash.

- He had a backup method of communicating with the conspiracy – his Necrophone. A suitable Push (**Intimidation** or **Negotiation**) could get him to hand it over, or Khan could just steal it. If she acquires it, she gets Edge 6, "The Necrophone." If she doesn't grab it, and Calatrava's still alive *and* doesn't have a reason to trust or aid her, give her Problem 17, "Whispers on the Wind."

THE NECROPHONE

This curious device was made by an eccentric conspiracy adept in the 1930s, and passed into Calatrava's hands through a dubious source. It was made by a servant of the Hungarian branch of the Linea Dracula, and is effectively an artificial way to compensate for the more potent sorcery of their Romanian counterparts. It consists of a heavy glass bell jar that's half-full of dirt, connected by a thick cable to an old-fashioned Bakelite telephone receiver. There's a small valve at the mouth of the jar that allows the user to add fresh blood. To use the device, connect it to a power source, top it up with some human blood to moisten the grave dirt, and speak into the receiver. If you're lucky, and if the spiritual currents are in alignment, your words will be heard by the vampire who sleeps on that native soil (Carlyle, in the case of Calatrava's Necrophone.)

It's a one-way channel; the vampire can't reply through this method. Listening at the receiver is not recommended, unless you like hearing the whispers of the unquiet dead.

FLIPPING CURTIS

If Curtis survives, and Khan convinces her that the attack on Calatrava's compound was no coincidence, that Hollister betrayed her, then Curtis becomes a Contact of Khan's.

She's good at following the money, and she's familiar with some of the conspiracy's internal financial channels. She can trace unusual transactions that point at *The Auction*, p. 187.

THE NEW BLOOD

Scene Type: Alternate
Lead-Ins: The Party, The Assassins, The Hare
Lead-Outs: The Middleman

The assassins who attacked the party work for the Moroccan drug lord Behar Tourabi, a rival of the Calatrava clan. Khan can track Behar down easily if she captured one of the assassins, or if she pushes **Criminology**. Merely locating Behar isn't enough – she needs a way to speak with him if she's to find out the truth behind the attack on Calatrava. A **Negotiation** or **Streetwise** Push can arrange a private meeting. Alternatively, a **Network** roll lets her track down a go-between who can put her in touch with Behar – give the player Tazi's Contact card.

If Khan's unwilling or unable to arrange a meeting, she can try breaking into Behar's compound.

FINDING BEHAR

NETWORK

Bonus: +2 if you Push **Charm**, **Negotiation**, or **Intimidation**.

Penalty: -1 per Heat Problem. -2 if you've got Problem 16, "Loose End."

Advance 7+: In a small flat in Casablanca, you meet your old contact Tazi, who has connections to smugglers and arms dealers across North Africa. Describe why Tazi owes you a favor – and then you can cash it in for a meeting with Behar.

Hold 4-6: You track down your old contact Tazi in Casablanca. He can get you a meeting with Behar, and the promise of safe passage – but you'll need to spend a Push to persuade Tazi to help. Alternatively, he can tell you where to find Behar's compound.

Setback 3 or less: As above, but gain Problem 16, "Loose End."

Extra Problem: None.

Stunt: No.

THE COMPOUND

Behar runs his operation from a compound in Casablanca. The place is a cross between a luxury villa and a fortress; high whitewashed walls surrounding lush green gardens. He's got plenty of bodyguards, his personal security reinforced after his strike at his rival Calatrava.

If Khan has a meeting arranged with the drug lord, she's escorted in and shown up to a dining room.

◆ If Khan's got Problem 16, "Loose End," then any surviving assassins are here in the villa; did Khan kill any of them in Spain?

◆ If Khan's got Problem 17, "Whisper on the Winds," then she arrives just as a vampire assassin eliminates Behar – see sidebar, p. 181.

BREAKING IN

If Khan doesn't have an invitation, she's got to sneak in.

SEARCHING FOR CLUES

Traffic Analysis or **Streetwise:** If Calatrava's dead, then there's a lot of activity around the compound, as Behar moves to consolidate his control of the drug trade in the region. If Calatrava survived, then there's an eerie stillness in the compound, a calm before the storm.

Notice: Khan spots one document among Behar's personal papers that's weirdly out of place – there's a business card from a "Doctor Jerik." It gives an English phone number, email, and street address (**Urban Survival:** the address is that of a cheap bedsit in North London). This is a core clue pointing at *The Middleman* (p. 182).

Accounting: Drug lords don't leave their financial records around for anyone to investigate, but if Khan manages to get into Behar's accounts (perhaps by using **Network** to hire a hacker, or by forcing Behar to reveal information at gunpoint), then she

discovers that Behar sent money to an account in a London bank connected to a private auction house – see *The Auction*, p. 187.

MEETING BEHAR

If Khan's gotten this far, then Behar assumes (correctly) that she's not someone he wants to piss off unnecessarily, and is willing to talk to her. Unlike his underlings, who probably want to kill Khan to get their revenge on the person who foiled their plans, Behar's more cautious and far-sighted; he wants to understand the situation fully before taking action.

◆ He'll start by apologizing for any "misunderstandings" in Girona – Khan wasn't the target of the assassins.

◆ He admits that his men followed Francesca Curtis, and hints that he knew that she would be making contact with Calatrava.

◆ Initially, he won't admit who tipped him off; he also won't admit that his attack was to enable him to take over the Calatrava distribution network. (If Calatrava's dead, then he'll boast about his new reach.)

◆ Behar doesn't know exactly who his ally in London is; it was arranged through an intermediary. He sent money to London; in exchange, he was sent a dossier on Curtis.

◆ This intermediary was a strange little man called Jerik (*The Middleman*, p. 182). Behar initially thought Jerik was insane, but he came with detailed information on the Calatrava operation.

INFILTRATING THE COMPOUND

INFILTRATION

Bonus: +2 if you Push **Architecture**.

Penalty: -2 if you've got Problem 16, "Loose End."

Advance 7+: You've broken into tougher places than this without being seen – and you can get out again. You automatically Advance on any **Evasion** tests needed to leave the compound.

Hold 4-6: You've made it in without being seen – at least for now. Your route in is compromised, though, so you may need to make some noise coming out.

Setback 3 or less: There's no way in that doesn't involve getting killed. You'll need to find another way to learn what Behar knows.

Extra Problem: If Khan has Tazi's contact card, then discard it after this operation – Behar's gang later kills Tazi for helping her.

Stunt: Yes (**Athletics**; **Cover**).

◆ If Khan hints at a supernatural connection, he's initially dismissive, but **Bullshit Detector** suggests that that's bravado – Behar doesn't know that Calatrava was working for vampires, but he's heard rumors about strange events.

◊ Using **Vampirology** or **Intimidation** can convince Behar that he's in danger, or at least dealing with unholy forces. If Behar's sufficiently alarmed about his new business parties, don't give the player Problem 19, "Forewarned."

◆ With a suitable Interpersonal Push or good roleplaying, Khan can convince Behar that he's best served by playing both sides. He'll tell Khan about his arrangement with London – but he'll also warn Hollister. He gives Khan the name of *The Middleman* (p. 182). After she leaves the compound, give the player Problem 19, "Forewarned."

ESCAPING THE COMPOUND

If Khan needs to make a hasty exit, she's got to make an **Evasion** test (9+). Success means she escapes both the compound and Casablanca without being spotted by Behar's men. If she fails, she's pursued through the streets of Casablanca. Have the player use one of her Mastery Edges to escape her pursuers; if she doesn't have any Masteries left, or if none of them are appropriate, then she gets a Hurt Problem instead.

DEAD MAN WALKING

If Calatrava warned his vampire masters about the attempt on his life, then Behar's doomed. The supernatural assassin – a summoned adzeh, a monstrous fly-demon – dispatched by Carlyle kills the drug lord moments before Khan meets him.

When Khan enters, she sees Behar's body crawling with thousands of fat black flies. His eyes bulge in terror as he asphyxiates on insects. His left eye bursts, and the adzeh crawls out of it. For an instant, Khan sees the outline of a stunted, semi-humanoid dwarf-thing in the middle of the insect cloud – and the adzeh-swarm flies towards her. Challenge time!

SURVIVING THE ADZEH SWARM
COOL

Advance 11+: You don't flinch when the adzeh races towards you. You freeze, letting the insect swarm land on you, crawl all over your skin. You know that the adzeh itself, the vampire controlling this swarm of filth, is in the middle of the insect cloud, using them to distract you. You feel it probing your lips, trying to force its way in – and you snap at it, biting its forelegs off. The adzeh shrieks, and the insects flee. Gain Edge 7, "Iron Will."

Hold 7-10: You grab a tablecloth and set fire to it. Alarms screech, but the smoke from the fire keeps the bug-vampire away. It screeches in pain and confusion.

Setback 6 or less: You scramble away from the bug-swarm, stumbling and clawing at your skin to get the bugs off. Gain Problem 20, "Adzeh, the Blood-Eater."

Extra Problem: Problem 19, "Forewarned".

Stunt: Yes (**Evasion**, to dodge; **Preparedness**, for bug spray).

If Khan hasn't found a core clue here already, Behar gasps Jerik's name before dying.

THE MIDDLEMAN

Scene Type: Alternate
Lead-Ins: The New Blood
Lead-Outs: The Auction, The Prince in Waiting

London.

Jerik's business card leads Khan to his small apartment. It's trivially easy to break in; it's clear no one has been here in several days. The apartment is filthy and dark. Jerik did everything he could to seal off any sources of natural light. The curtains are drawn tightly, and other windows have sheets of cardboard hastily taped over them. A profusion of flies buzz around the rooms, drawn by the rotten meat in the kitchen.

A quick search reveals the following:

♦ It looks like the apartment was abandoned quickly, but not in a panic; there's evidence that someone packed key belongings and left efficiently.

♦ Jerik's diet appears to consist almost entirely of raw meat – and from the state of the knives and the fur and bones in a black bag in the kitchen, he was also butchering stray cats.

♦ The clothing left behind is mostly once-expensive suits that have seen considerable wear and tear. At a guess, Jerik once had a considerably higher income than his present accommodation would suggest.

♦ The bedroom hasn't been used in weeks.

♦ There are several well-thumbed history books here; some were borrowed from various London libraries while others appear to belong to Jerik himself. They're all about archaeology and medieval history in Transylvania.

◊ Tucked into one book is a photograph, apparently being used as a bookmark: it's a print-out of a selfie taken from a camera phone. It's Jerik, looking tired but much happier, surrounded by three younger people – students, probably. They're all dressed in heavy jackets and high-visibility vests, and standing on a mountainside. The countryside suggests Transylvania to Khan. (One of the students in the photo is Carmen (p. 193).

◊ There are scraps of paper in the fireplace, suggesting that Jerik destroyed whatever notes he made.

◊ There's another folder, full of rejection letters from various universities and schools.

◊ There's a print-out of an email from a ""Dr. Graves," asking Jerik to meet Graves at his office. The address given is in Kensington (not far away from Hollister's offices). See *The Archivist*, p. 189.

◊ There's also a stack of business cards identical to the one Khan may have found in Morocco – the sad remnants of Jerik's attempt to rebuild his life after his breakdown.

◊ He also recently borrowed a Moroccan tourist guide and a Hungarian/French phrasebook.

♦ There's a catalogue from a private auction house, Cornet's. Notably, there's the upcoming auction of a number of medieval treasures from a private Russian collection. (*The Auction*, p. 187).

THE HIDDEN ROOM

There's a small hidden space above the bathroom – not an attic per se, but a little enclosed nook created when the building was converted into multiple small apartments. It's accessible by opening a little trapdoor in the ceiling and clambering up by means of a stepladder. The trapdoor is sticky with dried blood. Up there, next to the gurgling water tank, Khan finds a sleeping bag and a portable lamp. The walls of the little space are covered in scrawled markings, apparently written in dried blood.

♦ This room's nearly lightproof and soundproof; either Jerik was keeping someone imprisoned up here, or he retreated up here to hide from the light.

♦ The markings mostly depict leering faces, perhaps those of vampires. There's also the name "VORDENBURG" carved into one wooden beam, gouged into the wood as if with a knife.

♦ **Notice (core clue):** There's an envelope full of photographs; they look to be long-range surveillance photos of a youngish man leaving an office in central London. With a little legwork, Khan can identify the target of this surveillance as Hollister (*The Prince in Waiting*, p. 184)

◊ If Khan spends a push, give her Edge 8, "Memories of Hollister."

ASKING QUESTIONS

The flat is owned by a letting agency; with **Bureaucracy** or **Charm**, Khan learns that the lease is paid up until the end of the month. Jerik was previously several weeks behind on his rent, but recently settled his debts and paid the next month in advance.

His neighbors (**Streetwise**) recall him as a strange, unpleasant man.

♦ He was once a professor in some Eastern European university, but there must have been a scandal that forced him to leave.

♦ They rarely saw him during the day, only at night. When he did go out during the day, he always wore absurdly big, dark sunglasses, even in the depths of winter.

♦ He had no friends and few visitors.

♦ He surprised everyone by going away "on holiday" ten days ago. A weekend trip to Morocco, apparently. He certainly didn't catch a tan there.

♦ Several neighbors complain about the smell from his apartment. Others complain that they heard Jerik talking and even arguing with himself.

♦ No one's seen him in the last few days, but that's not unusual.

BACKGROUND CHECKS

If Khan does some background **Research** (she'll have to Take Time to do so), she can dig up details on Jerik's past.

♦ He was a lecturer in history at the University of Szeged until six months ago, when he was fired for improper behavior.

♦ The start of his decline can be traced back to a field trip into the Carpathians nine months ago.

♦ **History** or **Research** Push: Jerik was researching the life history of an Austrian nobleman, Baron Vordenburg, who traveled extensively in Transylvania in the 1870s. (His great-granduncle is mentioned in *Carmilla*). Vordenburg was wounded in the Russo-Turkish war.

♦ He tried to get work at various academic institutions in London, but was rejected. If Khan asks around, point her at *The Archivist* (p. 189).

FINDING JERIK

Jerik went into full-evasion mode after returning from Morocco; if Behar's attack on Calatrava failed and Carlyle investigates, the trail might lead back to Jerik. He cannot fail his master Kobori, so Jerik spends the time until the auction living on the streets of London. He keeps moving, crossing the Thames several times a day and traveling widdershins around the underground network to throw off any occult surveillance. He's picked up sufficient tradecraft to avoid being caught. Optionally, you can have him lurking on the fringes of scenes – maybe Khan spots from lurking outside the auction house, or Kastantev's hotel, but she shouldn't be able to catch him yet.

▼▼▼▼▼▼▼
THE PRINCE IN WAITING

Scene Type: Alternate
Lead-Ins: The Hare, The Middleman
Lead-Outs: The Auction, Adversary Mapping

Anthony Hollister's offices are in Kensington; the understated brass plaque on the door describes his business as a consultancy. Digging into Hollister's background by Taking Time for **Research** (or through a suitable Contact) reveals that he was a political fixer and PR handler for various up-and-coming politicians, but then took on a mysterious private client and dropped off the radar. Those who do business with him whisper that he's in control of a vast amount of wealth that he trades for political favors and assistance.

Personal security: Hollister never travels anywhere without a bodyguard, and his home and office both have state-of-the-art security systems. He also keeps a huge wolfhound as a pet, and brings it everywhere with him. The dog is oddly trained – it behaves with a lizard-like stillness, freezing in place before exploding into movement, and then freezing again. It also pays an unusual amount of attention to its surroundings, craning its head as though listening to conversations. Hollister doesn't seem to be an especially affectionate owner, either.

On occasions when the dog isn't allowed in, the beast waits outside, still as a statue.

OBSERVING HOLLISTER

▨▨▨▨▨▨
WATCHING HOLLISTER
SURVEILLANCE

Advance 7+: You monitor Hollister's movements. Most of it is exactly what you'd expect from a man in his position – meetings in various government departments and offices across London. You do spot two occasions when he deviates from this pattern. One afternoon, you see him send one of his bodyguards out to walk the freakish dog, and you spot Hollister watching through a window to ensure they're gone before making a phone call, as if he's eager to avoid being overheard. Later that evening, he takes a stroll with the dog and visits Highgate Cemetery; you're sure that's a vampire meetup. Gain Edge 9, "A Private Call."

Hold 4-6: Hollister is a hard man to keep tabs on; you have to be careful to stay clear of his bodyguards and that damn dog. Most of it is exactly what you'd expect from a man in his position – meetings in various government departments and offices across London.

Setback 3 or less: That dog can sense your presence, you swear. Even from a distance, it starts growling and staring right at you whenever you come near. Gain Problem 21, "The Hound of the Hollisters."

Extra Problem: You can Take Time to stake out Hollister's offices and home.

Stunt: Yes (**Cover** for a disguise; **Conceal** for a hiding place).

THE HOUND OF HOLLISTER

The huge and eerily pale wolfhound that pads silently after Hollister wherever he goes is, obviously, a vampiric monster, a gift from Carlyle. The vampire can possess the animal and see through its eyes whenever he needs to keep tabs on his servant. The dog has been used as a puppet by the vampire so many times that its natural instincts and impulses have been burned out of it; it's effectively a living robot now, a thing of fangs and sinews.

If Khan has no other leads to follow, then continued surveillance of Hollister leads her to *The Auction* (p. 187).

MEETING HOLLISTER

While Khan hasn't met Hollister before (or, at least, cannot *recall* meeting him), he's still a high-ranking conspiracy member connected to Carlyle, and there's a good chance that he's aware of the events in Budapest during *Never Say Dead*.

If Khan has the Problem "Stokovitch Survived" from that operation, then Hollister definitely knows that Leyla Khan is on the loose and is an active threat to the conspiracy; if Stokovitch is dead, but Khan's been making lots of noise since then, then that's also grounds for Hollister knowing who she is. At the same time, showing up at his home, pointing a gun at him and saying *"I'm infamous vampire hunter Leyla Khan. Let's talk"* definitely counts as **Intimidation**.

Oily and with intimidating confidence, Hollister isn't easily impressed by threats. He sees Khan as a creature like Stokovitch, a slave to the vampires. He doesn't want to end up as a thrall like them, which is why he's embarked on this quest to revive Kobori on his own terms. There's a discernible undercurrent of distaste when he talks to Khan.

Alternatively, Khan could use **Cover** to disguise herself, or **Network** to contact Hollister through an intermediary. An Interpersonal Push of some sort (**Charm**, **High Society**) is needed to convince Hollister to meet with someone he doesn't know.

The dog growls constantly at Khan; Hollister has one of his bodyguards take the animal outside into the hallway, but Khan can still hear it breathing and snuffling against the door throughout the conversation. The vampires are listening in; Hollister is aware he's under supernatural surveillance, so he speaks quietly when he discusses anything that might displease Carlyle.

Hollister responds to questions with deflections and stonewalling, or with threats of his own. He knows that she can't go to the police without exposing her own involvement in the conspiracy, and that if Khan stops moving long enough, Stokovitch or some other vampire assassin will track her down. If Khan's in disguise and threatens to go to the police, Hollister hints that doing so will end badly, and that his clients have the resources and reach to make problems disappear.

Specific denial for specific questions:

♦ He knows Francesca Curtis; she's a lawyer who has done work for his consultancy. He recently sent her to Spain to assist with a client who wished to buy property in London.

♦ He has no idea who Behar is. (**Bullshit Detector** doesn't work well on Hollister; he lies like fishes swim; at best, Khan spots a momentary smirk at Calatrava's misfortune.)
♦ Nor does he know who Dr. Jerik is. (**Bullshit Detector:** That question hit home.)

If the player mentions the auction at Cornet's, then Hollister admits that he's a collector of medieval art, and has an interest in some of the pieces in the auction. His *clients* (Carlyle and the other Hungarian-line vampires) are amused by this hobby of his; they lived through the Middle Ages that so fascinate him.

If the player has Edge 9, "A Private Call," and spends a Push, then Hollister offers a bargain – he won't report his meeting with Khan if she stays quiet. They're both humans trying to avoid divine retribution – or vampiric retribution, at any rate. He even hints that he will be in a position to help Khan if she waits a few days and doesn't interfere.

THE INVITATION

While meeting Khan, offer a Push of **Notice**: if the player accepts the offer, Khan spots a letter on Hollister's desk which she can grab with a Quick **Filch** Test (4+); if she fails, she needs to spend another Interpersonal Push to distract or deflect Hollister's attention (and if she fails to provide that, Hollister throws her out). The letter is an invitation to a private reception before *The Auction* (p. 187).

SEE YOU SOON

When the conversation ends, consider Hollister's response.

- If he thinks he can make use of Khan by playing her against Carlyle, give her Edge 10, "Hollister's Aid."
- If he believes that Khan's a danger to his plans, or if he needs to distract Carlyle from his own failings, give her Problem 22, "Targeted by the Conspiracy."

If the conversation goes *really* badly, it's time for "Evasive Measures" when Khan hears Hollister's bodyguards and the hound approaching.

EVASIVE MEASURES

EVASION

Advance 9+: You're able to vanish into London without being seen. Describe how you lose your pursuers in the Underground.

Hold 6-8: You escape your pursuers, but they've got connections in this city. Gain Problem 23, "London Heat."

Setback 5 or less: You dodge your pursuers, but that damnable dog keeps stalking you like a hound from Hell. You finally lose it on the Underground, but gain Problem 24, "It's Got Your Scent."

Extra Problem: None.

Stunt: Yes (**Athletics; Cover; Infiltration**).

ENOUGH TALK!

Khan's always got the option of pulling a gun and threatening Hollister. If she does so, skip straight to "Evasive Measures."

If Khan does kill Hollister, then most of his role in the narrative can be taken over by Dr. Jerik, who steals the key in *Bloody Murder,* p. 198 and then flees to Transylvania.

ADVERSARY MAPPING

Scene Type: Alternate
Lead-Ins: The Prince in Waiting
Lead-Outs: None

Once Khan learns (or suspects) that Hollister is plotting to betray his vampire master, she may decide that the best approach is to let the bad guys fight it out by informing Carlyle of his servant's treachery. **Tradecraft** tells Khan that directly approaching Carlyle is suicide. Carlyle was willing to tear up Budapest to steal Khan away from Jovitzo in *Never Say Dead*; if she approaches him in London, the best-case scenario is that he tries to enthrall her with his vampiric power. More likely, he'll try to kill her, and that's not a fight she wants to have unprepared.

If Khan has Edge 6, "The Necrophone," she can use that to contact Carlyle. If she has proof of Hollister's treachery and passes these on, give her Edge 11, ""Enemy of My Enemy." Without proof, she'll need to make an Interpersonal Push to prove her credentials.

If she doesn't have the Necrophone, then she'll need to make contact with Carlyle's operatives that aren't answerable to Hollister – and that means finding Stokovitch. If Khan *doesn't* have the Problem "Stokovitch Survived," then this line of action is shut down – she doesn't have time to identify a comparable figure in Carlyle's operation in time. If she does have that Problem, then she can try contacting the rival *sluger* with a **Network** test.

CONTACTING STOKOVITCH

NETWORK

Penalty: -1 per Heat Problem.

Advance 11+: You're able to arrange a meeting with Stokovitch on neutral ground – somewhere public, where she can't cause trouble. Describe where you arrange to meet her, and gain Edge 11, "Enemy of My Enemy."

Hold 7-10: As above, but Stokovitch isn't convinced – you've got to make an Interpersonal Push to persuade her to pass the message onto her master. If you don't make a Push, this becomes a Setback.

Setback 6 or less: It looks like Stokovitch has decided that taking you out is more valuable than the intel on Hollister. Run the Challenge "Revenge for Budapest."

Extra Problem: Problem 25, "Overexposed."

Stunt: No.

REVENGE FOR BUDAPEST

It's a set-up! You spot multiple hostiles moving through the crowd, trying to lock you down. You need to get out of here.

SENSE TROUBLE

Advance 12+: Describe how you vanish from the scene, leaving no trace behind you – other than a few unconscious goons. Gain Edge 12, "Bearded the Lion."

Hold 9-11: You're able to lose your pursuers, but not without cost. Discard any one Edge or Contact you've acquired that's connected to London. If you don't have any to discard, lose another Contact.

Setback 8 or less: Stokovitch's goons trap you in an alleyway. One of them's got vampire strength – he's blooded. You're able to take him down, but it hurts. Gain Problem 26, "Close to the Edge."

Extra Problem: Problem 27, "Calling Inspector Sands."

Stunt: Yes (**Evasion**; **Fighting**; **Preparedness**).

THE AUCTION

Scene Type: Core
Lead-Ins: The Middleman, The Prince in Waiting
Lead-Outs: The Archivist, The Heir, Attempted Burglary, Bloody Murder, Killing the Dog

Cornet's Auction House isn't a household name, like Christie's or Sotheby's. It's much more discrete, dealing in antiques and private collections; its clientele used to be ultra-wealthy aristocrats, but most of its dealings are bought by corporate investors. There are warehouses in Switzerland and Italy containing fortunes in art and antiques, held as an investment instead of stock or precious metals.

The upcoming auction at Cornet's is an unusual one. It's selling a large collection of antiques, some dating back to the 14th century. The collection belonged originally to a wealthy White Russian family, who fled Moscow in 1918. Now, the heir to the family fortune, Nestor Kastantev, is liquidating what remains of their collection.

Doing a little digging with **Research** turns up another odd fact – Nestor's uncle Mikhail vanished in 1974. He was last seen in the family mansion in Paris, reading in the library, but disappeared overnight. Police reports assumed he climbed out a window in the library – the room was soaked with rainwater – but there were no sightings of him after that.

(**Director's Eyes Only:** Kastantev's ancestor was one of the Russian soldiers who slew the vampire Count Kobori in Transylvania more than a century earlier. One of the relics in the collection is an old bookcase, and hidden in that case is a key that's needed to open up the route to Kobori's castle. Uncle Mikhail accidentally opened a portal to the castle.)

GETTING INTO THE AUCTION

With **High Society**, Khan can bluff her way into Cornet's, or get a meeting with Laura Burnwell, the house manager dealing with the Kastantev collection. Burnwell's charming but inconveniently discrete; she lets little information slip.

The items from the Kastantev collection are on display in a small private gallery attached to Cornet's until the upcoming auction is complete. Khan isn't an art expert, but the items are clearly labeled, so she can see that it's mostly Russian art from the turn of the century, and mid-century French pieces along with some antique furniture that must have been dragged from one side of Europe to the other. In one corner, there's a small collection of Transylvanian antiques, all easily transportable – some coins, some small jewels, a few daggers and other weapons.

Notice or **Vampirology:** There's a portrait in the collection that's of Transylvanian origin. It shows a stern-faced man with a ruddy moustache staring at the viewer. In one hand, he holds an ornate key; the other hand rests on the head of a hound that's eerily similar to the dog that accompanies Anthony Hollister.

If the player examines the portrait more closely, give her a Shadow Problem and tell her that she can tell the portrait is definitely that of a vampire. There's no name or any identifying details on the portrait.

FACES IN THE CROWD

Call for a **Sense Trouble** roll while at the auction.

HOSTILE EYES
SENSE TROUBLE

Bonus: If Khan's visited Jerik's flat (*The Middleman*, p. 182) and found the folder of photographs, she automatically gets Edge 13 regardless of her result on this test.

Advance 10+: You make two guys who might be Cornet's Auction House security, but might also be conspiracy goons. Better stay clear of them. If you want a better look around, you'll need to break in at night. You also spot someone out of place: a woman, early 20s, dressed like a student. She's watching the crowd, not examining the auction lots. Gain Edge 13, "The Other Woman."

If the player chooses to investigate the woman immediately, see *The Student*, p. 193.

Hold 4-9: You make two guys who might be Cornet's Auction House security, but might also be conspiracy goons. Better stay clear of them. If you want a better look around, you'll need to break in at night.

Setback 3 or less: Security at the auction house is tight – if you want a closer look at the lots, you'll need to break in at night. Gain Problem 28, "Under Surveillance."

Extra Problem: None.

Stunt: Yes (**Cover** for a good disguise).

GATHERING INTEL

Khan can pick up the following information by talking to Burnwell, or chatting to other antique collectors viewing the exhibits.

- The seller, Nestor Kastantev, is in London for the auction. (See *The Heir*, p. 190).
- The auction house consulted with a historian, Dr. Graves (see *The Archivist*, p. 189), to ensure all the items were genuine.
- Most bids are made by telephone or on the house's computer system. Anonymous bidding is the norm, and payment may be made electronically.
- Some of the pieces are likely to sell for tens of thousands of pounds.

THE PRICE OF INACTION

If Khan does nothing, then what happens next depends on the state of play.

- If Hollister has access to the payment from Behar, and the player isn't holding Edge 11, "Enemy of My Enemy," then an anonymous telephone bidder purchases the majority of the lots from the auction. Hollister obtains the key he needs, and heads to Transylvania with Dr. Jerik; run *Killing the Dog,* p. 194, as Hollister attempts to rid himself of his conspiracy handlers.
- If Hollister doesn't have access to the payment, or the player's got Edge 11, "Enemy of my Enemy," then Hollister's plan is foiled, and someone else buys the bookcase containing the key. Jerik goes for his backup option – see *Bloody Murder,* p. 198.

TRACKING THE AUCTION WINNER

Khan can identify the winner of the auction in several ways:

- Breaking into Cornet's, either before the auction and using **Electronic Surveillance** to plant a bug, or after the auction and digging through their records with **Data Recovery**.

- Coercing or deceiving a Cornet's employee with a suitable Interpersonal Push (**Charm** or **Intimidation** or a **Cover**).

- Using **Network** to get a computer hacker contact to hack into the auction house's systems.

- Tapping the phones.

All that gets Khan, though, is the name of a holding company based in Morocco (one owned by Behar, p. 168); it takes additional **Accounting** and some Taking Time for some digging to identify the actual buyer – Hollister. (Alternatively, if the player foiled Hollister's plan to get the money from Behar, then **Accounting** traces the purchase to a Russian oligarch living in London – see *Bloody Murder*, p. 198)

COUNTER-BIDDING

If Khan has access to disposable funds (through the Mastery Edge "Reptile Fund" or some other source), then she can try bidding herself. Hollister intended to purchase the majority of the lots as cover for his real target – the bookcase that conceals the key to Kobori's castle. If Khan bids strongly against the mysterious telephone bidder, then Hollister's forced to narrow the scope of his purchases, zeroing in on that bookcase. Khan can't beat this bid, but it does let her better target any *Attempted Burglary* (p. 191).

THE ARCHIVIST

Scene Type: Alternate
Lead-Ins: The Middleman, The Auction
Lead-Outs: The Heir, The Auction, The Middleman

Dr. Susan Graves is a writer and historian; she also works part-time for Cornet's as a valuer and antique expert. She was called in to examine the Kastantev collection. When appearing in public, Graves knows she has to look and act the part; she's got her respectably dour frock and can put on an Oxbridge accent. If visited at her offices in Kensington, she's more likely to be found wearing a ratty t-shirt. She's immensely enthusiastic about medieval history, and happily demonstrates the proper use of the replica battle axe she keeps on her wall at the slightest opportunity.

Information of relevance:

- Cornet's Auction House called her in to consult on some lots they're selling. Most of the Kastantev collection consists of Russian and French art, and some awful furniture – all very boring, not her field at all.

- One of Nestor Kastantev's ancestors, Vasily, was a Russian soldier, a *purochik* (lieutenant) in the 23rd Jägers during the Russo-Turkish war. He deserted along with a few other soldiers, but managed to bribe his way back into the army and avoided serious consequences. It appears that Kastantev and his compatriots looted some Romanian treasures, but it's never been clear where this treasure came from, or if Kastantev stole the treasures from some Romanian noble or if he reclaimed them from the Ottoman Turks.

  ◊ Kastantev kept a diary, although Graves suspects it's largely fanciful or forged; she took a brief look at it, but decided not to rely on it. The heir, Nestor, has the diary.

- Graves examined the medieval Romanian items included in the collection, and pronounced them genuine.

- If asked, she can give the player a full list of the items in the auction. Items that stand out:

  ◊ There were some knives and daggers that seemed very well used over an extended period of time – the sort of weapon you'd use for butchering animals. There's a Romanian term, *sluger*, that refers to a boyar who provided meat, especially beef, to a prince's court, and Graves speculates these daggers might have been a badge of office.

  ◊ There's a portrait of a nobleman with a key (p. 188). Graves has a photo of the portrait that she can show Khan. She guesses that this might be the nameless nobleman who owned the items.

  ◊ She suspects that the key in the portrait must have once existed, but is now lost.

- She can give Khan contact details for Cornet's manager, Laura Burnwell (*The Auction*, p. 187) or Nestor Kastantev (*The Heir*, p. 190).

If the player brings up the name of Dr. Jerik, or makes an Interpersonal Push using a suitable ability (**Interrogation**, **Charm**), then Graves relates a strange incident.

- She was contacted by Dr. Jerik, formerly of the University of Szeged.
- Graves knew of Jerik by reputation – indeed, she'd even referred to some of Jerik's papers when valuing the items in the collection.
- She knew that Jerik had left his position in the university under something of a cloud some months ago, but was still surprised when she met the man. Jerik struck her as a man in the middle of a complete breakdown; he was muttering to himself and largely incoherent.
- He tried to convince Graves to let him examine the collection as an expert in the field. When Graves refused, citing professional discretion and her contract with the auction house, Jerik tried to bribe her – he had an envelope full of cash, some five thousand pounds. Graves refused again, and Jerik threatened her, shouting that he had powerful friends and would ruin Graves.
- He left without Graves having to grab her trusty battle axe. Jerik left his business card; Khan can take it if she wants. (A core clue to *The Middleman*, p. 182).
- She didn't report the incident to Cornet's or to the police; Jerik needs help, she says, not more trouble. At the same time, it's not her problem.
- Shortly afterwards, one of Jerik's students tried to contact her; Graves rebuffed her, not wanting any further involvement with the man.
- If Khan wants to make Graves into a contact, she can do so with an Interpersonal spend.

THE HEIR

Scene Type: Alternate
Lead-Ins: The Auction, The Archivist
Lead-Outs: The Auction, Finding the Castle

Nestor Kastantev is Eurotrash – his name may be Russian, but French is his native language and he has homes in Munich and Italy, and a Swiss account. He has loyalty to no country; his family's traded on their inherited wealth for a century, and now it's running dry. Unloading some of his great-great-grandfather's junk to rich collectors is all he cares about.

Nestor's in London for the auction, and to party. Tracking him down requires either an introduction or a use of **High Society** or **Streetwise**. Once Khan finds him, getting him to talk requires either **Charm** or **Intimidation** (or a suitable **Cover**) depending on how she wants to play it.

He's aggressively incurious about his family history – it's long been suspected that his ancestor murdered and robbed some Transylvanian noble, and that the Kastantev fortune is founded on a crime. As far as he's concerned, his ancestor was a soldier who got rich in some war against the Turks, and that's that – why drag up the past? However, if Khan digs, she can learn some useful elements:

- Kastantev's great-uncle Mikhail vanished under mysterious circumstances in 1974. Mikhail also asked too many questions about the past, and read old Vasily Kastantev's diary. One night, everyone in the old family house in Paris was woken by screaming, and when they searched for Mikhail, he was gone. He was last seen in the library, and strangely the floor of that room was slick with rainwater, even though all the windows were closed. Ever after that, until they sold and demolished the house, there were stories about ghosts and strange chills in that room.
- If Khan can convince him to do so (Interpersonal Push or some other bribe), he can give her access to his ancestor's diary. It will take some time for him to find the diary – this counts as Taking Time.

THE DIARY

The campaign diary of Vasily Kastantev is a small, leatherbound notebook in surprisingly good condition considering its age. However, it suffered considerable water damage in 1974 when Mikhail Kastantev vanished. He accidentally activated the key and opened a partial door to Kobori's castle; however, as he wasn't in the right place, he perished horribly. Khan may find his remains in the castle on p. 198.

Reading the diary requires **Languages**, **Cryptography**, and **Archaeology** and a period of Taking Time. Khan doesn't have those Investigative abilities, so she'll need to recruit one or more Contacts or spend even more time doing **Research**.

The following clues can be found with it:

- Kastantev and some other soldiers somehow became entangled with the affairs of a "Baron Vordenburg."
- Vordenburg had a "blessing" that protected him; he'd sometimes tell the soldiers to stay behind, as they were vulnerable where he was not. (Director: hint that Vordenburg possessed either the Rosewater Potion or the Sykoran Crucifix, whichever protection Khan has or seeks. Draw a parallel between Vordenburg's vampire hunting and Khan's efforts.)

- During the Russo-Turkish war, Vordenburg led them to the "home of the Devil Kobori," a castle in the mountains above Sovata in Romania.
- They killed the devil as he slept, and then fled, taking with them "a tenth of the treasures of that place."
- Behind them, the castle "fell into the mist, as though the earth shook, but there was no sound."
- Vordenburg took with him a key from the castle, but when "black doors" pursued them, he gave it to Kastantev. Kastantev never saw the mysterious baron again, and believed him to have perished in the wilderness.

With **Research** (core clue), Khan can determine the location of the castle. See *Finding the Castle*, p. 198.

NESTOR AS AN OFFERING

As an optional scene, Hollister might try to abduct Kastantev. After all, how better to curry favor with Kobori than by resurrecting the vampire with the blood of one of its killers? Hollister needs to use conspiracy resources to grab Kastantev, so this takes place before *Killing the Dog* (p. 194). If he tries this, see *Stopping the Kidnapping*, p. 191. Hollister dispatches the same goons that Khan may have spotted at *The Auction*. The snatch team follows Kastantev's car from Cornet's, and waits until he's on his own before grabbing him, knocking him out, and bundling him into a van. If Khan nearby, **Notice** or **Sense Trouble** lets her intervene.

STOPPING THE KIDNAPPING
FIGHTING

Penalty: If Khan's got Problem 19, "Forewarned," Problem 22, "Targeted by the Conspiracy," Problem 25 "Overexposed," or Problem 28, "Under Surveillance," then the bad guys know she's there, and this is a trap for her. She's got a -4 penalty, and on a Setback she picks up Problem 30, "Left For Dead."

If she's got Problem 24, "It's Got Your Scent," then the dog is here too, giving Khan an additional penalty equal to her Shadow Score.

If Khan wants to ensure that the target isn't harmed, then she's at -1 dice.

Advance 11+: You spot the team shadowing the target. Describe how you intervene to take them out, and gain Edge 14, "Kastantev Owes You" or Edge 15, "Carmen Owes You."

Hold 7-10: You manage to stop the kidnappers, who drive off into the darkness. Kastantev, terrified, flees down the street. Carmen does the same, or runs to Khan if she knows her already.

Setback 6 or less: It happens too fast for you to intervene. They snatch their target and vanish.

Extra Problem: Problem 29, "Stuntwork"

Stunt: Yes (**Athletics**; **Shooting**; **Evasion**).

ATTEMPTED BURGLARY

Scene Type: Alternate
Lead-Ins: The Auction
Lead-Outs: The Student

Cornet's Auction House stores the Kastantev collection in a high-security vault on-site. Getting in will be challenging even for someone with Khan's skills; it's nigh-impossible for an amateur. Casing the vault notes the following security precautions:

- All windows and doors are locked and alarmed. The doors all use passcards and combination locks.
- Cameras everywhere, inside and out.
- There are four security guards on site at night: two patrolling the halls, and two monitoring the cameras in a security control room on the top floor.
- If any of the display cases are opened without an authorization code being entered from the control room, barred gates slam down.
- In the event of a power cut, those gates come down automatically too (they're held in place by electromagnets).

Architecture notes that the building itself is old, with plenty of hiding places and shadowy corridors. It should be possible to dodge most of the cameras.

Electronic Surveillance can bypass some of the security systems – enough to disarm the alarm on one window and squeeze in. Alternatively, some of those decorative skylights aren't alarmed, because no one would be crazy and agile enough to climb up there.

Khan could use **Filch** to steal someone's passcard, or visit the auction house during the day and hide until the place closes.

Once the player has briefly sketched out an intrusion plan, roll **Infiltration**.

BREAKING INTO CORNET'S

INFILTRATION

Bonus: +2 if the player Pushes **Architecture** or **Electronic Surveillance**.

Penalty: -4 if the player has no plan for how to deal with the security measures

Advance 7+: You make it into the main vault without being detected – and you've got a viable exit route, too. You've got a bonus die on any challenges to escape Cornet's.

Hold 4-6: You make it into the main vault without being detected – but getting out again is going to be a problem.

Setback 3 or less: You don't screw up – you know what you're doing. Someone else, though, doesn't, and the alarms go off half-way through your break-in. Skip the main vault and go straight to "The Other Intruder."

Extra Problem: Problem 31, "Break-in at Cornet's."

Stunt: Yes (**Athletics**; **Conceal**; **Filch**; **Preparedness**).

THE VAULT

Breaking into the vault gives Khan a chance to examine the items more closely. If she hasn't already spotted it, there's a portrait showing a stern-faced man with a ruddy moustache staring at the viewer. In one hand, he holds an ornate key; the other hand rests on the head of a hound that's eerily similar to the dog that accompanies Anthony Hollister.

If the player examines the portrait more closely, give her a Shadow Problem and tell her that she can tell the portrait is definitely that of a vampire.

There's no name or any identifying details on the portrait.

Several of the daggers bear the crest of the House of Dracula – it's certain that these treasures were looted from the lair of a vampire. From their age and design, likely one of the Hungarian line.

- There's a definite chill in one corner of the vault, near the antique furniture.
- Optionally, if the player hasn't visited *The Heir*, p. 190, move Vasily Kastantev's journal (p. 190) here and let her find it with **Notice**.

A Conceal Quick Test (9+) lets Khan spot that one of the heavy oak bookcases was repaired at some point in the past. It looks as though something was concealed within the frame of the case. Getting at it means taking the bookcase apart, and will take time and tools – but that secret might be what Hollister is after.

However, before Khan can disassemble the bookcase, the alarm goes off. Moments later, she hears someone running in a panic towards the vault.

SMASH AND GRAB

If Khan smashes the bookcase to get whatever's inside – discovering that "whatever" to be a mysterious iron key – then she gets Problem 34, "Spotted by Security." The theft of the key breaks up the partnership between Jerik and Hollister. Hollister tries to buy his way back into Carlyle's good graces by warning his current vampire master that Khan's in town; Jerik contacts Khan and tries to persuade her that her best chance for survival is to go to Transylvania and awaken Kobori (either to serve him, or to drain his blood for the Rosewater Potion – either way, Jerik's ultimate goal is to backstab Khan and offer her to Kobori as a "welcome-back-from-the-dead gift").

Run *Killing the Dog*, p. 194, but in this scenario, Hollister's trying to atone for his offenses against Carlyle, not using the strike on Khan as a distraction so he can flee London.

BURN IT ALL!

Aggressive players may think: *"Hey, the thing the bad guys want is in the vault. I don't have time to steal it, but I do have Preparedness and hence, explosives... so... boom?"* It's an extreme solution – and not an entirely unreasonable one. However, if the player tries this, then the explosion opens up a temporary and unstable gate between the key and Kobori's castle. A medieval Transylvanian castle briefly manifests in the middle of London, and Khan and Carmen are both dragged through the portal to Kobori's castle (p. 198). They're stuck in the dimensionally shifted ruin for several days until Hollister and/or Jerik arrive. See the "We Took a Short Cut" sidebar on p. 201, and unless the player spends a Push on **Outdoor Survival**, give her Problem 51, "Kobori's Guest."

MORE INTEL

Alternatively, sneaking into Laura Burnwell's office lets the player gather information about the auction. See *Tracking the Auction Winner*, p. 189.

THE OTHER INTRUDER

Carmen Vidraru, Jerik's former student, came to London looking for her professor. She failed to track down Jerik, but recognized the connection between Jerik's research and the Kastantev auction. She tried approaching Dr. Graves, but was rebuffed.

Breaking into the auction house was an impulsive decision on her part, and unfortunately she's ruined Khan's break-in. Time to run! Call for an **Evasion** Quick Test (8+); on a failure, give the player Problem 32, "Spotted by Security."

Assuming the player doesn't also choose to evade Carmen, segue into *The Student*, below.

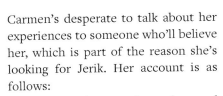

THE STUDENT

Scene Type: Alternate
Lead-Ins: The Auction, Attempted Burglary
Lead-Outs: The Archivist, Bloody Murder

Carmen Vidraru is in her mid-20s; she's a post-graduate student of history. She was one of Dr. Jerik's students, and accompanied him on the fateful field expedition to Transylvania. She came to London looking for her former teacher – and for more answers about what happened that night.

If Khan tracks Vidraru down after spotting her at the auction house, then Carmen's initially standoffish and paranoid. Mentioning that Khan knows something about Jerik, or using **Reassurance** convinces Carmen to listen. Mentioning the supernatural (or helping her escape the botched break-in at Cornet's) is like breaking a dam;

Carmen's desperate to talk about her experiences to someone who'll believe her, which is part of the reason she's looking for Jerik. Her account is as follows:

♦ Nine months ago, she and several other students accompanied their lecturer, Dr. Jerik, on a visit to Transylvania. Jerik was researching the life of occultist and historian Baron Vordenburg, and had discovered some accounts suggesting that during one undocumented gap in Vordenburg's life, he traveled with a band of Russian soldiers, including Vasily Kastantev. Jerik believed that

other clues might be found in Transylvanian records.

♦ Retracing the route taken by Kastantev's troops, they travelled into the mountains above Sovata, where one of the soldiers mentioned a castle. There are several ruins in that area; Jerik wanted to see which of them might be the castle described.

♦ They ran into difficulty on one mountainside; their phones and GPS systems led them astray, and they couldn't find the road as night approached. They had tents with them and it was a warm night, so they decided to make camp outdoors.

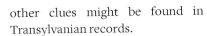

- That night, everyone in the group was afflicted by strange dreams. In Carmen's nightmares, she remembers knowing with that inexplicable dream-logic that there was a dead man buried under her tent, and that he was calling to her.
- The next morning, Dr. Jerik's tent was empty. They found him a short distance away, wandering through the stones, apparently sleepwalking and talking to himself.
- Afterwards, Jerik's behavior became erratic. He stopped showing up for lectures, got into fights with faculty staff. He refused to talk about his own experiences. She knows that he went to Paris for a few weeks, then there were rumors that he was in London.
- She has the same nightmare every few weeks of the dead man calling her from underground. So far, the dreams haven't taken that much of a toll on her sanity, but she's worried, so she came to London to look for her former lecturer. She discovered the existence of the Kastantev auction, and suspected that it would draw Jerik.
- She attempted to make contact with Dr. Graves (*The Archivist*) but was rebuffed.

Vidraru has no direct experience of the supernatural, but she's receptive to the idea. After that recurring nightmare, she's willing to believe that there might be vampires out there.

She can show Khan the approximate location of the ruin in Transylvania (core clue to *Finding the Castle*, p. 198), and will accompany Khan there if permitted. Give the player Carmen's Contact card. If the player doesn't think of pursuing Hollister to Romania, have Carmen prompt extending the chase overseas.

Carmen can't recall the exact location but she thinks she can retrace the expedition's steps if she returns to Transylvania.

CARMEN THE THRALL

The player may (correctly) suspect that Carmen's under the influence of the dead vampire Kobori. Note that there are several Shadow Blowback events (p. 206) connected to Carmen.

Carmen has no idea that the vampire is manipulating her from beyond the grave, and angrily rejects any such insinuation. If Khan has access to the Rosewater Potion, then she can use it to free Carmen. Khan has to push **Reassurance** to get Carmen to drink the potion (or use **Filch** to pour it into a drink). If Carmen's dosed with the potion, those Blowback events are averted.

KILLING THE DOG

Scene Type: Core
Lead-Ins: The Auction
Lead-Outs: To the Castle

Play this scene if Hollister has access to Behar's cash and can purchase the Kastantev collection without alerting his masters in the conspiracy. With the hidden key concealed in the bookcase, Hollister can go to Transylvania and reawaken Count Kobori, replacing his current master Carlyle with a more pliant vampire patron. To do that, though, he needs to get rid of his conspiracy watchdogs – including the literal hound from Hell that pads by his side.

If Khan's got Edge 11, "Enemy of My Enemy," then run "Carlyle's Turn" at this point.

His method for doing this is to target Leyla Khan.

If Hollister is already in contact with Khan, then luring her into a trap is easy – he contacts her and offers a trade. Both of them are servant or former servants of the conspiracy with... unusually fluid loyalty towards their vampiric patrons. They are kindred spirits of a sort – why not work together?

If Khan's Heat Score is 4 or more, then Hollister can use his contacts and pull with the British authorities to locate her. He'll then make contact with her and try to lure her into a trap.

Otherwise, he uses his police contacts and sway in the British government to track Khan down. Run the Challenge, "Stay Hiding in the Underbrush."

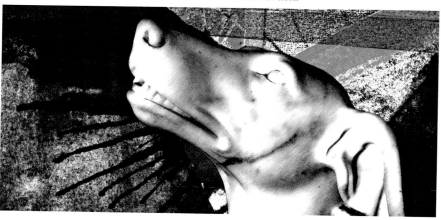

STAY HIDING IN THE UNDERBRUSH
COVER

Bonus: +2 if you Push **Streetwise** or **Tradecraft**.

Advance 9+: Your sources warn you that someone's looking for you – Anthony Hollister, a political fixer. He's been making calls to the police and to the home office, raising concerns about the presence of a potential terrorist in the UK.

Hold 6-8: Someone's looking for you. You've still got sources in the police and the intelligence community, and someone's put out a notice on you. You can't be sure who it is, yet, but they're trying to put pressure on you.

Setback 5 or less: Someone's looking for you, and the police are closing in. You're a person of interest in recent events, and they want to find you. Gain Problem 33, "Security Scrutiny."

Extra Problem: Discard a London Contact for the rest of this operation for an extra die.

Stunt: No.

THE ATTACK

Hollister dispatches a conspiracy kill team, and sends along the hound for supernatural backup so Carlyle can watch. While the hound's stalking Khan, Hollister can flee to Transylvania.

Frame the attack based on Khan's current circumstances. If Hollister's able to lure her into a trap, then he asks her to meet him at a location connected to the mystery, but not one that's directly linked to him (he intends to return to London after resurrecting Kobori, returning to his current life with a more pliable vampire master and hence more power in his own hands). Possible locations:

- Dr. Grave's offices
- The warehouse he's moved the Kastantev collection to
- An old MI6 safehouse familiar to Khan
- Highgate Cemetery

Alternatively, the attack might hit Khan's current safehouse, as she's tracked down by the authorities and the hound.

Start off with a **Sense Trouble** test.

SPOTTING THE AMBUSH
SENSE TROUBLE

Penalty: -1 per Shadow Problem, as the hound leads the enemy to Khan.

Advance 11+: You spot that monstrous pale hound skulking around the corners, its eyes gleaming red in the fog – and nearby, cars with tinted windows that weren't there a moment ago. It's a trap. You've got a choice – do you stand and fight, with a free bonus die for the next Challenge, or do you flee? Run either "The Jaws Close" or "Escaping the Trap."

Hold 7-10: You've got a little warning – not enough to get out in time, but at least you're not taken by surprise in the ambush.

Setback 6 or less: You're caught napping – you've got a -4 penalty to your next Challenge.

Extra Problem: None.

Stunt: No.

THE JAWS CLOSE
FIGHTING

Penalty: -4 if you failed in "Spotting the Ambush." -2 if your Heat is 4 or more (Hollister can risk bringing in police back-up). -2 if Stokovitch is still hunting Khan.

Advance 9+: They weren't expecting such a tough opponent. You wipe the floor with the thugs sent to capture you – but as the last bad guy falls, the hound attacks. Run "Hound from Hell."

Hold 6-8: You take down enough of them to spot an escape route. Run "Escaping the Trap."

Setback 5 or less: There are too many of them. Your only chance now is to ensure you get *arrested*, instead of murdered. You've got to get yourself into police custody. Gain Problem 34, "Nightsticks," Problem 37 "Still At Large," and see the sidebar *Arrested!*.

Extra Problem: None.

Stunt: Yes (**Athletics; Evasion; Shooting; Preparedness**).

HOUND FROM HELL

The hound stalks towards you – pale as death, jaws slavering, eyes glowing like hot coals. There's a terrible certainty about the way it moves, a conscious menace that tells you that the creature's in the thrall of a vampire. It's the occult equivalent of a remotely piloted drone.

FIGHTING

Bonus: +2 if the player has a suitable Vampire Block.

Advance 12+: The hound charges towards you. Describe how you kill the monster before it kills you. Gain Edge 16, "Death by Proxy."

Hold 9-11: The hound leaps on top of you, ripping at you with its teeth. You can smell its foul, sulfurous breath in your face. Just before it tears your throat out, it stops as though it's heard something beyond the range of your hearing – and then bolts off into the darkness. Something's gone wrong – but at least you're still alive.

Setback 8 or less: The beast's jaws close on you. It grabs your arm and shakes you like a rat, smashing you into a nearby car. Pain, then darkness broken by blue lights at the edge of your consciousness. Gain Problem 35, "Mauled" – and you've been arrested.

Extra Problem: Problem 36, "Clawed and Scraped."

Stunt: Yes (**Shooting**; **Evasion**).

ESCAPING THE TRAP
EVASION

Advance 9+: You run as though the hounds of Hell were on your tail – and they are. The animal pursues you for a short distance, but then suddenly gives up and bolts off. Something's gone wrong – there's a higher-priority target than you out there. At least you're clear for now – you may discard any one Heat Problem.

Hold 6-8: You lose most of your pursuers in a mad dash through the streets, but the hound keeps pace with you for several minutes – then suddenly gives up and bolts off. Something's gone wrong – there's a higher-priority target than you out there. Still, the monster has your scent. Gain Problem 38, "Still on the Loose."

Setback 5 or less: The hound catches you. Run the Challenge "Hound from Hell."

Extra Problem: None.

Stunt: Yes (**Athletics**; **Cover**).

ARRESTED!

If Khan's arrested during the *Killing the Dog* scene, then she can probably get away with claiming to be a bystander, or at the very least arguing that she was acting in self-defense. She may be able to get released without charge if her Heat Score is low enough (2 or less). As a former Secret Intelligence Service officer, Leyla Khan's fingerprints and other biometric data is on file, and her arrest may trigger secret alerts as soon as she's processed by the Metropolitan Police. The player has several options, depending on cards in hand.

♦ **Sit tight and hope her Cover holds.** If the player wants to avoid contact with her former colleagues in MI6, then she can hope that her cover identity is enough to get her through police detention. Have Khan make a **Cover** test (Difficulty 6, -1 per Heat Problem). If she passes, she's released without charge.

♦ **Call in an unofficial favor.** By making a **Network** test (Difficulty 8), Khan can call in a favor from her former contacts so they intercede on her behalf. She gets a +2 bonus to the roll if she pushes a suitable ability like **Tradecraft** or **Law**.

♦ **Get official help.** If the situation warrants, MI6 can intercede on a slightly more official level. They get any charges dismissed, and the player gains Problem 4, "Proving Ground." If the player already has this Problem, this option isn't available.

♦ **Get kicked out.** If MI6 deem the situation – and Khan – to be effectively unsalvageable, they just get rid of her. She's freed and given 24 hours to leave the UK; gain Problem 6, "Burned by MI6."

ALL A DISTRACTION

While the hound and the other security forces chase Khan, Hollister slips away from his remaining handlers and makes a break for the airport. Gathering rumors using **Traffic Analysis** or **Streetwise**, or visiting Hollister's home or office lets the player discover he's gone; his disappearance is mentioned in the newspapers the next day, so the player automatically learns that Hollister's gone missing after Taking Time.

If the player hasn't worked it out, **Vampirology** or **Tradecraft** suggests that Hollister was under some degree of vampiric influence, but has now broken free. That implies two things: first, that his master was one of the psychically less formidable Hungarian-line vampires, and two, his disappearance is probably connected to the sale of the Kastantev collection.

Professor Jerik disappears at the same time (possibly after *Bloody Murder*, p. 198).

CARLYLE'S TURN

If the player's managed to turn the tables on Hollister by acquiring Edge 11, "Enemy of My Enemy," here's how this scene plays out instead:

♦ Hollister sends his kill team to eliminate Khan.

♦ The kill team (ideally, led by Stokovitch) shows up – and asks Khan to accompany them. Stokovitch promises she won't be harmed, that her master Carlyle has given his word.

♦ Stokovitch brings Khan to Hollister's office, where Hollister is being held at gunpoint. They anticipated his attempt to escape.

♦ Hollister confesses everything – how he learned through Jerik that the vampire Kobori is still alive, how he intended to resurrect Kobori and rule through him. As soon as he's done confessing his treachery, the pale hound tears his throat out.

♦ Stokovitch's men search the body for the key; there's no sign of it. A few minutes' later, one of them reports that Jerik has fled the country. He must be on his way to Transylvania to resurrect Kobori.

♦ Carlyle doesn't want another Romanian-line vampire abroad in the world, but it's forbidden to attack a vampire directly. So, Stokovitch is authorized to send Khan to Romania to stop Jerik. Their interests align in this – both Khan and Carlyle want to prevent the rise of Count Kobori. Why, if only Khan had accepted Carlyle's kind offer back in *Never Say Dead*...

♦ Move onto *Finding the Castle*, p. 198; Jerik hires the Romanian mafia bodyguards using the last of the money.

BLOODY MURDER

Scene Type: Alternate
Lead-Ins: The Auction
Lead-Outs: Finding the Castle

If the player prevents Hollister from winning the auction, then the bulk of the Kastantev collection – including the bookcase containing the key – gets purchased by a Russian oligarch living in London named Vasily Kermanov.

The thought of the key to his master's resurrection being taken from him so horrifies Jerik that he breaks into the oligarch's house in Kensington and murders the Kermanov family. He then smashes the bookcase, retrieves the key, and vanishes. This is not a subtle crime; Jerik's caught on several CCTV cameras and leaves fingerprints all over the crime scene. His escape to Romania with Hollister only delays his inevitable arrest and conviction (and Hollister starts plotting how to eliminate Jerik as soon he learns of the murders).

Khan might learn of the killing in several ways:

- **Streetwise/Traffic Analysis:** News of the murders quickly circulates through London's underworld and through social media.
- **Cop Talk:** While the police quickly cordon off the scene, Khan can still learn of the killing through police contacts
- **Through the Auction House:** If Khan has access to the auction house's files, then she can track the buyer.
- **Tracking Hollister/Jerik:** Keeping tabs on either of these reprobates alerts Khan that something's happening. Unless she's very close at hand, she arrives too late to intervene; the two are on a plane to Romania before she discovers they've fled.

- **Heat 3+:** If the police are aware of Khan's connection to the auction, then she may be questioned about the death of Vasily Kermanov.

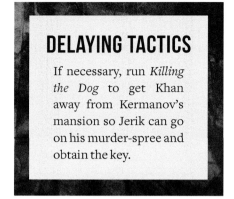

DELAYING TACTICS

If necessary, run *Killing the Dog* to get Khan away from Kermanov's mansion so Jerik can go on his murder-spree and obtain the key.

INSIDE THE MANSION

A **Cop Talk** Push or a successful **Infiltration** test (Difficulty 6) gets Khan into the mansion to take a look around. It's trivial to retrace the murder's path – one dead at the front door, another two in the drawing room, then clearing the house upstairs before toppling the antique bookcase down on Kermanov.

Weirdly, the library is soaking wet, as if a rainstorm blew through here. The raindrops are all on the back of the bookcase – the impossible indoor storm started when Jerik found the key. (See *Burn It All*, p. 192). The police's working theory is that the killer tried to burn the house down and was foiled by a sprinkler system.

- **Criminology** or **Electronic Surveillance:** There are plenty of cameras; the killer didn't care about being identified. Jerik's on a one-way trip. He either believes this is worth his life, or he thinks he can carry out a brutal murder in the middle of London and get away with it. Either option stinks of vampire.

- **Cryptography** or **Vampirology:** Scrawled above each victim is a pair of letters. If Khan's read the Kastantev diary (p. 190), or if she consults with Carmen, she realizes that Jerik's associated each of his victims with one of the Russian soldiers who defeated Count Kobori.
- **Forensics:** The attacker carried out the murders with a handgun, but there are tooth-marks on the bodies too. Post-mortem blood drinking and cannibalism.
- **Notice:** There's a hollow compartment in the frame of the old bookcase that the intruder smashed open with a crowbar.

If the player hasn't met her already, Khan spots Carmen in the crowd behind the police tape outside Kermanov's house (*The Student*, p. 193).

FINDING THE CASTLE

Scene Type: Alternate
Lead-Ins: The Auction, The Archivist
Lead-Outs: Opening the Gate

A flight from London to the airport in Bucharest takes about three hours. Remind the player that she can swap out unused Masteries if she wishes. She can't bring weapons through the airport without a **Conceal** or **Cover** test (Difficulty 7); a **Network** roll may be needed to make contact with Khan's friendly neighborhood weapons dealers.

From Bucharest, it's a connecting flight or long drive upcountry into Transylvania.

Photography: Satellite images of the ruins show no signs of unusual activity, other than some odd weather patterns. It's a cold and rain-swept land, only lightly inhabited. The nearest town of any size is twenty miles away.

If Carmen's with Khan, then she recalls the route to the castle – but run "Shadow of the Vampire," below.

If Khan's on her own, she has two options. The spy's solution is to track down Hollister and Jerik – they must be somewhere in this general area, and neither of the two have much in the way of tradecraft – they'll stick out and attract attention. The trouble with that option is that Hollister and Jerik have a considerable lead, and there's a risk that they'll find the castle before she finds their trail.

The other option is to open herself up to vampiric influence. **Vampirology** suggests that both Jerik and Carmen were contacted by the sleeping vampire when they rested here – and Khan's a walking wound, spiritually speaking. All she needs to do is not take the Rosewater Potion/ remove the Sykoran Crucifix, and then follow the psychic tugging as Kobori tries to claim her soul.

SHADOW OF THE VAMPIRE

As Carmen gets closer to the castle, she begins to fall under the sway of Kobori. At first, this is a subtle change – she becomes more certain about which way they should go, remembering how Jerik's field trip visited *that* desolate hillside and *this* crumbling ruin. She and Khan drive further up into the mountains, along narrow country roads that spiral around dark wooded hills. Describe how Carmen suddenly becomes talkative, almost manic, recalling details of the trip that she'd previously suppressed. Eagerly ask questions of the player – what's Khan going to do once they get to the castle site? Does she intend to dig up and destroy Count Kobori? How will she deal with Hollister and Jerik?

If the player asks, offer a Push of **Vampirology** to confirm that Carmen's under vampiric influence, giving a bonus in the Challenge to come.

As night draws in, Carmen suggests they sleep in the car or camp – there aren't any hotels or hostels in the region. During the night, Carmen – under Kobori's control – tries to incapacitate Khan by stunning her with a blow to the head from the tire iron.

After dealing with Carmen, Khan spots a strange light further up in the hills, and moments later heavy rain begins to splatter against the windshield. Run *Opening the Gate*.

STOPPING CARMEN
FIGHTING

Bonus: +2 if the player has advance warning. +2 if the player's current Shadow Score is 3 or less.

Advance 10+: You've been watching Carmen grapple with the vampire's unholy influence. You were waiting for something like this to happen, and it's easy to disarm her without hurting her. You knock her out. Gain Edge 17, "Parry and Riposte."

Hold 4-9: You wake just in time to spot Carmen swinging a tire iron at you. You grab her wrist and wrestle with her – her eyes blazing red, there's another soul behind them – and knock her out by slamming her head hard against the dashboard, several times. You're close to the vampire's castle, but you've got to leave Carmen behind.

Setback 3 or less: You wake – and then everything goes black and bloody again as Carmen smashes you in the face with something heavy and metal. Gain Problem 38, "Head Wound" and skip to "We Took a Short Cut," p. 201.

Extra Problem: Problem 39, "The Count's Call."

Stunt: Yes (**Sense Trouble; Evasion; Preparedness; Weapons**).

THE HILLS HAVE EYES

Tracking Hollister and Jerik by tracing their movements in Romania turns up some of the following clues.

- **Human Terrain:** As expected, it's easy for Khan enough to track their movements. Jerik's been here before and knows how to blend in, but Hollister's attempts to stay undercover are laughable. By following rumors and gossip, she knows she's only a day or so behind.

- **Streetwise:** Khan picks up rumors that someone's hired a bunch of low-grade mobsters from Romania's infamously Balkanized criminal underworld. From the sounds of it, she guesses that Hollister has recruited some local muscle. **Criminology** lets her identify the home town of the mobsters and pick up the trail there.

  ◊ A Push gets a little more information – Hollister's hired four mafia-types as bodyguards. A crook named Gheorghe "Surubelniţă" Popa leads the brute squad. Surubelniţă translates as "screwdriver," telling you everything you need to know about this charming individual.

Call for a **Network** test from Khan as she tracks Hollister through the criminal underworld.

TRACING HOLLISTER
NETWORK

Penalty: -1 per Heat or Shadow Problem.

Advance 7+: As per Hold, but you can also leverage your contacts for equipment if you need weapons or other supplies.

Hold 4-6: From your previous life as Jovitzo's enforcer, you still have contacts on the ground here. By playing your old role, you can shake them down for information – and some of them know where Count Kobori's castle once stood. One elderly man – his grandson's involved in human trafficking, bringing victims to the vampires – points to a desolate hillside in the distance and says that the "old master" lived there in his grandfather's time.

Setback 3 or less: One of your former contacts offers to help you. "Come up to the old farmhouse with me," he says, "I'll help you find the place you seek." It's a trap, and someone hits you from behind as you walk in the door. Gain Problem 38, "Head Wound" and skip to "We Took a Short Cut", p. 201.

Extra Problem: Problem 40, "Old Friends."

Stunt: Yes (**Cover; Sense Trouble**).

WALKING WOUNDED

Relying on her own vampiric connections requires a **Cool** test.

THE EDGE OF THE ABYSS
COOL

Penalty: -1 Shadow Problem.

Advance 9+: You open your mind to the vampire's uncanny call. It feels like you're sinking into the earth, the ground swallowing you, dragging you into the vampire's grave – but you hold fast, let the feeling guide you and draw you in instead of succumbing to it. You can feel, like a subsonic tremor, the vampire's fury as he fails to control you. Gain Edge 17, "Parry and Riposte."

Hold 6-8: You allow yourself to be drawn in by the vampire count. It feels like being drugged – you're not sure of anything. In a dream-like haze, you approach the appointed place. Your car is somehow a horse-drawn calèche; the mountainside ahead is both empty and dominated by a medieval castle. You are alone, and *he* is with you, his red eyes burning. Gain Problem 41, "Enthralled."

Setback 5 or less: You give in – and lose yourself. The last thing you remember is the sensation of being buried alive. Gain Problem 41, "Enthralled" and to go "We Took a Short Cut," p. 201.

Extra Problem: If Jovitzo is still alive, then Problem 42, "Your Former Master" is available.

Stunt: No.

WE TOOK A SHORT CUT

If Khan's captured by Hollister or Jerik, or otherwise incapacitated, she may be *brought* to the castle as an offering for Kobori instead of finding her own way there. In this case, Khan (and Carmen, if she's also a prisoner), wakes up in a prison cell in a crumbling tower of the castle. The door's firmly locked and secured, but the mortar on the window bars has crumbled. Outside's a howling darkness that might be a raging thunderstorm and might be some otherworldly abyss, but Khan can try climbing up the walls to escape her prison cell.

ESCAPING THE PRISON CELL
ATHLETICS

Penalty: -1 per Shadow Problem.

Advance 9+: It's a nerve-wracking climb, but you cling on to the crumbling stones of the castle, and make your way up to another window you can squeeze through. Go to *Exploring the Castle*.

Hold 4-8: You think you're about to fall, but then a gust of wind pushes you back against the wall, holding you there until you find your footing again. It's like a giant hand supporting you – and you glimpse eyes in the darkness. Gain Problem 41, "Enthralled" and go to *Exploring the Castle*.

Setback 3 or less: You slip. You try to grab onto the castle walls as you plummet, but they're slick with moss and rainwater. You fall into darkness – and smash into the mountainside, far below. As the blood leaks from your shattered body, the dark soil drinks it hungrily, and your last thought is that of the vampire Kobori – rising from his grave, given new life by your death.

Extra Problem: You have to drop your gun and gear as the wind tears at them. Gain Problem 43, "Disarmed."

Stunt: Yes (**Cool**; **Preparedness**).

Alternatively, if Khan remains in the cell, she'll be brought down to Kobori's grave at gunpoint by Hollister. Give her Problem 47, "Held at Gunpoint." and run *Bargaining*, p. 203.

201

OPENING THE GATE

Scene Type: Core
Lead-Ins: The Auction, Finding the Castle
Lead-Outs: Bargaining

The castle of Count Kobori is not wholly of this earth. When Baron Vordenburg and the Russian mercenaries defeated and entombed the vampire, his fortress vanished. Now, as Kobori comes closer to a blasphemous resurrection, so does his castle return to the material world.

Jerik walks up the hillside, leaning into the fierce and icy wind. He holds out one hand, pushing the key into empty air. As he approaches the edge of a precipice, it begins to rain again, a storm that howls around the mountainside, plunging everything into near-complete darkness. It's hard to tell, between the occluding cloud and the flashes of lightning, when the world changes, but it does. One moment, Jerik's walking off the edge of a cliff, and then suddenly he's crossing the courtyard of a medieval castle.

The hired goons are alarmed by the appearance of Kobori's castle, but a brief conversation between Hollister and Screwdriver, plus the promise of more money, convinces them to continue.

The five men follow Jerik as he heads straight into the main keep.

DEAD RUSSIANS

Searching around the courtyard, Khan finds two corpses.

One dead man's wearing a 19th-century Russian army uniform (**History:** from the era of the Russo-Turkish war; this guy must be one of the deserters recruited by Baron Vordenburg). He appears to have frozen to death, but his corpse is still quite fresh, as if he's been dead for hours, not more than a century. His hands are laden down with golden coins and jewels looted from the castle. (If Khan takes them, give her Edge 19, "Ill-Gotten Treasure"). Perhaps more usefully, he has three whittled stakes tucked into the belt of his great-coat, and the Berdan rifle strapped to his back is still, miraculously, usable.

Nearby is a second man, older, dressed in the remains of a dressing gown and silk pajamas. He resembles Nestor Kastantev – it's the corpse of his great-uncle Mikhail, who vanished mysteriously from their mansion in Paris in 1974. There's a copy of *Le Monde* from that year near his body. Mikhail committed suicide; he cut his wrists using a knife taken from the soldier's corpse.

EXPLORING THE CASTLE

Scene Type: Alternate
Lead-Ins: Opening the Gate
Lead-Outs: Bargaining

The action in the ruined castle is all in the cellars where Count Kobori sleeps, but exploring the upper levels gives Khan a chance to take out some of Hollister's bodyguards one-on-one before descending.

The castle was a grim ruin even before Kobori's defeat plunged it into the otherworld. It's a warren of empty rooms, decaying furniture, rat-chewed tapestries, and rain-drenched ruins. Parts of it appear to have been recently looted. Doors have been smashed in, boxes and wardrobes hastily pried open, and there are coins scattered on the floor – all evidence of the haste with which the Russian vampire slayers fled the castle after burying Kobori.

THE SHRINE TO DRACULA

If Khan has a Shadow Score of 3+, she feels drawn to one particular chamber in the case. This is a shrine to Dracula, Kobori's grandfather – and, effectively, patron deity. When Kobori was slain, Dracula was lost; either slumbering or dead, but no one knew for sure. While Kobori slept and the castle was locked away outside time, Dracula returned.

The shrine consists of a small altar with a brazier. A blue flame flickers in the brazier, without any visible fuel. Call for a **Cool** test.

SEEING THE BLUE FLAME

COOL

Penalty: -1 per Shadow Problem.

Advance 12+: You catch a glimpse in the flames of a face – an ageless man, neither old nor young, with a moustache and a scarred forehead. It is the man himself! Gain Edge 18, "The Face of Dracula."

Hold 9-11: The flame in the brazier flickers and dies as you approach it, leaving only a foul, sulfurous stench.

Setback 8 or less: You see a pair of terrible eyes in the depths of the flame. Gain Problem 44, "The Will of Dracula."

Extra Problem: Problem 45, "Burnt Hand."

Stunt: Yes (**Evasion** to flee; **Preparedness** for occult countermeasures).

CAT AND MOUSE

The sight of the scattered gold coins lures some of Hollister's hired goons off into the castle, while Hollister and Jerik descend into the depths. Khan can try to slip past these goons, or else take the time to eliminate them one by one.

This is an optional challenge – she can just head down to the basement and go for speed over thoroughness.

BARGAINING

When Baron Vorvdenburg and the Russian mercenaries slew Count Kobori, they hastily interred the vampire in a grave in the cellars of his own castle. They stuffed his mouth full of garlic and drove a stake through his heart, but that was not enough to completely destroy the monster.

Now, in those dark cellars, Hollister and Jerik (and any surviving mercenaries) dig up Kobori's remains. When Khan arrives, they've exposed the vampire's corpse. It's a horrific sight – a pale and bloody thing, dressed in rags, rent by many wounds. Jerik cradles the monster like a mother tending to her wounded child, while Hollister stands to one side (either coolly, if he's got the backup of his hired goons, or nervously with a gun in his hand if he's alone).

If there's a prisoner here to be sacrificed to the vampire, then they're here, tied up, at Hollister's feet. If Khan's a prisoner, then the guards hold her.

The two men have different plans for the vampire.

♦ Jerik wants to resurrect Kobori as quickly as possible by feeding the vampire blood. He'd prefer to feed someone else to his master so he can live on to serve Kobori, but right now, with the vampire's return at hand, he's sufficiently unstable to sacrifice himself if there are no other options. He's extremely intolerant of any delay.

♦ Hollister wants to bring Kobori back to the brink of consciousness, but no more. He wants to drip-feed the vampire, keeping the creature alive but helpless and in his power. Above all else, he wants to avoid Kobori regaining his full hypnotic power – Hollister was able to break free of Carlyle's control because Carlyle's from the weaker Hungarian line. The original Transylvanian-line vampires of the Linea Dracul have far greater spiritual strength; if Kobori wakes up and transfixes Hollister, he'll never be able to break free, and will have succeeded only in trading one master for a far worse one.

Jerik and Hollister don't trust each other; they had to work together to get this far, but now their aims diverge. Once she's free to act, Khan may be able to tip the balance one way or the other, either by convincing Jerik that his only chance to free his master is to kill himself immediately, or by pointing out to Jerik that Hollister intends to betray the vampire.

Bullshit Detector gives Khan insight into the motives of the two men; an Interpersonal Push lets her play into Jerik's madness or Hollister's fears.

First, though, she may need to deal with any remaining guards or break free.

TAKING DOWN HOLLISTER'S GUARDS
FIGHTING

Penalty: -4 if she's got Problem 47, "Held at Gunpoint."

Advance 11+: Hollister's hired goons are street thugs – they're not that tough. Describe how you take them down.

Hold 7-10: You take Hollister's goons down, but take a hit in the process. Gain Problem 48, "The Screwdriver."

Setback 6 or less: There are too many of them. When you attack, they grab you and drag you over to Kobori's grave. One of them pulls out a knife and is about to draw it across your throat. Unless you've got a clever way out of this one, they cut your throat and feed your blood to the vampire.

Extra Problem: Kobori's stirring in his slumber. Once you take out the goons, you'll have only a few seconds before the vampire wakes.

Stunt: Yes (**Shooting; Athletics**).

WAKING KOBORI

Neither Hollister nor Jerik is a match for Khan. Even wounded, she can take them out on her own – but not before one of them tries to reawaken the vampire. Her choice, therefore, is whether she wants to face the vampire physically (by manipulating events so that Jerik spills enough blood to resurrect Kobori) or psychically (by playing into Hollister's plan until she's close enough to eliminate both vampire and minions).

Other possible complications:

♦ If Carmen is still a factor, then she may be under the vampire's control like Jerik, or a trapped prisoner there to be sacrificed to the vampire.

♦ Khan might decide that explosives are the better part of valor, and decide to plant some C-4 charges and flee.

♦ Hollister may decide to switch sides and offer to help Khan – "Spare me," he pleads, "and I'll tell you everything about Carlyle! I ran his London operation! I know what you've forgotten!" A suitably karmic punishment for Hollister is to get eaten by Kobori – either the vampire rises up and kills him, or Hollister fall victims to "Kobori's Gaze," walks over and slits his own wrists to feed the vampire.

♦ If Khan has Edge 6, "The Necrophone," then the phone rings unexpectedly. On the other end of the line is Kobori, reaching out from beyond the grave through the necromantic device. He demands that Khan feed him blood; Jerik will do anything to get his hands on the Necrophone.

FROM HELL'S HEART

If no one spills blood on Kobori's grave, the vampire makes a last-ditch attempt to seize control of anyone nearby.

KOBORI'S GAZE

The vampire's dead eyes flick open, burning red in the darkness. You feel it trying to take control.

COOL

Bonus: Either the Sykoran Crucifix or Rosewater Potion from *Never Say Dead* can defend Khan against Kobori's commands.

Penalty: -1 per Shadow Problem. -1 die per other person you wish to protect from the vampire's gaze.

Advance 12+: You faced down Jovitzo when he was at full power; staring down his dead cousin isn't a problem for you. You push past the vampire's attempts to control you and stride across the room to his grave.

Hold 9-11: Moving as if you're fighting against a strong wind, you stagger across the room. Gain Problem 49, "Kobori's Death Curse."

Setback 8 or less: It's no good – you can't resist. Pick one – either someone else falls until Kobori's spell and kills themselves, spilling their blood on the vampire's grave and resurrecting him, or you do it. If you're still alive, you've got to fight or flee, *now*.

Extra Problem: None.

Stunt: Yes (**Evasion; Preparedness**).

FIGHTING KOBORI

The vampire has risen, but he's still weak. This is your only chance to take him out.

FIGHTING

Penalty: -2 if there are any of Kobori's minions present.

Advance 13+: You drive a stake into Kobori's heart. This time, you'll kill him properly. Vordenburg didn't finish the job – you will.

Hold 9-12: You attack the vampire, and you're winning – but then the earth shakes, and an icy wind blows through the cellar. The strange spell that brought the ruined keep back to Earth is collapsing. You've got to run, now (see the Challenge "Fleeing the Castle"), or you'll be trapped here in this Hell, this unspace with the vampire forever. There's no time to finish Kobori off *and* escape. What do you do?

Setback 8 or less: The vampire overpowers you and sinks his teeth into your throat. He's draining your life. Unless you've got some unexpected Edge or twist in hand, you're dead.

Extra Problem: Problem 50, "Claws of the Vampire."

Stunt: Yes (**Athletics; Evasion; Shooting; Preparedness**).

FLEEING THE CASTLE
EVASION

Penalty: -1 die for every other person you want to save.

Advance 9+: You sprint down the castle corridors as they collapse behind you. Kobori's spell is breaking, and the castle's falling back into the abyss. You cross the drawbridge just in time to see mists engulf the hillside behind you – and when they fade, the castle's gone.

Hold 6-8: As you flee, an iron hand grabs you and tries to drag you back into Hell. Run the Challenge "Fighting Kobori" again, but this time, there's no middle ground – it's Advance on 11+, and Setback on anything less.

Setback 5 or less: The mists close around you. If you've got the Kastantev key, you can use it to escape, tumbling out onto the hillside at the last moment. Otherwise, you're trapped in the vampire's castle forever – unless you've got some ally on the outside who can rescue you.

Extra Problem: None.

Stunt: Yes (**Athletics**).

AFTERMATH

The castle collapses, falling back into that howling netherworld. Whether Kobori's alive or dead, he's trapped in his demonic realm – assuming, of course, that Khan's got the key.

Any survivors cluster around Khan, or stumble off down the hillside in confusion. Jerik's incurably broken if he's still alive; Hollister's a dead man walking, doomed to spend the rest of his short life fleeing the conspiracy. He betrayed his master, and Carlyle is unforgiving. If Khan runs into him again, she finds Hollister to be a fugitive, paranoid wretch, skulking in alleyways and always on the run, always nervous that there's a hound from Hell on his trail.

Passing on intel to MI6 about Carlyle's network either buys off Problem 4, "Proving Ground" or earns Edge 20, "A Favor from Vauxhall Cross."

BLOWBACK

ANYWHERE

- **Problem 17, "Whispers on the Wind" or Problem 3 "Bad Dreams":** Khan suffers nightmares about Kobori – images of hands reaching out of the ground; of wandering endlessly through the corridors of a deserted castle, with weird winds howling outside; of a Russian soldier carrying away a key that drips blood. Khan's at -1 **Cool** die until she next Takes Time.

IN SPAIN

- **Problem 7, "Spotted":** Behar's men assume that Khan is working for Calatrava, and try to intimidate her by grabbing her and holding a knife to her throat. She can either play along and fool them with **Reassurance**, in which case she overhears them taking about Behar and discussing whether or not to kill her, or fight back with a **Fighting** Challenge (Advance 5+). On an Advance, Behar's men flee, and Khan gets Edge 1, "Who Are These Guys?" On a Setback, she picks up a Hurt Problem.
- **Problem 11, "Party Crasher":** Some of Calatrava's bouncers spot Khan; she needs to justify her presence at the party, perhaps by pushing **Charm** or **High Society**.

IN LONDON

- **Problem 19, "Forewarned":** The conspiracy knows Khan's coming, and have already circulated her description to the authorities. The first time Khan gains Heat in London, give her Problem 33, "Security Scrutiny" in addition to any other Heat Problems gained.
- **Problem #4, "It's Got Your Scent":** Hollister's hound tracks Khan to her hiding place; if she doesn't escape the hound's surveillance somehow, give her Problem 25, "Overexposed" and describe how the hound stalks her wherever she goes.
- **Problem 28, "Under Surveillance":** Having spotted her at Cornet's, Carmen Vidraru tries to follow Khan. It's trivially easier for Khan to evade the untrained student – if she talks to her instead, run *The Student*, p. 193.
- **Problem 31, "Break-In at Cornet's":** Cornet's tightens its security; if Khan returns there, she needs to spend an Interpersonal Push to get back in.
- **Problem 48 from *Never Say Dead*, "Stokovitch Survived":** Marina Stokovitch grabs and questions one of Khan's London contacts. Khan must spend a Push on **Reassurance** to keep the contact. Roleplay out the scene.

- **Heat Score 2+:** Whatever identity Khan used to enter the United Kingdom is compromised; she needs a new cover identity.
- **Heat Score 4+ and Problem 33, "Security Scrutiny":** Khan's arrested – but it's cover for an MI6 debriefing. Run the scene "Arrested."
- **Heat Score 5+:** Khan's gone beyond the pale; the cops now have an unofficial shoot-to-kill policy regarding her.
- **Shadow Score 4+:** Give Khan Problem 24, "It's Got Your Scent."

IN ROMANIA

- **Problem 35 from *Never Say Dead*, "Unfinished Business":** Sinclair discovers that Khan's returned to his territory. If Khan suffers a Setback on any **Network** rolls in Romania, then assume that the contact she's trying to contact is actually an assassin working for Sinclair who tries to eliminate her.
- **Shadow Score 2+:** Howling winds and foul weather make traveling perilous; Khan's at -2 to all **Driving** and **Athletics** rolls until she next Takes Time.
- **Shadow Score 4+:** Kobori tries to draw Khan to him; if she doesn't find a way to suppress her Shadow Score, run "We Took a Short Cut," p. 201, when she next Takes Time.

PROBLEMS

PROBLEM 1

The Dark Call

SHADOW

STARTING PROBLEM

You're still haunted by the vampires. You can sense them at the back of your mind, like voices calling you. The psychic wound has scabbed over, but it hasn't healed. You need more of the Rosewater Potion, and for that, you need vampire blood.

PROBLEM 2

The Best Defense

STARTING PROBLEM

The conspiracy – and especially, Carlyle, the vampire who tried to take you from Jovitzo – are still hunting you. You need to throw them off balance, to hit them where they're not expecting it. If you haven't Countered this card by the end of the operation, swap it for Problem 5, "Eliminate Her."

PROBLEM 3

Bad Dreams

SHADOW

STARTING PROBLEM

For the last few nights, you've been troubled by a memory from your fragmented past. Something about breaking into a house in Moscow. Blood on your hands, and a man running in terror as you hunt for him. To assuage your guilt, you've thrown yourself into your fight against your former masters.

PROBLEM 4

Proving Ground

STARTING PROBLEM

You've made tentative contact with your old employers at MI6. They're still very suspicious of you, considering how you left them, but they haven't cut you off entirely. If you don't produce useful intel by the end of the operation, swap this problem for Problem 6, "Burned by MI6."

PROBLEM 5

Eliminate Her

BLOWBACK

You've become a problem to the wider conspiracy, not just Carlyle and Jovitzo. You expect them to send a kill team to come after you.

PROBLEM 6

Burned by MI6

HEAT, CONTINUITY

You're a rogue in the eyes of both the conspiracy and MI6. You're solidly burned. As long as you hold this card, you've got to spend an extra Push when dealing with any members of the British intelligence community or their allies, and you're at +2 Heat when in the United Kingdom.

PROBLEM 7

Spotted

BLOWBACK

Whoever's following Curtis saw you.

PROBLEM 8

Sympathy for Curtis

She's like you in some ways; another tool of the conspiracy, to be used and discarded by unseen masters. Watching her brings up memories of your time as a thrall of the vampires. Maybe she too deserves a chance to break free...

PROBLEM 9

Car Crash Survivor

INJURY

You nearly died when your car was knocked off the road. This counts as an Injury, and you can't make Interpersonal Pushes until you Take Time to clean up.

PROBLEM 10

Need a Ride

HEAT

Not only is your car at the bottom of the cliff, you really don't want to hang around and answer awkward questions from the police.

PROBLEM 11

Party Crasher

BLOWBACK

You've infiltrated the party in the villa, so you've got to stay hidden. If you do anything to draw attention to yourself, you'll be in trouble. This may count as a Heat Problem at your GM's discretion.

PROBLEM 12

Bathroom Brawl

SERIOUS INJURY

You had to keep things quiet, and that meant no guns. Lots of smashed porcelain and blood, but no guns.

PROBLEM 12

Through and Through

SERIOUS INJURY

You've been shot. You can survive this, but you need Medical Attention and you're losing a lot of blood.

PROBLEM 13

Red Dot

There's a sniper out there, and they're trying to get a bead on you. You saw the red laser dot.

PROBLEM 14

Down

SERIOUS INJURY

You got hit badly enough to pass out. When you wake up, you're in the hands of the Calatrava gang.

PROBLEM 15

Loose End

BLOWBACK

The assassins who hit Calatrava's party want you dead. Counter by throwing them off the trail.

PROBLEM 16

Whispers on the Wind

SHADOW

The night after the party, you suddenly get a bone-deep chill, like someone's walking on your grave. When you next sleep, you dream of pale hands choking you.

PROBLEM 17

The Luciano Situation

HEAT

Describe how you escaped Luciano Calatrava's clutches – and how that escape raised your Heat Score.

PROBLEM 18

Forewarned

BLOWBACK

The conspiracy in London knows that you're coming. Expect trouble. Counter by ensuring you get to London undetected.

PROBLEM 19

Adzeh, the Blood-Eater

SHADOW, CONTINUITY

The monster tasted your blood. You can't counter this Shadow Problem until you kill the adzeh.

PROBLEM 20

The Hound of the Hollisters

SHADOW

That dog-thing can smell you coming.

PROBLEM 21

Targeted by the Conspiracy

You've got to assume that Hollister will inform his vampire masters of your meeting. Counter this problem by describing how you cover your tracks. If you've still got this card at the end of the next scene, it becomes a Heat and Shadow Problem.

PROBLEM 22

London Heat

HEAT

The police have been informed of a disturbance at the offices of respected political consultant Anthony Hollister.

PROBLEM 23

It's Got Your Scent

CONTINUITY, SHADOW

As long as that dog's alive, it'll keep hunting you. Counter by either sacrificing a Contact to sate its hungers, or killing the dog.

PROBLEM 24

Overexposed

SHADOW

You overplayed your hand in London, and Carlyle's minions are sniffing the streets for you.

PROBLEM 25

Close to the Edge

SERIOUS INJURY

You tangled with a Renfield. You've definitely got some cracked ribs, and it feels like you got run over by an elephant on meth.

PROBLEM 26

Calling Inspector Sands

HEAT

London's got more CCTV than anywhere else in the world – you've *definitely* been spotted.

PROBLEM 27

Under Surveillance

BLOWBACK

You've got a prickly feeling at the base of your spine; someone's watching you. Counter by Taking Time to lose any watchers.

PROBLEM 28

Stuntwork

INJURY

You caught the van, but like the dog that catches a car, there wasn't much you could do to stop it before they scraped you off a wall.

PROBLEM 29

Left for Dead

SERIOUS INJURY

You realize it's a trap an instant before the unseen shooter fires. You've been hit – you've got to get out of here and find Medical Attention immediately. If you don't, you'll die.

PROBLEM 30

Break-In at Cornet's

HEAT

You may discard this Heat Problem if you leave no trace of your presence and don't take anything from the auction house.

PROBLEM 31

Spotted by Security

HEAT

Your hasty exit from Cornet's was caught on camera. You may discard this Heat Problem if you allow Carmen Vidraru to be caught as you flee.

PROBLEM 32

Security Scrutiny

HEAT

The security services in London are looking for you. While you hold this Problem, you can't discard or counter other Heat Problems. Discard when you leave the UK.

PROBLEM 33

Nightsticks

INJURY

Kicking a police officer in the chest gets you arrested, but at the cost of a few bruises. You may push **Cop Talk** or **Charm** to Counter this card.

PROBLEM 34

Mauled

INJURY

By the time you wake up in the jail cell, someone's already treated the vicious dog bites on your forearms, but everything still aches and you're woozy from blood loss.

PROBLEM 35

Clawed and Scraped

INJURY

You've got dozens of scratches and cuts from the dog's assault. You can't make any Interpersonal Pushes until you Take Time to recover.

PROBLEM 36

Still At Large

SHADOW, CONTINUITY

The monstrous hound of the vampire Carlyle roams the streets of London, and the beast has your scent. This Shadow Problem only applies in London; counter by slaying Carlyle or the hound.

PROBLEM 37

Head Wound

INJURY

You were hit hard enough to knock you out, and you're bleeding from the scalp. Everything hurts.

PROBLEM 38

The Count's Call

SHADOW

Carmen's under Kobori's influence, just like you were controlled by Jovitzo. You can feel that psychic force again, like you're standing in the darkness on the edge of some terrible precipice. It takes all your courage to step back from the abyss.

PROBLEM 39

Old Friends

CONTINUITY

Some of Jovitzo's other servants know you're still alive, and they're on your trail again. While you hold this card, you've got a -2 penalty to all **Network** tests. Counter either by convincing them you're still connected by the conspiracy, or when you've acquired six new Contact cards.

PROBLEM 40

Enthralled

SHADOW

You're at least partially in the thrall of the vampire Count Kobori. Counter by killing the Count.

PROBLEM 41

Your Former Master

CONTINUITY

You sense, at the edge of perception, your former master Jovitzo roaring in anger as his cousin Kobori tries to claim "his" possession. Jovitzo still thinks he owns you – and he still has his hooks deep in your soul. This card counts as +2 Shadow in any situation involving Jovitzo.

PROBLEM 42

Disarmed

Your gun's somewhere at the bottom of a cliff in Transylvania – or in Hell. Either way, you can't use Shooting or Preparedness dice while you hold this card. Counter by obtaining a replacement weapon.

PROBLEM 43

The Will of Dracula

Dracula himself has sensed your presence in his land. While you hold this card, you automatically suffer a Setback on any contests with Kobori. Counter by discarding the Sykoran Crucifix or by reducing your Cool by 1 permanently.

PROBLEM 44

Burnt Hand

INJURY

You tipped over the brazier in horror, burning your hand badly.

PROBLEM 45

Gunshot

INJURY

One of the guards winged you with a bullet, and now blood's pouring down your arm. The castle's stones swallow the blood hungrily.

PROBLEM 46

Held at Gunpoint

Your captor's got a gun pointed right at you, and will shoot you if you make the slightest aggressive move. They don't care if you live or die – all that matters is your blood. Discard this card if you find a clever way to disarm your captor.

PROBLEM 47

The Screwdriver

SERIOUS INJURY

One of Hollister's goons lived up to his name, and now you've got a screwdriver in your stomach. Every time you roll a dice from one of your General abilities (including Stunts, but not Edges or Extra Problems), put a mark on this card. If you have more than six marks on the card before you get Medical Attention, you're dead.

PROBLEM 48

Kobori's Death Curse

CONTINUITY

The vampire cursed you with its last breath. Until you find a way to counter this card, you're in danger of slipping out of reality and back into the shadow dimension that contains his castle.

PROBLEM 49

Claws of the Vampire

INJURY, CONTINUITY

Kobori clawed your face and neck, and those wounds won't heal quickly. You'll bear the scars for the rest of your life, even after you counter this Injury card.

PROBLEM 50

Kobori's Guest

SHADOW

You've been trapped in a nightmare castle for days. Outside, there's nothing but a howling void, and it's well below zero. You've got a -2 penalty to your next three Challenges, then discard this card.

EDGES

EDGE 1
Who Are These Guys?

You've spotted Curtis' tail – four men, mostly Moroccan. You can discard this card and use a Contact or a **Criminology** Push to identify them, or discard it for a bonus die in any confrontation with these mysterious guys.

EDGE 2
Party Invitation

Francesca Curtis invited you to accompany her to a private party. Discard this for a free Push or a bonus dice in any Challenge at the party.

EDGE 3
En Garde

You can sense trouble coming. Discard this for a bonus die in any Challenge with the mysterious intruders.

EDGE 4
Indebted
CONTINUITY

You saved your target from the assassins, and that's a favor you can bank on in the future. Discard for a free Push when dealing with that individual.

EDGE 5
Drawing Fire

There's no way you should have made it through that barrage of sniper fire without getting hit, and yet, here you are, unscathed. Your luck's with you, tonight. Discard to Counter any Heat or Shadow Problem.

EDGE 6
The Necrophone

It's a jar filled with grave dirt connected to an old-fashioned telephone, and Calatrava treated it as though it was immensely valuable. Gain a Shadow Problem every time you activate it.

EDGE 7
Iron Will

You've stared death right in its million multifaceted eyes and you didn't blink. Discard for two bonus **Cool** dice in a Challenge.

EDGE 8
Memories of Hollister

You recognize his face; you've never dealt with him directly, but you know he's working for the conspiracy. Not at your former level, not a Slugeri, but just below that. Important enough to have considerable sway, a trusted servant of a vampire. Best to be on your guard. Discard this for a bonus **Sense Trouble** die in a Challenge, or for an Interpersonal Push when dealing with Hollister.

EDGE 9
A Private Call

You watched Hollister make a call, and you're sure he didn't want his vampiric masters eavesdropping on it. Mentioning that give you some leverage; you may discard this card for a free Interpersonal Push when dealing with Hollister.

EDGE 10
Hollister's Aid

In exchange for you backing off, Hollister's offered to help you in the future. He'll keep the conspiracy from finding you until then. While you hold this card, you may suppress your Heat and Shadow Scores by 1 each; discard this card if Hollister dies or at the end of the operation.

EDGE 11
Enemy of my Enemy

You've reported Hollister to Carlyle. Now to see if the vampire takes the bait…

EDGE 12
Bearded the Lion

You may not have accomplished what you set out to do, but you've caused enough chaos in your wake to make trouble for your enemies. Discard to Counter any one Heat or Shadow Problem.

EDGE 13

The Other Woman

You spotted someone out of place at the auction who warrants further investigation. As long as you hold this card, you've got a bonus dice when using **Surveillance** or **Infiltration** to watch her.

EDGE 14

Kastantev Owes You

CONTINUITY

You saved the life of Nestor Kastantev. Either discard for an Interpersonal Push when dealing with him, or for a bonus die in a **Network** test in Europe.

EDGE 15

Carmen Owes You

CONTINUITY

You saved the life of Carmen Vidraru. Either discard for an Interpersonal Push when dealing with her, or to gain her as a Contact.

EDGE 16

Death by Proxy

CONTINUITY

The pale hound was more than a servant of the vampire – it was an extension of Carlyle. A part of his unholy spirit was in the animal when you killed it. Discard this card to counter any one Vampire Problem connected to Carlyle.

EDGE 17

Parry and Riposte

The vampire's attempt to stop you failed, and you know you're getting close. Discard this card to counter any one Shadow Problem connected to Kobori, or for a bonus die in any Contest in Kobori's castle.

EDGE 18

The Face of Dracula

CONTINUITY

You've seen the face of the Count himself, the father of vampires. You know he's got to die. Once per game, you can draw on this well of determination for +1 **Cool**. Discard this card if you ever abandon the quest to kill Dracula.

EDGE 19

Ill-Gotten Treasure

CONTINUITY

You've got a bag full of antique gold coins and other treasures. You'll need to find a specialist fence to turn it all into something more usable, but it should still translate to a considerable amount of walking-around money.

EDGE 20

A Favor from Vauxhall Cross

CONTINUITY

MI6 owes you a favor. Discard this card to cash it in. You can use this to clear all Heat Problems when in England.

CONTACTS

CONTACT 1

Francesca Curtis, Lawyer

London. Ex-conspiracy bagman and unwitting agent.

Accounting, Criminology, High Society.

CONTACT 2

Tazi, Arms Dealer

Morocco.
Military Science, Streetwise.
Mechanics 2, Shooting 2.

CONTACT 3

Susan Graves, Historian

Archaeology, History, Languages, Research.

CONTACT 4

Carmen Vidraru, Archaeology Student

Archaeology, History, Languages, Vampirology.

Infiltration 1.

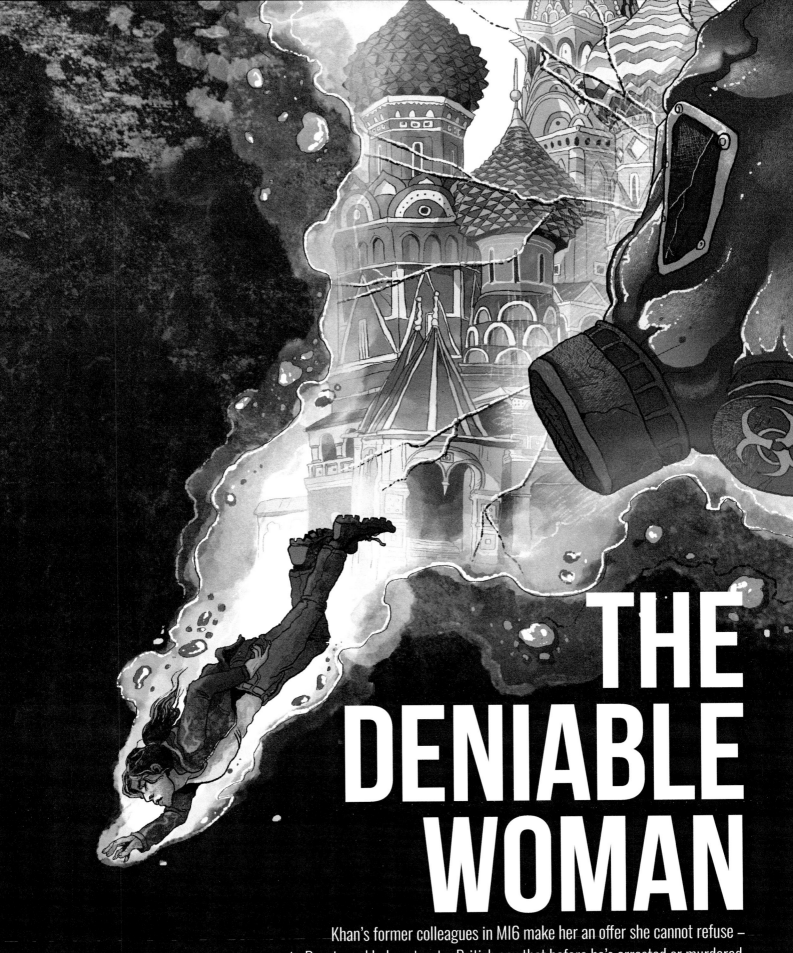

THE DENIABLE WOMAN

Khan's former colleagues in MI6 make her an offer she cannot refuse –
go to Russia and help extract a British spy that before he's arrested or murdered.

BACKSTORY

During the 1970s, Russian scientists following notes left by Baron Vordenburg (see p. 183) managed to resurrect and capture a Romanian-line vampire, which they codenamed Koschei. They brought the creature to an isolated laboratory in Kostroma. The creature soon broke out of their control and turned the research facility into its new lair. This vampire isn't part of the wider conspiracy – it's an independent horror concerned only with its own appetites and delusions. It has a few mortal servants, agents well-placed to either provide Koschei with victims or conceal its existence.

One of these agents is an FSB officer, Nina Rozhkova. She tries to balance her loyalty to two masters – the Russian state and the vampire. When she became aware of a British spy asking questions about the vampire, she lured the spy into a trap and gave him to Koschei.

Khan's mission is to rescue this spy, Harry Coleman.

However, there are two other hurdles that must be overcome. First, Coleman was betrayed by his colleagues at a Moscow-based MI6 cut-out called Cathedral Dome; one of those colleagues, the roguish Linklathe, hires Khan to find Coleman in the hope she'll fail to find the missing spy.

Second, Coleman's girlfriend in Moscow, Olga Agrapova, is secretly working for the vampire Carlyle (p. 126), and is using Coleman to investigate Project KOSCHEI.

OVERVIEW

To successfully complete the operation, Khan must:

◆ Travel to Moscow
◆ Identify Olga Agrapova
◆ Locate the secret British safehouse
◆ Find her way to the secret research facility
◆ Destroy Koschei

CAST LIST

Key non-player characters in the operation:

MI6

Harry Coleman: An MI6 spy, a former associate of Khan's. He's come to share her secret crusade against the vampires. Currently, he's assigned to a British investment firm/cut-out called Cathedral Dome.

Jimmy Linklathe: A diplomatic attaché and spy at the British embassy in Moscow. Linklathe doesn't believe in vampires, and helped push Coleman out of his post in Cathedral Dome to open up a space for his buddy Michael Hestridge.

LONDON

Angela Coleman: Harry's estranged wife.

CATHEDRAL DOME MOSCOW

Aaron Shawler: The chummy, ineffectual head of Cathedral Dome; a good source of local intel, but not otherwise useful.

Michael Hestridge: Ambitious college friend of Jimmy Linklathe, eager to turn the cut-out into a genuine moneymaking company.

Tara Tallwood: Coleman's secretary and confidante.

MOSCOW

Olga Agrapova: Coleman's girlfriend (and secret agent of Carlyle).

Eduard Morozov: A former researcher on Project KOSCHEI, now hiding in a Moscow safehouse.

Borya Ignatiev: Industrialist and party animal; also, an unwilling servant of Koschei.

Nina Rozkhova: FSB officer and agent of Koschei.

THE COURT OF KOSCHEI

Maria Rozkhova: A former researcher, Nina Rozkhova's mother, now a bolotnik.

"Koschei": a Romanian-line vampire captured and experimented upon during the Cold War.

THE THIRST FOR…PERFLUORODECALIN?

When Koschei was a prisoner of the Soviet researchers, they experimented with keeping the vampire in a quasi-coma using a blood substitute based on a chemical called perfluorodecalin. One of the virtues of the perfluorodecalin compound is that it's better than normal blood at traveling through damaged blood vessels.

The vampire was horribly damaged when it broke free of the Soviet researchers. Half of Koschei's body was crushed and he was severely burned. He needs a large supply of perfluorodecalin to temporarily restore his strength. He mixes the blood of his victims with the chemical so the stolen vitality can suffuse his body.

THE BOLOTNIKI

In Slavic myth, the *bolotnik* is a swamp monster, a grotesque old man who drags travelers to their deaths in the mire. In this operation, the term refers to the monsters controlled by Koschei. These unfortunate souls were once the researchers at the bioweapons lab, now transformed into zombie-like monsters controlled by the vampire's psychic powers. They shamble around the island in Kostroma. By day, they're uncontrolled and feral, rooting around the island or just staring at the lake-water. By night, Koschei drags them into his own delusions, and makes the ruined lab into a parody of a medieval court.

TIMELINE

1984: Soviet researchers using the Vordenburg diary discover the tomb of "Koschei", a Romanian-line vampire. They bring the slumbering vampire to a research facility on an island in the forests northeast of Moscow.

1987: Koschei escapes from his confinement and turns the research laboratory into his new castle.

1996: Koschei forces Borya Ignatiev to provide him with a supply of perfluorodecalin.

Four years ago: MI6 sets up Cathedral Dome Investments as a front for spying on Moscow.

Three years ago: Harry Coleman leaves MI6 and joins Cathedral Dome.

One year ago: Coleman meets Tara Tallwood and deals with her abusive boyfriend.

Nine months ago: Coleman starts a relationship with Olga Agrapova.

One month ago: Coleman meets the informant, Morozov, who tells him about the existence of Koschei.

Three weeks ago: Nina Rozhkova, one of the vampire's thralls, discovers Morozov's treachery. She attempts to kill Morozov; he escapes and is put in a safehouse by Coleman.

Two weeks ago: Linklathe reveals Coleman's relationship to Rozhkova in exchange for a bribe.

One week ago: Rozkhova convinces Coleman to meet her by revealing her knowledge of his relationship with Olga Agrapova. He leaves a letter for Olga in his apartment. At the meeting, Coleman's captured and brought to Koschei's lair.

Four days ago: Before Olga can retrieve the letter, Michael Hestridge breaks into the apartment looking for Coleman's files. He steals the letter.

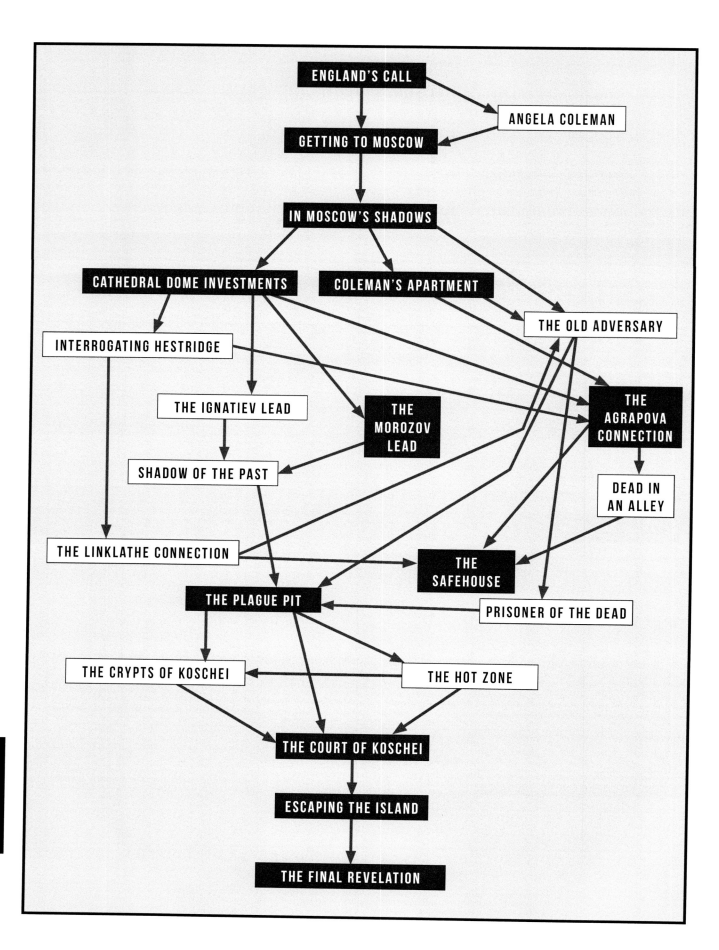

ENGLAND'S CALL

ANGELA COLEMAN

GETTING TO MOSCOW

IN MOSCOW'S SHADOWS

CATHEDRAL DOME INVESTMENTS

COLEMAN'S APARTMENT

THE OLD ADVERSARY

INTERROGATING HESTRIDGE

THE IGNATIEV LEAD

THE MOROZOV LEAD

THE AGRAPOVA CONNECTION

SHADOW OF THE PAST

DEAD IN AN ALLEY

THE LINKLATHE CONNECTION

THE SAFEHOUSE

THE PLAGUE PIT

PRISONER OF THE DEAD

THE CRYPTS OF KOSCHEI

THE HOT ZONE

THE COURT OF KOSCHEI

ESCAPING THE ISLAND

THE FINAL REVELATION

ENTRY VECTORS

The default entry vector is for Khan to be contacted by her former employers in MI6, as described in *England's Call*, p. 218.

Other possible vectors:

- If you're running this on the heels of *Never Say Dead,* then Khan might seek out MI6 if she's being pursued by Jovitzo.

- Jean Hulier (p. 126) might have uncovered something about Russian vampire/biochemistry experiments in the 1980s; digging around puts Khan in touch with her old friend Angela Coleman.

- The Vordenburg diary from *No Grave for Traitors* was reviewed by the FSB; tracking their research into that document brings Khan to Moscow, where she runs into Coleman shortly before he vanishes.

- Harry Coleman could be established as a contact of Khan's in a previous adventure, long before he disappears.

- Digging up dirt on Hestridge in *No Grave for Traitors* might expose a connection to Cathedral Dome Investments.

- Investigating Jovitzo's connections might put Khan on Koschei's trail.

STARTING PROBLEMS

Optionally, offer the four Starting Problems to the player and ask her to pick whichever one best reflects Khan's current situation, or pick the most apt Problem yourself and give it to the player. If you've already played through *Never Say Dead* or another Leyla Khan adventure, and your player already has a hand full of ongoing Problems, you don't need to add another.

1. **Building Bridges. Starting Problem.** You need allies and reliable sources; that means rebuilding your connection to MI6.

You need to end this operation in MI6's good graces.

2. **Shelter in a Storm. Starting Problem.** The conspiracy's closing in on you – you need to lie low out of your usual haunts, or lose some of the monsters on your trail. If you don't find a way to counter this problem, gain Problem 5, "At Your Throat."

3. **Out of Blood. Starting Problem.** You've exhausted the last of the Rosewater Potion. You need more vampire blood to make more of your protective elixir.

4. **Voice Message. Starting Problem.** A few days ago, you got a brief and confused message from Harry Coleman. He's MI6, you worked with him when you were in the service. Moscow desk. He sounds terrified, drunk. He said you were right, said that he needed to talk to you – but he didn't leave any way to contact him. Discard this for a free Interpersonal Push when dealing with Harry. While you hold this card, you've got a -1 penalty to any **Cool** tests.

ENGLAND'S CALL

Scene Type: Core
Lead-Outs: Getting to Moscow

Let the player describe where Khan is when the adventure begins. Is she on the trail of some vampire? Investigating some facet of the conspiracy? Lying low under an assumed identity in some obscure Provençal village? Visiting her estranged family in Lebanon?

Wherever she is, she's contacted by her former colleagues in MI6. They might:

♦ Contact her via an encrypted email channel that's been inactive for years

♦ Get a message to her via a dead drop that she used when she was working for MI6

♦ Connect to her via a Contact she has in hand

♦ Connect to her via a trusted intermediary

♦ Send a young MI6 handler, **Jimmy Linklathe**, to track her down

Pick a channel that the player seems willing to trust. The message, however it gets to her, arranges a meeting between Khan and Jimmy Linklathe on suitably neutral ground – a café or hotel bar is ideal.

THE NEW HANDLER

Jimmy Linklathe is frighteningly young and precocious; he looks like he's still in university, and makes Khan feel ancient. He speaks with a plummy Oxbridge accent, and has a shock of wild blonde hair. He exudes confidence, if not competence.

His mission here is to handle a dangerous and unreliable asset – Leyla Khan. He's been told that she left MI6 under unusual circumstances, and that she's obsessed with an international occult conspiracy of some sort. (Linklathe has no idea that vampires are real.) However, he's perfectly willing to indulge Khan's "delusions" for the moment – all he needs from her are her undeniable skills as a field operative.

Linklathe explains the following:

♦ A British MI6 officer, Harry Coleman, has gone missing in Moscow. He was operating without diplomatic cover from the embassy, and his activities were a little... self-directed, as Linklathe delicately puts it. They need to find him and bring him home quietly and deniably, without the Russian FSB getting involved.

♦ So, they want to bring in someone from outside, someone they can rely on but aren't directly associated with – Leyla Khan.

♦ Khan's assignment is to sneak into Moscow, track Coleman down, and get him out of the country quietly.

♦ In exchange, they'll owe Khan a favor, and will pay her a reasonable fee for her services. (She'll gain Edge 1, "Coin of the Realm" and Edge 2. "A Favor from Vauxhall Cross" at the end of the mission.)

- Linklathe pauses: *"You knew Coleman back when you were still with us, didn't you?"* Let the player decide what relationship, if any, Khan had with Coleman.
  - ◊ Coleman's married; his wife lives in London. At least, he was married when Khan knew him, before Jovitzo stole five years of her life and free will.
  - ◊ She recalls Coleman as dogged and professional. Once he had a lead, he'd follow it to the ends of the earth. He's average height, bearded, charming when he wants to be, callous by instinct.

Possible Investigative ability uses:

- **Bullshit Detector:** Linklathe's telling the truth – he's clearly skeptical about Khan, and sees her as a disposable, deniable asset. However, this doesn't seem to be a trap or anything more sinister.
  - ◊ A Push of **Bullshit Detector** picks up that Linklathe has a personal interest in Coleman's fate. He seems a little eager to have the whole matter wrapped up, as if confirming that Coleman is dead will somehow benefit him. (Linklathe has plans to profit from Coleman's Cathedral Dome Investments, see "Jimmy's Game," p. 235).
- **Negotiation:** A **Negotiation** Push can extract a bigger payment from Linklathe, giving Khan an extra copy of either Edge 1 or Edge 2 once she extracts Coleman.
- **Tradecraft:** Linklathe's only marginally qualified for this; it suggests that that MI6 have already given Coleman up for dead, and are sending her as a last-ditch attempt to bring him back alive. She's not expected to survive.

LIKELY QUESTIONS

- **What was Coleman's cover in Moscow?** He's running a brokerage that connects wealthy Russians with investment and property opportunities overseas. Sanctioned money laundering, basically, but Vauxhall Cross can track the money.
- **What exactly was he doing there? How was he "self-directed?"** Coleman's actual mission was to look at the Russian military-industrial complex, especially high-tech or unusual weapons developments. Cyber-intrusions, psychological ops, non-linear warfare – that sort of thing. He'd become rather obsessed with it – much like Khan.
- **Is this connected to the conspiracy?** Linklathe pauses before answering, obviously trying to decide how much to indulge what he sees as Khan's delusions. He finally settles on being evasive. "Oh, I'm hardly an expert on that... theory. Possibly, I suppose. You'll have to look into that on the ground."
  - ◊ **Bullshit Detector:** Linklathe doesn't believe in vampires in the slightest, and sees Coleman and Khan as cut from the same paranoid cloth.
- **When did he disappear?** He's missed a scheduled check-in a week ago, and hasn't responded to attempts to contact him. MI6 is cautious about trying too hard to find him through, ah, non-deniable channels.

DEPARTURES

Once Khan's agreed to take the mission, Linklathe visibly relaxes. "I'll be in Moscow too, at the embassy. The FSB will have me under surveillance, of course, but I'm sure I can slip them for a quick meeting if you need a steer. I've taken the liberty of procuring a passport and papers for you, as well as flights to Moscow. I'll see you there." Give the player Edge 3, "Linklathe's Folder."

If the player goes to consult with Linklathe, run the scene *The Linklathe Connection* (p. 233).

▰ ▰ ▰ ▰ ▰ ▰

ANGELA COLEMAN

Scene Type: Alternate
Lead-Ins: England's Call
Lead-Outs: Getting to Moscow

Khan recalls that Coleman was married, and that his wife Angela is a cardiologist living in London. If she wants to track Angela down, she can do so with **Research**.

Angela's in her mid-40s; while she and Harry have a house in Sussex, she lives in a flat in London near the hospital where she works. (If Khan's played through *No Grave for Traitors*, p. 167, she may have some ongoing Problems associated with London like "Still At Large").

Angela tries to avoid associating with Harry's work; a push of **Charm** or **Reassurance** (or breaking into the flat and using **Intimidation**) is needed for her to talk. Ask the player if Angela would remember Khan, and what sort of relationship they had.

Under questioning, Angela reveals the following:

- Harry told her he that he was leaving MI6, and that a new opportunity had opened up for him in Moscow.
- They tried to make a long-distance relationship work, but they've grown apart. She blames him for the breakdown in their marriage.
- They still talk regularly – mostly about their children, both of whom live with Angela's mother in Sussex. A secure, encrypted line – Harry might be out of MI6, but he still takes precautions, maintains good tradecraft, and it's become second

nature to her too in some ways.

- She doesn't know much about his work in Moscow, and is unaware he's gone missing.
- She last talked to Harry about a week ago (shortly before he vanished). He said that he had to take a trip, and that he wouldn't be around for some time. He also asked her a lot of questions about medical topics – about how blood is stored, about synthetic blood products, about tissue regeneration. She had the impression that he was grappling with some sort of technical document in Russia, and was using her to parse unfamiliar jargon. When she asked why he was asking such odd questions, he just said that a client had left him some interesting material.
- Specifically, she asked him about perfluorodecalin, a compound that was used as the key ingredient in various synthetic blood substitutes in the 1990s. She's heard that the Russians are continuing to experiment with perfluorodecalin-based substances.
- A push of **Charm**, or finding a Contact with **Pharmacy**, discovers that perfluorodecalin-based synthetics have shown some promise in treating damaged or crushed tissue. As the perfluorodecalin molecules are much smaller than hemoglobin, a perfluorodecalin fluid can carry oxygen through damaged blood vessels that normal blood cannot traverse. It's more commonly found in various high-end cosmetics.

GETTING TO MOSCOW

Scene Type: Core
Lead-Ins: England's Call
Lead-Outs: In Moscow's Shadows

Linklathe's dossier contains flights to Moscow; Khan may prefer to arrange her own transport, and might prefer to take a slower, less conspicuous route in (train or driving). Khan has fragmentary memories from her time as Jovitzo's thrall about operations she carried out in Russia at his behest – ask the player to describe these memories (they're not germane to this adventure, but can lay seeds for future interactions).

While traveling, Khan has another memory – or a dream – about her first meeting with Jovitzo. Frame the scene as you wish – is Khan falling asleep on a plane? Driving through the night? Hiding the back of a truck heading for Moscow? Walking through some concrete tunnel deep in the Moscow subway?

FLASHBACK: FIVE YEARS GONE

Five years ago, MI6 sent Khan to Hungary to investigate John Sinclair, a former SAS officer who'd vanished into the criminal underworld in Budapest. British intelligence feared that Sinclair was a security risk, that he intended to sell secret information to some criminal syndicate or hostile intelligence service. Khan trailed Sinclair into tunnels under the city.

Segue into actual play – instead of Khan just *remembering* going into the tunnel, present it as happening in real time. Ask the player what she's doing – how is she following Sinclair? Is he just ahead of her? Has she planted a tracking device? Is she in disguise?

The concrete of the tunnel walls gives away to stone; she's entered a medieval section of the underworld. There are ancient carvings and symbols daubed on the walls – bizarre alchemical symbols, Satanic imagery, coats of arms.

The tunnel opens into a larger chamber. It looks like a medieval banqueting hall, torch-lit, with benches and low trestle tables. There are about two dozen people there, each of whom has a metal cup in front of them. Some wear hooded robes; others business suits or street clothes. Politicians and senior police officers rub elbows with drug dealers and terrorists.

Sinclair's there too, at the high table, kneeling before a throne. And seated on that throne is a figure who seems to have stepped straight out of some medieval painting – long-haired, greasy, harsh-featured, but possessed of an inhuman charisma, as though some unnatural light blazes through his veins.

Call for a **Cool** test as Jovitzo turns his gaze upon Khan. He gestures to a table place set at his side. "Join me."

EYES OF THE VAMPIRE

He saw you, even though you were hidden in the shadows. His eyes, burning like red suns... the taste of blood in your mouth as you fell into darkness for years....

COOL

Advance 9+: You managed to turn and run before Jovitzo ensorcelled you with his gaze. They chased you through the tunnels like a pack of wolves at your heels. You nearly made it back to the surface, and you're not sure how many of them you took down in your escape. You fought tooth and nail, but they dragged you back. Gain Edge 4, "Defiant to the Last."

Hold 6-8: You couldn't resist his unnatural will. The vampire's gaze paralyzed you, held you fixed in place while his minions dragged you up to his throne.

Setback 5 or less: You only remember it now for the first time – you *chose* not to resist the vampire. Some dark impulse in you took over, and you walked willingly towards his throne. Gain Problem 6, "Born in Darkness."

Extra Problem: None.

Stunt: Yes (**Cover** for disguise; **Evasion** to escape; **Fighting** to punch your way out; **Sense Trouble** for advance warning).

The flashback ends as Khan's brought to Jovitzo's side, and the vampire bears his fangs...

When the flashback ends, Khan's back where she was when you first framed the scene – on an airplane, a train, walking through the Moscow subway. In that liminal moment between dreaming and waking, Khan has the unsettling sensation that someone's watching her from close by. Give the player the opportunity to push **Notice**; if the player accepts, she gets Edge 5, "The Watcher."

MOSCOW CENTRAL

There's an obligatory **Cover** test as Khan arrives in Moscow. She can use Edge 3, "Linklathe's Folder," to automatically Hold on this test, or rely on her own contacts and resources to get into the city undetected. If Khan does use "Linklathe's Folder," make note of it.

ENTERING MOSCOW

You're not MI6 anymore, but you never really leave – any more than t he other side can really change. It's still the Great Game, played in the shadows.

COVER

Advance 9+: You've got some old identities you established when you were working for Jovitzo that are still active. Passports, money, a base of operations – a life you can slip on like a winter jacket. Gain Edge 6, "The Moscow Identity."

Hold 4-8: You make it through security without being flagged. You're not safe – you can't be certain the FSB haven't chosen you at random for scrutiny – but you don't think they know who you are. Yet.

Setback 3 or less: You're detained and questioned. You can either lull them into complacency by Taking Time, or else Gain Problem 7, "Troublemaker."

Extra Problem: Problem 8, "Marked."

Stunt: No.

IN MOSCOW'S SHADOWS

Scene Type: Core
Lead-Ins: Getting to Moscow
Lead-Outs: Cathedral Dome Investments, The Old Adversary, Coleman's Apartment

Ask the player what cover identity Khan is using, and where she's staying. Pretending to be a tourist is the easiest way to stay off the FSB's radar, but may limit her ability to investigate without drawing suspicion. Going in as a wealthy investor makes it more plausible for her to visit Cathedral Dome Investments, but requires a more elaborate cover identity for Khan. Pretending to be, say, a Europol detective or private investigator gives her more flexibility, but draws more attention from the authorities – especially if she's exposed.

Khan has two obvious leads to follow:

♦ (core clue) Coleman's cover in Moscow is that he's running *Cathedral Dome Investments*, p. 224.

♦ (core clue) **Tradecraft** or **Criminology**: Even if the FSB don't know that Coleman's actively working for MI6, it's certain they'd keep tabs on him. Khan has connections in the FSB that might be willing to trade intel for intel (*The Old Adversary*, p. 238)

Some lines of inquiry are dead ends, so you can play through them quickly in a montage as Khan works her contacts and informants. Remember, Khan can use Network to create a contact with any Investigative abilities listed below that she doesn't possess herself.

Bureaucracy: Cathedral Dome Investments is a small but highly profitable company. Unlike some of its competitors, it's avoided scrutiny and interference from European regulators. (**Tradecraft** or **Criminology** guesses that's down to Coleman's contacts – if he's using the company as a front for espionage activities, he could ensure his allies give it a clean bill of health).

Cop Talk: Coleman hasn't been reported as a missing person, and there are no reports of violence or disturbance at his apartment or at the Cathedral Dome offices. Khan doesn't have **Cop Talk**, so she'll need to use **Network** to create a local contact. If the player doesn't have anyone in mind, her contact is Yuri Fokine, a gruff Moscow Police detective whose main goal is ensuring that Khan doesn't leave a trail of bodies behind her.

♦ A Push does get one interesting piece of intel – a year ago, there was an odd incident involving Coleman and two English students. One of them accused Coleman of assaulting him, then dropped the charges and said he'd fallen down a flight of stairs. The other student was a girl called Tallwood; she's now Coleman's assistant.

High Society (or Criminology): Cathedral Dome's one of a number of channels for taking Russian oil and gas money and investing it in the West. It's on the fringes of legality – it's not one of the major money-laundering routes, but it'd certainly be easy to use it as such.

♦ A push of **Reassurance** or **Charm** convinces one Russian investor to confide to Khan that the person to talk to about the firm's special policies is Harry Coleman – he handles, ah, major investments that require a personal touch.

♦ A push of **Charm** discovers that Harry Coleman has a Russian girlfriend, **Olga Agrapova**. Tracking her down leads to *The Agrapova Connection*, p. 231.

Research: Cathedral Dome's run by Aaron Shawler. Shawler's been in Moscow for more than thirty years, since the fall of the Soviet Union. He lost a lot of money on a bad deal a few years ago that brought down his former company, Shawler Property. He's the official owner of Capital Dome – but reading between the lines, he's semi-retired and leaves running the company to his partners.

COLEMAN'S APARTMENT

Scene Type: Alternate
Lead-Ins: In Moscow's Shadows, Cathedral Dome Investments
Lead-Outs: The Old Adversary, The Agrapova Connection

Coleman's official residence in Moscow is an expensive apartment in a bloc favored by Western ex-pats and under surveillance by the authorities.

♦ **Urban Survival:** Coleman would have known that this apartment isn't secure. There may not be much of value here – but it might be worth working some of your Russian security contacts for intel. Dealing with the FSB always comes at a cost… (see *The Old Adversary*, p. 238).

The apartment is securely locked; if Khan doesn't have a key, she'll need to sneak in with an **Infiltration** Challenge.

First impressions: the apartment's been recently searched. Clothes and belongings everywhere, books strewn around the floor. There aren't any signs of a struggle. Judging from the food in the refrigerator, Coleman hasn't been back here in some time.

BREAKING INTO COLEMAN'S APARTMENT

INFILTRATION

You're almost certainly under surveillance here, so you need to be quick about this. If you're caught, you'll blow the whole operation.

Bonus: +2 if you Push **Urban Survival**.

Advance 7+: You get in easily without being spotted, and have plenty of time to search the apartment thoroughly.

Hold 4-6: You get in – but you're sure that she got picked up by a security camera. You can't stay long – if you linger here more than two minutes, gain Problem 9, "Moscow Heat."

Setback 2-3: Just as you're about to break in, a police patrol walks by outside. It's too hot – they're watching this place.

Extra Problem: Problem 9, "Moscow Heat."

Stunt: Yes (**Cover** to disguise yourself; **Preparedness** or **Filch** for lockpicks; **Athletics** to climb in window eight stories up).

◆ **Tradecraft:** It's a common KGB trick to hassle suspected spies and journalists by breaking into their apartments or hotel rooms and leaving some trace of their presence – muddy footprints on the mat, a broken vase or painting, a turd in the toilet. This isn't that – someone hastily searched this apartment, and did it sloppily. (The apartment was searched by Hestridge on Linklathe's instructions, but he was disturbed by Olga Agrapova.)

◆ The lock wasn't forced; whoever got in here had access to the key.

◆ **Notice:** There's a framed photograph on the desk. It's strange – there are two photos in the frame. The original photograph, the one that actually fits the frame, is a photograph of two young children; Harry's kids back in London, who are in the custody of his estranged wife Angela. It's an old photograph, taken ten or twelve years ago; the two children run through a park, kicking at autumn leaves. A happy memory.

◆ Someone's opened the frame and put another photograph in front of the first one. This second photo is a print-out of a long-distance surveillance camera; it shows a dark-haired young woman (Olga Agrapova) coming out of an apartment building. On the back of the photo is a handwritten message: *Gorky Park, Saturday, 3pm.* The message is dated – two days before Coleman disappeared. Give Khan Edge 7, "The Mysterious Note."

◇ If Khan Takes Time to do some **Research**, or Pushes **Urban Survival**, she can identify the apartment building in question, giving her a lead to find *The Agrapova Connection* (p. 231).

A more thorough search turns up the following:

◆ You don't think Coleman's here very often. The apartment is oddly soulless.

◆ There's a blank spot at the back of the wardrobe, the sort of place you'd keep a go-bag packed with cash and other necessities like a false passport. Coleman knew he was leaving.

◆ Looking through emails on the computer, it's obvious that Coleman doesn't trust this machine – there's little of interest here. The computer has likely been compromised by the FSB. However, there are files and photographs of a factory in Moscow that produces a chemical called perfluorodecalin – an ingredient in blood substitutes. A little digging (**Research**) discovers the factory is owned by Ignatiev (see *The Ignatiev Connection*, p. 230).

◆ A Push of **Electronic Surveillance:** There's a security camera, feeding into Coleman's computer. Accessing the footage turns up the following:

◇ There's a suspicious blank period nine days ago. There might be some supernatural element to the way the screen's suddenly bathed in darkness, but it could equally be some high-tech counter-surveillance gadget. (This is when Nina Rozkhova visited and left "The Mysterious Note").

◇ A week ago, Coleman writes a note and leaves it on the table. He then makes a brief phone call. The camera doesn't record sound.

◇ Four days ago, someone enters the apartment – a young man, his face half-hidden by a scarf. (Khan may recognize him as Michael Hestridge. He hastily searches the apartment. He finds the letter, but before he can read it, the door opens again and a woman enters (Olga Agrapova). She screams and runs; the male intruder also flees a moment later, taking the letter with him.

◇ Fast-forwarding – the last person to enter the apartment was Khan herself.

CATHEDRAL DOME INVESTMENTS

Scene Type: Core
Lead-Ins: In Moscow's Shadows
Lead-Outs: The Agrapova Connection, Interrogating Hestridge, Coleman's Apartment

Cathedral Dome's offices in central Moscow are blandly corporate – all plate glass and polished steel and concrete. Etchings of 17th- and 18th-century architectural drawings decorate the walls. The office isn't open to the public – if Khan's got a suitable **Cover**, she can get an appointment. Otherwise, a Push of **High Society** or **Charm** gets her past the front desk.

The company's relatively small, employing a dozen people. Most of Cathedral Dome's activities are entirely legal and unremarkable, and most of the staff are unaware that their office was created as a front for British Intelligence. Looking around, the office seems to have been deliberately engineered as an outpost of England in the heart of Moscow; most of the staff are from the United Kingdom.

Human Terrain identifies three key figures in the office who might be worth questioning.

- ♦ **Aaron Shawler:** The elderly owner of Cathedral Dome.
- ♦ **Michael Hestridge:** One of the junior partners, running Harry Coleman's portfolio in his absence.
- ♦ **Tara Tallwood:** Coleman's personal assistant and secretary.

Khan can either manipulate the situation so she gets to talk to any of these three potential sources, or make contact with them outside the office. It's trivially easier for her to follow any of them home, or find Michael Hestridge in some Moscow nightclub.

AARON SHAWLER

Shawler landed in Moscow in December of 1989, convinced that communism was about to collapse and that capitalism was about to march east. He was right on the money – Shawler was right there as Russia went through reforms, and was one of the flock of vultures that hopes to make a fortune in the transition from communism to hyper-capitalism. He never quite made it, never landed the right deal or make the right connections to state security. He got wealthy, but not super-rich – and then lost most of that money trying to keep up with his super-rich drinking pals from the wild days of the mid-90s.

Cathedral Dome is the third act of his life in Moscow. He was secretly bailed out by a British bank with connections to MI6 – to set up Cathedral Dome as a plausible front, MI6 needed someone to be the face of the company. Shawler was ideal – well-established, well-connected, but enough of a screw-up that the authorities wouldn't look too closely. Shawler knows that part of his value is that he's deliberately ignorant of what's really going on.

Play him as a lecherous, somewhat tipsy old rogue.

- Harry Coleman? The chap hasn't turned up in the office for weeks, but... well, Shawler isn't always punctilious about showing up for work either. One has to have a certain flexibility here, you know. Hestridge is handling Coleman's portfolio in his absence – if Khan has any questions, ask him.
- **Bullshit Detector:** Shawler appears to be a designated mushroom, kept in the dark about anything important. He's not lying when he says he doesn't know anything, but he's also avoiding asking questions.
- **Human Terrain:** Shawler's out of touch with the day to day running of the company. He refers any questions to Hestridge or Tara Tallwood.
- **Charm:** If flattered, Shawler mentions that he knows that Coleman has a girlfriend or mistress here in Moscow. He doesn't know the details – Harry's charmingly old-fashioned about such affairs. Tara knows, though, no doubt. Coleman runs his life through Ms. Tallwood.
- A push of **Charm** convinces Shawler to tell his employees to cooperate fully with Khan's questions. Give the player Edge 8, "Shawler's Assistance."

MICHAEL HESTRIDGE

Young Michael Hestridge instantly reminds Khan of Jimmy Linklathe – they both have the same plummy Oxbridge accent, the same cocky attitude, the same outrageously youthful ambition. Hestridge introduces himself as the "chap who's taking over from Coleman."

Notice spots that he's got the same school tie pin as Linklathe; alternatively, **Research** can turn up the same intel. He and Jimmy Linklathe were at school and Cambridge together. This is a clue pointing to "Jimmy's Game" (p. 235).

If Khan's visited Coleman's apartment and found the security camera, she recognizes Hestridge as the man who broke in four days ago.

- He doesn't know where Coleman is, and honestly, he doesn't care. He and Coleman never got, and he thinks Coleman was a drag on the company's success. He rarely brought in useful clients. Look at this portfolio, he says – it's full of shit. He brandishes a print-out of Coleman's recent clients. (See "The Portfolio," p. 227).
  - ◊ **Bullshit Detector:** Hestridge becomes nervous and defensive when discussing Coleman. He's eager to heap dirt on his predecessor, as if trying to justify his lack of concern.
- **Bullshit Detector** or **Tradecraft:** Hestridge seems to know, or at least, suspect, that Cathedral Dome is a cover for something more than investment banking. However, he's definitely not a spy and seems to have absolutely no loyalty or sense of high purpose.
- A Push of **Charm** or **Reassurance** (or getting him when he's relaxed) gets more information out of him.
  - ◊ He despises both Shawler and Coleman. Shawler's an old fraud,

Coleman's a former spy who never really left. You can't rely on either of them – Shawler might get drunk and sink a deal, and Coleman's still seeing monsters in every shadow. The company would do much better – and more importantly, Hestridge would be a lot richer – if both of them left.

◊ Why doesn't he leave himself? Because he wants Cathedral Dome's portfolio of clients and its reputation. He's willing to hold out until Shawler kicks the bucket.

◊ Privately, he believes that Coleman ran afoul of the FSB. He was always poking his nose where it didn't belong, and that's dangerous.

Khan's likely to question Hestridge again, more forcefully. See *Interrogating Hestridge*, p. 232.

TARA TALLWOOD

Tallwood is Harry Coleman's personal assistant and secretary. As her name might imply, she's pale and willowy, with a dancer's grace. She's came to Moscow on a holiday after graduation from university, and ended up getting a job here in Cathedral Dome. She speaks highly of Mr. Coleman.

Play her as defensive and guarded; she's worried about Harry Coleman, but also wants to protect his secrets.

♦ **Bullshit Detector:** Tallwood's choosing her words very carefully. She's not necessarily lying, but she's trying to shield Coleman from close scrutiny. She may know that Harry's still working for MI6 in some capacity.

♦ She hasn't seen Coleman in a week, but he sometimes takes unexpected breaks. Maybe he's had to return to England unexpectedly, or maybe he's off on some client's yacht.

♦ A suitable Interpersonal Push gets her to hand over the spare key and entry code to Coleman's apartment (*Coleman's Apartment*, p. 222).

♦ Mr. Hestridge is handling Coleman's clients in his absence. Tallwood can provide a copy of the portfolio (p. 227) if the player uses a suitable Interpersonal Push.

♦ (core clue) She knows that Coleman has a girlfriend here in Moscow, a Russian girl named Olga Agrapova. However, she won't reveal Agrapova's contact details unless Khan uses a suitable Interpersonal ability (**Reassurance** or **Interrogation** both work, albeit in very different ways).

◊ If Khan uses **Reassurance**, then Tallwood first confides why she's so protective of Coleman. When Tallwood first came to Moscow, she was travelling with her boyfriend, Raymond. He was abusive and violent – he had problems with drugs. Coleman spotted that Raymond was causing trouble in a nightclub,

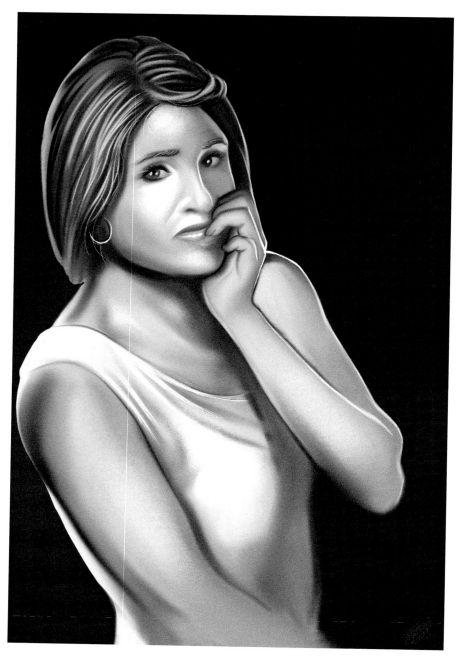

and... convinced him to leave. Coleman, she insists, is a good man. She trusts him – if he's gone missing, there's a good reason for it.

◊ If Khan uses **Interrogation**, then Tallwood tries to stall by saying that Coleman is a very private individual, and dislikes having his personal life being made the topic of discussion. It's clear that Tallwood's trying to protect Agrapova; when pressed, Tallwood admits that Coleman hinted that Agrapova might be in danger because of their relationship. He was very careful when meeting her; she never visited the office, or Coleman's apartment. She recalls one incident where Agrapova telephoned the office looking for Coleman, and he made her hang up immediately, as if worried that someone was listening in on the line.

◊ Either way, she knows Agrapova's address. See *The Agrapova Connection*, p. 231.

THE PORTFOLIO

Going through Coleman's portfolio of clients means Taking Time and using **Research** to correlate names and account numbers. (**Accounting** gets it done faster.) The following clues can be extracted:

♦ Cathedral Dome Investments is definitely a profitable concern.

♦ Coleman was definitely using it as a cover for meeting informants and agents. His clients fall into two categories – genuine investors who are ploughing hundreds of thousands of pounds into the market, and a smaller number of clients who are dealing in smaller sums, or not investing at all.

Two clients in particular are of interest.

♦ (core clue) The first is a Russian named Dr. Eduard Morozov. Coleman had several meetings with him in the last few weeks. Morozov hasn't invested anything in Cathedral Dome, but after Coleman first met Morozov, Coleman set up an account named "Fund V." Several weeks later, immediately after another meeting according to the file, someone deposited 20,000 pounds in the Fund V account. The bank transfer traces back to an account in London.

◊ **Tradecraft:** Morozov is likely an informant, being paid by Coleman.

◊ **Research:** Morozov is a part-time lecturer at First Moscow State Medical University. See *The Morozov Lead*.

♦ The second suspect client is Borya Ignatiev, a wealthy timber and chemical magnate based in the city of Kostroma. Borya suddenly moved a sizeable amount of money into Cathedral Home's accounts a week ago, just around the time that Coleman disappeared. See *The Ignatiev Lead*, p. 230.

◊ **Tradecraft:** Ignatiev's rumored to have connections to the FSB.

◊ **Traffic Analysis:** While the account is marked as being opened by Coleman, it was opened *after* he was last seen. If asked, Tara Tallwood confirms that she logged in as Coleman; Hestridge told her to do so. Hestridge, she says, told her that Coleman arranged the deal with Borya, and that it should be put in under his name to count for year-end bonuses.

▰▰ ▰▰ ▰▰

THE MOROZOV LEAD

Scene Type: Core
Lead-Ins: Cathedral Dome
Lead-Outs: Shadow of the Past, Prisoner of the Dead

Coleman's investment portfolio notes a sum of money invested on behalf of a Doctor Eduard Morozov, and Khan's experience as a spy makes her think that this Morozov might be one of Coleman's informants.

BACKGROUND CHECKS

Born in 1962, Morozov is a specialist in blood diseases. Most of his biography is vague, with considerable gaps in his public record, implying that he was involved in secret military work in some capacity. Reading the pattern of gaps suggests that there was some sort of scandal or disgrace that ended Morozov's career in the 1980s. **Research** also digs up a death notice for his wife Marya around that time.

For the last decade, he's been a poorly paid part-time lecturer.

THE UNIVERSITY

Contacting First Moscow State Medical University is a dead end – they report that Dr. Morozov's contract has been terminated, effective immediately, and they don't know where he is. However, they can give Khan Morozov's home address here in Moscow.

MOROZOV'S HOME

Morozov lived in a small townhouse in an old district of the city. From outside, the house looks deserted; there's no movement inside.

Questioning neighbors yields little information – no one wants to talk to strangers. A **Streetwise** or **Reassurance** push gets the following:

- Morozov was a quiet man; he kept to himself and rarely spoke to anyone. He always seemed to be looking over his shoulder.
- One neighbor recalls seeing a strange man leave Morozov's house in the dead of night a few weeks ago. She doesn't know who this stranger was, but from her description, it sounds like it might have been Harry Coleman.
- Two weeks ago, there was a fight of some sort in Morozov's. People heard shouting, a gunshot, and this unearthly scream. The police were called, but there was no sign of Morozov, and no one's told the public what happened. Morozov hasn't been seen.

- However, the locals warn, there have been government men here on several nights since. The house is being watched, they suspect.

The house isn't locked. Entering, it's clear (**Tradecraft**) that someone hastily cleared the place out, professionally – there are the ashes of a fire in the grate, suggesting someone burnt documents and stirred the remains. The house was cleared of fingerprints and other evidence.

The house was subsequently searched, clumsily, presumably by the police.

- Searching around, Khan finds a set of photographs from the 1980s, showing Morozov as a young man. In some of them, he's wearing a lab coat or a biohazard suit; in others, he's palling around with co-workers out in the woods.
  - ◊ Digging into this lead through research is covered in *Shadow of the Past*, p. 237.

- Another photograph shows a young couple with a baby. On the back is written "Rozkhova, 3/5/84". The mother, in particular, reminds Khan of Nina Rozkhova if she's met her. Give Khan Edge 9, "The Rozkhova Photograph."
- **Notice:** There's a bullet hole in one wall that someone's hastily filled in with plaster.

Tradecraft (core clue) guesses that someone took Morozov. Maybe Coleman smuggled him out; maybe some government security agency spirited him away. This house is a dead end, but Morozov's definitely connected to Coleman's disappearance. Give the player Edge 10, "The Morozov Question."

Call for a **Sense Trouble** test if Khan declares she's leaving the house without searching it thoroughly.

LOOSE ENDS
SENSE TROUBLE

The house is under surveillance, you're sure of it. You shouldn't linger here – but there's something here you're missing.

Advance 5+: You freeze, then move quietly through the house. There's something moving in the attic. Something alive up there. Choose now – investigate, and get a bonus dice on any Challenge you face up there, or sneak out now without being seen.

Hold 3-4: There's something moving in the attack. You hear rattling, shallow breathing, something groaning. Do you investigate or not?

Setback 2 or less: Everything's fine. Nothing to see here. Oh, gain Problem 8, "Marked." If you already have it, gain Problem 9, "Moscow Heat" instead.

Extra Problem: None.

Stunt: No.

THE HORROR IN THE ATTIC

Morozov was attacked by a monstrous servant of Koschei, a bolotnik. The creature was originally one of the researchers at the Project KOSCHEI labs, but is now a shambling disease-filled zombie animated by the vampire's will. After Morozov shot it, shattering the bolotnik's spine, it crawled up into the attic of his house to hide. Rozkhova intends to collect the bolotnik and return it to her master's lair in the future.

If Khan does climb into the attack, she finds the thing huddled in a corner. It looks like a rotted corpse, milky eyes staring blindly into the darkness. There's a recent bullet wound in its chest, but surely it died long before that.

- The creature's flesh is weirdly mottled and discolored – diseased, maybe. It's leaking some sort of yellowish-brown fluid.
  - After the fight, **Chemistry** can identify it as a perfluorodecalin-derived compound, a sort of synthetic blood.
- It's wearing the tattered remains of what looks like a plastic boiler suit – maybe a hazmat suit.
- If approached, the creature flinches and growls, shuffling back deeper into the corner and waving its hands feebly at Khan.
- Then, suddenly, it cocks its head. The milky eyes seem to focus on her. It exhales, sending a cloud of foul-smelling gas into the confined space of the attic. The zombie is temporarily possessed by Koschei's consciousness.
- It speaks. What it says depends on Khan's previous adventures.
  - If she's still on the run from Jovitzo and Carlyle, then it threatens to return her to her former master or the vampire who covets her. "*A runaway servant... a disloyal Slugeri. Intolerable. I shall ransom you to your master, girl, and he shall whip you for your disobedience. Come to me, and meet your punishment.*"

◇ If she's killed a vampire like Jovitzo or Kobori, then Koschei is furious. "*I smell the death on you. You have sinned against the House of Dracul, killed my kin. Come to me, if you think there is death in me.*"

◇ Either way, give Khan Problem 11, "Zombie Minions."

With that, or if Khan tries to leave or attack, the bolotnik flings itself towards her.

WRESTLING THE BOLOTNIK

FIGHTING

The thing lurches towards you in a sudden burst of speed.

Advance 11+: You manage to dodge the creature's initial attack, and take it out. Gain Edge 11, "The Things Can Die."

Hold 7-10: The zombie-thing leaps on top of you, dragging you down the stairs from the attic. You land heavily, painfully – something cracks. Gain Problem 12, "Cracked Ribs." Choose what happens next: either you manage to kill the monster, but gain Problem 13, "Concussion," or you escape, but the thing's still alive, and you gain Problem 8, "Marked."

Setback 6 or less: The zombie pushes you down the stairs. You land badly, and everything goes dark. Skip to the scene *Prisoner of the Dead*, p. 244.

Extra Problem: Problem 14, "Infected."

Stunt: Yes (**Athletics**; **Evasion**; **Sense Trouble**).

THE IGNATIEV LEAD

Scene Type: Alternate
Lead-Ins: Cathedral Dome
Lead-Outs: The Old Adversary, The Plague Pit

Borya Ignatiev isn't quite rich enough to qualify as an oligarch, but he's still immensely wealthy. He controls vast forests in Kostroma Oblast, north-east of Moscow, and earns a huge amount of money from the timber industry. He's also diversified into various chemical industries – including a factory in Moscow that produces industrial quantities of perfluorodecalin.

While he's based in the small city of Kostroma, he spends most of his time in Moscow.

♦ **Criminology** or **Streetwise:** Ignatiev's generally believed to be connected to the FSB. Indeed, given his behavior, it's possible that he's a puppet, a walking rubber-stamp who's only job is to be the legal owner of the Kostroma timber company. He certainly spends as little time as possible at home.

♦ **Tradecraft:** If Ignatiev is that strongly connected to the FSB, it's suspicious that he's on Cathedral Dome's client list – unless he's an informant, and that's out of character for him. He seems quite cowed and servile.

♦ **Research:** Before building the perfluorodecalin factory, Kostroma imported a large quantity of the substance each year. There's no obvious connection between Kostroma's activities and perfluorodecalin.

◇ With a Push, Khan discovers that foreign investment firm recently made a bid for the perfluorodecalin factory. If Khan's played through *No Grave for Traitors*, then she recognizes some of the names associated with the bid – it's part of the same money laundering apparatus operated by Hollister Consulting. If Khan hasn't played through *No Grave for Traitors*, give her Edge 12, "Financial Irregularities."

♦ **Traffic Analysis:** Ignatiev has a private jet that regularly flies back and forth between Moscow and a private airfield outside Kostroma.

♦ A Push of **Research** or **Streetwise:** Apparently, Ignatiev had an older brother, Vasily, who died in a hunting accident in the woods thirty years ago. The incident changed Ignatiev; people used to say he was haunted by his brother's ghost.

♦ Pushing **High Society** can get Khan into the same nightclubs that Ignatiev favors. The aging timber magnate is vulnerable to **Charm**, but panics and clams up at any mention of vampires, perfluorodecalin, bioweapons research or anything related. If pushed, he tells Khan to talk to Nina Rozkhova – she handles "the island." See *The Old Adversary* (p. 238). If Khan continues to pursue him, he becomes aggressive, shouting that she'll "get us all killed" and ordering his security to get rid of her.

THE AGRAPOVA CONNECTION

Scene Type: Core
Lead-Ins: Cathedral Dome, Interrogating Hestridge
Lead-Outs: The Safehouse, Interrogating Hestridge, Dead In An Alley

The elusive Olga Agrapova is an academic and folklorist. She's twenty years younger than Harry Coleman, but as soon as Khan tracks her down, she's struck by Olga's similarity in demeanor, if not in appearance, to Harry's estranged wife Angela. Both women are a little distant, as if their thoughts are far away, but intimidatingly intense when their attention is focused on you.

She speaks excellent English; she studied in London for a few months.

Olga lives in a brutalist concrete residential block across the city from Cathedral Dome offices or Harry Coleman's modern apartment.

Reassurance or a solid cover story is needed to convince Agrapova to meet; Harry warned her to be wary of people asking questions about him.

OLGA'S STORY

When questioned, Olga reveals the following:

- She met Harry Coleman nine months ago. They met in a bar, and she mentioned that she was a student of Russian history, especially the Russo-Turkish war. Soon after, he contacted her to ask her about her research into a 19th-century Russian military officer, Vasily Kastantev. (If Khan's played through *No Grave for Traitors*, she recognizes that name as Nestor Kastantev's ancestor.) She doesn't know why Coleman was interested in such a figure, although she knows the Kastantevs are a wealthy White Russian family.

- As far as she's aware, Harry works as an investment banker at Cathedral Dome. She's has no idea he's a spy, but now that it's been pointed out to her, it's not surprising. (**Bullshit Detector** suggests she's lying; if pressed, she shrugs and says that everyone's got secrets in this city, and that the way Harry acted, she guessed he was a spy.)

- Harry told her not to contact him at the office. He said that it could cause problems for her, and that it was better if he kept his work and personal lives completely separate.

- She and Harry began seeing each other romantically after a few weeks.

- She doesn't know Harry's married. If Khan reveals this to her, then Olga's thrown off balance; the player gains a free Interpersonal Push that can only be used on interactions with Olga. At first, they'd meet at Harry's apartment, but he became nervous about that, and instituted a new policy for their relationship. They met at bars, instead, and never the same one twice. He was worried about 'gossips and tattletales', as he put it. (See "Olga and the Safehouse," below.) **Bullshit Detector** suggests that Olga's being a little evasive.

- Two weeks ago, Harry brought her to a concert, and there they ran into one of Harry's co-workers, who he introduced as Mike (Michael Hestridge). She didn't like him very much, but Mike seemed very interested in Olga. He kept buying her drinks, asking her questions about herself, flirting with her – as though he was trying to provoke Harry.

- Harry was furious after that. He said he'd call her in a few days.

- She hasn't seen Harry in a week, and he hasn't answered his phone.

With a **Reassurance** Push, or if the player brings up the video recording from *Coleman's Apartment*, p. 222, she volunteers a little more information:

- She went to Harry's apartment a few days ago, to see if there was any sign of him. There was a man there, Harry's colleague Mike – she ran away before he could talk to her. She remembers seeing Mike take something off the table.

- After that, she started carrying a gun that Harry gave her.
  - ◊ **Tradecraft:** It's bad tradecraft to hand firearms out to untrained civilians. Coleman was paranoid, unhinged, or desperate.

OLGA AND THE SAFEHOUSE

There's a key piece of testimony from Olga that she tries to keep hidden. She knows the location of a safehouse in Moscow, but Coleman told her to not reveal the location of the safehouse under any circumstances. She and Coleman used the flat for their trysts.

There are three ways that Khan can get this core clue from Olga.

- If Khan has Edge 14, "Coleman's Note," she can question Olga about it, and Olga reveals the location of the safehouse.

- A Push of **Interrogation** or **Reassurance** can press Olga into revealing what she knows. **Reassurance** only works if Khan first convinces Olga that she's an old friend of Coleman's and has his best interests at heart.

- Optionally, if the player misses both these options, run *Dead in an Alley* (p. 235).

OLGA'S SECRET

Olga's secretly an agent of the vampire Carlyle (p. 126); her vampire master wanted to discover the truth behind Koschei, and sent her to secretly direct an investigation into him. Carlyle planted the suggestion in Coleman's mind, and used Olga to cultivate that obsession. There's no way for Khan to discover Olga's connection to Carlyle at this point, but you can subtly foreshadow Olga's eventual betrayal in several ways:

♦ Olga's unfazed if Khan starts talking about vampires.

♦ Olga may express curiosity about the Rosewater Potion or Sykoran Crucifix, if Khan has either of these items.

♦ It's slightly odd that Olga ran into Coleman at a bar; they appear to move in very different social circles.

INTERROGATING HESTRIDGE

Scene Type: Core
Lead-Ins: Cathedral Dome, Coleman's Apartment, The Agrapova Connection
Lead-Outs: The Agrapova Connection, The Linklathe Connection

Various clues point towards Hestridge's involvement in Coleman's disappearance – he's caught on camera at Coleman's flat (p. 222), and there are some suspicious transactions in Coleman's portfolio.

If he can, Hestridge tries to lie his way out; he insists that his visit to Coleman's apartment was completely innocent (*"just there to water his plants"*), and that the Ignatiev account is entirely above board (*"well, as legitimate as any of our deals, I suppose"*). He'll call Linklathe as soon as he can (see "Jimmy's Game," p. 235).

◊ **Bullshit Detector** can tell that Hestridge is lying.

Getting Hestridge alone is tricky. Khan could try breaking into his apartment and ambushing him there, grabbing him on the street, or luring him into a compromising situation. If the player tries this, call for a **Surveillance** test (or **Infiltration**, or **Cover**, or even **Fighting**, as appropriate).

SNATCHING HESTRIDGE

SURVEILLANCE

You need to have a little chat with Hestridge. Just you, him, and no lines of retreat.

Advance 7+: It all goes smoothly. You spirit Hestridge away without anyone seeing you. Gain Edge 13, "In Over His Head."

Hold 4-6: Not quite textbook, but you still manage to grab Hestridge.

Setback 3 or less: You grab Hestridge, but you can't shake the feeling that you got spotted. Gain Problem 8, "Marked."

Extra Problem: None.

Stunt: No.

If Khan questions Hestridge when he can't deny everything and walk away (then **Interrogation** gets the following:

♦ He and Linklathe know each other from university. They help each other out – Linklathe introduced him to Cathedral Dome, and he buys property in Linklathe's name. Civil service pay is awful, you know.

♦ They both think that Cathedral Dome can be much more profitable – make them both astoundingly rich – if the people holding the company back are removed. Shawler's only a few bottles of vodka away from an early grave, so it's just Coleman who needs to be convinced to retire.

♦ Linklathe said that he could force Coleman out if Hestridge could give him some leverage. Anything even slightly scandalous would be enough, given Coleman's questionable behavior and Linklathe's connections back in London. Hestridge found out through Tara Tallwood that Coleman was seeing some Russian woman, Olga Agrapova, and he passed this information onto Linklathe.

♦ A few days later, Coleman disappeared. Linklathe asked Hestridge to check out Coleman's apartment, to make sure nothing untoward had happened. Olga Agrapova interrupted Hestridge while he was there, and fled. There was a note for her on the counter, but Hestridge couldn't make much of it. "I'll see you in a few weeks," or something like that.

o A Push of **Intimidation** or **Interrogation** gets Hestridge to hand over the actual note. It's Edge 14, "Coleman's Note."

If Khan doesn't somehow silence Hestridge (either by killing him, kidnapping him, or pushing **Intimidation** to ensure his silence), he'll report his contact with her to Linklathe.

THE LINKLATHE CONNECTION

Scene Type: Alternate
Lead-Ins: Any
Lead-Outs: The Safehouse, The Old Adversary

Khan's temporary handler Linklathe works at the British Embassy in Moscow under diplomatic cover. The embassy's under constant watch; if Khan visits her, give her Problem 9, "Moscow Heat."

Linklathe brought in Khan to search for Coleman not because he thought she'd be able to find him, but because hiring a former officer who was considered disgraced and deniable let him say he was doing something about Coleman's disappearance. He doesn't want results from Khan – his optimum outcome from hiring her is that she conveniently vanishes, or comes back with a lot of rambling nonsense about vampires and conspiracies. He doesn't want to find the truth.

Of course, if Khan does uncovers something about Coleman's disappearance, then the other virtue of hiring someone who's disgraced and deniable is that they're also *disposable*.

Tradecraft warns Khan not to approach Linklathe openly, but she can easily set up a meeting with him under some Cover, or track him down outside the embassy. His response to her depends on how much she's found out:

- If Khan hasn't found out anything that connects Linklathe to Coleman's disappearance, then Linklathe tries to get her to shut down the investigation. He'll ask her leading questions – "*Do you think there could have been something supernatural involved? Do you believe Coleman was, ah, free of influence?*" He cautions her against digging too deep – "*can't upset the Russians too much, even now, not without cause*" and hints that whatever happened to Coleman is probably his own fault. "*You and I both knew – ah, know the man. He's a good chap, but not the most, ah, discrete, now, is he? And once he gets an idea in his head, there's no changing his mind. Who knows what trouble he got himself into? This might all be something of a fool's errand.*" **Bullshit Detector** or **Tradecraft** picks up that Linklathe's trying to get her to drop the investigation.
- If she's on Hestridge's trail, or has other suspicions of foul play in Coleman's disappearance, then Linklathe is more interested, and asks her to keep talking, to give him a full description on everything she's seen. He then warns her that because of the sensitivity of the situation, and the need to keep Cathedral Dome secure, she shouldn't speak of this to anyone. He urges her to keep looking, and to report back as soon as she has more information. As soon as she leaves, he'll alert Rozhkova that they have a problem (see *Blowback*, p. 250). If the player already suspects Linklathe and tries following him, run "Tracking Linklathe," below.

TRACKING LINKLATHE

TRACKING LINKLATHE
SURVEILLANCE

There's something off about Linklathe. Keeping eyes on him seems like a good idea.

Bonus: +2 if you Push **Urban Survival**.

Penalty: -1 per Heat Problem.

Advance 9+: You follow Linklathe without being spotted. See "The Meeting," below.

Hold 4-8: You try to follow Linklathe through the streets of Moscow, but cops show up, making following him risky. He definitely has protection from local authorities – but does he know that? Is he being set up, or is he complicit? You can keep following him, but gain Problem 15, "Exposed."

Setback 3 or less: You try to follow Linklathe through the streets of Moscow, but you're ambushed as you follow him into a subway. Run the Challenge "Harassing the Opposition."

Stunt: Yes (**Athletics; Cover; Driving**).

A Push of **Streetwise** IDs Khan's attackers as Night Wolves, a large and aggressive biker gang with ties to the Kremlin. Patches tie these particular members to the Kostroma region.

THE MEETING

Successfully tracking Linklathe without being spotted lets Khan follow him to a meeting in Gorky Park with Nina Rozkhova. The two meet in the open, walking amid the trees and weaving in and out of crowds. **Tradecraft** lets Khan guess that Rozkhova's an officer of the Russian domestic intelligence agency, the FSB.

If Khan sneaks close enough to eavesdrop, or uses a directional microphone or other surveillance tool, she can overhear snatches of the conversation. Linklathe complains to Rozkhova that the "mad woman" he hired is proving less broken and more competent than he anticipated; Rozkhova is initially dismissive of Linklathe's concerns, but becomes more attentive when he mentions Khan's name. Clearly, Rozkhova has heard of Khan before.

CONFRONTING LINKLATHE

Once she's got the evidence of corruption in Cathedral Dome, or Linklathe's secret association with Rozkhova, Khan can try confronting Linklathe about his involvement in the scheme. Linklathe's response depends on Khan's approach:

♦ If she puts pressure on him quietly, threatening him with exposure instead of death, then she can use **Interrogation** to get him to co-operate. (And a Push converts him into an unwilling and unreliable Contact.)

HARASSING THE OPPOSITION
FIGHTING

Four of them grab you as you come down the stairs. Street toughs, but this isn't a random mugging. You saw a cop on the street a moment ago, but he just turned away and walked in the opposite direction. This is a hit on you, with official sanction.

Anyway, enough contemplating the political ramifications of this – one of them's trying to hit you in the face with a bike chain.

Advance 11+: You take them out cleanly, without breaking stride. You can follow Linklathe to "The Meeting," below.

Hold 7-10: You take them out, but by the time the last of them's unconscious and bleeding on the floor, you've lost Linklathe.

Setback 6 or less: This is their turf, and they knew you were coming. You're lucky to escape alive. Gain Problem 16, "A Hell of a Beating" (or go to *Prisoner of the Dead*, p. 244).

Extra Problem: Problem 17, "Hit in the Face with a Bike Chain."

Stunt: Yes (**Athletics**; **Evasion**; **Shooting**; **Weapons**).

- If she threatens him, then he panics and tries to run to safety. If confronted in the British Embassy, then Linklathe calls security; if on the streets, he shouts that she's trying to murder him and runs screaming for the police. Either way, a quick punch is enough to shut him up (if the player hesitates, Khan may need to grab Linklathe and abduct him in order to question him – see the Challenge below).

ABDUCTING LINKLATHE

EVASION

Trouble's on the way. You've got to get out of here if you're going to question Linklathe.

Advance 11+: You grab Linklathe and escape with him. He struggles, but never breaks free. You hustle him into an alleyway and vanish into the city.

Hold 7-10: You've got to dump Linklathe, but you make a clean getaway.

Setback 6 or less: Security shows up. You can't keep hold of Linklathe, and you're hit a few times, but you manage to get away. Gain Problem 18, "Tangled with Security."

Extra Problem: If you let Linklathe go, you may roll an extra die, but cannot Advance.

Stunt: Yes (**Athletics**; **Fighting**).

JIMMY'S GAME

Once Khan's in a position to **Interrogate** Linklathe, and if he's got nowhere left to run, he confesses.

- SIS set up Cathedral Dome as a cover for operations in Russia. It was designed to be a way to move money around covertly and set up meetings with potential sources and informants.
- Harry Coleman was a headache. He was off on some wild goose chase about secret Soviet-era weapons projects and monsters, and he wouldn't listen when someone tried to shut him down.
- At the same time, Linklathe's friend Hestridge pointed out the genuine commercial potential in Cathedral Dome.
- Linklathe tried to get Coleman fired by exploiting his relationship with a Russian girl, Olga Agrapova, to the FSB. He thought that the FSB would try to recruit Agrapova, Linklathe would then expose Coleman as having an affair with a Russian swallow. Coleman would be fired or sent back to England, and Hestridge would get control of Cathedral Dome.
- He doesn't know where Coleman is.
- (core clue) SIS operate a safehouse in Moscow – it's not connected to Cathedral Dome. It's run through another cut-out. Coleman used it from time to time. There might be a clue there. (*The Safehouse*, p. 236).
- Linklathe's FSB contact is Nina Rozkhova (*The Old Adversary*, p. 238).

DEAD IN AN ALLEY

Scene Type: Alternate
Lead-Ins: The Agrapova Connection
Lead-Outs: The Safehouse

Run this scene if the player failed to follow up on leads pointing to Agrapova, and you want to move the game on.

Worried by Coleman's absence, Agrapova went looking for him. She tried to find the safehouse where they slept together several times. She knew its approximate location, but not the exact address. She wandered the streets, looking for the apartment block, and nearly found it – but realized she was being followed by Rozkhova's minions (the same goons that Khan may encounter in "Harassing the Opposition," p. 234. When she tried to flee, they attempted to intercept her. In the ensuing struggle, Agrapova got shot with her own weapon, and the attackers fled.

Khan can learn about Agrapova's death in several ways:

- Revisiting Agrapova's apartment: the place is now sealed off, with a pair of cops searching for clues. **Cop Talk** discovers that Agrapova's body was found on the streets last night.
- At Cathedral Dome, Tara Tallwood might see a news report about the death and inform Khan that Coleman's girlfriend is dead.
- Rumors from local street-level contacts picked up with **Streetwise**. If Khan investigates:

- The crime scene itself is closed off, but **Cop Talk** gets the basics. A young woman, killed in what looks to be a mugging gone wrong. She was attacked by a gang, pulled a gun on them, and got killed by her own weapon when they tried to wrestle it off her.

- Breaking into the morgue for some **Forensic Pathology** confirms the police account; there's nothing obviously supernatural about how Agrapova died. However, her body's gone from the morgue, and there are no records of who took it or where it was moved to.

- **Streetwise** gets eye-witness accounts of Agrapova's fate. She seemed to be looking for a particular address, then noticed she was being followed and walked away. Accounts vary as to what happened then, as no-one wanted to involved. Some say she shot herself, others that she was attacked and the gun when off by mistake, other claim she was killed. All accounts agree, though, that the attackers were members of a branch of the Night Wolves.

- **Notice (core clue):** As Khan searches the scene, she sees a curtain across the street twitch – a third-floor apartment in a tower bloc - and glimpses a face for an instant. If she's got Edge 10 – "The Morozov Question," she immediately recognizes Dr. Morozov. If she doesn't, **Tradecraft** still tells her that the man in the window was watching her, and that he might know something about Agrapova's death.

- That third-floor apartment is *The Safehouse*, below.

THE SAFEHOUSE

Scene Type: Core
Lead-Ins: The Agrapova Connection, The Linklathe Connection, Dead in an Alley
Lead-Outs: The Old Adversary, The Plague Pit, Shadow of the Past

The Moscow safehouse is a drab, run-down apartment, one of hundreds in this one anonymous tower block. It's owned by an SIS cut-out, with nothing to tie it back to British intelligence.

Coleman knew about the safehouse from earlier assignments in Moscow, and used it occasionally to meet with informants who weren't suitable for Cathedral Dome. He also used it, illicitly, for his meetings with Olga Agrapova.

For the last two weeks, he's stashed Dr. Eduard Morozov here. The doctor fled an attempt to silence him in his own home (p. 228) and has stayed here ever since. He hasn't been outside in weeks, living off stockpiled supplies in the apartment's meagre kitchen.

Morozov pretends to be the resident of the apartment, introducing himself as 'Borya' and pretending to be ill and infectious, explaining why he never leaves. **Bullshit Detector** proves he's lying; **Reassurance**, **Tradecraft** or just mentioning Harry Coleman's name gets access to the flat.

MOROZOV'S TESTIMONY

After his long isolation, every day spent waiting for the hammer to fall, every car going by or footstep on the stairs heralding a hit squad, Morozov's exhausted and on edge. Confessing is balm; it's easy to get him talking.

Play Morozov as a tired old man.

At this point, he's convinced that he's doomed, and has lost all hope of escaping to England or getting out of this unscathed. He considers himself to be a dead man walking.

Morozov explains the following:

- He worked in biological weapons research when he was a young man.

- He was a lab assistant at Project KOSCHEI. It was an attempt to isolate, extract and weaponize a psychoactive agent – a mind control drug.

- They told him that the original sample was dug out of the permafrost, but he knows that was a cover story – the KOSCHEI sample came from Transylvania, and was connected to the work of a 19th-century occultist, Dr. Vordenburg.

  ◊ **Research:** Vordenburg was a 19th-century occultist and vampire hunter. If Khan's played through *No Grave for Traitors* (p. 167), she recognizes Vordenburg as the hunter who orchestrated the defeat of Count Kobori.

- **Core clue:** KOSCHEI was located in a laboratory in Kostroma; the site was an island in the middle of a lake, surrounded by thick forests. Miles from anywhere.

  ◊ With **Research**, Khan can easily locate the site of the lab from those clues.

  ◊ **Criminology:** If Khan's encountered the Night Wolf biker gang, she knows that particular branch of the gang is headquartered in Kostroma.

- Another project underway at the site were experiments in creating artificial blood substitutes. The researchers claimed they were working on ways to treat victims of chemical and biological attacks. These experiments were based around a chemical called perfluorodecalin.

- In 1992, there was an accident at the laboratory where Project KOSCHEI and several other bioweapons projects were conducted. The lab was evacuated and shut down. Many of the researchers were infected and couldn't be saved.

- As Morozov fled the scene, he saw *something* he cannot explain. A human shape, moving amid the debris in the hot zone, in a place where nothing human could live.
- They told him the lab site was destroyed to prevent infection spreading.
- Morozov was contacted by Coleman a few months ago. Coleman already knew something about KOSCHEI, and was willing to pay for information.
- Initially, Morozov was hesitant to assist a man he suspected to be a British spy, and refused.
- Shortly after that initial meeting, Morozov was interviewed at the university where he worked by an FSB agent named Nina Rozhkova. (*The Old Adversary*, p. 238). She wanted to know about his contact with Coleman, and questioned him about his experiences with Project KOSCHEI.
  - ◊ **Bullshit Detector:** He's holding something back about Rozkhova. A push of **Reassurance** or **Interrogation**, or showing him Edge 9 – The Rozkhova Photograph gets him to admit that he knew two researchers at the site who were named Rozkhova – they had a baby daughter. Both of them died when the lab was destroyed. He doesn't know what happened to the child, but it's possible that she was evacuated and grew up to join the FSB.
  - ◊ The co-incidence – or connection – unsettled him, and he instinctively denied knowing anything about Coleman.
- Later, Coleman contacted him again, and showed him aerial photographs of the laboratory site. It wasn't destroyed – it was left to rot. There's

still something *living* there on that island.

- Two weeks ago, Morozov was attacked at his home by a bizarre creature. He shot it with a gun that Coleman gave him, and fled. Coleman brought him here, to this safehouse.
- After his encounter with the creature, he became ill. A strong dose of a phage therapy cured the bacterial infection. He has cultured more of the same phages (and can cure Problem 14, "Infected" if Khan has that card). Phages, by the by, are bacteria-eating organisms that kill a particular strain of a bacterial infection. The Soviet Union experiments with phages when they could not obtain antibiotics from the West during the Cold War.
  - ◊ If Khan asks for a supply of phages, give her Edge 16, "Phage Culture."
- Coleman said he'd be back to check on Morozov in a few days, but that was more than a week ago, and there's been no sign or word from the British spy since.

THE NEXT MOVE

Morozov wants to be smuggled out of Moscow, back to England – or at least, to somewhere safer. Khan could arrange that through Linklathe – if she trusts him. More plausibly, she could use **Network** to arrange an extraction, or just have Morozov sit tight for now if the safehouse is still a secret. One option is to send him to Julian Hulier, the biochemist encountered in *Never Say Dead* (p. 123).

If Khan gets Morozov out of Russia safely, she can claim him as a contact.

Khan could contact the FSB Agent (*The Old Adversary*, p. 238), or head to the ruins of Project KOSCHEI (*The Plague Pit*, p. 240).

SHADOW OF THE PAST

Scene Type: Alternate
Lead-Ins: The Safehouse, The Morozov Lead
Lead-Outs: The Plague Pit

Morozov worked at Project KOSCHEI, a Soviet-era bioweapons research facility. Even thirty years later, it's not easy for Khan to get intel on the site. Possible options:

- If she Takes Time and spends a Push on **Research**, she can dig up some information, poorly sourced and full of conspiracy theories and false leads.
- She could use Network to create a contact who's an expert on Russian bioweaponry, or a contact within the post-*biopreparat* Russian weapons industry who's willing to talk.
- Nina Rozkhova or Jimmy Linklathe could both produce files on KOSCHEI – if Khan can force them to do so.

However she gets the intel, it's fragmentary. Most of it just confirms Morozov's testimony – there was a bioweapons research facility out in Kostroma, on an island in the woods. They were looking into synthetic blood, blood-borne diseases, or mind control depending on which rumor you believe. The lab was destroyed in a fire in 1984 and the project shut down.

There's one key piece of intel that Khan can obtain through research – the location of the base, complete with recent satellite photography. Khan doesn't have **Photography**, so she'll have to use Network to create a Contact to assist her.

- It's in the wilderness beyond the city of Kostroma – there's what looks like a logging road that goes near the lake.

- There's a structure near the lakeside that looks like a boathouse.
- **Photography** notes that the site on the island is overgrown, but may still be largely intact – it definitely wasn't demolished.
- A push of **Photography** spots an outlet pipe that may be a back entrance into the main building. Give the player Edge 16, "The Back Door."

If the player wants to head straight there, see *The Plague Pit*, p. 240.

THE OLD ADVERSARY

Scene Type: Alternate
Lead-Ins: The Safehouse, Coleman's Apartment, The Ignatiev Lead
Lead-Outs: Prisoner of the Dead, The Plague Pit

Nina Rozkhova haunts the mystery of Harry Coleman's disappearance. She interrogated Olga Agrapova and Eduard Morozov; she's the one who left the note in Coleman's apartment. She's Borya Ignatiev's FSB handler. Her parents were part of the research team on Project KOSCHEI.

Digging into her background with a push of **Tradecraft** or a local contact digs up the following details on her:
- Rozkhova's in her late 30s; she was raised by an aunt, and recruited into the FSB after university.
- She's a mid-ranking officer in the Economic Security Service, responsible for investigating financial crimes and money transfers.
- She's got a reputation as a prickly, standoffish analyst; she operates mostly alone, and is unpopular and unlikely to ever be promoted. However, she's proved herself to be highly competent. She's seen as an attack dog, used to take down troublemakers, especially foreign ones.

ROZKHOVA'S SECRETS

When Nina Rozkhova was in her teens, she was contacted by her dead mother, a bolotnik sent by the vampire Koschei. Her "mother" said that she would watch over her and protect her, if only Nina would swear eternal fealty to the devil who held her mother's soul. For more than twenty years, Nina has been a servant of the vampire. It's not the same relationship that Khan had to Jovitzo; Nina's not a thrall or Sluger, as the resurrected vampire can't create such things any more. She covers up the vampire's murders, and ensures he has a ready supply of perfluorodecalin.

MEETING ROZKHOVA

If Khan's Heat is 2 or less, she can arrange an off-the-books meeting with Rozkhova with a push of **Tradecraft.** Otherwise, she'll need to stalk Rozkhova with **Surveillance** until she finds an opportunity to intercept her (see sidebar).

The FSB operates out of the old Lubyanka building, the former headquarters of the infamous KGB, but if Khan ends up there, things have gone horribly wrong for her. Rozkhova prefers to meet Khan in the open, at Gorky Park.

Play Rozkhova as unfriendly and cold; her initial goal in any meeting is to shut Khan's investigation down through threats.
- Initially, Rozkhova says she's unwilling to discuss anything related to Harry Coleman. The Russian authorities will, of course, investigate his disappearance if the

WATCHING ROZKHOVA
SURVEILLANCE

You need to ambush an FSB officer who's got supernatural backup, and you need to do it in Moscow. This is going to be tough.

Bonus: +2 if you discard Edge 6, "The Moscow Identity."

Penalty: -1 per Heat Problem.

Advance 12+: You find your opening, grabbing Rozkhova when she's off guard.

Hold 9-11: Security's too tight. You've got to find an alternate approach.

Setback 8 or less: It's a trap! You're picked up by FSB security! A bag goes over your head, and someone hits you with a taser. You're down. Go to *Prisoner of the Dead*, p. 244.

Extra Problem: Problem 9, "Moscow Heat."

Stunt: Yes (**Cover; Driving; Infiltration**).

man is indeed missing. Mostly likely, she says, he has succumbed to some drug addiction or other depravity, and will be found dead. A report will be issued in due course.

◊ If Khan presses her without the benefit of any hard evidence, Rozkhova stonewalls, turning the questions back on Khan. Who is Khan anyway? What is her interest in Coleman? What will the FSB find if they dig into Khan's background?

♦ If presented with evidence of her involvement (Edge 7, "The Mysterious Note," Linklathe's confession), she admits that she knows Coleman; she was investigating him on suspicion of being an illegal British spy. She claims that she did not injure Coleman. In fact, she brought him where he wanted to go.

◊ **Bullshit Detector:** She's telling the truth – she didn't hurt or kill Coleman. However, she's definitely not worried about Coleman coming back to trouble her again. Whatever Coleman went, she doesn't expect him to ever return.

◊ Rozkhova also hints that she had sanction from *Coleman's* superiors. "Your Harry Coleman had fewer friends than you think – and even fewer will mourn him. You are, I think, not meant to succeed in your mission. Go home, Leyla Khan – wherever that is."

◊ In response to any further questions, Rozkhova offers to bring Khan to the same place she brought Coleman. If Khan accepts, see *The Plague Pit*, p. 240.

◊ If Coleman refuses, give her Problem 8, "Marked."

♦ If Khan has Edge 9, "The Rozkhova Photograph" and guesses that the photo shows the infant Nina and her parents, Rozkhova's shaken. She admits that there are powerful creatures in the world that her superiors in the FSB know nothing about, and that her mother was caught up in the machinations of these things. She suspects that Khan was similarly consumed by the vampires. Out of a sense of... professional courtesy, she will explain what's going on.

◊ Rozkhova admits that she is in the service of a creature that lives on an island hidden in the forests beyond Kostroma. She has never met Koschei face to face – the monster is so riddled with plague that it is dangerous for anyone to be in proximity to it. It communicates with her through her mother.

◊ She supplies Koschei with what he desires. She's covered up disappearances in the woods near Kostroma, and helped conceal the continued existence of the bioweapons site.

◊ If asked, she also admits that Koschei requires a supply of a chemical called perfluorodecalin, supplied by Borya Ignatiev's factory. Give Khan Edge 17, "Perfluorodecalin Habit."

◊ With a Push of **Reassurance or Negotiation**, Rozkhova admits she can't act against the monster.

It controls her mother and holds her soul captive. The best she can do is tell her mother to let Khan onto the island safely. Give Khan Edge 18, "Cold Welcome."

◊ Rozkhova is willing to tell Khan all this to make it clear that her mission is hopeless. Harry Coleman is a dead man, even if he's not actually dead yet. He went looking for a vampire, and found one. Does Khan want to follow him down that path? If she does, run *The Plague Pit*.

GETTING THERE

Koschei's lair in the forests beyond Kostroma is a seven-hour drive from Moscow; it's faster to get a flight to the airport at Yaroslavl and drive from there. Either way, the trip counts as Taking Time.

Solo: If Khan's traveling alone, then flying there is her best route. Once she hits the wilderness, she needs **Outdoor Survival** to find her way; if she doesn't have access to that ability, then she gets Problem 19, "Lost in the Woods."

With Rozkhova: Borya Ignatiev has a private airfield outside Kostroma, large enough for his jet to land. He uses that to transfer supplies of perfluorodecalin to the island; when Rozkhova needs to make trips to the site, she hitches a ride on Ignatiev's plane. This is how she brought Coleman to Koschei.

Captured: If captured by the bad guys at any point, Khan's smuggled to the island via plane and left in the shack on the lakeshore. Run *Prisoner of the Dead*, p. 244.

THE TIME OF DAY

If Khan's in control of her movements (i.e. she's not a prisoner) and doesn't have Problem 19, "Lost in the Woods," then she can time her travel so she arrives at the island during daytime or night-time as she wishes. If she's a prisoner, she's woken at twilight and brought to the island in the darkness and she must face the vampire by night. If she manages to find a place to hide, she can try Taking Time if she wants to wait until dawn.

THE PLAGUE PIT

Scene Type: Core
Lead-Ins: The Informant
Lead-Outs: The Hot Zone, The Court of Koschei

The former research base is on an island surrounded by a lake, surrounded by almost impenetrable forests. There's a small transit station on the lakeshore, now mostly overgrown. When the lab was operational, supplies arrived at the transit station and crossed to the island by boat.

From the shore, it's hard to tell that there was ever anything on the wooded island. The lab's almost completely hidden by vegetation and debris. Examining it through binoculars does reveal some signs that the place was once inhabited – there are a few overgrown structures by the shore, the sunken remains of a jetty, trash half-buried in the mud.

◆ **Notice:** There are fresh marks gouged in the mud near the old jetty. Several heavy things (canisters of perfluorodecalin) were dragged up from the shore and into the woods.

◆ **Outdoor Survival:** The lake is dead – no fish, no insects. The water is almost certainly poisoned with toxins leeching from the lab.

THE TRANSIT STATION

The station is in ruins – it looks like no-one's been here in thirty years. There's a warehouse whose roof has collapsed, several sheds full of abandoned and rusted machinery, and an empty boathouse. However, under a tarpaulin,

Khan discovers a modern motorboat with a full tank of gas. Near the boat is a locker with several protective hazmat suits. Clearly, someone is still crossing over to the island.

A shed next to the boathouse is also still in use. There are a few cheap folding chairs, several coils of nylon rope and duct tape – ideal for restraining prisoners – and a telephone on a small table. This is where Rozkhova and Ignatiev come for their orders from Koschei, and where they keep prisoners that are to be fed to the monster.

THE PHONE CALL

If Khan picks up the phone, she hears the rhythmic bleeping of a call being connected – there's no need to dial. This phone is directly connected to its counterpart on the island. After a few moments, it's picked up. The voice on the other end is a sepulchral groan – it's the bolotnik that used to be Maria Rozkhova, Nina's mother.

- If Khan identifies herself, then the voice changes as Koschei takes possession of Maria's body. (It's the same voice as Khan heard in "The Horror in the Attic", p. 229.) "Come across, disloyal Sluger. Your friend is here. I have questions for you. I have a death for you."
- If Khan pretends to be Nina, or is evasive, then unMaria groans at her. "Nina... child... the master has a plaything. Stay away." A push of **Reassurance** convinces the zombie that Khan is Nina, and Maria says "I shall meet you... on the shore. Do not go to the castle."

If Nina Rozkhova is present, she can arrange with her mother for Khan to have a safe landing. Before talking to the bolotnik, she points out to Khan that she has to be very careful; the vampire holds her mother's soul hostage, and doesn't dare openly cross Koschei.

CROSSING THE LAKE

The only way across the lake is to take the boat (Khan could swim across the lake, but the water's poisonous, so it would be very unwise – give her Problem 14, "Infected," if she has to take a swim. She can't swim in a hazmat suit.)

If Nina Rozkhova's here, this is as far as she goes – she won't cross the lake.

The boat starts smoothly. The equipment lying in the boat gives clues about the vessel's usual cargo. Bloodstained ropes, scraps of duct tape, cleaning supplies – the spoor of vampire victims. A chemical smell, and scrape marks from plastic drums – the vital perfluorodecalin shipments.

As she crosses the lake, call for a Cool test from Khan.

THE WELCOMING COMMITTEE

As Khan approaches the shore, she spots a figure moving through the underbrush. Hunched, flesh half-rotten, dressed in tattered plastic rags, it moves more like a wild animal, but it's clearly human, or at least humanoid. It's one of Koschei's bolotniks. It sniffs the air, peering half-blind across the lake, sheltering its eyes from the sun.

If Maria knows that Khan's coming (Edge 18, "Cold Welcome"), then the creature waves at Khan, gesturing towards a low beach where she should land the boat.

Otherwise, it's a feral bolotnik. Does Khan want to take the creature out with a gunshot, or try to hide, either by steering the boat into a patch of mist or lying down in the boat so it looks like it broke free of its moorings and drifted across the water?

THE EDGE OF THE UNHOLY
COOL

You can sense the darkness in this place. It may be far from the crumbling castles and underground lairs preferred by the vampires you've known, but the stench is the same. Unholy. Undead.

Bonus: +2 if you've got the Sykoran Crucifix.

Penalty: -1 per Shadow Problem.

Advance 9+: You're not going to turn aside from this. Discard any one Shadow Problem.

Hold 4-8: A chill runs down your spine as you approach the island, but you swallow your fears. You've fought the undead before and survived. Maybe your luck will carry you through one more encounter.

Setback 3 or less: For a moment, you imagine Jovitzo sitting opposite you in the boat, draped in furs, a cold sneer on his face. You're not free of the vampires yet. They're in you, infecting you, corrupting every drop of blood, every cell of your being. Gain Problem 20, "Need a Win."

Extra Problem: None.

Stunt: No.

SNIPER SHOT
SHOOTING

You've got one shot to put the monster down before it raises the alarm.

Advance 7+: Breath. Relax. Aim. Slack. Squeeze. And it's a perfect shot. The creature crumples to the ground. Birds rise up in alarm from the trees on the shore, but there's no movement on the island. You reach the shore without further problems.

Hold 4-6: You take the monster down cleanly, but the noise of the shot draws more of the zombie-things out of the woods. Run the Challenge "Swarmed by Bolotniki," but gain a free bonus die.

Setback 3 or less: You miss your first shot, hit with the second, but by then the woods are swarming with the monsters. Run the Challenge "Swarmed by Bolotniki."

Extra Problem: None.

Stunt: No.

GHOSTING IN
CONCEAL

These monsters aren't that bright when the vampire isn't controlling them directly. Maybe you can drift to the shore without being spotted.

Bonus: +2 if you've got Problem 11, "Zombie Minions."

Advance 7+: You conceal yourself in the boat, and let the current carry you, watching through a small gap in the tarpaulin. The zombie-thing on the shore vanishes back into the trees. You reach the shore without further problems.

Hold 4-6: The bolotnik stays watching you drift for some time. You're forced to Take Time, but can't use this time to do anything. After what feels like an eternity of being watched, the monster gives up and retreats.

Setback 3 or less: You've been spotted. The monster wakes through the water towards your boat – and it's not alone! Run the Challenge "Swarmed by Bolotniki."

Extra Problem: None.

Stunt: No.

SWARMED BY BOLOTNIKI
FIGHTING

A dozen of the creatures stumble out of the forest and swarm towards you, wading through the shallow waters. You can't shoot them all before they reach the boat.

Advance 7+: It's a bloody, nasty fight, but you walk away and they don't. Gain Edge 19, "No Quarter."

Hold 4-6: You survive, barely. Gain Edge 19, "No Quarter," but also Problem 21, "Bleeding Badly."

Setback 3 or less: You're torn limb from limb by the mob of monsters. It's over.

Extra Problem: Problem 14, "Infected". If you already have this problem, add a mark.

Stunt: Yes (**Driving; Evasion; Shooting; Weapons**).

LANDING ON THE BEACH

If Khan makes it to the shore alive, run *The Hot Zone*, p. 244.

MEETING MARIA

If Khan's to be met by Maria, the bolotnik helps draw the boat up onto the shore. Up close, the face of the creature is clearly visible – the rotten, diseased flesh still bears an uncanny resemblance to Nina Rozkhova's features, but what really haunts Khan are the eyes. Even after death, Maria has the same haunted, furtive expression that Khan sees when she looks in the mirror. Both women were the thralls of monsters; both have won some small measure of freedom, but where

ESCAPE ATTEMPT
ATHLETICS

You're bound hand and foot, but there are enough jagged bits of metal on that rusty junk for you to cut your way free – if you've got time.

Advance 10+: You easily cut your way clear with time to spare. Discard Problem 23, "Bound." You can either climb out that window and steal the boat, or get the drop on Nina Rozkhova when she comes to get you. If you take the latter option, gain a bonus die in any challenges to subdue her.

Hold 4-9: You manage to get free just as Rozkhova opens the door to your prison. Discard Problem 23, "Bound," and run the Challenge "Fighting Nina."

Setback 3 or less: You cut your hands free just as Nina opens the door. If you score an Advance or Hold on the next Challenge, you can discard Problem 23, "Bound." Run the Challenge "Fighting Nina."

Extra Problem: Problem 24, "Deep Cut."

Stunt: Yes (**Conceal** to have a blade hidden in your clothes; **Filch** to dexterously reach your bonds; **Mechanics** to spot a piece of machinery well suited to the task).

FIGHTING NINA
FIGHTING

Nina Rozkhova has a gun. You don't. This could end really badly.

Penalty: -4 if you've got Problem 23, "Bound."

Advance 9+: You wrestle Nina to the ground and take her gun. Do you want to kill her or question her?

Hold 4-8: There's a brief, vicious struggle for Rozkhova's gun, and it goes off as you wrestle. She's dead.

Setback 3 or less: Rozkhova gets the drop on you, and foils your escape attempt. She drags you out to the boat and ferries you across to the island. Welcome to *The Court of Koschei*, p. 247.

Extra Problem: Problem 25, "Shot."

Stunt: Yes (**Athletics** to charge her; **Mechanics** for an improvised weapon).

Khan strives to escape fully, Maria's desperate to conserve the tiny amount of free will left to her.

Khan has only a brief moment to act – if she hesitates too long, Maria will raise the alarm (run the Challenge "Swarmed by Bolotniki," above.)

Possible options:

♦ **Eliminate Maria:** A snap-shot or sudden strike can kill the bolotnik while it stares at her in confusion

♦ **Ask to be taken to the Master:** Maria visibly relaxes – this is what the bolotnik expects. Victims go to the Master, yes yes. This way, to *The Court of Koschei* (p. 247).

- **Share Protection:** If Khan has a spare dose of the Rosewater Potion or is willing to part temporarily with the Sykoran Crucifix, she can free the bolotnik from Koschei's control. Maria asks for a few minutes to have a brief conversation with her daughter by telephone, if Nina's in the transit station on the shore. After that, she tells Khan about the secret entrance into Koschei's castle (p. 245), then walks into the water to drown. She dies while the vampire has no claim on her soul.
- **Persuade Maria to help:** An Interpersonal Push and reminding Maria of her relationship with Nina (or, using Cover to pretend to be Nina) can convince Maria to guide Khan to the secret entrance.

PRISONER OF THE DEAD

Scene Type: Alternate
Lead-Ins: The Morozov Lead
Lead-Outs: The Plague Pit, The Court of Koschei

If Khan was captured at any point in this adventure, then she wakes up locked in a shed in the transit station. Her hands and feet are tied, and she's got no equipment (give her Problem 22, "Stolen Gear" and Problem 23, "Bound"). There's a small, grimy window that gives her a view of the lake and the island. A small motorboat bobs up and down, ready to depart.

From the boathouse next door, she hears part of a muffled conversation – Nina Rozkhova's voice, on the telephone to her mother the bolotnik. Khan catches the words *"another spy"* and something about a *"crossing,"* then *"All right, I'll put her on the boat."*

- **Bullshit Detector** picks up on an unusual amount of emotion; Nina's voice cracks several times, as if she's on the verge of tears.

Does Khan try to escape, or does she just wait and see what happens? If she tries to break free, run the "Escape Attempt" Challenge below.

If Khan doesn't try to escape, then Nina unlocks the door to the shed and brings her out at gunpoint. She orders Khan into the motorboat, and loads a plastic barrel drum full of perfluorodecalin into the boat too. During this time, Khan can try talking to Nina.

- By default, Nina largely ignores Khan, treating her as another victim of the vampire who must be disappeared. Once they're ready to depart, she brings Khan across to the island, leaving Khan and the barrel of chemicals on the shore. She leaves without a word or a glance back. The bolotniki soon emerge from the trees, and take both Khan and the chemical supplies to *The Court of Koschei*, p. 247.
- An Interpersonal Push (**Charm, Tradecraft**) gets Nina talking. She admits that she brought Harry Coleman here and sent him to the island; he went looking for answers, and found the vampire. She believes he's still alive – just like her mother is still alive.
- If Khan has leverage (Edge 9, "The Rozkhova Photograph," for example, or couples an Interpersonal Push with questioning Nina about the telephone conversation), then Nina admits that she's forced to serve Koschei not because she's his thrall, but because her mother was one of the victims of the disaster in 1984 and the monster controls her soul. If Khan can convince her that there's a chance of saving Maria Rozkhova, give the player Edge 18, "Cold Welcome."

THE HOT ZONE

Scene Type: Alternate
Lead-Ins: The Plague Pit
Lead-Outs: The Court of Koschei, The Crypts of Koschei

The island is small and heavily overgrown. The old research lab is in the middle of the island; around the edges, mostly lost in the trees, are outbuildings and the ruins of storerooms and accommodation for the scientists who once worked here.

The forest is tainted. The roots of the trees intertwine with broken concrete and debris from the old laboratory. The vegetation grows strangely. The trees are misshapen, their bark or leaves discolored by chemicals leeched from the soil. There's no movement in the woods except the rustling of the leaves in the wind; not even an insect buzzes through the air.

- If Khan has Edge 19, "No Quarter," she can move about the island freely, having eliminated most of the bolotniki. Otherwise, she needs to pass the *Exploring the Island* challenge to move through the woods.
- If she also has Edge 16, "The Back Door" then she can make her way to the secret entrance to Koschei's lair. If she doesn't have that Edge, then she can obtain it by Taking Time to search the island thoroughly.
- If she's guided by Maria Rozkhova, then she's both safe from attack by other bolotniki *and* gets brought straight to the secret entrance.

You may be the only living thing on this island. You've got to keep quiet if you want to stay that way.

Bonus: +2 if you Push **Outdoor Survival**.

Advance 10+: You move through the dying forest, looking for signs of the vampire and its servants. Gain either Edge 16, "The Back Door" or Edge 20, "The Drop" – your choice.

Hold 4-9: You avoid contact with the zombies that stumble blindly through the woods, hiding in the mud and undergrowth. The island's crawling with the dead.

Setback 3 or less: As you sneak through the woods, you're grabbed by a half-dead zombie lurking in the undergrowth. If you fight back, you kill the creature, but gain Problem 26, "Limping." If you let it drag you away, go to the scene *The Court of Koschei*.

Extra Problem: Problem 14, "Infected." If you already have this problem, add a mark.

Stunt: No.

THE SECRET ENTRANCE

Koschei's established his vampiric court in the heart of the old laboratory. The main entrance to the lab is easily found once you're in the woods – just follow the tracks in the mud dug by three decades of dragging perfluorodecalin barrels up the slope. The secret entrance, though, is harder to find. It's a former ventilation shaft that was mostly destroyed in the fires, but it's possible to climb down the blacked metal of the shaft into the lower sections of the lab – *The Crypts of Koschei*.

THE CRYPTS OF KOSCHEI

Scene Type: Alternate
Lead-Ins: The Hot Zone
Lead-Outs: The Court of Koschei, Escaping the Island

These "crypts" were once the laboratories and storerooms under the main lab. It's a half-flooded, lightness maze of concrete-walled and corridors that somehow echoes a medieval dungeon. Koschei, in his madness, has improvised torture chambers and cells, twisting pipes and laboratory equipment into manacles and spikes, and hung sheets of rotten cloth or plastic up as tapestries.

Notice (**core clue**): Notably, there's a storeroom where the barrel drums of perfluorodecalin are kept.

The action in the crypts varies depending on whether it's day or night.

BY NIGHT

The crypts are empty at night, as Koschei and his minions gather in *The Court of Koschei* (p. 247) on the level above. The sound of their 'revels' – and Coleman's suffering – can be heard echoing down through the concrete corridors from above.

BY DAY

Koschei sleeps in his 'coffin' – the remains of a device similar in appearance to a hyperbaric chamber from the 1960s. The coffin was partially crushed when the lab was destroyed, but Koschei has repaired it as best he can. The floor of the chamber contains native soil from his homeland in Transylvania; pipes connected to the machine once pumped in a solution of artificial blood to keep the vampire in a constant state of bloated satisfaction.

Coleman's kept chained in the same room, manacled to the wall. Koschei keeps the key to the manacles in the 'coffin' with him.

The bolotniki are allowed roam the island by day. The undead creatures have little will or purpose of their own without Koschei's mind directing them, so they just wander around staring at the sky, chasing gusts of wind, or murdering anyone foolish enough to cross the poisoned lake.

STACKING THE PERFLUORODECALIN

If Khan's realized the importance of the perfluorodecalin drums to the vampire, she can stop to interfere with the chemical stock. Some options:

♦ If she's got access to a supply of the Rosewater Potion, dumping the potion into the perfluorodecalin will temporarily disrupt Koschei's control of his minions once

the vampire ingests the tainted chemical. Once Koschei consumes the drum, the bolotniki will turn on him.

- More prosaically, make a Preparedness roll to have a flask of strong acid, or holy water to hand.
- Even more prosaically, puncturing the drums or blowing up the storeroom works to deny Koschei the chemicals he needs.

RESCUING COLEMAN

Coleman's barely sane. He's been a prisoner of the vampire for days, kept trapped here as Koschei questions him about the wider world and tries to turn him into a thrall. He drifts in and out of consciousness, hallucinating wildly. He's running a high fever, suggesting he's been infected by some of the biological weapons present on the island. When he sees Khan, he raves that she was right, she was right, and that brought him here.

Reassurance calms him down enough to recognize Khan.

- Coleman cautions that he's been compromised by the vampire. The thing's in his head. He's like the *bolotniki* – he can't disobey.
- The vampire nearly drained him dry, and tried to feed him blood, but there's something *wrong* with Koschei. The blood just made Coleman sick instead of turning him into a vampire, too.
- Koschei's trapped on the island, and dependent on the supplies and equipment here to keep him alive –

or undead, or whatever he is.

- The vampire's trying to control him – he doesn't know why.

Coleman's manacles can't be unlocked easily (simple Mechanics test, 10+). Khan can try to Filch the key from the vampire if she wishes (use the Challenge *Opening the Coffin*, below).

If Khan successfully frees Coleman, she can flee the island – run *The Final Revelation*, p. 249.

If Khan gets a Setback, but she's poisoned the perfluorodecalin, then she achieves a partial victory – the vampire, exhausted by the battle, has to take a massive dose of the chemical to animate its damaged organs, and so suffers whatever fate Khan's prepared.

If she manages to kill the vampire, then the *bolotniki* run wild. She'll still have to succeed at *Escaping the Island* (p. 249).

STAKING KOSCHEI

OPENING THE COFFIN

MECHANICS

Penalty: -1 per Shadow Problem.

Advance 10+: You open Koschei's coffin without attracting attention. If you attempt to kill the vampire as he sleeps, you've got a bonus die. Alternatively, you can steal the key to the shackles.

Hold 4-9: You struggle to open the coffin, and Koschei's stirring by the time you work out how to open the heavy lid. If you want to steal the key to the shackles, you can do so now and let the lid fall back.

Setback 3 or less: As you're struggling to open the bizarre 'coffin', it's flung open from within. Koschei's awake! There's no chance to escape – it's fight or die. Run the Challenge "Fighting Koschei."

Extra Problem: Problem 27, "Creeeeaaakk."

Stunt: Yes (**Cool; Infiltration**).

WAKING KOSCHEI

WEAPONS

Bonus: +1 die if you scored an advance on "Opening the Coffin."

Advance 13+: Koschei's half-dead already, and you use that to your advantage, staying on the vampire's blind side and pummeling him with your blows. He stumbles, and you press the advantage, leaping on him so he impales himself on a jagged spike of metal from his broken coffin. The horror's tainted ichor – a thin slurry of poisoned blood and chemicals – spew from his ruined body. He's dead.

Hold 9-12: This is hopeless – you can't beat him in this fight. He flings you across the room. Gain Problem 28, "Broken Arm," and choose: do you surrender, do you try to escape, or do you fight on, for a lucky break?

If you fight on, run "Fighting Koschei" on p. 248, but no Extra Problems are available.

Setback 8 or less: You woke a sleeping monster. The vampire's iron hand clutches your throat and squeezes the life from you. You're dead.

Extra Problem: Problem 29, "Claws of the Vampire."

Stunt: Yes (**Athletics; Evasion**).

THE COURT OF KOSCHEI

Scene Type: Core
Lead-Ins: The Hot Zone, Prisoner of the Dead, The Crypts of Koschei
Lead-Outs: Escaping the Island

During the night – or, if Khan's discovered and captured by Koschei – the vampire hosts a bizarre, madcap court in the ruins of the old laboratory. Koschei still thinks and acts like a medieval warlord; it takes a considerable effort of will (and a dose of perfluorodecalin) for him to focus on what's really going on, instead of indulging in his recurring fantasy that it's still the 13th century. He sits on a throne of rubble and has his *bolotniki* act as knights and courtiers at an imaginary feast, while drinking a mix of blood and perfluorodecalin from a "goblet" that's actually a chemistry flask.

If Coleman's still his prisoner, then Koschei seats him in a place of honor at the right hand of his throne. Koschei isn't the vampire he once was; he couldn't turn Coleman into an Assign, so he's now trying to summon what remains of his powers to turn Coleman into a thrall instead. Coleman spends his nights slumped in his chair, muttering the names of tube stations in London like a mantra in an attempt to stay sane.

KHAN AS A PRISONER

If Khan's brought in as a prisoner, then Koschei jeers at her and has her dragged before his throne by the bolotniki. He demands to know who she is and what she is doing in his "castle." If she reveals nothing useful, then he declares that he'll feast upon her tomorrow night, once he feels strong enough to feed – i.e., once a fresh drum of perfluorodecalin arrives so he can temporarily restore the crushed half of his body.

If Khan reveals that she's a former spy, or that she's here to rescue Coleman, then Koschei is intrigued – could she be more useful as a servant than the Englishman? What talents does Khan offer? Will she trade herself for him?

BREAKING FREE

If Khan can't talk her way out of her predicament, then Coleman attempts to help. His plan is to slip her a knife so she can cut open her bonds without anyone seeing. He rises from his chair and stumbles towards her, pretending that he's mistaken her for Olga Agrapova. When he gets close to her, he pretends to recoil in alarm, overacting to distract Koschei as he drops a knife on the floor nearby and kicks it under a chair. It's up to Khan to grab the weapon without being spotted.

REACHING FOR THE KNIFE
FILCH

Advance 10+: You manage to get to the knife and cut the ropes holding you without anyone noticing. Surprise may be your only advantage – gain a bonus die in your next Challenge.

Hold 4-9: You grab the knife and cut yourself free, but you don't have much time before they realize you're no longer restrained. Do you attempt to escape immediately, or attack the vampire in front of all his minions?

Setback 3 or less: Koschei spots you reaching for the weapon, and suddenly he's at your side. "What's this?" he roars, his mangled face flushed red with anger, "a traitor in my court." Choose – either he kills you, or he kills Harry.

Extra Problem: None.

Stunt: No.

KHAN AS A GUEST

If Khan just walks in, or if she pushes **High Society** while a prisoner, then Koschei greets her as an honored guest. He can smell the blood of one of his noble cousins (Jovitzo) on her, even though he cannot recall the names of his kin right now. He treats her as a knight, an emissary sent to his court from one of his peers. As a guest, Khan won't be immediately attacked by Koschei or his minions.

What does Khan want?

♦ With **Negotiation,** she can trade herself for Coleman; the vampire is disappointed with his prisoner. Khan's already been a thrall, so she must be psychically compromised already, and a lot more alluring and competent than Coleman. He'll offer to set Coleman free in exchange for Khan.

♦ With **Charm,** she can lull Koschei into a false sense of security, convincing him that she's not a threat to him. She can establish herself as a guest in his court, allowing her to move freely about the lab (down to *The Crypts of Koschei*, p. 245). Once the compound's spiked, all she needs to do is stall until Koschei refreshes his goblet of blood mixed with perfluorodecalin.

♦ With **Intimidation**, she can challenge Koschei for Coleman. Khan has no chance of beating the vampire in a one-on-one combat. However, if she's already spiked his supply of perfluorodecalin, then the vampire poisons himself when he uses the chemical to prepare for battle. He bleeds Coleman into a goblet of perfluorodecalin, then drinks the bloody potion.

FIGHTING KOSCHEI

There are three likely circumstances under which Khan fights Koschei. She might have poisoned him and just needs to force him to exert himself to win. She might be launching a one-woman assault on his "castle", armed with whatever weapons she's been able to source from her contacts. Or, she might simply have no choice but to fight the monster.

FINDING THE DEATH
FIGHTING

Bonus: +4 if she's poisoned the perfluorodecalin. +2 if she's got Edge 19, "No Quarter."

Advance 13+: Koschei's already wounded. You wear him down, striking at his wounded side until he falls. You've done the impossible and killed the dead. Remove any one Shadow or Injury Problem.

Hold 9-12: You manage to exhaust Koschei. If you've poisoned the perfluorodecalin, then his bolotniki turn on him and kill him for you. Otherwise, you've got a chance to escape with Coleman as the vampire roars in pain and confusion.

Setback 8 or less: The vampire charges towards you, roaring in fury. You think you mortally wounded the monster, but you can't be sure – and you'll never know, as he rips you to pieces.

Extra Problem: If Khan has a gun, gain Problem 30, "Disarmed." Otherwise, gain Problem 28, "Broken Arm."

Stunt: Yes (**Shooting** if Khan has access to firearms; **Mechanics** if she has access to explosives).

ESCAPING THE ISLAND

Scene Type: Core
Lead-Ins: The Hot Zone, Prisoner of the Dead, The Crypts of Koschei
Lead-Outs: Escaping the Island

If Khan's managed to turn the bolotniki on Koschei, then she can easily flee down to the shore. A quick search discovers an old but still usable rowboat, hidden in the weeds.

However, if the bolotniki are still a threat, then Khan needs to evade the feral monsters as she flees with Coleman.

ESCAPING THE ISLAND

EVASION

Bonus: +4 if she's got Edge 19, "No Quarter." +2 if she Pushes **Outdoor Survival.**

Advance 10+: You cross the island without being detected by the monsters, and find a rowboat hidden in the undergrowth. You're off the cursed island before they find your scent.

Hold 6-9: You race down to the shore, but you're ambushed by one last creature. Gain Problem 14, "Infected" and if you already have this problem, add a mark.

Setback 5 or less: You nearly make it to the shore, but you're ambushed by a swarm of the creatures. Without the vampire's psychic restraint, the monsters are savage, feral – and cannibalistic.

Extra Problem: If you're accompanied by Coleman, abandon him to get a bonus die. Alternatively, you can take Problem 30, "Disarmed."

Stunt: Yes (**Fighting**).

THE FINAL REVELATION

Scene Type: Finale
Lead-Ins: Escaping the Island

As Khan approaches the lakeshore, she spots an unfamiliar car parked by the boathouse. Waiting nearby, watching Khan's boat cross the poisoned water, is Olga Agrapova. Nina Rozkhova lies on the ground in front of her – unconscious or dead, it's hard to tell.

◆ If Khan has Problem 48 from *Never Say Dead*, "Stokovitch Survived," then Stokovitch is also waiting in the car, with a sniper rifle to hand.

◆ If Agrapova was "killed'" (in *Dead in an Alley*, p. 235), then she's clearly been brought back by vampiric magic. She's deathly pale, and in constant pain. She's a Renfield now, dependent on a regular supply of vampire blood to stay alive.

Agrapova levels a gun at Khan. "Carlyle sent me," she admits. "The master wants to know what became of his cousin."

◆ If Koschei is dead, and Khan admits that, then they either attempt to kill Khan, or take her prisoner back to Carlyle. Pick whichever option fits better with the previous interactions between Khan and the two other women.

◆ If Khan lies or Koschei is still alive, and she has Coleman with her, then Agrapova orders Khan to hand Coleman over. Carlyle intends to interrogate Coleman back in London, and use him as a conduit to control the wounded vampire.

◆ If Koschei is alive and Coleman's dead, then Agrapova asks if she should cross to the island and take his place. She's clearly scared, but determined to complete her mission if it's at all possible. She asks Khan for advice – after all,

Khan also knows the terrible power of a vampire's command. If there's any hope that she survives a visit to Koschei's court, she has to try. What does Khan tell her? Does she send her to her likely death, or tell her that it's hopeless?

If Khan has Problem 30, "Disarmed," and Agrapova shoots at her, then she has no way to fight back. All she can do is dodge, throwing herself into the water and swimming for cover. By the time she recovers, Agrapova's gone.

If Khan freed the soul of Maria Rozkhova, then the bolotnik emerges from the water and drags Agrapova away, giving Khan a chance to escape and rescue Nina Rozkhova. Khan may take Rozkhova as a Contact.

If Khan's still armed, she can return fire.

ONE LAST SHOT

SHOOTING

Penalty: -2 if Stokovitch is present.

Advance 9+: You snap off one last shot, killing Agrapova. If present, Stokovitch flees in the car before you reach the shore. You bury Agrapova in a shallow grave by the lakeside. She was never here, and neither were you. Gain Nina Rozkhova as a Contact.

Hold 6-8: If he's with you, then Coleman grabs your gun and wades towards Agrapova, giving you covering fire and a chance to escape. If he's dead, then it's a bloody shootout on the shore. Gain Problem 31, "Crawling Away."

Setback 5 or less: Agrapova fires first. You're dead.

Extra Problem: If Coleman's present, gain an extra die by sacrificing him.

Stunt: Yes (**Evasion**).

AFTERMATH

Has Khan put an end to the monster, or is Koschei still alive? The monster can be contained indefinitely by Nina Rozkhova and Borya Ignatiev, given regular supplies of blood and perfluorodecalin. While that's a poor solution, it's better than having him under the control of Carlyle.

If Carlyle does gain control of Koschei, it'll take him several months to prepare an extraction plan for the broken vampire. He'll relocate Koschei from the Kostroma site to somewhere closer to Carlyle's base of operations in England. Following the financial ties can point Khan at the entry vectors for *No Grave for Traitors*, p. 167.

If Coleman survived, then he can expose Linklathe's schemes with Cathedral Dome and re-establish himself in MI6 and be Khan's man on the inside (give her Coleman as a Contact).

BLOWBACK

IN MOSCOW:

♦ **Heat 3+:** Khan's questioned by the police. Make a quick **Cover** test; if she fails to get 6+, gain Problem 8, "Marked."

♦ **Problem 6, "Born in Darkness":** Khan's beset by nightmares and waking visions; she's at -2 to all Social Challenges until she suppresses her Shadow Score.

♦ **Problem 8, "Marked":** Khan's attacked, either by a bolotnik or a gang of thugs. Use "Wrestling the Bolotnik" (p. 230) if you haven't already; if you have, use the Challenge "Ambushed!"

AMBUSHED!
DRIVING

A biker gang tries to intercept you.

Advance 9+: You evade the bikers.

Hold 4-8: You evade them, but take a beating. Gain Problem 17, "Hit in the Face with a Bike Chain."

Setback 3 or less: They drag you out of the car. Go to *Prisoner of the Dead*, p. 244.

Extra Problem: None

Stunt: Yes (**Shooting**; **Sense Trouble**).

ON THE ISLAND:

♦ Khan needs to make a Conceal test (8+) to hide. If she fails, run the Challenge "Swarmed by Bolotniki," p. 243.

PROBLEMS

PROBLEM 1
Building Bridges
STARTING PROBLEM

You need allies and reliable sources; that means rebuilding your connection to MI6. You need to end this operation in MI6's good graces.

PROBLEM 2
Shelter in a Storm
STARTING PROBLEM

The conspiracy's closing in on you – you need to lie low out of your usual haunts, or lose some of the monsters on your trail. If you don't find a way to counter this problem, gain Problem 5, "At Your Throat."

PROBLEM 3
Out of Blood
STARTING PROBLEM

You've exhausted the last of the Rosewater Potion. You need more vampire blood to make more of your protective elixir.

PROBLEM 4
Voice Message
STARTING PROBLEM

A few days ago, you got a brief and confused message from Harry Coleman. He's MI6, you worked with him when you were in the service. Moscow desk. He sounds terrified, drunk. He said you were right, said that he needed to talk to you – but he didn't leave any way to contact him. Discard this for a free Interpersonal Push when dealing with Harry. While you hold this card, you've got a -1 penalty to any Cool tests.

PROBLEM 5
At Your Throat
CONTINUITY, HEAT

The conspiracy's closing in. You start every mission with some Heat from now on.

PROBLEM 6
Born in Darkness
SHADOW

You have a memory of *willingly* submitting to Jovitzo the vampire. Some part of you chose the path of evil – at least, that's how you remember it, but can you trust your own memories.

PROBLEM 7
Troublemaker
HEAT

You had to argue, threaten and bribe to get through security, and now you've pissed off the Moscow Police.

PROBLEM 8
Marked

Your movements are being tracked. You can throw them off by Taking Time – discard this card if you do so.

PROBLEM 9
Moscow Heat
HEAT

It's Moscow, so live by Moscow rules – "you are never completely alone." You're being watched.

PROBLEM 10
Shaken

That hallucination has unnerved you. Something strange is going on. You can't make any Interpersonal Pushes until you Take Time to rest or find some other way to work off your stress. When you do, discard this card.

PROBLEM 11
Zombie Minions
VAMPIRE

This vampire has some sort of diseased zombie servants. Possibly lots of them. You may need to be loaded for bear.

PROBLEM 12
Cracked Ribs
INJURY

You definitely heard several ribs snap there.

PROBLEM 13
Concussion
INJURY

You're dazed. While you hold this card, apply the penalty from Injuries to all Challenges.

PROBLEM 14
Infected

You've been exposed to a Soviet-era bioweapon. Every time you Take Time, put a mark on this card. You've got a -1 penalty to all Physical Challenges for each mark on this card. If you have five marks on this card, you die. Counter by obtaining Medical Attention from a doctor equipped to deal with such a plague.

PROBLEM 15

Exposed

HEAT

You've been spotted by whoever's protecting Linklathe. You can't Advance on any Cover or Network tests in Moscow while you hold this card.

PROBLEM 16

A Hell of a Beating

SERIOUS INJURY

You can barely move. You're at -4 to all Physical Challenges until you Take Time for Medical Attention.

PROBLEM 17

Hit in the Face with a Bike Chain

INJURY

You've been hit in the face by a bike chain.

PROBLEM 18

Tangled with Security

You just made a scene in the British Embassy in Moscow. If you don't end this operation on good terms with MI6, this becomes a Heat Problem next time you visit the United Kingdom.

PROBLEM 19

Lost in the Woods

You've taken a wrong turn, and you probably won't make it to the island before nightfall. Counter by spending a Push.

PROBLEM 20

Need a Win

SHADOW

Apply your Shadow Score as a penalty to all Challenges. Discard when you next score an Advance.

PROBLEM 21

Bleeding Badly

INJURY

If this is the only Injury card you hold, you can't discard it unless you get Medical Attention.

PROBLEM 22

Stolen Gear

You've got no equipment. You can't use Preparedness or Shooting until you find some supplies.

PROBLEM 23

Bound

You're tied hand and foot with zip-ties.

PROBLEM 24

Deep Cut

INJURY

You sliced your arm open on some rusty metal, but tetanus is the least of your worries right now.

PROBLEM 25

Shot

SERIOUS INJURY

If you don't get medical treatment by the end of this operation, you'll bleed out and die.

PROBLEM 26

Limping

INJURY

This penalty only applies to Evasion.

PROBLEM 27

Creeeeakk

You've just alerted any monsters in the area to your presence. While you hold this card, you've got a -2 penalty to any Infiltration Challenges. Counter by Taking Time to hide.

PROBLEM 28

Broken Arm

SERIOUS INJURY

He nearly tore your arm off.

PROBLEM 29

Claws of the Vampire

SERIOUS INJURY

Koschei clawed your face and neck, and those wounds won't heal quickly. You'll bear the scars for the rest of your life, even after you counter this Injury card.

PROBLEM 30

Disarmed

You can't use Shooting until you find another gun.

PROBLEM 31

Crawling Away

CONTINUITY

You nearly died on the shore, and it takes you time to recover. Permanently reduce any two of your General abilities by one die each.

EDGES

EDGE 1
Coin of the Realm
CONTINUITY

You've got access to funds from the Single Intelligence Account – discard this card to draw down several thousand pounds in untraceable cash.

EDGE 2
A Favor from Vauxhall Cross
CONTINUITY

MI6 owes you a favor. Discard this card to cash it in.

EDGE 3
Linklathe's Folder

MI6 have provided you with a passport and cover – but do you trust MI6? You may discard this card to automatically Hold on any **Cover** test in Moscow. If you do so, gain Problem 8, "Marked."

EDGE 4
Defiant to the Last

You remember fighting against Jovitzo's control for as long as you could. Draw on that memory of your courage and discard this card to counter any Shadow Problem.

EDGE 5
The Watcher

You had a vision? A memory? An intuition of someone watching you, a pale and hungry figure. While you hold this card, you cannot suppress your Shadow Score. Discard to automatically Advance in a **Sense Trouble** test, or Counter by dismissing the experience as a hallucination.

EDGE 6
The Moscow Identity

You've already established a cover identity in Moscow. Discard this card to automatically Hold on any one **Network**, **Cover**, or **Preparedness** test made in the city.

EDGE 7
The Mysterious Note
CLUE

Someone arranged a clandestine meeting with Coleman just before he vanished, using his girlfriend Olga as leverage. There's definitely foul play going on.

EDGE 8
Shawler's Assistance

You have one free Interpersonal Push per employee when questioning any employee of Cathedral Dome. Discard this card when you leave Moscow, or if you lose Shawler's favor.

EDGE 9
The Rozkhova Photograph
CLUE

A photo of two scientists and their infant child. On the back, it says "Rozkhova" and a date in 1984. Who are these people? Your intuition tells you this is an important clue.

EDGE 10
The Morozov Question

Morozov's disappearance is definitely connected to Coleman – you're on the right track. Discard to gain a bonus Push when you find Morozov.

EDGE 11
These Things Can Die

Nothing brightens your day like killing a zombie. Discard for a bonus die in any contest with these zombies.

EDGE 12
Financial Irregularities
CONTINUITY

Borya Ignatiev gave you details of some suspicious money transfers out of Switzerland and London that you need to look into later.

EDGE 13
In Over His Head

You've got Hestridge off balance. Discard for a free Push when dealing with him.

EDGE 14

Coleman's Note

CLUE

You've found a note from Coleman to his girlfriend, directing her to "check on our place. I'll explain when I'm back." Where is "their place"? You need to talk to Olga.

EDGE 15

Culture

An experimental antibiotic. Discard to Counter Problem 14, "Infected" or to get a bonus die on any Medic test.

EDGE 16

The Back Door

CLUE

You've spotted what appears to be an alternative entrance to the ruined Soviet bioweapons lab.

EDGE 17

Perfluorodecalin Habit

CLUE

You know that the Koschei entity's reliant on a chemical called perfluorodecalin to enable it to digest blood. There's got to be a way to exploit this dependency.

EDGE 18

Cold Welcome

Maria Rozkhova died in 1987, but apparently, she'll be waiting for you when you get to Koschei's island. That's really not very reassuring.

EDGE 19

No Quarter

You've killed a hell of a lot of the zombie creatures that infest the island. You don't know if you've taken them all out, but you've definitely made a dent in their numbers.

EDGE 20

The Drop

You've made it into Koschei's lair without being spotted. Discard for +1 die on any Challenge.

CONTACTS

CONTACT 1

Harry Coleman, MI6 Officer

You knew Harry when you were both at MI6. Whatever else you can say about him, he comes through in the end.
Accounting, Criminology, Tradecraft, Traffic Analysis.

Infiltration 2, Shooting 2.

CONTACT 2

Jimmy Linklathe, "Diplomat"

He hired you to investigate Harry Coleman's disappearance.

Bureaucracy, High Society.

CONTACT 3

Yuri Fokine, Moscow Cop

Cop Talk, Negotiation, Streetwise.

Fighting 1, Surveillance 2

CONTACT 4

Tara Tallwood, Personal Assistant

Coleman's secretary.

CONTACT 5

Eduard Morozov, Scientist

He worked on Project KOSCHEI.

Chemistry, Diagnosis, Pharmacy, Vampirology.

Medic 1.

CONTACT 6

Nina Rozkhova, FSB

Your counterpart in Moscow.

Cop Talk, Criminology, Electronic Surveillance, Tradecraft, Streetwise, Vampirology.

Surveillance 2.

CONTACT 7

Angela Coleman

Harry Coleman's estranged wife.

Diagnosis, Forensic Pathology, Pharmacy.

Medic 2.

BACKMATTER

CONTACTS AND CARDS

Grab an entry from this list of generic Contacts when the player unexpectedly uses **Network** to create a Contact. Each Contact specializes in one particular Investigative field, but we also list the Contact's other Investigative and General abilities.

CONTACT

Sam Eczes, Fixer

BUDAPEST, HUNGARY.

Sleazy and crooked, but Eczes has plenty of underworld connections that aren't tied to the vampires.

Accounting, Forgery, Streetwise.

Surveillance 1.

CONTACT

Accounting –
Terry Belcher,
Crooked Accountant

Belcher specializes in quick turnaround money laundering; if you need ready cash, lean on him.

Accounting, Criminology, Law, Streetwise.

Network 1.

CONTACT

Archaeology –
Dr. Margene Garris,
Archaeologist

Specialist in medieval Europe; has connections to fringe occult groups.

Archaeology, History, Occult Studies.

CONTACT

Architecture –
Henry Stroud, Burglar

No one knows a city's architecture like an academically minded burglar.

Architecture, Art History, Forgery, High Society, Urban Survival.

Filch 2, Infiltration 2.

CONTACT

Art History –
Sister Ivona Cristea, Nun

Curator of the Church's private art collection; here to save Leyla's soul, or a corrupt art dealer?

Art History, History, Human Terrain, Research.

CONTACT

Astronomy —
Professor Seriwasa Sen,
Astronomer

Comes from a wealthy family; his sister was kidnapped and ransomed by conspiracy-associated criminals.

Astronomy, Data Recovery, Photography

CONTACT

Bullshit Detector —
Alice Carriway, Psychologist

Treated Khan while she was at MI6.

Bullshit Detector, Diagnosis, Pharmacy.

Medic 2.

CONTACT

Bureaucracy –
Olly Bracken, Bureaucrat

"Oily" Olly is easily bribed, and knows how to grease the wheels of the bureaucracy.

Bureaucracy, Negotiation, Law, Streetwise.

CONTACT

Charm –
Lisa Duclos, Con Artist

She won't dare cross a vampire, but Duclos may be a willing partner in smaller-scale grifts and heists.

Charm, Forgery, Streetwise.

Cover 2, Filch 2.

CONTACT
Chemistry – Ziyan Menouar, Criminal

Former bomb-maker turned criminal supplier.

Chemistry, Urban Survival.

Mechanics 2, Surveillance 1.

CONTACT
Data Recovery – Vayu Patel, GCHQ Contractor

A contact of Khan's from her MI6 days.

Cryptography, Data Retrieval, Tradecraft, Traffic Analysis.

Hacking 2.

CONTACT
Forgery – Honna Kritikou, Activist

Makes false passports and documentation for refugees and other people trying to stay under the radar.

Bureaucracy, Data Recovery, Forgery, Streetwise.

Cover 2.

CONTACT
Cop Talk – Leonhard Conzelmann, Ex-Cop

A former police officer, fired on corruption charges, Conzelmann still has connections in the force.

Cop Talk, Criminology, Streetwise.
Fighting 1, Preparedness 1, Surveillance 2, Shooting 1.

CONTACT
Diagnosis – Dr. Kasper Meert, Clinician

Runs a back-alley clinic in Switzerland; asks no questions.

Diagnosis, Forensic Pathology, Pharmacy, Streetwise.

Medic 2.

CONTACT
High Society – David Sitchwel, Gossip Columnist

Sitchwel's got the connections to open almost any door – in exchange for something suitable scandalous.

Charm, High Society, Human Terrain.

CONTACT
Criminology – Dr. Roosje Broekotte, Europol Analyst

An expert in mapping criminal conspiracies – or the conspiracy's spy in Europol?

Criminology, Human Terrain, Languages, Traffic Analysis.

CONTACT
Electronic Surveillance – Ed Visner, Technical Expert

Sells black-market surveillance and counter-surveillance equipment

Architecture, Electronic Surveillance, Photography, Urban Survival.
Hacking 1, Infiltration 1, Mechanics 2.

CONTACT
History – Professor Nancy Bell, Academic

MI6 recruiter at Cambridge, teaching military and political history.

History, Military Science, Tradecraft.

CONTACT
Cryptography – Rytin Igorevich, Mathematician

Rytin specializes in encryption on the dark web – he's an eccentric shut-in, extremely paranoid.

Cryptography, Data Retrieval, Forgery, Traffic Analysis, Streetwise.

Mechanics 1.

CONTACT
Forensic Pathology – Dr. Olga Karwacka, Pathologist

Runs the city morgue, and knows what when Khan's in town, some unusual corpses are about to hit the table.

Chemistry, Criminology, Diagnosis, Forensic Pathology.

Medic 2.

CONTACT
Human Terrain – Julius Schurmann, Political Fixer

Election fixer and middle-man across Eastern Europe.

Accounting, Human Terrain, Law, Negotiation.

CONTACT

Interrogation –
Detective Klara Skalova,
Police Detective

Knows of Khan's connections to MI6 – does she still believe Khan's working for them?

Cop Talk, Criminology, Law, Interrogation, Streetwise.

Fighting 1, Medic 1, Surveillance 2, Shooting 2.

CONTACT

Military Science –
Sadiqe Razavian,
NATO Analyst

Civilian analyst and expert on NATO and former Warsaw Pact militaries.

History, Human Terrain, Military Science, Photography, Tradecraft.
Shooting 1.

CONTACT

Outdoor Survival –
Nadja Havarsdottir,
Survivalist

Former scientist, now convinced the planet is doomed and human civilization is over. Lives off the grid.

Chemistry, Outdoor Survival.

Mechanics 1, Medic 2, Preparedness 1, Shooting 1.

CONTACT

Intimidation –
Mosin Gleb, Enforcer

Mosin looks like he could go toe-to-toe with a monster – and would too, if it amused him.

Cop Talk, Intimidation, Streetwise, Urban Survival.

Fighting 2.

CONTACT

Negotiation –
Terrence Singer,
Arms Dealer

Salesman for several black-market weapons-smuggling groups.

Criminology, Military Science, Negotiation, Streetwise.

Shooting 1, Preparedness 2.

CONTACT

Pharmacy –
Zdenko Smolic, Researcher

Smolic's aware of the supernatural, and intends to come up with a scientific theory of vampirism.

Chemistry, Pharmacy, Vampirology.

Medic 2.

CONTACT

Languages –
Doria Meldeer, Interpreter

Works for the European Parliament, so has access to corridors of bureaucracy, if not power.

Bureaucracy, Human Terrain, Languages, Research.

CONTACT

Notice –
Petra Sandor, Journalist

Freelances for various investigative newspapers; the conspiracy has considered eliminating her if she gets too close

Criminology, Human Terrain, Notice, Streetwise, Traffic Analysis.

CONTACT

Photography –
Aline Cabral,
Photojournalist

Works in warzones and dangerous places across the world; very well connected.

Art History, Military Science, Negotiation, Photography.

CONTACT

Law –
Paul Grepper,
Crooked Lawyer

On retainer for the mob.

Cop Talk, Criminology, Law, Negotiation.

CONTACT

Occult Studies –
Barnabas Eschem,
Gravedigger

Caretaker of an ancient graveyard; claims the dead talk to him.

Architecture, History, Languages, Occult Studies, Vampirology.

CONTACT

Reassurance –
Fr. Bernard Bray, Priest

Aware of the supernatural; may have Vatican connections.

Human Terrain, Languages, Reassurance, Occult Studies.

CONTACT

Research – "Crow" Bryant, Information Broker

Crow's a professional rumor-monger, and scrupulously neutral in the underworld.

Criminology, Cryptography, Data Retrieval Forgery, Negotiation, Notice, Research.

CONTACT

Tradecraft – Angela McRoss, Retired MI6 Mentor

Used to run the Eastern Europe desk at MI6, now runs a private consultancy firm.

Bureaucracy, Criminology, Human Terrain, Negotiation, Tradecraft.

Cover 2, Network 2.

CONTACT

Urban Survival – Morisha Malik, Social Worker

Former victim of human trafficking, now helps other survivors.

Bureaucracy, Languages, Reassurance, Streetwise, Urban Survival.

Evasion 2.

CONTACT

Streetwise – Cyprien Fokaides, Fence

Deals in stolen goods – art, mostly, but a growing sideline in software and industrial prototypes.

Accounting, Negotiation, Law, Streetwise.

Cover 2, Filch 1.

CONTACT

Traffic Analysis – Gavin Tyler, Hacker

Criminal hacker for hire.

Cryptography, Data Recovery, Military Science, Research, Traffic Analysis.

Hacking 2.

CONTACT

Vampirology – Dr. Morgens, Scholar

Unbearable pretentious Van Helsing-wannabe, but has genuine knowledge of the occult

History, Occult Studies, Research, Vampirology.

Preparedness 2.

INJURY PROBLEMS

PROBLEM

Winded
INJURY

That fall knocked the air out of you.

PROBLEM

Clawed
INJURY

Nothing vital got hit, but you're bleeding badly.

PROBLEM

Hard Impact
INJURY

Maybe you cracked a rib. It certainly feels like you did.

PROBLEM

Bruised
INJURY

You've been battered and bloodied. You can clean up the worst of the marks with a few minutes in a bathroom, but you'll be feeling that effects of that beating for a while.

PROBLEM

Punched
INJURY

Your ears are ringing, and you're unsteady on your feet. That one hurt.

PROBLEM

Through and Through
INJURY

You got lucky – the bullet missed any bones or major organs. A clean hit, all things considered. Still hurts like hell, though.

PROBLEM

Bludgeoned

INJURY

You haven't been hit by one of *those* before, but it turns out one heavy blunt improvised weapon hurts just as much as any other.

PROBLEM

Bleeding

INJURY

You're bleeding badly. If you don't Take Time at the end of the current scene to stop the bleeding, this becomes a Serious Injury instead.

PROBLEM

Bullet in the Side

INJURY

You've been shot. If this is the only Injury card you have when you Take Time, you still get a Hurt card – it ignores the usual rule that a single Injury can be shrugged off.

PROBLEM

Broken Fingers

INJURY

You heard the bones snap. You can strap them once you're out of this mess.

PROBLEM

Nearly Broken

INJURY

You've got to fight to stay conscious. Either choose to black out now, or else this card becomes a Serious Injury instead.

PROBLEM

Hurt

It's only blood.
Maybe not even your blood.

The accumulation of injuries slows you down. While you hold this card, you're at -1 to all Physical rolls. Discard at the end of the adventure.

PROBLEM

Concussion

INJURY

You're stunned. You've got a -2 to all Mental tests for the rest of the scene.

HEAT PROBLEMS

PROBLEM

Police Attention

HEAT

The cops stop you and ask you a few questions. Name, address, business in the city. Your cover holds... for now.

PROBLEM

Media Reports

HEAT

The media speculates about terrorists, criminals, political unrest, but you know the truth behind the front-page stories.

PROBLEM

Fingerprints

HEAT

You didn't have time to wipe the room down, and you left prints behind. Counter by pushing Forensic Pathology.

PROBLEM

Rising Tension

HEAT

You can sense the tension on the streets; the city's bracing itself for impact.

PROBLEM

Security Cameras

HEAT

The place sprouts security cameras like weeds. You're certain you were spotted. Counter by Pushing **Electronic Surveillance**.

PROBLEM

Triggered Alarm

HEAT

There go the sirens and burglar alarms. Counter by Pushing **Electronic Surveillance**.

PROBLEM
Under Surveillance
HEAT

You've seen that car before. The faces on the street are a little too familiar, as if they're repeating on you. You're being watched.

PROBLEM
Crime Scene
HEAT

You fled a crime scene, and the police find that suspicious. Of course, they'd be a lot more suspicious if they knew what you actually did there.

PROBLEM
Poking the Hornet's Nest
HEAT

You asked the right questions of the right people, and you're getting close to the truth. If you're facing incoming fire, you're heading in the right direction.

PROBLEM
Political Connections
HEAT

You've pissed off the wrong people, connected people, and they've brought the police down on you.

PROBLEM
Noisy
HEAT

It's not a textbook infiltration. It got messy, and that'll draw attention.

PROBLEM
Tip-Off
HEAT

Someone betrayed you, gave your details to the authorities. The streets aren't a friendly place for you, tonight.

SHADOW PROBLEMS

PROBLEM
Uncanny Chill
SHADOW

Someone just walked on your grave.

PROBLEM
The Shadows Move
SHADOW

The shadows in the room wheel and seethe, as if they're somehow alive. You're at -1 to any **Infiltration** tests for the rest of this scene.

PROBLEM
Calling the Blood
SHADOW

While you hold this card, your wounds bleed more than they should. Round up, instead down, when swapping Injuries for Hurt cards. If your Shadow Score is suppressed, ignore this effect.

PROBLEM
Moths on the Window
SHADOW

A series of quiet thumps and chirps against the glass. The outside of the window is crawling with fat moths. *Acherontia Atropos*, the Death's-head.

PROBLEM
Whispers of Madness
SHADOW

You can hear voices that aren't there, the dead whispering beneath the city streets. You've got a -2 penalty to any **Cool** rolls while you hold this card; Counter by Taking Time to sleep, or else by atoning to someone whose death you're responsible for.

PROBLEM
Wheeling Bats
SHADOW

A flock of bats wheels overhead, distracting you. While you hold this card, reroll any dice that come up 6s. Counter by getting away from the shrieking bats.

PROBLEM
Bad Dreams
SHADOW

You suffer from nightmares of previous encounters with vampires.

PROBLEM
Unholy Portents
SHADOW

Steam rises from the holy water fonts in the church. A lame dog lies in the middle of the street, blocking traffic. An icy rain suddenly bombards the city, bringing with it an ungodly stench. The forces of evil are abroad...

PROBLEM
The Shadow of the Past
SHADOW

For a moment, the city around you changes. It's like you slip back in time, the cafes and office blocks replaced with churches and tenements. This is how the vampires saw it, when last they looked on it with living eyes.

PROBLEM
Eyes in the Dark
SHADOW

Tiny eyes gleam in the shadows, reflecting the lights from passing cars. The rats are watching you.

PROBLEM
A Sudden Silence
SHADOW

Suddenly, there's a gap in the city's noise. In the same instant, the cars all happened to be stopped. All conversations just happened to pause. The construction workers picked that moment to down tools. "An angel passed," says someone nearby, but you don't think it was an angel.

PROBLEM
Bugged
SHADOW

There's a pile of dead insects in here, hundreds of them. All piled up in one corner, like filings attracted to a magnet. Drawn by some unearthly force...

BLANK PROBLEM, EDGE & CONTACT CARDS

PROBLEM
Problem

PROBLEM
Problem

PROBLEM
Problem

PROBLEM
Problem

PROBLEM
Problem

PROBLEM
Problem

PROBLEM
Shadow

PROBLEM
Shadow

PROBLEM
Shadow

PROBLEM
Shadow

PROBLEM
Shadow

PROBLEM
Shadow

PROBLEM

Heat

PROBLEM

Heat

PROBLEM

Heat

PROBLEM

Heat

PROBLEM

Heat

PROBLEM

Heat

PROBLEM

Injury

PROBLEM

Injury

PROBLEM

Injury

PROBLEM

Injury

PROBLEM

Injury

PROBLEM

Injury

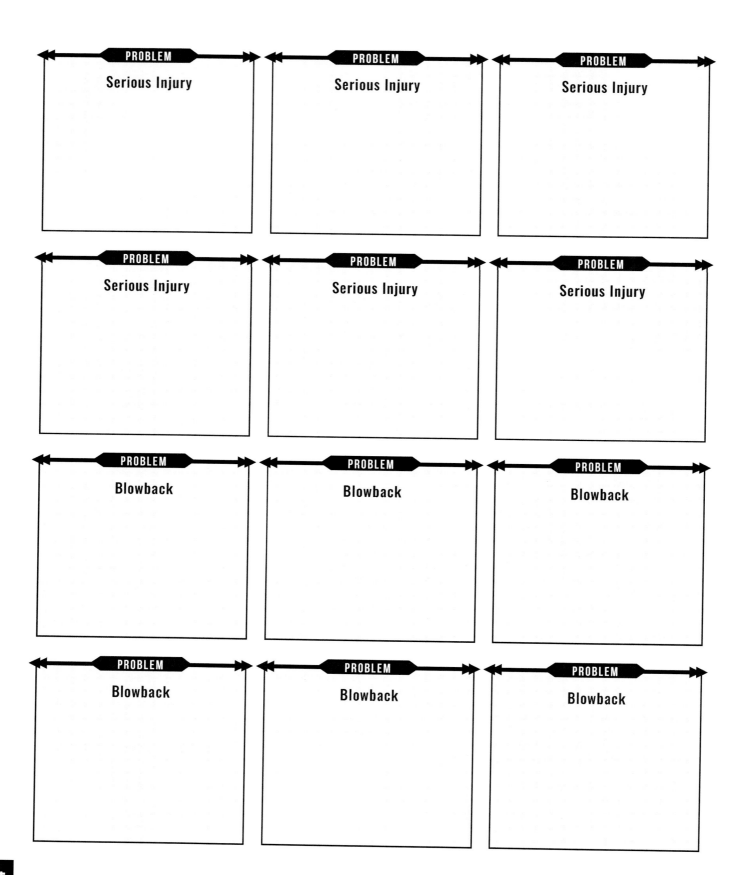

PROBLEM

Serious Injury

PROBLEM

Serious Injury

PROBLEM

Serious Injury

PROBLEM

Serious Injury

PROBLEM

Serious Injury

PROBLEM

Serious Injury

PROBLEM

Blowback

PROBLEM

Blowback

PROBLEM

Blowback

PROBLEM

Blowback

PROBLEM

Blowback

PROBLEM

Blowback

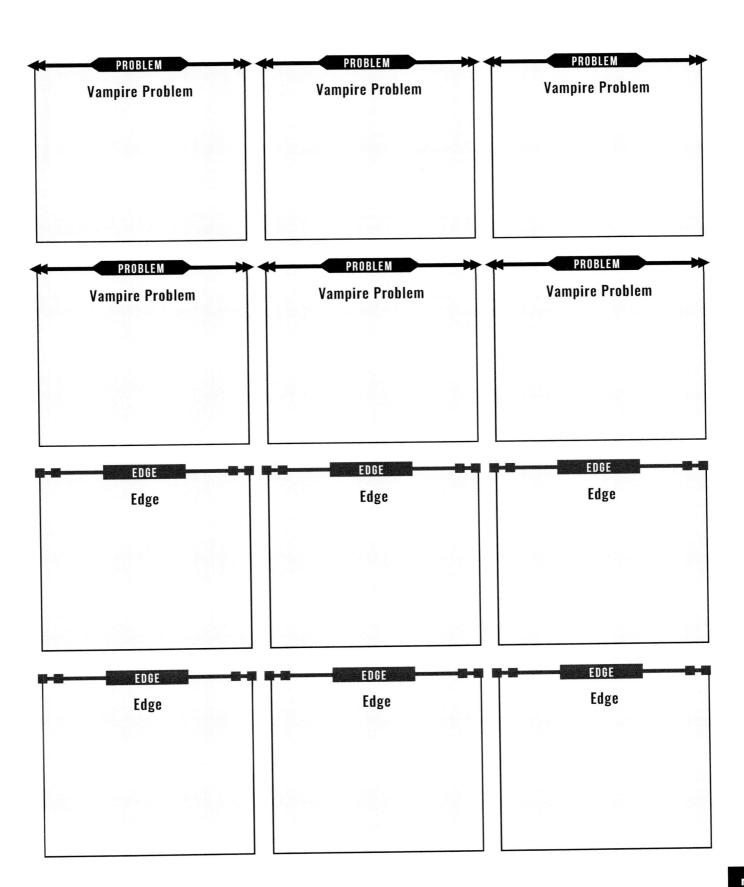

PROBLEM

Vampire Problem

PROBLEM

Vampire Problem

PROBLEM

Vampire Problem

PROBLEM

Vampire Problem

PROBLEM

Vampire Problem

PROBLEM

Vampire Problem

EDGE

Edge

EDGE

Edge

EDGE

Edge

EDGE

Edge

EDGE

Edge

EDGE

Edge

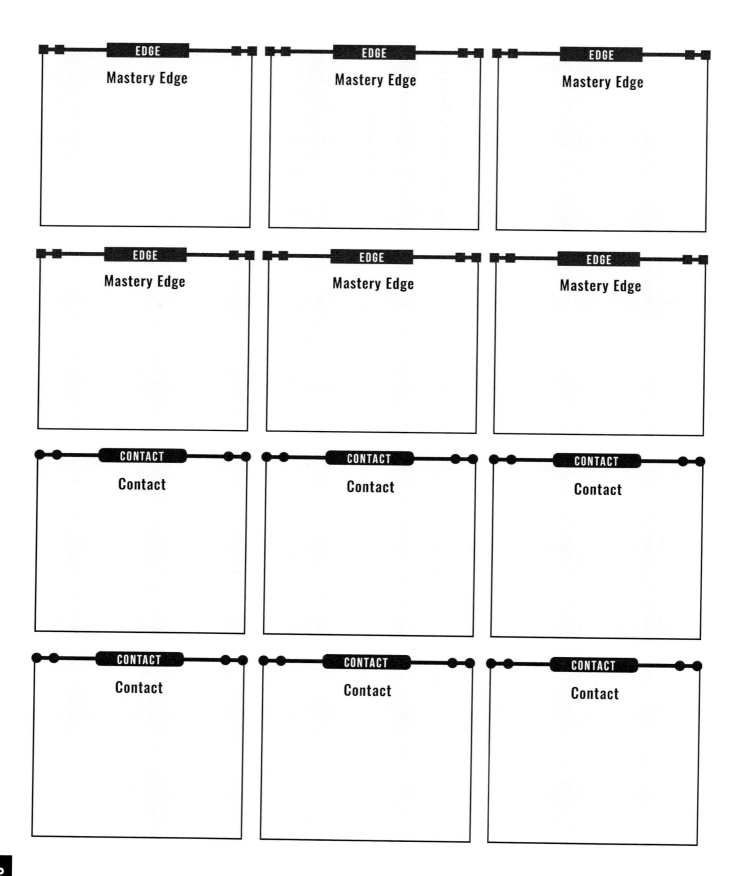

Mastery Edge

Mastery Edge

Mastery Edge

Mastery Edge

Mastery Edge

Mastery Edge

Contact

Contact

Contact

Contact

Contact

Contact

NBA: SOLO OPS CHARACTER SHEET

NAME:_____

CONTACTS:_____

_____

_____

INVESTIGATIVE ABILITIES

☐ Accounting **A**	☐ Diagnosis **A**	☐ Notice **T**
☐ Archaeology **A**	☐ Electronic Surveillance **T**	☐ Occult Studies **A**
☐ Architecture **A**	☐ Forensic Pathology **T**	☐ Outdoor Survival **T**
☐ Art History **A**	☐ Forgery **T**	☐ Pharmacy **T**
☐ Astronomy **T**	☐ High Society **I**	☐ Photography **T**
☐ Bullshit Detector **I**	☐ History **A**	☐ Reassurance **I**
☐ Bureaucracy **I**	☐ Human Terrain **A**	☐ Research **A**
☐ Charm **I**	☐ Interrogation **I**	☐ Streetwise **I**
☐ Chemistry **T**	☐ Intimidation **I**	☐ Tradecraft **I**
☐ Cop Talk **I**	☐ Languages **A**	☐ Traffic Analysis **T**
☐ Criminology **A**	☐ Law **A**	☐ Urban Survival **T**
☐ Cryptography **T**	☐ Military Science **A**	☐ Vampirology **A**
☐ Data Recovery **T**	☐ Negotiation **I**	

GENERAL ABILITIES

STUNT USE

☐ Athletics	☐ ☐
☐ Conceal	☐ ☐
☐ Cool	☐ ☐
☐ Cover	☐ ☐
☐ Driving	☐ ☐
☐ Evasion	☐ ☐
☐ Fighting	☐ ☐
☐ Filch	☐ ☐
☐ Infiltration	☐ ☐
☐ Mechanics	☐ ☐
☐ Medic	☐ ☐
☐ Network	☐ ☐
☐ Preparedness	☐ ☐
☐ Sense Trouble	☐ ☐
☐ Shooting	☐ ☐
☐ Surveillance	☐ ☐

HEAT TRACKER

0	1	2	3	4	5

INJURY TRACKER

0	1	2	3	4	5

SHADOW TRACKER

0	1	2	3	4	5

BACKSTORY

LEYLA KHAN BACKSTORY

You're waking up from a nightmare.

Things you're certain about: your name is Leyla Khan. Your father was British; your mother Lebanese. You grew up in England, and got recruited by MI6. You used to be a spy.

And then... the nightmare.

It's not amnesia. It's not that simple. Something broke your mind. Something made you a different person, forced you to serve them. Forced you to be their enforcer, their monster. You did horrible things in the shadows across Europe. You can't recall – can't let yourself recall – the details. Not yet.

It's like someone set fire to your old house, and you're walking around in the burnt-out ruins. You know the layout of the place perfectly, but everything's changed on the inside – it's scorched, or covered in thick soot, or burnt away entirely. Some of it might be salvageable if you carefully rebuild it, but other parts are now treacherous – step on the wrong floorboard, and it'll collapse under your weight and send you plunging into catatonia.

Sometimes, you'll find intact chains of memories. You'll run into a familiar face, and be able to *pull* up a memory that's entangled with other facts and flashbacks, but you don't have a complete picture of either your former life *or* the mysterious master you were forced to serve. Just the memory of eyes in the darkness, and the taste of blood.

You can't trust your memories. What did this to you? Are you compromised? Can you rebuild your identity – or should you raze it all and start again?

One thing you do remember, one thing you hold onto despite everything – you're going to get revenge.

LEYLA KHAN CHARACTER SHEET

NAME: LEYLA KHAN

CONTACTS:_____

_____

_____

_____

_____

INVESTIGATIVE ABILITIES

☐ Accounting **A**	☐ Diagnosis **A**	■ Notice **T**
☐ Archaeology **A**	■ Electronic Surveillance **T**	☐ Occult Studies **A**
☐ Architecture **A**	☐ Forensic Pathology **T**	■ Outdoor Survival **T**
☐ Art History **A**	☐ Forgery **T**	☐ Pharmacy **T**
☐ Astronomy **T**	■ High Society **I**	☐ Photography **T**
■ Bullshit Detector **I**	☐ History **A**	■ Reassurance **I**
☐ Bureaucracy **I**	■ Human Terrain **A**	■ Research **A**
■ Charm **I**	☐ Interrogation **I**	■ Streetwise **I**
☐ Chemistry **T**	■ Intimidation **I**	■ Tradecraft **I**
☐ Cop Talk **I**	☐ Languages **A**	■ Traffic Analysis **T**
■ Criminology **A**	☐ Law **A**	■ Urban Survival **T**
☐ Cryptography **T**	☐ Military Science **A**	☐ Vampirology **A**
☐ Data Recovery **T**	☐ Negotiation **I**	

GENERAL ABILITIES

STUNT USE

- ☐ Athletics ⚁⚁
- ☐ Conceal ⚁⚁
- ☐ Cool ⚁⚁
- ☐ Cover ⚁⚁
- ☐ Driving ⚁⚁
- ☐ Evasion ⚁⚁
- ☐ Fighting ⚁⚁
- ☐ Filch ⚁⚁
- ☐ Infiltration ⚁⚁
- ☐ Mechanics ⚁⚁
- ☐ Medic ⚁⚁
- ☐ Network ⚁⚁
- ☐ Preparedness ⚁⚁
- ☐ Sense Trouble ⚁⚁
- ☐ Shooting ⚁⚁
- ☐ Surveillance ⚁⚁

HEAT TRACKER

0	1	2	3	4	5

INJURY TRACKER

0	1	2	3	4	5

SHADOW TRACKER

0	1	2	3	4	5

NOTES

STARTER NOTES FOR EXPERIENCED GUMSHOE GMS

Already an experienced *Night's Black Agents* Director and want to get to grips with *Night's Black Agents: Solo Ops* quickly? Here's the bottom line up front.

- Investigative abilities don't have pools. In place of point spends, the player spends **Pushes**, which can be applied to any investigative ability. The character starts with three Pushes and can earn additional ones during play.
- General abilities don't use pools, either. Instead, each is associated with a number of dice – usually 2 – you roll in an attempt to hit a difficulty number.
- Cherries have become **Mastery Edges** – the player gets to pick three cards from a deck of special abilities, and can swap these in and out over the course of the mission.
- In place of the basic pass-fail outcomes of General ability tests, One-2-One uses a more detailed story-branching format called the **Challenge**. Here, the player can achieve great, okay or disastrous results. In that order, they're called Advances, Holds, or Setbacks. Difficulty thresholds are customised for each challenge.
- Some Challenges let a player take on Extra Problems or draw on other abilities (**Stunts**) to get extra dice in a challenge.
- The player receives cards as reminders of ongoing advantages (**Edges**) and impediments (**Problems**).
- Some Edges have to be spent to gain the offered benefit; others give an ongoing advantage.
- Some Problems require the player to take action to Counter (discard) them.
- There are three special types of problem - **Injury**, **Heat** and **Shadow** (reflecting the vampire's awareness or influence over the character). These problems stack – so, if you're holding multiple Heat cards, you add them up to work out your overall Heat score.
- There's no Health ability, and Stability's replaced by Cool. The character cannot usually be eliminated in the middle of an operation. However, some Problems will eliminate the character at the end of the story unless Countered.
- Instead of a Vampyramid, some Problem cards trigger later in the story as **Blowback**.

RULES QUICK REFERENCE

Investigative Abilities (p. 11) allow you to gather information. The animating principle behind GUMSHOE is that *failing to get key information is never interesting*. If you have the right ability and you look in the right place for the clues you need to solve the mystery, you will always find the information you seek. If you lack the relevant ability, your character can use Network to obtain a Contact (p. 45), who might also provide guidance and assurance as needed.

In some situations, you can spend a resource called a Push (p. 13) to gain an additional benefit.

You start the game with **3 Pushes**, and can gain others during play.

In addition, you start with **3 Mastery Edges**, special edges representing your Agent's intensive training and expertise. Each Mastery Edge describes what it does on the card.

General Abilities (p. 25) determine whether you succeed or fail when trying to take actions other than gathering information, usually in an event called a test. The most important kind of test is the Challenge (p. 34).

The game uses standard six-sided dice, which roleplayers sometimes refer to as d6s.

You've got two dice in all General Abilities.

Challenges

In a Challenge, you roll dice from the specified General Ability. If your total fails to reach the lower threshold for the challenge, you suffer a Setback. If you meet the lower threshold, you Hold. If you cross the higher threshold, you Advance.

You can earn more dice in a challenge

♦ by taking on Extra Problems,

♦ or tapping your other abilities to perform dramatic Stunts.

When rolling multiple dice, roll one at a time: you may succeed without having to roll all of them.

♦ On an Advance you will probably gain an Edge (p. 38): an advantage you can use later in the scenario. As a reminder, you gain an Edge card. The card's text will tell you how it works. Often, you must discard the card to gain the advantage.

♦ If you reached the Advance threshold *without* rolling all of the dice you were entitled to, you *also* gain a Push.

♦ On a Setback, you often gain a Problem (p. 38), representing a dilemma that might cause trouble for you later. Again, you receive a card to remember it by — a Problem card. Certain cards might lead to a terrible end for your agent should you fail to get rid of, or Counter, them (p. 39) before the scenario concludes.

Every so often you'll make a simple roll, called a Quick Test (p. 40), to see if you succeed or fail, without the possibility of Advances, Edges, Setbacks, or Problems.

The rest is detail. You don't have to learn any special rules for combat or mental distress, as you would in standard GUMSHOE and most other roleplaying games. The Challenge system, with its descriptions of outcomes, and its resulting Edges and Problems, handles it all.

Cumulative Problems

Some Problems stack with one another.

♦ The more *Heat* problems you have, the more attention you draw from law enforcement

♦ The more *Shadow* problems you have, the more you're vulnerable to supernatural threats

♦ The more *Injury* problems you have, the bigger your penalty to physical Challenges. You can Take Time to turn Injuries into Hurt cards – Hurt cards have a smaller penalty, but last for the rest of the story.

Taking Time

Some actions, like resting to recover from injuries, lying low, travelling, conducting lengthy surveillance or research, or other prolonged actives are considered to Take Time. Some special Problems only kick in when you Take Time.

LIST OF GENERAL ABILITIES

ABILITY	CATEGORY	ICON
Athletics	Physical	▲
Conceal	Manual	■
Cool	Mental	★
Cover	Social	●
Driving	Manual	■
Evasion	Physical	▲
Fighting	Physical	▲
Filch	Manual	■
Infiltration	Physical	▲
Mechanics	Manual	■
Medic	Manual	■
Network	Social	●
Preparedness	Mental	★
Sense Trouble	Mental	★
Shooting	Physical	▲
Surveillance	Social	●

LIST OF MASTERY EDGES

MASTERY EDGE	GENERAL ABILITY	TYPE	PAGE NUMBER
Trained Reflexes	Athletics	Physical	26
Unstoppable	Athletics	Physical	26
Perfect Conceal	Conceal	Manual	26
Cache	Conceal	Manual	26
Unshakable	Cool	Mental	26
Ice Cold	Cool	Mental	26
Connected Cover	Cover	Social	27
Quick Disguise	Cover	Social	27
Grand Theft Auto	Driving	Manual	27
Wheel Artist	Driving	Manual	27
Vanish	Evasion	Physical	28
Dodge This	Evasion	Physical	28
Martial Arts Expert	Fighting	Physical	29
Weapons Expert	Fighting	Physical	29
Grit	Fighting	Physical	29
Sleight of Hand	Filch	Manual	29
No Slip-Ups	Filch	Manual	29
Open Sesame	Infiltration	Physical	29
Stealth Operator	Infiltration	Physical	29
Boom	Mechanics	Manual	30
Duct Tape Ninja	Mechanics	Manual	30
Painkillers and Vodka	Medic	Manual	30
Battlefield Medic	Medic	Manual	30
What Are You Doing Here?	Network	Social	30
You Never Knew Me	Network	Social	30
The Nick of Time	Preparedness	Mental	31
The Reptile Fund	Preparedness	Mental	31
Intuition	Sense Trouble	Mental	31
En Garde	Sense Trouble	Mental	31
Sniper	Shooting	Physical	32
Two Guns Blazing	Shooting	Physical	32
Pavement Artist	Surveillance	Social	32
Total Situational Awareness	Surveillance	Social	32

LIST OF INVESTIGATIVE ABILITIES

ABILITY	TYPE	ICONS
Accounting	Academic	A C
Archaeology	Academic	A C
Architecture	Academic	A C
Art History	Academic	A C
Astronomy	Technical	T C
Bullshit Detector	Interpersonal	I
Bureaucracy	Interpersonal	I C
Charm	Interpersonal	I
Chemistry	Technical	T C
Cop Talk	Interpersonal	I C
Criminology	Academic	A
Cryptography	Technical	T C
Data Recovery	Technical	T C
Diagnosis	Academic	A C
Electronic Surveillance	Technical	T
Forensic Pathology	Technical	T C
Forgery	Technical	T C
High Society	Interpersonal	I C
History	Academic	A C
Human Terrain	Academic	A
Interrogation	Interpersonal	I C
Intimidation	Interpersonal	I
Languages	Academic	A C
Law	Academic	A C
Military Science	Academic	A
Negotiation	Interpersonal	I
Notice	Technical	T
Occult Studies	Academic	A C
Outdoor Survival	Technical	T C
Pharmacy	Technical	T C
Photography	Technical	T C
Reassurance	Interpersonal	I
Research	Academic	A
Streetwise	Interpersonal	I
Tradecraft	Interpersonal	I
Traffic Analysis	Technical	T C
Urban Survival	Technical	T
Vampirology	Academic	A C

INDEX